Confucianism and Ecology

Harvard University
Center for the Study of World Religions
Publications

General Editor: Lawrence E. Sullivan
Senior Editor: Kathryn Dodgson

Religions of the World and Ecology
Series Editors:
Mary Evelyn Tucker and John Grim

Cambridge, Massachusetts

ᴄ

Confucianism and Ecology
The Interrelation
of Heaven, Earth, and Humans

edited by
Mary Evelyn Tucker
and
John Berthrong

Distributed by Harvard University Press
for the
Harvard University Center for the Study of World Religions

Grateful acknowledgment is made for permission to reprint the following:

Portions of Huey-li Li, "A Cross-Cultural Critique of Ecofeminism," in *Ecofeminism: Women, Animals, Nature*, edited by Greta Gaard. Copyright © 1993 Temple University Press. Reprinted by permission of Temple University Press.

Tu Wei-ming, "The Continuity of Being: Chinese Visions of Nature," in *On Nature*, edited by Leroy S. Rouner. Copyright © 1984 University of Notre Dame Press.

Portions of Mary Evelyn Tucker, "An Ecological Cosmology: The Confucian Philosophy of Material Force," in *Ecological Perspectives*, edited by Christopher Key Chapple, pages 105–125. Copyright © 1994 State University of New York Press.

Portions of Tu Wei-ming, "Beyond the Enlightenment Mentality," in *Worldviews and Ecology: Religion, Philosophy, and the Environment*, edited by Mary Evelyn Tucker and John A. Grim, pages 19–29. Maryknoll, N.Y.: Orbis Books, 1994 (copyright © 1994 Associated University Presses, Inc.; Orbis edition by license from Associated University Presses).

Library of Congress Cataloging-in-Publication Data

Confucianism and ecology : the interrelation of heaven, earth, and humans / edited by Mary Evelyn Tucker and John Berthrong.
    p.   cm. — (Religions of the world and ecology)
  Includes bibliographical references and index.
  ISBN 0-945454-15-5 (hardcover : alk. paper)
  ISBN 0-945454-16-3 (pbk. : alk. paper)
  1. Philosophy, Confucian. 2. Ecology—China—Philosophy.
3. Environmental ethics—China. I. Tucker, Mary Evelyn.
II. Berthrong, John H. III. Series.
B127.C65C64 1998
179'.1'0951—dc21   98-18767
                                         CIP

Acknowledgments

The series of conferences on religions of the world and ecology will take place from 1996 through 1998, with supervision at the Harvard University Center for the Study of World Religions by Don Kunkel and Malgorzata Radziszewska-Hedderick and with the assistance of Janey Bosch, Naomi Wilshire, and Lilli Leggio. Narges Moshiri, also at the Center, was indispensable in helping to arrange the first two conferences. A series of volumes developing the themes explored at the conferences will be published by the Center and distributed by Harvard University Press under the editorial direction of Kathryn Dodgson and with the skilled assistance of Eric Edstam.

These efforts have been generously supported by major funding from the V. Kann Rasmussen Foundation. The conference organizers appreciate also the support of the following institutions and individuals: Aga Khan Trust for Culture, Association of Shinto Shrines, Nathan Cummings Foundation, Dharam Hinduja Indic Research Center at Columbia University, Germeshausen Foundation, Harvard Buddhist Studies Forum, Harvard Divinity School Center for the Study of Values in Public Life, Jain Academic Foundation of North America, Laurance Rockefeller, Sacharuna Foundation, Theological Education to Meet the Environmental Challenge, and Winslow Foundation. The conferences were originally made possible by the Center for Respect of Life and Environment of the Humane Society of the United States, which continues to be a principal cosponsor. Bucknell University, also a cosponsor, has provided support in the form of leave time from teaching for conference coordinators Mary Evelyn Tucker and John Grim as well as the invaluable administrative assistance of Stephanie Snyder. Her thoughtful attention to critical details is legendary. President William Adams of Bucknell University and Vice-President for Academic Affairs Daniel Little have also granted travel funds for faculty and students to attend the conferences. Grateful acknowledgment is here made for the advice from key area specialists in shaping each conference and in editing the published volumes. Their generosity in time and talent has been indispensable at every step of the project. Finally, throughout this process, the support, advice, and encouragement from Martin S. Kaplan has been invaluable.

Contents

Preface

Lawrence E. Sullivan

Religion distinguishes the human species from all others, just as human presence on earth distinguishes the ecology of our planet from other places in the known universe. Religious life and the earth's ecology are inextricably linked, organically related.

Human belief and practice mark the earth. One can hardly think of a natural system that has not been considerably altered, for better or worse, by human culture. "Nor is this the work of the industrial centuries," observes Simon Schama. "It is coeval with the entirety of our social existence. And it is this irreversibly modified world, from the polar caps to the equatorial forests, that is all the nature we have" (*Landscape and Memory* [New York: Vintage Books, 1996], 7). In Schama's examination even landscapes that appear to be most free of human culture turn out, on closer inspection, to be its product.

Human beliefs about the nature of ecology are the distinctive contribution of our species to the ecology itself. Religious beliefs— especially those concerning the nature of powers that create and animate—become an effective part of ecological systems. They attract the power of will and channel the forces of labor toward purposive transformations. Religious rituals model relations with material life and transmit habits of practice and attitudes of mind to succeeding generations.

This is not simply to say that religious thoughts occasionally touch the world and leave traces that accumulate over time. The matter is the other way around. From the point of view of environmental studies, religious worldviews propel communities into the world with fundamental predispositions toward it because such religious worldviews are primordial, all-encompassing, and unique. They are *primordial* because they probe behind secondary appearances and stray thoughts to rivet human attention on realities of the first order: life at its source, creativity in its fullest manifestation, death and destruction at their origin, renewal and salvation in their germ. The revelation of first things is compelling and moves communities to take creative action. Primordial ideas are prime movers.

Religious worldviews are *all-encompassing* because they fully absorb the natural world within them. They provide human beings both a view of the whole and at the same time a penetrating image of their own ironic position as the beings in the cosmos who possess the capacity for symbolic thought: the part that contains the whole—or at least a picture of the whole—within itself. As all-encompassing, therefore, religious ideas do not just contend with other ideas as equals; they frame the mind-set within which all sorts of ideas commingle in a cosmology. For this reason, their role in ecology must be better understood.

Religious worldviews are *unique* because they draw the world of nature into a wholly other kind of universe, one that appears only in the religious imagination. From the point of view of environmental studies, the risk of such religious views, on the one hand, is of disinterest in or disregard for the natural world. On the other hand, only in the religious world can nature be compared and contrasted to other kinds of being—the supernatural world or forms of power not always fully manifest in nature. Only then can nature be revealed as distinctive, set in a new light startlingly different from its own. That is to say, only religious perspectives enable human beings to evaluate the world of nature in terms distinct from all else. In this same step toward intelligibility, the natural world is evaluated in terms consonant with human beings' own distinctive (religious and imaginative) nature in the world, thus grounding a self-conscious relationship and a role with limits and responsibilities.

In the struggle to sustain the earth's environment as viable for future generations, environmental studies has thus far left the role of religion unprobed. This contrasts starkly with the emphasis given, for example, the role of science and technology in threatening or sustaining the ecology. Ignorance of religion prevents environmental studies from achieving its goals, however, for though science and technology share many important features of human culture with religion, they leave unexplored essential wellsprings of human motivation and concern that shape the world as we know it. No understanding of the environment is adequate without a grasp of the religious life that constitutes the human societies which saturate the natural environment.

A great deal of what we know about the religions of the world is new knowledge. As is the case for geology and astronomy, so too for religious studies: many new discoveries about the nature and function of religion are, in fact, clearer understandings of events and processes that began to unfold long ago. Much of what we are learning now about the religions of the world was previously not known outside of a circle of adepts. From the ancient history of traditions and from the ongoing creativity of the world's contemporary religions we are opening a treasury of motives, disciplines, and awarenesses.

A geology of the religious spirit of humankind can well serve our need to relate fruitfully to the earth and its myriad life-forms. Changing our habits of consumption and patterns of distribution, reevaluating modes of production, and reestablishing a strong sense of solidarity with the matrix of material life—these achievements will arrive along with spiritual modulations that unveil attractive new images of well-being and prosperity, respecting the limits of life in a sustainable world while revering life at its sources. Remarkable religious views are presented in this series—from the nature mysticism of Bashō in Japan or Saint Francis in Italy to the ecstatic physiologies and embryologies of shamanic healers, Taoist meditators, and Vedic practitioners; from indigenous people's ritual responses to projects funded by the World Bank, to religiously grounded criticisms of hazardous waste sites, deforestation, and environmental racism.

The power to modify the world is both frightening and fascinating and has been subjected to reflection, particularly religious reflection, from time immemorial to the present day. We will understand ecology better when we understand the religions that form the rich soil of memory and practice, belief and relationships where life on earth is rooted. Knowledge of these views will help us reappraise our ways and reorient ourselves toward the sources and resources of life.

This volume is one in a series that addresses the critical gap in our contemporary understanding of religion and ecology. The series results from research conducted at the Harvard University Center for the Study of World Religions over a three-year period. I wish especially to acknowledge President Neil L. Rudenstine of Harvard University for his leadership in instituting the environmental initiative at Harvard and thank him for his warm encouragement and characteristic support of our program. Mary Evelyn Tucker and John Grim of Bucknell University coordinated the research, involving the direct participation of some six hundred scholars, religious leaders, and environmental specialists brought to Harvard from around the world during the period of research and inquiry. Professors Tucker and Grim have brought great vision and energy to this enormous project, as has their team of conference convenors. The commitment and advice of Martin S. Kaplan of Hale and Dorr have been of great value. Our goals have been achieved for this research and publication program because of the extraordinary dedication and talents of Center for the Study of World Religions staff members Don Kunkel, Malgorzata Radziszewska-Hedderick, Kathryn Dodgson, Janey Bosch, Naomi Wilshire, Lilli Leggio, and Eric Edstam and with the unstinting help of Stephanie Snyder of Bucknell. To these individuals, and to all the sponsors and participants whose efforts made this series possible, go deepest thanks and appreciation.

Series Foreword

Mary Evelyn Tucker and John Grim

The Nature of the Environmental Crisis

Ours is a period when the human community is in search of new and sustaining relationships to the earth amidst an environmental crisis that threatens the very existence of all life-forms on the planet. While the particular causes and solutions of this crisis are being debated by scientists, economists, and policymakers, the facts of widespread destruction are causing alarm in many quarters. Indeed, from some perspectives the future of human life itself appears threatened. As Daniel Maguire has succinctly observed, "If current trends continue, we will not."[1] Thomas Berry, the former director of the Riverdale Center for Religious Research, has also raised the stark question, "Is the human a viable species on an endangered planet?"

From resource depletion and species extinction to pollution overload and toxic surplus, the planet is struggling against unprecedented assaults. This is aggravated by population explosion, industrial growth, technological manipulation, and military proliferation heretofore unknown by the human community. From many accounts the basic elements which sustain life—sufficient water, clean air, and arable land—are at risk. The challenges are formidable and well documented. The solutions, however, are more elusive and complex. Clearly, this crisis has economic, political, and social dimensions which require more detailed analysis than we can provide here. Suffice it to say, however, as did the *Global 2000 Report*: ". . .once such global environmental problems are in motion they are difficult to reverse. In fact few if any of the problems addressed in the *Global 2000 Report* are amenable to quick technological or policy fixes; rather, they are inextricably mixed with the world's most perplexing social and economic problems."[2]

Peter Raven, the director of the Missouri Botanical Garden, wrote in a paper titled "We Are Killing Our World" with a similar sense of urgency regarding the magnitude of the environmental crisis: "The world that provides our evolutionary and ecological context is in serious trouble, trouble of a kind that demands our urgent attention. By formulating adequate plans for dealing with these large-scale problems, we will be laying the foundation for peace and prosperity in the future; by ignoring them, drifting passively while attending to what may seem more urgent, personal priorities, we are courting disaster."

Rethinking Worldviews and Ethics

For many people an environmental crisis of this complexity and scope is not only the result of certain economic, political, and social factors. It is also a moral and spiritual crisis which, in order to be addressed, will require broader philosophical and religious understandings of ourselves as creatures of nature, embedded in life cycles and dependent on ecosystems. Religions, thus, need to be re-examined in light of the current environmental crisis. This is because religions help to shape our attitudes toward nature in both conscious and unconscious ways. Religions provide basic interpretive stories of who we are, what nature is, where we have come from, and where we are going. This comprises a worldview of a society. Religions also suggest how we should treat other humans and how we should relate to nature. These values make up the ethical orientation of a society. Religions thus generate worldviews and ethics which underlie fundamental attitudes and values of different cultures and societies. As the historian Lynn White observed, "What people do about their ecology depends on what they think about themselves in relation to things around them. Human ecology is deeply conditioned by beliefs about our nature and destiny—that is, by religion."[3]

In trying to reorient ourselves in relation to the earth, it has become apparent that we have lost our appreciation for the intricate nature of matter and materiality. Our feeling of alienation in the modern period has extended beyond the human community and its patterns of material exchanges to our interaction with nature itself. Especially in technologically sophisticated urban societies, we have become removed from the recognition of our dependence on nature. We no longer know who we are as earthlings; we no longer see the earth as sacred.

Thomas Berry suggests that we have become autistic in our interactions with the natural world. In other words, we are unable to value the life and beauty of nature because we are locked in our own egocentric perspectives and shortsighted needs. He suggests that we need a new cosmology, cultural coding, and motivating energy to overcome this deprivation.[4] He observes that the magnitude of destructive industrial processes is so great that we must initiate a radical rethinking of the myth of progress and of humanity's role in the evolutionary process. Indeed, he speaks of evolution as a new story of the universe, namely, as a vast cosmological perspective that will resituate human meaning and direction in the context of four and a half billion years of earth history.[5]

For Berry and for many others an important component of the current environmental crisis is spiritual and ethical. It is here that the religions of the world may have a role to play in cooperation with other individuals, institutions, and initiatives that have been engaged with environmental issues for a considerable period of time. Despite their lateness in addressing the crisis, religions are beginning to respond in remarkably creative ways. They are not only rethinking their theologies but are also reorienting their sustainable practices and long-term environmental commitments. In so doing, the very nature of religion and of ethics is being challenged and changed. This is true because the reexamination of other worldviews created by religious beliefs and practices may be critical to our recovery of sufficiently comprehensive cosmologies, broad conceptual frameworks, and effective environmental ethics for the twenty-first century.

While in the past none of the religions of the world have had to face an environmental crisis such as we are now confronting, they remain key instruments in shaping attitudes toward nature. The unintended consequences of the modern industrial drive for unlimited economic growth and resource development have led us to an impasse regarding the survival of many life-forms and appropriate management of varied ecosystems. The religious traditions may indeed be critical in helping to reimagine the viable conditions and long-range strategies for fostering mutually enhancing human-earth relations.[6] Indeed, as E. N. Anderson has documented with impressive detail, "All traditional societies that have succeeded in managing resources well, over time, have done it in part through religious or ritual representation of resource management."[7]

It is in this context that a series of conferences and publications exploring the various religions of the world and their relation to ecology was initiated by the Center for the Study of World Religions at Harvard. Directed by Lawrence Sullivan and coordinated by Mary Evelyn Tucker and John Grim, the conferences will involve some six hundred scholars, graduate students, religious leaders, and environmental activists over a period of three years. The collaborative nature of the project is intentional. Such collaboration will maximize the opportunity for dialogical reflection on this issue of enormous complexity and will accentuate the diversity of local manifestations of ecologically sustainable alternatives.

The conferences and the volumes are intended to serve as initial explorations of the emerging field of religion and ecology while pointing toward areas for further research. We are not unaware of the difficulties of engaging in such a task, yet we are encouraged by the enthusiastic response to the conferences within the academic community, by the larger interest they have generated beyond academia, and by the probing examinations gathered in the volumes. We trust that this series and these volumes will be useful not only for scholars of religion but also for those shaping seminary education and institutional religious practices, as well as for those involved in public policy on environmental issues.

We see these conferences and publications as expanding the growing dialogue regarding the role of the world's religions as moral forces in stemming the environmental crisis. While, clearly, there are major methodological issues involved in utilizing traditional philosophical and religious ideas for contemporary concerns, there are also compelling reasons to support such efforts, however modest they may be. The world's religions in all their complexity and variety remain one of the principal resources for symbolic ideas, spiritual inspiration, and ethical principles. Indeed, despite their limitations, historically they have provided comprehensive cosmologies for interpretive direction, moral foundations for social cohesion, spiritual guidance for cultural expression, and ritual celebrations for meaningful life. In our search for more comprehensive ecological worldviews and more effective environmental ethics, it is inevitable that we will draw from the symbolic and conceptual resources of the religious traditions of the world. The effort to do this is not without precedent or problems, some of which will be signaled below. With this volume and with this series we hope the field of reflection and discussion regarding religion and ecology will begin to broaden, deepen, and complexify.

Qualifications and Goals

The Problems and Promise of Religions

These conferences and volumes, then, are built on the premise that the religions of the world may be instrumental in addressing the moral dilemmas created by the environmental crisis. At the same time we recognize the limitations of such efforts on the part of religions. We also acknowledge that the complexity of the problem requires interlocking approaches from such fields as science, economics, politics, health, and public policy. As the human community struggles to formulate different attitudes toward nature and to articulate broader conceptions of ethics embracing species and ecosystems, religions may thus be a necessary, though only contributing, part of this multidisciplinary approach.

It is becoming increasingly evident that abundant scientific knowledge of the crisis is available and numerous political and economic statements have been formulated. Yet we seem to lack the political, economic, and scientific leadership to make necessary changes. Moreover, what is still lacking is the religious commitment, moral imagination, and ethical engagement to transform the environmental crisis from an issue on paper to one of effective policy, from rhetoric in print to realism in action. Why, nearly fifty years after Fairfield Osborne's warning regarding *Our Plundered Planet* and more than thirty years since Rachel Carson's *Silent Spring*, are we still wondering, is it too late?[8]

It is important to ask where the religions have been on these issues and why they themselves have been so late in their involvement. Have issues of personal salvation superseded all others? Have

divine-human relations been primary? Have anthropocentric ethics
been all-consuming? Has the material world of nature been devalued
by religion? Does the search for otherworldly rewards override
commitment to this world? Did the religions simply surrender their
natural theologies and concerns with exploring purpose in nature
to positivistic scientific cosmologies? In beginning to address these
questions, we still have not exhausted all the reasons for religions'
lack of attention to the environmental crisis. The reasons may not
be readily apparent, but clearly they require further exploration and
explanation.

In discussing the involvement of religions in this issue, it is also
appropriate to acknowledge the dark side of religion in both its
institutional expressions and dogmatic forms. In addition to their
oversight with regard to the environment, religions have been the
source of enormous manipulation of power in fostering wars, in
ignoring racial and social injustice, and in promoting unequal gender
relations, to name only a few abuses. One does not want to
underplay this shadow side or to claim too much for religions'
potential for ethical persuasiveness. The problems are too vast and
complex for unqualified optimism. Yet there is a growing consensus
that religions may now have a significant role to play, just as in the
past they have sustained individuals and cultures in the face of
internal and external threats.

A final caveat is the inevitable gap that arises between theories
and practices in religions. As has been noted, even societies with
religious traditions which appear sympathetic to the environment
have in the past often misused resources. While it is clear that
religions may have some disjunction between the ideal and the real,
this should not lessen our endeavor to identify resources from within
the world's religions for a more ecologically sound cosmology and
environmentally supportive ethics. This disjunction of theory and
practice is present within all philosophies and religions and is
frequently the source of disillusionment, skepticism, and cynicism.
A more realistic observation might be made, however, that this
disjunction should not automatically invalidate the complex worldviews and rich cosmologies embedded in traditional religions.
Rather, it is our task to explore these conceptual resources so as to
broaden and expand our own perspectives in challenging and
fruitful ways.

In summary, we recognize that religions have elements which are both prophetic and transformative as well as conservative and constraining. These elements are continually in tension, a condition which creates the great variety of thought and interpretation within religious traditions. To recognize these various tensions and limits, however, is not to lessen the urgency of the overall goals of this project. Rather, it is to circumscribe our efforts with healthy skepticism, cautious optimism, and modest ambitions. It is to suggest that this is a beginning in a new field of study which will affect both religion and ecology. On the one hand, this process of reflection will inevitably change how religions conceive of their own roles, missions, and identities, for such reflections demand a new sense of the sacred as not divorced from the earth itself. On the other hand, environmental studies can recognize that religions have helped to shape attitudes toward nature. Thus, as religions themselves evolve they may be indispensable in fostering a more expansive appreciation for the complexity and beauty of the natural world. At the same time as religions foster awe and reverence for nature, they may provide the transforming energies for ethical practices to protect endangered ecosystems, threatened species, and diminishing resources.

Methodological Concerns

It is important to acknowledge that there are, inevitably, challenging methodological issues involved in such a project as we are undertaking in this emerging field of religion and ecology.[9] Some of the key interpretive challenges we face in this project concern issues of time, place, space, and positionality. With regard to time, it is necessary to recognize the vast historical complexity of each religious tradition, which cannot be easily condensed in these conferences or volumes. With respect to place, we need to signal the diverse cultural contexts in which these religions have developed. With regard to space, we recognize the varied frameworks of institutions and traditions in which these religions unfold. Finally, with respect to positionality, we acknowledge our own historical situatedness at the end of the twentieth century with distinctive contemporary concerns.

Not only is each religious tradition historically complex and culturally diverse, but its beliefs, scriptures, and institutions have themselves been subject to vast commentaries and revisions over time. Thus, we recognize the radical diversity that exists within and among religious traditions which cannot be encompassed in any single volume. We acknowledge also that distortions may arise as we examine earlier historical traditions in light of contemporary issues.

Nonetheless, the environmental ethics philosopher J. Baird Callicott has suggested that scholars and others "mine the conceptual resources" of the religious traditions as a means of creating a more inclusive global environmental ethics.[10] As Callicott himself notes, however, the notion of "mining" is problematic, for it conjures up images of exploitation which may cause apprehension among certain religious communities, especially those of indigenous peoples. Moreover, we cannot simply expect to borrow or adopt ideas and place them from one tradition directly into another. Even efforts to formulate global environmental ethics need to be sensitive to cultural particularity and diversity. We do not aim at creating a simple bricolage or bland fusion of perspectives. Rather, these conferences and volumes are an attempt to display before us a multiperspectival cross section of the symbolic richness regarding attitudes toward nature within the religions of the world. To do so will help to reveal certain commonalities among traditions, as well as limitations within traditions, as they begin to converge around this challenge presented by the environmental crisis.

We need to identify our concerns, then, as embedded in the constraints of our own perspectival limits at the same time as we seek common ground. In describing various attitudes toward nature historically, we are aiming at *critical understanding* of the complexity, contexts, and frameworks in which these religions articulate such views. In addition, we are striving for *empathetic appreciation* for the traditions without idealizing their ecological potential or ignoring their environmental oversights. Finally, we are aiming at the *creative revisioning* of mutually enhancing human-earth relations. This revisioning may be assisted by highlighting the multiperspectival attitudes toward nature which these traditions disclose. The prismatic effect of examining such attitudes and relationships may provide some necessary clarification and symbolic resources for reimagining our own situation and shared concerns at the end of the twentieth century. It will also be sharpened by identifying the multilayered symbol systems in world religions which have traditionally oriented humans in establishing relational resonances between the microcosm of the self and the macrocosm of the social and natural orders. In short, religious traditions may help to supply both creative resources of symbols, rituals, and texts as well as inspiring visions for reimagining ourselves as part of, not apart from, the natural world.

Aims

The methodological issues outlined above are implied in the overall goals of the conferences, which are described as follows:

1. To identify and evaluate the *distinctive ecological attitudes*, values, and practices of diverse religious traditions, making clear their links to intellectual, political, and other resources associated with these distinctive traditions.

2. To describe and analyze the *commonalities* that exist within and among religious traditions with respect to ecology.

3. To identify the *minimum common ground* on which to base constructive understanding, motivating discussion, and concerted action in diverse locations across the globe; and to highlight the specific religious resources that comprise such fertile ecological ground: within scripture, ritual, myth, symbol, cosmology, sacrament, and so on.

4. To articulate in clear and moving terms *a desirable mode of human presence with the earth;* in short, to highlight means of respecting and valuing nature, to note what has already been actualized, and to indicate how best to achieve what is desirable beyond these examples.

5. To outline the most significant areas, with regard to religion and ecology, in need of *further study*; to enumerate questions of highest priority within those areas and propose possible approaches to use in addressing them.

In these conferences and volumes, then, we are not intending to obliterate difference or ignore diversity. The aim is to celebrate plurality by raising to conscious awareness multiple perspectives regarding nature and human-earth relations as articulated in the religions of the world. The spectrum of cosmologies, myths, symbols, and rituals within the religious traditions will be instructive in resituating us within the rhythms and limits of nature.

We are not looking for a unified worldview or a single global ethic. We are, however, deeply sympathetic with the efforts toward formulating a global ethic made by individuals, such as the theologian, Hans Küng, or the environmental philosopher, J. Baird Callicott, and groups, such as Global Education Associates and United Religions. A minimum content of environmental ethics needs to be seriously considered. We are, then, keenly interested in the contribution this series might make to discussions of environmental policy in national and international arenas. Important intersections may be made with work in the field of development ethics.[11] In addition, the findings of the conferences have bearing on the ethical formulation of the Earth Charter that will be presented to the United Nations for adoption by the end of the century. Thus, we are seeking both the grounds for common concern and the constructive conceptual basis for rethinking our current situation of estrangement from the earth. In so doing we will be able to reconceive a means of creating the basis not just for sustainable development, but also for sustainable life on the planet.

As scientist Brian Swimme has suggested, we are currently making macrophase changes to the life systems of the planet with microphase wisdom. Clearly, we need to expand and deepen the wisdom base for human intervention with nature and other humans. This is particularly true as issues of genetic alteration of natural processes are already available and in use. If religions have traditionally concentrated on divine-human and human-human relations, the challenge is that they now explore more fully divine-human-earth relations. Without such further exploration, adequate environmental ethics may not emerge in a comprehensive context.

Resources: Environmental Ethics Found in the World's Religions

For many people, when challenges such as the environmental crisis are raised in relation to religion in the contemporary world, there frequently arises a sense of loss or a nostalgia for earlier, seemingly less complicated eras when the constant questioning of religious beliefs and practices was not so apparent. This is, no doubt, something of a reified reading of history. There is, however, a decidedly anxious tone to the questioning and soul-searching that appears to haunt many contemporary religious groups as they seek to find their particular role in the midst of rapid technological change and dominant secular values.

One of the greatest challenges, however, to contemporary religions remains how to respond to the environmental crisis, which many believe has been perpetuated because of the enormous inroads made by unrestrained materialism, secularization, and industrialization in contemporary societies, especially those societies arising in or influenced by the modern West. Indeed, some suggest that the very division of religion from secular life may be a major cause of the crisis.

Others, such as the medieval historian Lynn White, have cited religion's negative role in the crisis. White has suggested that the emphasis in Judaism and Christianity on the transcendence of God above nature and the dominion of humans over nature has led to a devaluing of the natural world and a subsequent destruction of its resources for utilitarian ends.[12] While the particulars of this argument have been vehemently debated, it is increasingly clear that the environmental crisis and its perpetuation due to industrialization, secularization, and ethical indifference present a serious challenge to the world's religions. This is especially true because many of these religions have traditionally been concerned with the path of personal salvation, which frequently emphasized otherworldly goals and rejected this world as corrupting. Thus, as we have noted, how to adapt religious teachings to this task of revaluing nature so as to prevent its destruction marks a significant new phase in religious thought. Indeed, as Thomas Berry has so aptly pointed out, what is necessary is a comprehensive reevaluation of human-earth relations if the human is to continue as a viable species on an increasingly degraded planet. This will require, in addition to major economic and political changes, examining worldviews and ethics among the world's religions that differ from those that have captured the imagination of contemporary industrialized societies which regard nature primarily as a commodity to be utilized. It should be noted that when we are searching for effective resources for formulating environmental ethics, each of the religious traditions have both positive and negative features.

For the most part, the worldviews associated with the Western Abrahamic traditions of Judaism, Christianity, and Islam have created a dominantly human-focused morality. Because these worldviews are largely anthropocentric, nature is viewed as being of secondary importance. This is reinforced by a strong sense of the transcendence of God above nature. On the other hand, there are rich resources for rethinking views of nature in the covenantal tradition of the Hebrew Bible, in sacramental theology, in incarnational Christology, and in the vice-regency (*khalifa Allah*) concept of the Qur'an. The covenantal tradition draws on the legal agreements of biblical thought which are extended to all of creation. Sacramental theology in Christianity underscores the sacred dimension of material reality, especially for ritual purposes.[13] Incarnational Christology proposes that because God became flesh in the person of Christ, the entire natural order can be viewed as sacred. The concept of humans as vice-regents of Allah on earth suggests that humans have particular privileges, responsibilities, and obligations to creation.[14]

In Hinduism, although there is a significant emphasis on performing one's *dharma*, or duty, in the world, there is also a strong pull toward *mokṣa*, or liberation, from the world of suffering, or *saṃsāra*. To heal this kind of suffering and alienation through spiritual discipline and meditation, one turns away from the world (*prakṛti*) to a timeless world of spirit (*puruṣa*). Yet at the same time there are numerous traditions in Hinduism which affirm particular rivers, mountains, or forests as sacred. Moreover, in the concept of *līlā*, the creative play of the gods, Hindu theology engages the world as a creative manifestation of the divine. This same tension between withdrawal from the world and affirmation of it is present in Buddhism. Certain Theravāda schools of Buddhism emphasize withdrawing in meditation from the transient world of suffering (*saṃsāra*) to seek release in *nirvāṇa*. On the other hand, later Mahāyāna schools of Buddhism, such as Hua-yen, underscore the remarkable interconnection of reality in such images as the jeweled net of Indra, where each jewel reflects all the others in the universe. Likewise, the Zen gardens in East Asia express the fullness of the Buddha-nature (*tathāgatagarbha*) in the natural world. In recent years, socially engaged Buddhism has been active in protecting the environment in both Asia and the United States.

The East Asian traditions of Confucianism and Taoism remain, in certain ways, some of the most life-affirming in the spectrum of world religions.[15] The seamless interconnection between the divine, human, and natural worlds that characterizes these traditions has been described as an anthropocosmic worldview.[16] There is no emphasis on radical transcendence as there is in the Western traditions. Rather, there is a cosmology of a continuity of creation stressing the dynamic movements of nature through the seasons and the agricultural cycles. This organic cosmology is grounded in the philosophy of *ch'i* (material force), which provides a basis for appreciating the profound interconnection of matter and spirit. To be in harmony with nature and with other humans while being attentive to the movements of the *Tao* (Way) is the aim of personal cultivation in both Confucianism and Taoism. It should be noted, however, that this positive worldview has not prevented environmental degradation (such as deforestation) in parts of East Asia in both the premodern and modern period.

In a similar vein, indigenous peoples, while having ecological cosmologies have, in some instances, caused damage to local environments through such practices as slash-and-burn agriculture. Nonetheless, most indigenous peoples have environmental ethics embedded in their worldviews. This is evident in the complex reciprocal obligations surrounding life-taking and resource-gathering which mark a community's relations with the local bioregion. The religious views at the basis of indigenous lifeways involve respect for the sources of food, clothing, and shelter that nature provides. Gratitude to the creator and to the spiritual forces in creation is at the heart of most indigenous traditions. The ritual calendars of many indigenous peoples are carefully coordinated with seasonal events such as the sound of returning birds, the blooming of certain plants, the movements of the sun, and the changes of the moon.

The difficulty at present is that for the most part we have developed in the world's religions certain ethical prohibitions regarding homicide and restraints concerning genocide and suicide, but none for biocide or geocide. We are clearly in need of exploring such comprehensive cosmological perspectives and communitarian environmental ethics as the most compelling context for motivating change regarding the destruction of the natural world.

Responses of Religions to the Environmental Crisis

How to chart possible paths toward mutually enhancing human-earth relations remains, thus, one of the greatest challenges to the world's religions. It is with some encouragement, however, that we note the growing calls for the world's religions to participate in these efforts toward a more sustainable planetary future. There have been various appeals from environmental groups and from scientists and parliamentarians for religious leaders to respond to the environmental crisis. For example, in 1990 the Joint Appeal in Religion and Science was released highlighting the urgency of collaboration around the issue of the destruction of the environment. In 1992 the Union of Concerned Scientists issued a statement of "Warning to Humanity" signed by over 1,000 scientists from 70 countries, including 105 Nobel laureates, regarding the gravity of the environmental crisis. They specifically cited the need for a new ethic toward the earth.

Numerous national and international conferences have also been held on this subject and collaborative efforts have been established. Environmental groups such as World Wildlife Fund have sponsored interreligious meetings such as the one in Assisi in 1986. The Center for Respect of Life and Environment of the Humane Society of the United States has also held a series of conferences in Assisi on Spirituality and Sustainability and has helped to organize one at the World Bank. The United Nations Environmental Programme in North America has established an Environmental Sabbath, each year distributing thousands of packets of materials for use in congregations throughout North America. Similarly, the National Religious Partnership on the Environment at the Cathedral of St. John the Divine in New York City has promoted dialogue, distributed materials, and created a remarkable alliance of the various Jewish and Christian denominations in the United States around the issue of the environment. The Parliament of World Religions held in 1993 in Chicago and attended by some 8,000 people from all over the globe issued a statement of Global Ethics of Cooperation of Religions on Human and Environmental Issues. International meetings on the environment have been organized. One example of these, the Global Forum of Spiritual and Parliamentary Leaders held in Oxford in 1988, Moscow in 1990, Rio in 1992, and Kyoto in

1993, included world religious leaders, such as the Dalai Lama, and diplomats and heads of state, such as Mikhail Gorbachev. Indeed, Gorbachev hosted the Moscow conference and attended the Kyoto conference to set up a Green Cross International for environmental emergencies.

Since the United Nations Conference on Environment and Development (the Earth Summit) held in Rio in 1992, there have been concerted efforts intended to lead toward the adoption of an *Earth Charter* by the year 2000. This *Earth Charter* initiative is under way with the leadership of the Earth Council and Green Cross International, with support from the government of the Netherlands. Maurice Strong, Mikhail Gorbachev, Steven Rockefeller, and other members of the Earth Charter Project have been instrumental in this process. At the March 1997 Rio + 5 Conference a benchmark draft of the *Earth Charter* was issued. The time is thus propitious for further investigation of the potential contributions of particular religions toward mitigating the environmental crisis, especially by developing more comprehensive environmental ethics for the earth community.

Expanding the Dialogue of Religion and Ecology

More than two decades ago Thomas Berry anticipated such an exploration when he called for "creating a new consciousness of the multiform religious traditions of humankind" as a means toward renewal of the human spirit in addressing the urgent problems of contemporary society.[17] Tu Weiming has written of the need to go "Beyond the Enlightenment Mentality" in exploring the spiritual resources of the global community to meet the challenge of the ecological crisis.[18] While this exploration is also the intention of these conferences and volumes, other significant efforts have preceded our current endeavor.[19] Our discussion here highlights only the last decade.

In 1986 Eugene Hargrove edited a volume titled *Religion and Environmental Crisis.*[20] In 1991 Charlene Spretnak explored this topic in her book *States of Grace: The Recovery of Meaning in the Post-Modern Age.*[21] Her subtitle states her constructivist project clearly: "Reclaiming the Core Teachings and Practices of the Great

Wisdom Traditions for the Well-Being of the Earth Community."
In 1992 Steven Rockefeller and John Elder edited a book based on
a conference at Middlebury College titled *Spirit and Nature: Why
the Environment Is a Religious Issue.*[22] In the same year Peter
Marshall published *Nature's Web: Rethinking Our Place on Earth,*[23]
drawing on the resources of the world's traditions. An edited volume
on *Worldviews and Ecology*, compiled in 1993, contains articles
reflecting on views of nature from the world's religions and from
contemporary philosophies, such as process thought and deep
ecology.[24] In this same vein, in 1994 J. Baird Callicott published
Earth's Insights which examines the intellectual resources of the
world's religions for a more comprehensive global environmental
ethics.[25] This expands on his 1989 volumes, *Nature in Asian
Traditions of Thought* and *In Defense of the Land Ethic.*[26] In 1995
David Kinsley issued a book titled *Ecology and Religion: Ecological
Spirituality in a Cross-Cultural Perspective*[27] which draws on
traditional religions and contemporary movements, such as deep
ecology and ecospirituality. Seyyed Hossein Nasr wrote a comprehensive study of *Religion and the Order of Nature* in 1996.[28] Several
volumes of religious responses to a particular topic or theme have
also been published. For example, J. Ronald Engel and Joan Gibb
Engel compiled a monograph in 1990 on *Ethics of Environment and
Development: Global Challenge, International Response*[29] and in
1995 Harold Coward edited a volume on *Population, Consumption
and the Environment: Religious and Secular Responses.*[30] Roger
Gottlieb edited a useful source book, *This Sacred Earth: Religion,
Nature, Environment.*[31] Single volumes on the world's religions and
ecology were published by the Worldwide Fund for Nature.[32]

   The conferences and volumes in the series Religions of the World
and Ecology are thus intended to expand the discussion already
under way in certain circles and to invite further collaboration on a
topic of common concern—the fate of the earth as a religious
responsibility. To broaden and deepen the reflective basis for mutual
collaboration has been an underlying aim of the conferences
themselves. While some might see this as a diversion from pressing
scientific or policy issues, it is with a sense of humility and yet
conviction that we enter into the arena of reflection and debate on
this issue. In the field of the study of world religions, we see this
as a timely challenge for scholars of religion to respond as engaged

intellectuals with deepening creative reflection. We hope that these conferences and volumes will be simply a beginning of further study of conceptual and symbolic resources, methodological concerns, and practical directions for meeting this environmental crisis.

Notes

1. He goes on to say, "And that is qualitatively and epochally true. If religion does not speak to [this], it is an obsolete distraction." Daniel Maguire, *The Moral Core of Judaism and Christianity: Reclaiming the Revolution* (Philadelphia: Fortress Press, 1993), 13.

2. Gerald Barney, *Global 2000 Report to the President of the United States*, (Washington, D.C.: Supt. of Docs. U.S. Government Printing Office, 1980–1981), 40.

3. Lynn White, Jr., "The Historical Roots of Our Ecologic Crisis," *Science* 155 (March 1967):1204.

4. Thomas Berry, *The Dream of the Earth* (San Francisco: Sierra Club Books, 1988).

5. Brian Swimme and Thomas Berry, *The Universe Story* (San Francisco: Harper San Francisco, 1992).

6. At the same time we recognize the limits to such a project, especially because ideas and action, theory and practice do not always occur in conjunction.

7. E. N. Anderson, *Ecologies of the Heart: Emotion, Belief, and the Environment* (New York and Oxford: Oxford University Press, 1996), 166. He qualifies this statement by saying, "The key point is not religion per se, but the use of emotionally powerful symbols to sell particular moral codes and management systems" (166). He notes, however, in various case studies how ecological wisdom is embedded in myths, symbols, and cosmologies of traditional societies.

8. *Is It Too Late?* is also the title of a book by John Cobb, first published in 1972 by Bruce and reissued in 1995 by Environmental Ethics Books.

9. Because we cannot identify here all of the methodological issues that need to be addressed, we invite further discussion by other engaged scholars.

10. See J. Baird Callicott, *Earth's Insights: A Survey of Ecological Ethics from the Mediterranean Basin to the Australian Outback* (Berkeley: University of California Press, 1994).

11. See, for example, *The Quality of Life*, ed. Martha C. Nussbaum and Amartya Sen, WIDER Studies in Development Economics (Oxford: Oxford University Press, 1993).

12. White, "The Historical Roots of Our Ecologic Crisis," 1203–7.

13. Process theology, creation-centered spirituality, and ecotheology have done much to promote these kinds of holistic perspectives within Christianity.

14. These are resources already being explored by theologians and biblical scholars.

15. While this is true theoretically, it should be noted that, like all ideologies, these traditions have at times been used for purposes of political power and social control. Moreover, they have not been able to prevent certain kinds of environmental destruction, such as deforestation in China.

16. The term "anthropocosmic" has been used by Tu Weiming in *Centrality and Commonality* (Albany: State University of New York Press, 1989).

17. Thomas Berry, "Religious Studies and the Global Human Community," unpublished manuscript.

18. Tu Weiming, "Beyond the Enlightenment Mentality," in *Worldviews and Ecology*, ed. Mary Evelyn Tucker and John Grim (Lewisburg, Pa.: Bucknell University Press, 1993; reissued, Maryknoll, N.Y.: Orbis Books, 1994).

19. This history has been described more fully by Roderick Nash in his chapter entitled "The Greening of Religion," in *The Rights of Nature: A History of Environmental Ethics* (Madison: University of Wisconsin Press, 1989).

20. *Religion and Environmental Crisis*, ed. Eugene C. Hargrove (Athens: University of Georgia Press, 1986).

21. Charlene Spretnak, *States of Grace: The Recovery of Meaning in the Post-Modern Age* (San Francisco: Harper San Francisco, 1991).

22. *Spirit and Nature: Why the Environment Is a Religious Issue*, ed. Steven Rockefeller and John Elder (Boston: Beacon Press, 1992).

23. Peter Marshall, *Nature's Web: Rethinking Our Place on Earth* (Armonk, N.Y.: M. E. Sharpe, 1992).

24. *Worldviews and Ecology*, ed. Mary Evelyn Tucker and John Grim (Lewisburg, Pa.: Bucknell University Press, 1993; reissued, Maryknoll, N.Y.: Orbis Books, 1994).

25. Callicott, *Earth's Insights*.

26. Both are State University of New York Press publications.

27. David Kinsley, *Ecology and Religion: Ecological Spirituality in a Cross-Cultural Perspective* (Englewood Cliffs, N.J.: Prentice Hall, 1995).

28. Seyyed Hossein Nasr, *Religion and the Order of Nature* (Oxford: Oxford University Press, 1996).

29. *Ethics of Environment and Development: Global Challenge, International Response*, ed. J. Ronald Engel and Joan Gibb Engel (Tucson: University of Arizona Press, 1990).

30. *Population, Consumption, and the Environment: Religious and Secular Responses*, ed. Harold Coward (Albany: State University of New York Press, 1995).

31. *This Sacred Earth: Religion, Nature, Environment*, ed. Roger S. Gottlieb (New York and London: Routledge, 1996).

32. These include volumes on Hinduism, Buddhism, Judaism, Christianity, and Islam.

Introduction:
Setting the Context

Mary Evelyn Tucker and John Berthrong

Confucian Ecology

Confucianism has significant intellectual and spiritual resources to
offer in the emerging discussions regarding attitudes toward nature,
the role of the human, and environmental ethics. Its dynamic,
organismic worldview, its vitalist understanding of *ch'i* (material
force), its respect for the vast continuity of life, its sense of
compassion for suffering, its desire to establish the grounds for just
and sustainable societies, its emphasis on holistic, moral education,
and its appreciation for the embeddedness of life in interconnected
concentric circles are only some examples of the rich resources of
the Confucian tradition in relation to ecological issues. A more
detailed discussion follows of some of the key ideas of Confucianism regarding cosmology and ethics.

It should be noted that we are using the term Confucianism
broadly, to cover the entire tradition. In a historical framework,
however, Confucianism generally refers to the early part of the
tradition in the Classical era (first millennium B.C.E.) through the
Han (206 B.C.E.–220 C.E.) and T'ang (618–907 C.E.) dynasties up
until the ninth century. Neo-Confucianism is a later development
of the tradition that arose in the tenth, eleventh, and twelfth centuries
and continued down to the twentieth century. A twentieth-century
form of Confucianism, arising in Hong Kong, Taiwan, and the
United States, is known as the New Confucianism.

Naturalistic Cosmology

Chinese naturalism as a primary ingredient of Confucianism in its
broadest sense is characterized by an organic holism and a dynamic
vitalism. The organic holism of Confucianism refers to the fact that
the universe is viewed as a vast integrated unit, not as discrete
mechanistic parts. Nature is seen as unified, interconnected, and
interpenetrating, constantly relating microcosm and macrocosm.
This interconnectedness is already present in the early Confucian
tradition in the *I ching*, or *Book of Changes*, and in the Han correspondences of the elements with seasons, directions, colors, and
even virtues.

This sense of naturalism and holism is distinguished by the view
that there is no Creator God; rather, the universe is considered to
be a self-generating, organismic process.[1] Confucians are traditionally concerned less with theories of origin or with concepts of
a personal God than with what they perceive to be the ongoing
reality of this self-generating, interrelated universe. This interconnected quality has been described by Tu Weiming as a "continuity of being."[2] This implies a great chain of being, which is in
continual process and transformation, linking inorganic, organic, and
human life-forms. For the Confucians this linkage is a reality
because all life is constituted of *ch'i*, the material force or psycho-
physical element of the universe. This is the unifying element of
the cosmos and creates the basis for a profound reciprocity between
humans and the natural world.

This brings us to a second important characteristic of Confucian
cosmology, namely, its quality of dynamic vitalism inherent in *ch'i*.
It is material force as the substance of life that is the basis for the
continuing process of change and transformation in the universe.
The term *sheng sheng* (production and reproduction) is used in
Confucian and Neo-Confucian texts to illustrate the ongoing
creativity and renewal of nature. Furthermore, it constitutes a
sophisticated awareness that change is the basis for the interaction
and continuation of the web of life systems—mineral, vegetable,
animal, and human. And finally, it celebrates transformation as the
clearest expression of the creative processes of life with which
humans should harmonize their own actions. In essence, human

beings are urged to "model themselves on the ceaseless vitality of the cosmic processes."[3] This approach is an important key to Confucian thought in general, for a sense of holism, vitalism, and harmonizing with change provides the metaphysical basis on which an integrated morality can be developed. The extended discussions of the relationship of *li* (principle) to *ch'i* (material force) in Neo-Confucianism can be seen as part of the effort to articulate continuity and order in the midst of change. *Li* is the pattern amidst flux which provides a means of establishing harmony.

The Ethics of Self-Cultivation

For the Confucian tradition as a whole, the idea of self-cultivation implies a "creative transformation"[4] such that one forms a triad with Heaven and Earth. This dynamic triad underlies the assumption of our interconnectedness to all reality and acts as an overriding goal of self-cultivation. Thus, through the deepening of this creative linkage with all things, human beings may participate fully in the transformative aspects of the universe. In doing so, they are participating in an *anthropocosmic* worldview rather than in an anthropocentric one. Tu Weiming uses this term to indicate that the human is a microcosm situated in the macrocosm of the universe itself.[5] This calls for a sense of relational resonance of the human with the cosmos rather than domination or manipulation of nature.

In cultivating their moral nature within this triad, then, human beings are entering into the cosmological processes of change and transformation. Just as the universe manifests this complex pattern of flux and fecundity, so do human beings nurture the seeds of virtue within themselves and participate in the human order in this process of ongoing transformation. This is elaborated especially by the Han Confucians and Sung Neo-Confucians through a specific understanding of a correspondence between virtues practiced by humans as having their natural counterpart in cosmic processes. For example, in his "Treatise on Humaneness" Chu Hsi (1130–1200) speaks of the moral qualities of the mind of Heaven and Earth as four, namely, origination, flourish, advantage, and firmness. These correspond to the four moral qualities of humans, namely, humaneness, righteousness, propriety, and wisdom. The cosmological and the human virtues are seen as part of one dynamic process of transformation in the universe. In Han Confucian thought these virtues are coordinated with seasons, directions, and colors.

The *anthropocosmic* view, then, of the human as forming a triad with Heaven and Earth and, indeed, affecting the growth and transformation of things through human self-cultivation and human institutions originates in Classical Confucianism, especially in Hsün Tzu (310–213 B.C.E.), and finds one of its richest expressions in Chang Tsai's *Western Inscription* (*Hsi ming*) in the eleventh century. This relationship of Heaven, Earth, and human becomes expressed as a parental one, and central to this metaphor is the notion of humans as children of the universe and responsible for its care and continuation.

To summarize, then, Confucianism may be a rich source for rethinking our own relationships between cosmology and ethics in light of present ecological concerns. Its organic holism and dynamic vitalism give us a special appreciation for the interconnectedness of all life-forms and renews our sense of the inherent value of this intricate web of life. The shared psycho-physical entity of *ch'i* becomes the basis for establishing a reciprocity between the human and nonhuman worlds. In this same vein, the ethics of self-cultivation and the nurturing of virtue in the Confucian tradition provide a broad framework for harmonizing with the natural world and completing one's role in the triad. This is only suggestive of the rich possibilities available within the Confucian tradition for creating a more comprehensive ecological worldview and effective environmental ethics. The essays in this volume point toward such a range of intellectual resources in Confucianism for rethinking human-earth relations. This volume is but a beginning for future exploration.

Volume Overview

In order to demonstrate the past, present, and potential Confucian contributions to contemporary ecological discussions, this volume is thematically organized into five major sections. The first section presents two leading Confucian scholars' analyses of the present ecological crisis in relation to Enlightenment values. The second section outlines the context of Confucianism's response to the contemporary debate on ecology in terms of worldviews, ethics, and philosophical reconceputalization. The third section presents a partial catalogue of conceptual resources for the task of critique and reconstruction. These materials are drawn from the long history of Confucianism within the East Asian cultural matrix. The fourth section presents a series of philosophic reflections on how Confucianism can add its distinctive voice to the growing global conversation about ecology. The fifth section demonstrates how Confucianism can cope with some very specific contemporary issues, critiques, and case studies.

The volume begins with a foreword to the entire series on religions of the world and ecology, in which the series editors remind us that Confucianism is only one of a number of religious traditions struggling to come to grips with contemporary environmental degradation. Religions have been continually challenged historically to respond to crisis and change. Yet the modern ecological crisis is unique in its scope and destructiveness. Never before has humankind had to question, as Tu Weiming warns, whether or not the human is a viable species. Furthermore, it is now clear that any long-term solution to the ecological crisis will be based on reformulating human values to include the relation of humans to nature. Consequently, religions, as one of the principle civilizational repositories of shared human values, must find ways individually and collectively to address the ecological crisis as a matter of fundamental moral principles and attitudes.

This volume on Confucianism and ecology focuses on the specific contributions of Confucianism to the present debate. The five sections address the ecological crisis in three overlapping modes. These are historical, dialogical, and engaged. A number of the essays approach the question of Confucianism from a historical perspective and describe how Confucianism in East Asia developed views of nature, social ethics, and cosmology, which may now shed light on contemporary problems. Chapters with a dialogical approach link the history of Confucianism to other philosophic and religious traditions. The most pertinent dialogue is that of Confucianism and modernity as embodied in the Enlightenment project. The third mode displays how Confucianism has been and is now involved in concrete ecological issues ranging from economic and industrial development to the role of women as agents of ecological transformation.

The volume begins with Tu Weiming's critique of the Enlightenment mentality. Tu argues that the modern Enlightenment project is the dominant human ideology for any analysis of the present ecological crisis. In fact, according to Tu, there has never been a more pervasive human ideology. The Enlightenment project created the modern world, which has become slowly aware that its technology has let the genie of ecological disaster out of the bottle of modernity. What began in the West as a search for liberty, equality, and fraternity has led to unrestrained industrialization and unsustainable urban sprawl on both sides of the Pacific Rim and beyond.

Wm. Theodore de Bary's response to Tu Weiming isolates two of Tu's main points, the need for rootedness and localization. From de Bary's point of view, one of the main problems of the Enlightenment is that our easy sense of being rooted in the cosmos was one of the casualties of modernization. We have lost a feeling of connectedness with our world and with humanity. De Bary reminds us that many modern Western thinkers have lamented the loss of community and cosmic solidarity as well. To prove his point, de Bary cites a long passage from Wendell Berry, the American poet-farmer turned ecological activist. Berry himself was stimulated by readings from the Confucian tradition. In the end, de Bary argues that both Berry and Tu follow the classic teaching of the *Great Learning (Ta hsüeh)* that moves from the cultivation of the self to the proper ordering of the world. In this context, any ordering of the world begins with relearning to protect our local bioregion, cherish our families, and find a way to live in a harmonious manner with the larger cosmos.

The second group of essays, by Rodney Taylor, P. J. Ivanhoe, and Michael Kalton, situates the Confucian response to the ecological crisis within the larger discussion of religion and the environment. Taylor, by reviewing how Confucians such as Tu Weiming and Okada Takehiko look at humanity's place in the cosmos, comes to the conclusion that Confucianism has the resources for serving as a modern environmental philosophy. Although Confucianism is traditionally considered to be humanistic in focus, Confucians such as Chang Tsai (1020–1077) always viewed human beings as part of the larger cosmos. Taylor locates Confucianism's contribution both in its historical past and as a dialogue partner for Western philosophers and theologians. Ivanhoe extends the discussion to relate early Confucian reflections on nature to contemporary theories of environmental philosophy. Ivanhoe shows how it is possible to link the thought of Hsün Tzu to the analytical side of modern philosophy. Here again we see how Confucianism, although deeply committed to human flourishing, is always embedded in a primordial cosmic reality. Ivanhoe explains how Hsün Tzu was deeply impressed with the coordination of nature and how human beings must learn to play a role within the larger web of life. This is described in the Confucian cosmology of the interaction of Heaven, Earth, and humans.

Kalton moves on from the historical richness of the Confucian tradition to ask how it can be reconceptualized for the twenty-first century. Kalton builds on the history of Confucian thought and envisions what a modern Confucian philosophy would have to look like in order to be sensitive to the ecological crisis. He shows how this can be done by taking key Neo-Confucian ideas such as principle (*li*), material force (*ch'i*), and self-cultivation and applying them to the contemporary situation. He underscores the importance of Confucian reflections on principle and the vital matrix of material force for constructively reconceptualizing our relations with the natural world.

The next section deals in greater detail with various conceptual resources drawn from the Chinese, Korean, and Japanese contexts. Tu Weiming begins with a classic statement of the Confucian concern for the continuity of being. It is this Chinese Confucian focus on the relatedness of being that Tu holds up as the foundation for future Confucian ecological speculations. It is a statement of Tu's vision of the anthropocosmic nature of Confucianism as an inclusive humanism that is rooted in the regenerative rhythms of the cosmos.

Joseph Adler returns to one of the founding figures of Neo-Confucianism, Chou Tun-i (1017–1073). Adler attends to a key cosmological metaphor of responsiveness (*ying*) as a method to unlock Chou's vision of nature and humanity. Adler provides us with careful readings of some of Chou's texts that reveal how this seminal thinker demonstrated that Confucian social ethics ought to be expanded to include the natural world as well. As Adler reminds

us, the Neo-Confucians were famous for their sensitive understanding of living things, so much so that it was reported that Chou
was worried about cutting the grass outside the window of his study.

Toshio Kuwako focuses his attention on the thought of Chu Hsi
(1130–1200), the grand synthesizer of the Northern and Southern
Sung Neo-Confucian philosophy. According to Kuwako, Chu's
genius lay in his ability to take the more random reflections of his
Sung colleagues and weave them into a coherent philosophic whole.
One of Chu's chief concerns was to demonstrate that the virtue of
humaneness (*jen*) not only refers to humanity but to the correlation
of all living beings and nature.

The next two essays, by Young Chan Ro and Mary Evelyn
Tucker, continue the historical discussion of the Confucian resources
for ecology through the exploration of the crucial concept of
material force (*ch'i*). In addition to being one of the paramount
concepts in the pan–East Asian philosophic lexicon, *ch'i* functions
as a prime resource for reflections on nature and cosmology. Ro
guides us through an examination of the Korean Yi Yulgok (1536–
1584), one of the most famous of the Yi dynasty Neo-Confucian
philosophers. As Ro explains, Yulgok was known for his balanced
presentation of *ch'i* as the connective cosmological link between
all beings. *Ch'i* operates as a foundation for all ecosystems and
allows for a place for both humanity and all other entities. In fact,
if we consider Yulgok's arguments seriously, then we must attend
to nature as an interconnected web of nature that we disregard at
our own peril. Tucker's essay surveys the broad theme of *ch'i* in
key Chinese Neo-Confucian figures. She then discusses how the
Japanese Neo-Confucian Kaibara Ekken (1630–1714) developed an
ecological philosophy based on *ch'i* theory. As with Kuwako and
Ro, Tucker makes the case that reflection on *ch'i* is not only
important for our understanding of the East Asian development of
Neo-Confucianism but may also provide us with a way to think
about humanity and nature in a global context.

The next three chapters are broad-ranging philosophic reflections
on contemporary ecological concerns. Chung-ying Cheng attempts
a complex interweaving of cosmology, ecology, and ethics. Cheng
argues that at the heart of the Confucian vision lies an inclusive
humanism based on the relational patterns of the *Book of Changes*
(*I ching*). Cheng believes that, if we can revive this kind of

relational, processive axiology, then we have an opportunity to reverse the dualistic and agonistic patterns of thought that have dominated Western philosophy since the Enlightenment. In much the same spirit, John Berthrong tries to show how Classical Confucian metaphors can be employed by modern New Confucians as they seek to respond to the ecological crisis. Building on the work of Mou Tsung-san, one of the most important of the New Confucians, Berthrong illustrates how the fundamental trait of concern-consciousness can guide the tradition into a strengthened understanding of nature. Robert Neville concludes the trio of philosophic studies by advancing the notion of "posture," or "orientation," as important for Confucian ecological reflection. For Neville, posture is related to the notion of ritual or habit, namely, how a human being relates effectively and reciprocally to the wider world, including both humans and nature. Clearly, one of the pressing concerns of the modern world is for humanity to find a balanced way or structure, such as is suggested in the *Doctrine of the Mean* (*Chung yung*), that allows for the intrinsic value of nature to be preserved and enhanced as it pertains to human flourishing.

The final triad of essays, by Huey-li Li, Seiko Gotō and Julia Ching, and Robert Weller and Peter Bol, move from the theoretical to the practical. As Li notes, whatever rich resources the Confucian tradition might have to contribute to contemporary concerns, many feminists remain unconvinced. Feminists often charge that Confucianism is incurably patriarchal in structure. Li underscores the inevitable contradictions between theories and practices. She observes that despite numerous Taoist and Confucian texts focusing on the unity of nature and humanity, modern East Asia is as highly industrialized and polluted as many other parts of the world. However, Li argues that if we pay proper attention to the notion of heaven (*t'ien*), we might find a means to address ecofeminist critiques of Confucianism in a constructive manner.

Gotō and Ching remind us that not all cultural exchanges occur exclusively through the medium of ideas. They provide us with a study of two famous parks, Kusihikawa Korakuon Park in Japan and the Wörlitzer Park in Germany. In outlining some of the Confucian influences on landscape gardening, Gotō and Ching underscore the broader cultural and aesthetic matrix in which Confucianism spread beyond China to East Asia and even to the West.

The final chapter, by Robert Weller and Peter Bol, directly addresses the present ecological crisis by asking: How is it possible to promote sound ecological attitudes and policies in contemporary China? They point out that Chinese cosmology is based on a theory of cosmic resonances that shows nature is best understood in terms of pulsating harmonies. Another feature of the Weller and Bol essay is an exploration of popular culture as illustrated by the continued use of traditional almanacs and the persistence of *feng shui*, or geomancy. The authors note that, as modern Taiwanese try to deal with ecological degradation, they often resort to the language of kinship and cosmic resonance. Whatever ideological means the Chinese may involve in formulating sound ecological policies, some of the underlying motivations and explanations will, no doubt, continue to rely on traditional sources.[6]

The essays in this volume, then, show a living Confucian tradition seeking to find a useful retrieval of resources to respond adequately to the growing destruction of the environment in Asia and beyond. Of course, the Confucian world is not alone in this task. All the major religious traditions have become more aware in recent years of the challenge presented by unrestrained development and subsequent pollution. Moreover, they are ever more conscious that, although they may have resources to construct better attitudes and policies toward nature, they have not done so adequately in the past. While further research and discussion is vital, this volume is meant to be an initial step toward lessening the divide between rich conceptual resources and efficacious environmental practices in the contemporary world.

Notes

1. Frederick F. Mote, *Intellectual Foundations of China* (New York: Alfred A. Knopf, 1971), 17–18.

2. See Tu Weiming's article, included in this volume, "The Continuity of Being: Chinese Visions of Nature"; originally published in Tu Wei-ming, *Confucian Thought: Selfhood as Creative Transformation* (Albany: State University of New York Press, 1985).

3. Tu, *Confucian Thought: Selfhood as Creative Transformation*, 39. Professor Tu notes, "For this reference in the *Chou I*, see *A Concordance to Yi-Ching*, Harvard Yenching Institute Sinological Index Series Supplement no. 10 (reprint; Taipei: Chinese Materials and Research Aids Service Center, Inc., 1966), 1/1."

4. See Tu Weiming's essays in *Confucian Thought: Selfhood as Creative Transformation*.

5. Tu Weiming uses the term "anthropocosmic" widely. See especially *Confucian Thought: Selfhood as Creative Transformation* and *Centrality and Commonality: An Essay on Confucian Religiousness* (Albany: State University of New York Press, 1989).

6. The understanding of the ecological role of traditional sources, such as geomancy and Chinese medicine, is discussed by E. N. Anderson in *Ecologies of the Heart* (Oxford: Oxford University Press, 1996).

The Nature of the Critique

Beyond the Enlightenment Mentality

Tu Weiming

The Enlightenment mentality underlies the rise of the modern West as the most dynamic and transformative ideology in human history.[1] Virtually all major spheres of interest characteristic of the modern age are indebted to or intertwined with this mentality: science and technology, industrial capitalism, market economy, democratic polity, mass communication, research universities, civil and military bureaucracies, and professional organizations. Furthermore, the values we cherish as definitions of modern consciousness— including liberty, equality, human rights, the dignity of the indivi- dual, respect for privacy, government for, by, and of the people, and due process of law—are genetically, if not structurally, inseparable from the Enlightenment mentality. We have flourished in the spheres of interest and their attendant values occasioned by the advent of the modern West since the eighteenth century. They have made our life-world operative and meaningful. We take if for granted that, through instrumental rationality, we can solve the world's major problems and that progress, primarily in economic terms, is desirable and necessary for the human community as a whole.

We are so seasoned in the Enlightenment mentality that we assume the reasonableness of its general ideological thrust. It seems self-evident that both capitalism and socialism subscribe to the aggressive anthropocentrism underlying the modern mind-set: man is not only the measure of all things but also the only source of power for economic well-being, political stability, and social development. The Enlightenment faith in progress, reason, and individualism may have been challenged by some of the most brilliant minds in the modern Western academy, but it remains a standard of inspiration for intellectual and spiritual leaders throughout the world. It is inconceivable that any international project, including those in ecological sciences, not subscribe to the theses that the human condition is improvable, that it is desirable to find rational means to solve the world's problems, and that the dignity of the person as an individual ought to be respected. Enlightenment as human awakening, as the discovery of the human potential for global transformation, and as the realization of the human desire to become the measure and master of all things is still the most influential moral discourse in the political culture of the modern age; for decades it has been the unquestioned assumption of the ruling minorities and cultural elites of developing countries, as well as highly industrialized nations.

A fair understanding of the Enlightenment mentality requires a frank discussion of the dark side of the modern West as well. The "unbound Prometheus," symbolizing the runaway technology of development, may have been a spectacular achievement of human ingenuity in the early phases of the industrial revolution. Despite impassioned reactions from the romantic movement and insightful criticisms of the forebears of the "human sciences," the Enlightenment mentality, fueled by the Faustian drive to explore, to know, to conquer, and to subdue, persisted as the reigning ideology of the modern West. It is now fully embraced as the unquestioned rationale for development in East Asia.

However, a realistic appraisal of the Enlightenment mentality reveals many faces of the modern West incongruous with the image of "the Age of Reason." In the context of modern Western hegemonic discourse, progress may entail inequality, reason, self-interest, and individual greed. The American dream of owning a car and a house, earning a fair wage, and enjoying freedom of privacy, expression, religion, and travel, while reasonable to our (American) sense of what ordinary life demands, is lamentably unexportable as a modern necessity from a global perspective. Indeed, it has now been widely acknowledged as no more than a dream for a significant segment of the American population as well.

An urgent task for the community of like-minded persons deeply concerned about ecological issues and the disintegration of communities at all levels is to insure that both the ruling minorities and cultural elites in the modern West actively participate in a spiritual joint venture to rethink the Enlightenment heritage. The paradox is that we cannot afford to accept uncritically its inner logic in light of the unintended negative consequences it has engendered on the life-support systems; nor can we reject its relevance, with all of the fruitful ambiguities this entails, to our intellectual self-definition, present and future. There is no easy way out. We do not have an "either-or" choice. The possibility of a radically different ethic or a new value system separate from and independent of the Enlightenment mentality is neither realistic nor authentic. It may even appear to be either cynical or hypercritical. We need to explore the spiritual resources that may help us to broaden the scope of the Enlightenment project, deepen its moral sensitivity, and, if necessary, transform creatively its genetic constraints in order to realize fully its potential as a worldview for the human condition as a whole.

A key to the success of this spiritual joint venture is to recognize the conspicuous absence of the idea of community, let alone the global community, in the Enlightenment project. Fraternity, a functional equivalent of community in the three cardinal virtues of the French Revolution, has received scant attention in modern Western economic, political, and social thought. The willingness to tolerate inequality, the faith in the salvific power of self-interest, and the unbridled affirmation of aggressive egoism have greatly poisoned the good well of progress, reason, and individualism. The need to express a universal intent for the formation of a "global village" and to articulate a possible link between the fragmented world we experience in our ordinary daily existence and the imagined community for the human species as a whole is deeply felt by an increasing number of concerned intellectuals. This requires, at a minimum, the replacement of the principle of self-interest, no matter how broadly defined, with a new Golden Rule: "Do not do unto others what you would not want others to do unto you."[2] Since the new Golden Rule is stated in the negative, it will have to be augmented by a positive principle: "in order to establish myself, I have to help others to enlarge themselves."[3] An inclusive sense of community, based on the communal critical self-consciousness of reflective minds, is an ethico-religious goal as well as a philosophical ideal.

The mobilization of at least three kinds of spiritual resources is necessary to ensure that this simple vision is grounded in the historicity of the cultural complexes informing our ways of life today. The first kind involves the ethico-religious traditions of the modern West, notably Greek philosophy, Judaism, and Christianity. The very fact that they have been instrumental in giving birth to the Enlightenment mentality makes a compelling case for them to reexamine their relationships to the rise of the modern West in order to create a new public sphere for the transvaluation of typical Western values. The exclusive dichotomy of matter/spirit, body/ mind, sacred/profane, human/nature, or creator/creature must be transcended to allow supreme values, such as the sanctity of the earth, the continuity of being, the beneficiary interaction between the human community and nature, and the mutuality between humankind and Heaven, to receive the saliency they deserve in philosophy, religion, and theology.

The Greek philosophical emphasis on rationality, the biblical image of man having "dominion" over the earth, and the Protestant work ethic provided necessary, if not sufficient, sources for the Enlightenment mentality. However, the unintended negative consequences of the rise of the modern West have so undermined the sense of community implicit in the Hellenistic idea of the citizen, the Judaic idea of the covenant, and the Christian idea of fellowship that it is morally imperative for these great traditions, which have maintained highly complex and tension-ridden relationships with the Enlightenment mentality, to formulate their critique of the blatant anthropocentrism inherent in the Enlightenment project. The emergence of a communitarian ethic as a critique of the idea of the person as a rights-bearing, interest-motivated, rational economic animal clearly indicates the relevance of an Aristotelian, Pauline, Abrahamic, or Republican ethic to current moral self-reflexivity in North America. Jürgen Habermas's attempt to broaden the scope of rational discourse by emphasizing the importance of "communicative rationality" in social intercourse represents a major intellectual effort to develop new conceptual apparatuses to enrich the Enlightenment tradition.[4]

The second kind of spiritual resource is derived from non-Western, axial-age civilizations, which include Hinduism, Jainism, and Buddhism in South and Southeast Asia, Confucianism and Taoism in East Asia, and Islam. Historically, Islam should be considered an essential intellectual heritage of the modern West because of its contribution to the Renaissance. The current practice, especially by the mass media of North America and Western Europe, of consigning Islam to radical otherness is historically unsound and culturally insensitive. It has, in fact, seriously undermined the modern West's own self-interest as well as its own self-understanding. Islam and these non-Western ethico-religious traditions provide sophisticated and practicable resources in worldviews, rituals, institutions, styles of education, and patterns of human-relatedness. They can help to develop ways of life, both as continuation of and alternative to the Western European and North American exemplification of the Enlightenment mentality. Industrial East Asia, under the influence of Confucian culture, has already developed a less adversarial, less individualistic, and less self-interested modern civilization. The coexistence of market economy with government leadership, democratic polity with meritocracy, and individual initiatives with group orientation has, since the Second World War, made this region economically and politically the most dynamic area of the world. The significance of the contribution of Confucian ethics to the rise of industrial East Asia offers profound possibilities for the possible emergence of Hindu, Jain, Buddhist, and Islamic forms of modernity.

The Westernization of Confucian Asia (including Japan, the two Koreas, mainland China, Hong Kong, Taiwan, Singapore, and Vietnam) may have forever altered its spiritual landscape, but its indigenous resources (including Mahāyāna Buddhism, Taoism, Shintoism, shamanism, and other folk religions) have the resiliency to resurface and make their presence known in a new synthesis. The caveat, of course, is that, having been humiliated and frustrated by the imperialist and colonial domination of the modern West for more than a century, the rise of industrial East Asia symbolizes the instrumental rationality of the Enlightenment heritage with a vengeance. Indeed, the mentality of Japan and the Four Mini-Dragons (South Korea, Taiwan, Hong Kong, Singapore) is characterized by mercantilism, commercialism, and international competitiveness. The People's Republic of China (the motherland of the Sinic world) has blatantly opted for the same strategy of development and has thus exhibited the same mentality since the reform was set in motion in 1979. Surely the possibility for these nations to develop more humane and sustainable communities should not be exaggerated; nor should it be undermined.

The third kind of spiritual resource involves the primal traditions: Native American, Hawaiian, Maori, and numerous tribal indigenous religious traditions. They have demonstrated, with physical strength and aesthetic elegance, that human life has been sustainable since Neolithic times. The implications for practical living are far-reaching. Their style of human flourishing is not a figment of the mind but an experienced reality in our modern age.

A distinctive feature of primal traditions is a deep experience of rootedness. Each indigenous religious tradition is embedded in a concrete place symbolizing a way of perceiving, a mode of thinking, a form of living, an attitude, and a worldview. Given the unintended disastrous consequences of the Enlightenment mentality, there are obvious lessons that the modern mind-set can learn from indigenous religious traditions. A natural outcome of indigenous peoples' embeddedness in concrete locality is their intimate and detailed knowledge of their environment; indeed, the demarcations between their human habitat and nature are muted. Implicit in this model of existence is the realization that mutuality and reciprocity between the anthropological world and the cosmos at large is both necessary and desirable. What we can learn from them, then, is a new way of perceiving, a new mode of thinking, a new form of living, a new attitude, and a new worldview. A critique of the Enlightenment mentality and its derivative modern mind-set from the perspective of indigenous peoples could be thought-provoking.

An equally significant aspect of indigenous lifeways is the ritual of bonding in ordinary daily human interaction. The density of kinship relations, the rich texture of interpersonal communication, the detailed and nuanced appreciation of the surrounding natural and cultural world, and the experienced connectedness with ancestors point to communities grounded in ethnicity, gender, language, land, and faith. The primordial ties are constitutive parts of their being and activity. In Huston Smith's characterization, what they exemplify is participation rather than control in motivation, empathic understanding rather than empiricist apprehension in epistemology, respect for the transcendent rather than domination over nature in worldview, and fulfillment rather than alienation in human experience. As we begin to question the soundness or even sanity of some of our most cherished ways of thinking—such as regarding knowledge as power rather than wisdom, asserting the desirability of material progress despite its corrosive influence on the soul, and justifying the anthropocentric manipulation of nature even at the cost of destroying the life-support system—indigenous perspectives emerge as a source of inspiration.

Of course, I am not proposing any romantic attachment to or nostalgic sentiments for "primal consciousness," and I am critically aware that claims of primordiality are often modernist cultural constructions dictated by the politics of recognition. Rather, I suggest that, as both beneficiaries and victims of the Enlightenment mentality, we show our fidelity to our common heritage by enriching it, transforming it, and restructuring it with all three kinds of spiritual resources still available to us for the sake of developing a truly ecumenical sense of global community. Indeed, of the three great Enlightenment values embodied in the French Revolution, fraternity seems to have attracted the least attention in the subsequent two centuries. The re-presentation of the *Problematik* of community in recent years is symptomatic of the confluence of two apparently contradictory forces in the late twentieth century: the global village as both a virtual reality and an imagined community in our information age and the disintegration and restructuring of human togetherness at all levels, from family to nation.

It may not be immodest to say that we are beginning to develop a fourth kind of spiritual resource from the core of the Enlightenment project itself. Our disciplined reflection, a communal act rather than an isolated struggle, is a first step toward the "creative zone" envisioned by religious leaders and teachers of ethics. The feminist critique of tradition, the concern for the environment, and the persuasion of religious pluralism are obvious examples of this new corporate critical self-awareness. The need to go beyond the Enlightenment mentality, without either deconstructing or abandoning its commitment to rationality, liberty, equality, human rights, and distributive justice, requires a thorough reexamination of modernity as a signifier and modernization as a process.

Underlying this reexamination is the intriguing issue of traditions in modernity. The dichotomous thinking of tradition and modernity as two incompatible forms of life will have to be replaced by a much more nuanced investigation of the continuous interaction between modernity as the perceived outcome of "rationalization" defined in Weberian terms and traditions as "habits of the heart" (to borrow an expression from Alexis de Tocqueville), enduring modes of thinking, or salient features of cultural self-understanding. The traditions in modernity are not merely historical sedimentation passively deposited in modern consciousness. Nor are they, in functional terms, simply inhibiting factors to be undermined by the unilinear trajectory of development. On the contrary, they are both constraining and enabling forces capable of shaping the particular contour of modernity in any given society. It is, therefore, conceptually naïve and methodologically fallacious to relegate traditions to the residual category in our discussion of the modernizing process. Indeed, an investigation of traditions in modernity is essential for our appreciation of modernization as a highly differentiated cultural phenomena rather than as a homogeneous integral process of Westernization.

Talcott Parsons may have been right in assuming that market economy, democratic polity, and individualism are three inseparable dimensions of modernity.[5] The post–Cold War era seems to have inaugurated a new world order in which marketization, democratization, and individualism are salient features of a new global village. The collapse of socialism gives the impression that market rather than planned economy, democratic rather than authoritarian polity, and individualist rather than collectivist style of life symbolize the wave of the future. Whether or not we believe in the "end of history," a stage of human development in which only advanced capitalism—characterized by multinational corporations, information superhighways, technology-driven sciences, mass communication, and conspicuous consumption—dominates, we must be critically aware of the globalizing forces which, through a variety of networks, literally transform the earth into a wired discourse community. As a result, distance, no matter how great, does not at all inhibit electronic communication and, ironically, territorial proximity does not necessarily guarantee actual contact. We can be frequent conversation partners with associates thousands of miles apart, yet we are often strangers to our neighbors, colleagues, and relatives.

The advent of the global village as virtual reality rather than authentic home is by no means congenial to human flourishing. Contrary to the classical Confucian ideal of the "great harmony" (*ta-t'ung*), what the global village exhibits is sharp difference, severe differentiation, drastic demarcation, thunderous dissonance, and outright discrimination. The world, compressed into an interconnected ecological, financial, commercial, trading, and electronic system, has never been so divided in wealth, influence, and power. The advent of the imagined, and even anticipated, global village is far from a cause for celebration.

Never in world history has the contrast between the rich and the poor, the dominant and the marginalized, the articulate and the silenced, the included and the excluded, the informed and the uninformed, and the connected and the isolated been so markedly drawn. The rich, dominant, articulate, included, informed, and connected beneficiaries of the system form numerous transnational networks making distance and, indeed, ethnic boundary, cultural diversity, religious exclusivism, or national sovereignty inconsequential in their march toward domination. On the other hand, residents of the same neighborhood may have radically different access to information, ideas, tangible resources (such as money), and immaterial goods (such as prestige). People of the same electoral district may subscribe to sharply conflicting political ideologies, social mores, and worldviews. They may also experience basic categories of human existence (such as time and space) in incommensurable ways. The severity of the contrast between the haves and the have-nots at all levels of the human experience— individual, family, society, and nation—can easily be demonstrated by hard empirical data. The sense of relative deprivation is greatly intensified by the glorification of conspicuous consumption by the mass media. Even in the most economically advanced nations, notably North America, the Scandinavian countries and other nations of Western Europe, and Japan and the Mini-Dragons, the pervasive mood is one of discontent, anxiety, and frustration.

If we focus our attention exclusively on the powerful megatrends that have exerted shaping influences on the global community since the end of the Second World War—science, technology, communication, trade, finance, entertainment, travel, tourism, migration, and disease—we may easily be misled into believing that the world has changed so much that the human condition is being structured by newly emerging global forces without any reference to our inherited historical and cultural praxis. One of the most significant *fin-de-siècle* reflections of the twentieth century is the acknowledgment that globalization does not mean homogenization and that modernization intensifies as well as lessens economic, political, social, cultural, and religious conflict in both inter- and intranational contexts. The emergence of primordial ties (ethnicity, language, gender, land, class, and faith) as powerful forces in constructing internally defensive cultural identities and externally aggressive religious exclusivities compels practical-minded global thinkers to develop new conceptual resources to understand the spirit of our time. The common practice of internationalists, including some of the most sophisticated analyzers of the world scene, of condemning the enduring strength of primordial ties as a parochial reaction to the inevitable process of globalization is simple-minded and ill-advised. What we witness in Bosnia, Africa, Sri Lanka, and India is not simply "fragmentization" as opposed to global integration. Since we are acutely aware of the explosive potential of ethnicity in the United States, language in Canada, and religious fundamentalism in all three major monotheistic religions, we must learn to appreciate that the quest for roots is a worldwide phenomenon.

Nowadays we are confronted with two conflicting and even contradictory forces in the global community: internationalization (globalization) and localization (communization). The United Nations, which came into being because of the spirit of internationalization, must now deal with issues of rootedness (all those specified above as primordial ties). While globalization in science, technology, mass communication, trade, tourism, finance, migration, and disease is progressing at an unprecedented rate and to an unprecedented degree, the pervasiveness and depth of communal (or tribal) feelings, both hidden and aroused, cannot be easily transformed by the Enlightenment values of instrumental rationality, individual liberty, calculated self-interest, material progress, and rights consciousness. The resiliency and explosive power of human-relatedness can be better appreciated by an ethic mindful of the need for reasonableness in any form of negotiation, distributive justice, sympathy, civility, duty-consciousness, dignity of person, sense of intrinsic worth, and self-cultivation.

In the Confucian perspective, human beings are not merely rational beings, political animals, tool-users, or language-manipulators. Confucians seem to have deliberately rejected simplistic reductionist models. They define human beings in terms of five integrated visions:

1. Human beings are sentient beings, capable of internal resonance not only between and among themselves but also with other animals, plants, trees, mountains, and rivers, indeed nature as a whole.

2. Human beings are social beings. As isolated individuals, human beings are weak by comparison with other members of the animal kingdom, but if they are organized to form a society, they have inner strength not only for survival but also for flourishing. Human-relatedness as exemplified in a variety of networks of interaction is necessary for human survival and human flourishing. Our sociality defines who we are.

3. Human beings are political beings in the sense that human-relatedness is, by biological nature and social necessity, differentiated in terms of hierarchy, status, and authority. While Confucians insist upon the fluidity of these artificially constructed boundaries, they recognize the significance of "difference" in an "organic" as opposed to "mechanic" solidarity—thus the centrality of the principle of fairness and the primacy of the practice of distributive justice in a humane society.

4. Human beings are also historical beings sharing collective memories, cultural memories, cultural traditions, ritual praxis, and "habits of the heart."

5. Human beings are metaphysical beings with the highest aspirations not simply defined in terms of anthropocentric ideas but characterized by the ultimate concern to be constantly inspired by and continuously responsive to the Mandate of Heaven.

The Confucian way is a way of learning, learning to be human. Learning to be human in the Confucian spirit is to engage oneself in a ceaseless, unending process of creative self-transformation, both as a communal act and as a dialogical response to Heaven. This involves four inseparable dimensions—self, community, nature, and the transcendent. The purpose of learning is always understood as being for the sake of the self, but the self is never an isolated individual (an island); rather, it is a center of relationships (a flowing stream). The self as a center of relationships is a dynamic open system rather than a closed static structure. Therefore, mutuality between self and community, harmony between human species and nature, and continuous communication with Heaven are defining characteristics and supreme values in the human project.[6]

Since Confucians take the concrete living human being here and now as their point of departure in the development of their philosophical anthropology, they recognize the embeddedness and rootedness of the human condition. Therefore, the profound significance of what we call primordial ties—ethnicity, gender, language, land, class, and basic spiritual orientation—which are intrinsic in the Confucian project, is a celebration of cultural diversity (this is not to be confused with any form of pernicious relativism). Often, Confucians understand their own path as learning of the body and mind (*shen-hsin-chih-hsüeh*) or learning of nature and destiny (*hsing-ming-chih-hsüeh*). There is a recognition that each one of us is fated to be a unique person embedded in a particular condition. By definition, we are unique particular human beings, but at the same time each and every one of us has the intrinsic possibility for self-cultivation, self-development, and self-realization. Despite fatedness and embeddedness as necessary structural limitations in our conditionality, we are endowed with infinite possibilities for self-transformation in our process of learning to be human. We are, therefore, intrinsically free. Our freedom, embodied in our responsibility for ourselves as the center of relationships, creates our worth. That alone deserves and demands respect.

In discussing the "spirit" of the Five Classics in the concluding section of *The World of Thought in Ancient China*, Benjamin Schwartz, referring to the central issue of the Neo-Confucian project, observes:

> In the end the root problem was to be sought where Confucius and
> Mencius had sought them—in the human heart/mind. It is only the
> human heart/mind. . .which possesses the capacity to "make itself

sincere" and having made itself sincere to extend this transcendent capacity to realize the *tao* within the structures of human society. When viewed from this perspective, this is the essential gospel of the Four Books. At a deeper level, the Four Books also point to an ontological ground for the belief in this transcendental ethical capacity of the individual in the face of the ongoing challenge of a metaethical Taoist and Buddhist mysticism.[7]

The ontological grounding of the Neo-Confucian project on the learning of the heart-and-mind enabled Confucian intellectuals in late imperial China, premodern Vietnam, Chosŏn Korea, and Tokugawa Japan to create a cultural space above the family and below the state. This is why, though they never left home, actively participated in community affairs, or deeply engaged themselves in local, regional, or "national" politics, they did not merely adjust themselves to the world. Max Weber's overall assessment of the Confucian life-orientation misses the point. The spiritual resources that sustained their social activism came from minding their own business and included cultivating themselves, teaching others to be good, "looking for friends in history," emulating the sages, setting up cultural norms, interpreting the Mandate of Heaven, transmitting the Way, and transforming the world as a moral community.

As we are confronted with the issue of a new world order in lieu of the exclusive dichotomy (capitalism and socialism) imposed by the super powers, we are easily tempted to come up with facile generalizations: "the end of history,"[8] "the clash of civilizations,"[9] or "the Pacific century." The much more difficult and, hopefully, in the long haul, much more significant line of inquiry is to address truly fundamental issues of learning to be human: Are we isolated individuals, or do we each live as a center of relationships? Is moral self-knowledge necessary for personal growth? Can any society prosper or endure without developing a basic sense of duty and responsibility among its members? Should our pluralistic society deliberately cultivate shared values and a common ground for human understanding? As we become acutely aware of our earth's vulnerability and increasingly wary of our own fate as an "endangered species," what are the critical spiritual questions to ask?[10]

Since the Opium War (1840–1842), China has endured many holocausts. Prior to 1949, imperialism was the main culprit, but

since the founding of the People's Republic of China, erratic
leadership and faulty policies must also share the blame. Although
millions of Chinese died, the neighboring countries were not
seriously affected and the outside world was, by and large, oblivious
to what actually happened. Since 1979, China has been rapidly
becoming an integral part of the global economic system. More than
30 percent of the Chinese economy is tied to international trade.
Natural economic territories have emerged between Hong Kong and
Chuan Chou, Fujian and Taiwan, Shantung and South Korea.
Japanese, European, and American, as well as Hong Kong and
Taiwanese, investments are present in virtually all Chinese pro-
vinces. The return of Hong Kong to the PRC, the conflict across
the Taiwan Straits, the economic and cultural interchange among
overseas Chinese communities and between them and the motherland, the intraregional communication in East Asia, the political and
economic integration of the Association for Southeast Asian
Nations, and the rise of the Asia-Pacific region will all have
substantial impact on our shrinking global community.

The revitalization of the Confucian discourse may contribute to
the formation of a much needed communal critical self-consciousness among East Asian intellectuals. We may very well be in the
very beginning of global history rather than witnessing the end of
history. And, from a comparative cultural perspective, this new
beginning must take as its point of departure dialogue rather than
clash of civilizations. Our awareness of the danger of civilizational
conflicts, rooted in ethnicity, language, land, and religion, makes
the necessity of dialogue particularly compelling. An alternative
model of sustainable development, with an emphasis on the ethical
and spiritual dimensions of human flourishing, must be sought.

The time is long overdue to move beyond a mind-set shaped by
instrumental rationality and private interests. As the politics of
domination fades, we witness the dawning of an age of communication, networking, negotiation, interaction, interfacing, and
collaboration. Whether or not East Asian intellectuals, inspired by
the Confucian spirit of self-cultivation, family cohesiveness, social
solidarity, benevolent governance, and universal peace, will articulate an ethic of responsibility as Chinese, Japanese, Koreans, and
Vietnamese emigrate to other parts of the world is profoundly
meaningful for global stewardship.

We can actually envision the Confucian perception of human flourishing, based upon the dignity of the person, in terms of a series of concentric circles: self, family, community, society, nation, world, and cosmos. We begin with a quest for true personal identity, an open and creatively transforming selfhood which, paradoxically, must be predicated on our ability to overcome selfishness and egoism. We cherish family cohesiveness. In order to do that, we have to go beyond nepotism. We embrace communal solidarity, but we have to transcend parochialism to realize its true value. We can be enriched by social integration, provided that we overcome ethnocentrism and chauvinistic culturalism. We are committed to national unity, but we ought to rise above aggressive nationalism so that we can be genuinely patriotic. We are inspired by human flourishing, but we must endeavor not to be confined by anthropocentrism, for the full meaning of humanity is anthropocosmic rather than anthropocentric. On the occasion of the international symposium on Islamic-Confucian dialogue organized by the University of Malaya (March 1995), the Deputy Prime Minister of Malaysia, Anwar Ibrahim, quoted a statement from Huston Smith's *The World's Religions*. It very much captures the Confucian spirit of self-transcendence:

> In shifting the center of one's empathic concern from oneself to one's family one transcends selfishness. The move from family to community transcends nepotism. The move from community to nation transcends parochialism and the move to all humanity counters chauvinistic nationalism.[11]

We can even add: the move towards the unity of Heaven and humanity (*t'ien-jen-ho-i*) transcends secular humanism, a blatant form of anthropocentrism characteristic of the Enlightenment mentality. Indeed, it is in the anthropocosmic spirit that we find communication between self and community, harmony between human species and nature, and mutuality between humanity and Heaven. This integrated comprehensive vision of learning to be human serves well as a point of departure for a new discourse on the global ethic.

The case against anthropocentrism through the formulation of an anthropocosmic vision embodied in the Neo-Confucian learning of the heart-and-mind is succinctly presented by Wang Yang-ming. Let me conclude with the opening statement in his *Inquiry on the Great Learning*:

> The great man regards Heaven and Earth and the myriad things as one body. He regards the world as one family and the country as one person. . . . That the great man can regard Heaven, Earth, and the myriad things as one body is not because he deliberately wants to do so, but because it is natural to the humane nature of his mind that he do so. Forming one body with Heaven, Earth, and the myriad things is not only true of the great man. Even the mind of the small man is no different. Only he himself makes it small. Therefore when he sees a child about to fall into a well, he cannot help a feeling of alarm and commiseration. This shows that his humanity (*jen*) forms one body with the child. It may be objected that the child belongs to the same species. Again, when he observes the pitiful cries and frightened appearance of birds and animals about to be slaughtered, he cannot help feeling an "inability to bear" their suffering. This shows that his humanity forms one body with birds and animals. It may be objected that birds and animals are sentient beings as he is. But when he sees plants broken and destroyed, he cannot help. . .feeling. . .pity. This shows that his humanity forms one body with plants. It may be said that plants are living things as he is. Yet even when he sees tiles and stones shattered and crushed, he cannot help. . .feeling. . .regret. This shows that his humanity forms one body with tiles and stones. This means that even the mind of the small man necessarily has the humanity that forms one body with all. Such a mind is rooted in his Heaven-endowed nature, and is naturally intelligent, clear and not beclouded. For this reason it is called "clear character."[12]

For Confucians to fully realize themselves, it is not enough to become a responsible householder, effective social worker, or conscientious political servant. No matter how successful one is in the sociopolitical arena, the full measure of one's humanity cannot be accommodated without a reference to Heaven. The highest Confucian ideal is the "unity of man and Heaven," which defines humanity not only in anthropological terms but also in cosmological terms. In the *Doctrine of the Mean* (*Chung yung*), the most authentic manifestation of humanity is characterized as "forming a trinity with Heaven and Earth."[13]

Yet, since Heaven does not speak and the Way in itself cannot make human beings great—which suggests that although Heaven is omnipresent and may be omniscient, it is certainly not omnipotent—our understanding of the Mandate of Heaven requires that we fully appreciate the rightness and principle inherent in our heart-minds. Our ability to transcend egoism, nepotism, parochialism, ethnocentrism, and chauvinistic nationalism must be extended to anthropocentrism as well. To make ourselves deserving partners of Heaven, we must be constantly in touch with that silent illumination that makes the rightness and principle in our heart-minds shine forth brilliantly. If we cannot go beyond the constraints of our own species, the most we can hope for is an exclusive, secular humanism advocating man as the measure of all things. By contrast, Confucian humanism is inclusive; it is predicated on an "anthropocosmic" vision. Humanity in its all-embracing fullness "forms one body with Heaven, Earth, and the myriad things." Self-realization, in the last analysis, is ultimate transformation, that process which enables us to embody the family, community, nation, world, and cosmos in our sensitivity.

The ecological implications of the Confucian anthropocosmic worldview are implicit, yet need to be more carefully articulated. On the one hand, there are rich philosophical resources in the Confucian triad of Heaven, Earth, and human. On the other hand, there are numerous moral resources for developing more comprehensive environmental ethics. These include textual references, ritual practices, social norms, and political policies. From classical times Confucians were concerned with harmonizing with nature and accepting the appropriate limits and boundaries of nature. This concern manifested itself in a variety of forms cultivating virtues that were considered to be both personal and cosmic. It also included biological imagery used for describing the process of self-cultivation. To realize the profound and varied correspondences of the person with the cosmos is a primary goal of Confucianism: it is a vision with vital spiritual import and, at the same time, it has practical significance for facing the current ecological crisis. This volume itself begins to chart a course for realizing the rich resources of the Confucian tradition in resituating humans within the rhythms and limits of the natural world.

Notes

1. I wish to acknowledge, with gratitude, that Mary Evelyn Tucker and John Berthrong were instrumental in transforming my oral presentation into a written text. I would also like to note that materials from three published articles of mine have been used in this paper: "Beyond the Enlightenment Mentality," in *Worldviews and Ecology: Religion, Philosophy, and the Environment*, ed. Mary Evelyn Tucker and John A. Grim (Maryknoll, N.Y.: Orbis Books, 1994), 19–28; "Global Community as Lived Reality: Exploring Spiritual Resources for Social Development," *Social Policy and Social Progress: A Review Published by the United Nations, Special Issue on the Social Summit, Copenhagen, 6–12 March 1995* (New York: United Nations Publications, 1996), 39–51; and "Beyond the Enlightenment Mentality: A Confucian Perspective on Ethics, Migration, and Global Stewardship," *International Migration Review* 30 (spring 1996):58–75.

2. *Analects*, 12:2.

3. *Analects*, 6:28.

4. Jürgen Habermas, "What Is Universal Pragmatics?" in his *Communication and the Evolution of Society*, trans. Thomas McCarthy (Boston: Beacon Press, 1979), 1–68.

5. Talcott Parsons, "Evolutionary Universals in Sociology," in his *Sociological Theory and Modern Society* (New York: The Free Press, 1967), 490–520.

6. See Thomé H. Fang, "The Spirit of Life," in his *The Chinese View of Life: The Philosophy of Comprehensive Harmony* (Taipei: Linking Publishing, 1980), 71–93.

7. Benjamin I. Schwartz, *The World of Thought in Ancient China* (Cambridge, Mass.: Belknap Press of Harvard University Press, 1985), 406.

8. Francis Fukuyama's use of this Helena expression may have given the misleading impression that, with the end of the Cold War, the triumph of capitalism necessarily led to the homogenization of global thinking. Dr. Fukuyama's recent emphasis on the idea of "trust" by drawing intellectual resources from East Asia clearly indicates that, so far as shareable values are concerned, the West can hardly monopolize the discourse.

9. Samuel P. Huntington, "The Clash of Civilizations?" *Foreign Affairs* 72, no. 3 (summer 1993):22–49.

10. These questions are critical issues for my course, "Confucian Humanism: Self-Cultivation and the Moral Community," offered in the "moral reasoning" section of the core curriculum program at Harvard University.

11. Quoted by Anwar Ibrahim in his address at the opening of the international seminar entitled "Islam and Confucianism: A Civilizational Dialogue," sponsored by the University of Malaya, 13 March 1995. It should be noted that Huston Smith's remarks, in this particular reference to the Confucian project, are based on my discussion of the meaning of self-transcendence in Confucian humanism.

If we follow my "anthropocosmic" argument through, we need to transcend "anthropocentrism" as well. See Huston Smith, *The World's Religions* (San Francisco: Harper San Francisco, 1991), 182, 193, and 195 (notes 28 and 29).

12. *A Source Book in Chinese Philosophy*, trans. Wing-tsit Chan (Princeton: Princeton University Press, 1963), 659–60.

13. *Chung yung* (Doctrine of the Mean), chap. 22. For a discussion of this idea in the perspective of Confucian "moral metaphysics," see Tu Wei-ming, *Centrality and Commonality: An Essay on Chung-yung* (Honolulu: The University Press of Hawaii, 1976), 100–141.

"Think Globally, Act Locally," and the Contested Ground Between

Wm. Theodore de Bary

Tu Weiming's article "Global Community as Lived Reality: Exploring Spiritual Resources for Social Development" opens with a statement on our current social and ecological problems "that what we have been doing to nature and to our global community in the past two centuries, since the French Revolution, especially in the last four decades, since the Second World War, has resulted in a course of self-destruction and instilled in us a sense of urgency."[1] I share that sense of urgency, and since I agree with his general characterization of the problem, I will not belabor his basic points.

Taking as his baseline the Enlightenment and the French Revolution, Tu proceeds to characterize the Enlightenment mentality in terms of the values of "liberty, equality, human rights, the dignity of the individual, respect for privacy, government for, by and of the people"—all values which he accepts and recognizes as "genetically, if not structurally, inseparable from the Enlightenment mentality." Also genetically related to that mentality, but which he tends to question, are the values of instrumental rationality, faith in progress, reason, and individualism.

"Genetically" speaking, however, I am mindful that these values are also rooted in other pre-Enlightenment traditions, such as the Judeo-Christian, the classical civilizations of Greece and Rome, the mercantile economy and culture of the Mediterranean world, and the canon law of medieval Christendom.

It is true that these values, as listed by Tu, were given their specific modern formulation by the Enlightenment, but if we are talking about roots, as Tu goes on to do, then we have to think of these values in their historical evolution, which presents us with a real difficulty in retracing and recovering one's roots.

Take for instance the idea of progress. It is true that the idea of progress as *unlimited* is very much a product of the Enlightenment, but the idea of living for the future, of history as cumulative and leading to some promised fulfillment, is also rooted in covenantal, messianic conceptions that lie at the heart, as well as the roots, of the Judeo-Christian tradition. These go as far back as the idea of the Exodus to the promised land but can be found, too, in the Greco-Roman epics of the *Odyssey* and the *Aeneid*, which so reflect the maritime adventures and adventurousness of the Mediterranean peoples, with their idealizations of the heroic values of a migrant people, personified by the epic journeying of Ulysses and Aeneas. Exploration and expansion—the planting of Greek colonies all around the Mediterranean and Black Seas, the expansion of the Roman imperium throughout the civilized world, and the carrying of that civilization (Roman law and engineering especially) into the far reaches of barbarian Europe—such long-term historical movements energized and inspirited Europe. Moreover, they contributed to the ambitions and optimism of the Enlightenment and to the outburst of European expansionism in the seventeenth, eighteenth, and nineteenth centuries. Indeed, Western imperialism draws its very name from the Roman imperium.

There are profound ambiguities in all of these developments, for good and ill, and ultimately perhaps profound, almost impenetrable mysteries. But one thing is clear: these movements eventually brought a new view of past, present, and future to Asia and, in the twentieth century, the dominance of many features of the Enlightenment mentality that Tu has described in the following passage from his article:

> A fair understanding of the Enlightenment mentality requires a frank discussion of the dark side of the modern West as well. The "unbound Prometheus", symbolizing the runaway technology of development, may have been a spectacular achievement of human ingenuity in the early phases of the industrial revolution. Despite impassioned reactions from the Romantic movement and insightful criticisms of the forefathers of the "human sciences", the Enlightenment mentality, fueled by the Faustian drive to explore, to know,

to conquer and to subdue, persisted as the reigning ideology of the modern West. It is now fully embraced as the unquestioned rationale for development in East Asia.[2]

I agree with all of this, and with the inventory which Tu goes on to present of the unhappy, untoward, incongruous outcomes from this so-called Age of Reason, and with the unintended consequences of the changes it wrought all over the world. But if we are going to do what Tu later calls us to do, get back to our roots, I do not see how this retracing of our steps can avoid confronting many historical ambiguities that will present a great challenge to both our faith and intelligence.

In going on to discuss the "need to explore the spiritual resources that may help us to broaden the scope of the Enlightenment project," Tu cites "the conspicuous absence of the idea of community, let alone the global community, in the Enlightenment project."[3] I do not know by what criteria we do or do not attribute such conceptions to the Enlightenment, but concomitant with the rise of the Enlightenment in the late eighteenth and early nineteenth century was a great deal of communitarian activity. This was manifest in the attempts to create utopian communities in the settling of America, all up and down the eastern seaboard of the United States (the Mennonites, Quakers, and Shakers, the Ephrata community in Pennsylvania, Salem in North Carolina). Another aspect of it is shown in the socialist, communist, and anarchist movements, all of which envisioned, in their early forms, the "withering away of the state," leaving nothing but self-governing, cooperative communities. Certainly the early appeal of communism in China and Japan was of this sort, as shown in the writings of Liu Shih-p'ei and Li Ta-chao in the early decades of this century. Moreover, when Tu laments "the scant attention given to the idea of 'fraternity' among the slogans of the French Revolution," he overlooks the great play on "comrade" ship in the socialist movement, which lasted almost a hundred years over half the world until everyone came to recognize it as a hollow euphemism: comradeship with the Party or the so-called proletariat did not help much once one was denounced as a rightist or declared an enemy of the people. In such a situation one would be glad to have just one friend, let alone a comrade or brother. That is one example of what became of the great revolutionary ideal of fraternity and its symbiotic relationship with Western individualism and instrumental rationality. World revolution did it in, and what has now taken over, the industrial-technological revolution, is not going to remedy things, for all of its instant communications.

But I go on to what I think emerges as Tu's main point: the need for rootedness and localization. The idea of going back to the sources of our primal energies has been with us for some time—for a long time if you want to go back to the Romantics of the late eighteenth or early nineteenth century, and more recently in the trend sloganized in the phrase, "Think globally, act locally." It is nothing new, but I would like to suggest a somewhat different approach to the matter, one that I think answers to Tu's call for an ethic of human relatedness and communal responsibility. I offer it as a suggestion, as a guideline, for what might be considered practicable, both for the model it proposes and the lessons that can be learned from past failures.

Let me start first with the great Neo-Confucian Chu Hsi (1130–1200), who had tried to recover China's cultural, and especially moral, roots from the devastating effects of a shortsighted political opportunism and utilitarianism, abetted as he saw it—and this may surprise you—by a Buddhist idealism that was easy prey, via the principle of "adaptive" or "expedient" means, to that utilitarianism. Chu Hsi's starting point was close to what Tu has set forth at the conclusion of his paper:

> A possible Confucian contribution to this joint venture [that is, an
> effort to deal with "localism, nativism, tribalism" (at one end of the
> spectrum) and "globalism, cosmopolitanism and internationalism"
> (at the other end)] is the faith in human self-transformation as a
> corporate enterprise. The Confucian insistence that the ultimate
> meaning of life ought to be realized in practical living on a daily
> basis enjoins us to take self-cultivation and family life as the roots
> of self-realization.[4]

Chu Hsi himself started from the same standpoint as Tu (which is of course also the standpoint of Confucius and Mencius), but the great thing about Chu Hsi, coming a millennium and a half later than they, is that he took into account the intervening history, especially China's experience with the great centralized dynasties that Confucius and Mencius had never themselves had to face. It was not enough, as he saw it, to start with self-cultivation in the context of family life (though he devoted extraordinary attention to this himself). Nor would it suffice to frame self and family in a global—indeed cosmic—philosophical vision (though this too he did most impressively). What he saw as most needed was the community as an organized *infrastructure* with self and family on one side and state on the other.

Chu Hsi studied, discussed, and wrote trenchantly on at least five key community organizations or processes that were needed to bridge the gap between family and state. First was a community-wide cooperative organization for mutual aid, encouragement, and edification, or *hsiang-yüeh*. The second was for charitable granaries for the storing and distribution of seed and food grain. The third involved techniques for the development and sharing of improved agricultural methods. Fourth was the maintenance of local schools (community schools, or *she hsüeh*), so that public education would be available to all and not just those well-to-do families or lineages that were able to maintain their own private schools. The fifth was academies for the discussion of learning and public issues among the educated. Chu Hsi thought of these measures as serving the public interest (*kung*), and his whole method of self-cultivation (self-scrutiny of the mind-and-heart) was based on the need for each individual to examine his own intentions with regard to whether or not he was pursuing his own personal interests beyond what was fair to others, at the expense of the public good.

Chu Hsi's advocacy of such community infrastructures became well known throughout East Asia—not just in China but in Korea and Japan. Because of Chu's enormous prestige as a philosopher and scholar, most scholars after him endorsed these measures: ruler after ruler and dynasty after dynasty in China sanctioned them, but, to make the story short, very little came of it. If one could assign one principle reason for this disappointing outcome among several relevant factors, it would be that these infrastructural institutions were undermined, eroded, or ground to pieces in the unceasing struggle between the bureaucratic state above and private interest groups below.

Much the same situation prevails in China today, and the same is increasingly true in the United States, as big business, big mergers, bigger shopping malls, multinational organizations, to say

nothing of hegemonic ideologies on the left and right, swamp or
suffocate almost all efforts to preserve local economies and local
cultures.

In his paper Tu concludes by welcoming the rising tide of
nongovernmental organizations (NGOs) in the world today. I myself
am all for the work of NGOs, and for some time I have argued that
our chief resource in the struggle for human rights must be the long-
term, persistent efforts of the NGOs and United Nations–related
organizations, not United States foreign policy and diplomatic
negotiations. But I am taken aback by Tu's astounding confidence
in what NGOs are going to do for us in this situation. Here is what
he says:

> The dynamism of the NGOs, as glaringly displayed in Rio, Egypt,
> Copenhagen and Beijing, sends a loud and clear message that an
> unprecedented participatory democracy as a global phenomenon is
> unfolding like a mighty tide. Any attempt, organizational, ideologi-
> cal or strategic, to stop it will be overwhelmed.[5]

Chu Hsi himself was much less optimistic than Tu about the
assured success of such efforts. He may have shared the confidence
expressed by Tu in the quotation above, namely, "the faith in human
self-transformation as a corporate enterprise." But Chu Hsi's faith
was tempered by his knowledge of history and his awareness of the
weakness and fallibility of humankind, what he called "the precariousness of the human mind-and-heart"—that is, precariously
poised between self-interest and the public interest, between
legitimate self-regard and selfishness.

I am reminded of a long conversation I once had with the late
William Hung on the precariousness of the human mind as well as
the fallibility of humankind. Professor Hung was a classically
educated scholar, quite familiar with what Chu Hsi had said on the
subject in his preface to the *Doctrine of the Mean* (*Chung yung*).
We were talking about, among other things, Confucian and Christian
views of human nature and sin, and Hung took issue with the notion
that they were so far apart—that Confucians, as followers of
Mencius and believers in the goodness of human nature, were
inherently optimistic whereas, according to a simplistic view of
Christianity, Christians were pessimistic about human nature and
preoccupied with the sinfulness of man. Hung recalled what Chu

Hsi had said about the "precariousness of the human mind" in relation to the "mind of the Way" and Chu Hsi's keen sense of human fallibility, a sense which not only balanced but was integral with the human moral sense (that is, what constituted goodness) as represented by the "mind of the Way." Hung came from the last generation of Chinese whose early educational formation was shaped by the traditional Four Books and was thus still informed by such awarenesses. Hardly any Chinese since then, with a few exceptions like T'ang Chün-i, would have so readily expressed themselves in those terms. As an accompaniment to the teachings of the *Chung yung*, Chu's emphasis on the precariousness of the human mind underscored the need for a kind of religious awe and trepidation as enjoined by the *Chung yung*'s injunction to be watchful over oneself and be cautious lest one overstep the bounds ordained by Heaven.

This classic, balanced view of human nature, of the human potential for self-transformation as expressed by Tu, and yet at the same time the human susceptibility to error and sense of limitation, reminds me of an American Confucian/Christian, the farmer-poet Wendell Berry. In his powerful, prophetic book, *The Unsettling of America*, Berry addresses a wide range of economic, social, and cultural problems that have accompanied the despoliation of the environment, not only in America but worldwide, which arose with the idea that humans beings are entitled to exploit nature mercilessly for the sake of unlimited economic development and their futuristic vision of unlimited progress.

Chu Hsi's universe was an ordered one—the universe as an ordered life process, in which the mind of the Way provided the direction for human creative activity in keeping with the larger life process. Similarly, in his critique of the modern view of humankind as totally liberated from any such limitation, and now a law only unto itself, Berry invokes a more traditional Christian view of humans as delicately balanced between the animal and angelic. Not content with this limitation, modern human beings have usurped the sovereignty of the divine and claimed dominion over all. Here is the way he puts it:

But our experience of sovereignty suggests that it becomes dangerous when it defines itself exclusively in terms of what is inferior to it, neglecting or ignoring what is superior to it. That is to say that sovereignty is a safe concept only when its place is symmetrically defined. Thus, once, the place of humans was thought to be above the animals and below the angels—between the natural and the divine. Then, by understanding and accepting that human place in the order of things, people could see that their privileges were limited and safeguarded by certain responsibilities. They could see, moreover, that only evil could be the result of the transgression of these limits: one could not escape the human condition except sinfully, by pride or by degradation.

The growth of what is called the Modern World has been, by turns, both the cause and the effect of the destruction of that old sense of universal order. The most characteristically modern behavior, or misbehavior, was made possible by a redefinition of humanity which allowed it to claim, not the sovereignty of its place, neither godly nor beastly, in the order of things, but rather an absolute sovereignty, placing the human will in charge of itself and of the universe.

And having thus usurped the whole Chain of Being, conceiving itself, in effect, both creature and creator, humanity set itself a goal that in those circumstances was fairly predictable: it would make an Earthly Paradise. This projected Paradise was no longer that of legend: the lost garden that might be rediscovered by some explorer or navigator. This new Paradise was to be invented and built by human intelligence and industry. And by machines. For the agent of our escape from our place in the order of Creation, and of our godlike ambition to make a Paradise, was the machine—not only as instrument, but even more powerfully as metaphor. Once, the governing human metaphor was pastoral or agricultural, and it clarified, and so preserved in human care, the natural cycles of birth, growth, death, and decay. But modern humanity's governing metaphor is that of the machine. Having placed ourselves in charge of Creation, we began to mechanize both the Creation itself and our conception of it. We began to see the whole Creation merely as raw material, to be transformed by machines into a manufactured Paradise. . . .

But total human control is just as impossible now as it ever was. . . . In the modern city unprecedented organization and unprecedented disorder exist side by side; one could argue that they have a symbiotic relationship, that they feed and thrive upon each other. It is not difficult to think of any number of such examples in government, education, industry, medicine, agriculture—wherever the specialist has come with his controls.

The reason would seem to be that the specialist and the idea of total control also have a symbiotic relationship, that neither can exist without the other. The specialist puts himself in charge of *one* possibility. By leaving out all other possibilities, he enfranchises his little fiction of total control. Leaving out all the "non-functional" or otherwise undesirable possibilities, he makes a rigid, exclusive boundary within which absolute control becomes, if not possible, at least conceivable.

But what the specialist never considers is that such a boundary is, in itself, profoundly disruptive. Its first disruption is in his mind, for having enclosed the possibility of control that is within his competence to imagine and desire, he becomes the enemy of all other possibilities. And, secondly, having chosen the possibility of total control within a small and highly simplified enclosure, he simply abandons the rest, leaves it totally *out* of control; that is, he forsakes or even repudiates the complex, partly mysterious patterns of interdependence and cooperation, controllable only within limits, by which human culture joins itself to its sources in the natural world.[6]

Wendell Berry is not a sinologue. He comes to his Confucianism by way of the translations of Ezra Pound, and Pound by way of Ernest Fenellosa, the American student of Japanese and Chinese art, who, in order to pursue his researches had to become knowledgeable about Oriental philosophy and religion. In the course of doing so, Fenellosa and Pound encountered the Confucian Four Books, the primers for all nineteenth-century Japanese, as they were for all educated East Asians from the fourteenth to the nineteenth centuries. What many of them—Fenellosa, Pound, and probably even Berry— did not realize was the extent to which this particular version of the Confucian canon was shaped and informed by Chu Hsi, es- pecially in its focus on the *Great Learning* (*Ta hsüeh*) and the *Doctrine of the Mean* (*Chung yung*).

It is quite striking to me, however, how the approaches of both Wendell Berry and Tu Weiming to the modern crisis are structured on the *Great Learning*. They use somewhat different language: Tu speaks of self-transformation, whereas Berry talks of "self-discipline" and "character formation."[7] They both go on, then, to family, community, state, and the larger world.

In some ways, however, the work of Wendell Berry addresses the matter in a more down-to-earth way. As a farmer he addresses first of all the fundamental problem of agriculture, its ruination by industrialization, the effect of this on humankind and the human community, and so on. He really goes to the grass roots of the matter. That is what his book *The Unsettling of America* is about, namely, the uprooting of settled communities and of American culture by the destruction of any sustainable agriculture. But when one considers this in relation to China (as neither Berry nor Tu do), one can appreciate even more the Confucian significance of Berry's own project. Chinese and Confucian culture, traditionally, was about settled communities living on the land, nourishing themselves and the land. It is this natural, organic process that Confucian self-cultivation draws upon for all its analogies and metaphors and that quite as naturally appeals to the farmer Wendell Berry. One can also find in Confucian literature a close analogue to Berry's strictures regarding specialization.

Without going on at much greater length and in more detail, I cannot do justice to the full scope and depth of Wendell Berry's critique of the American situation. I wonder, however, whether any Chinese Confucian of the present day has engaged the problem in as down-to-earth, practical, and penetrating a way as he. Now that Mao and Deng have inflicted on China the same industrialization of agriculture and exploitation of nature as the West, it may be only fair for the West, in the person of the American Confucian Wendell Berry, to stand as a Confucian prophet for China as well.

In an earlier essay Berry wrote about the Confucian virtue of trustworthiness, *hsin*, following Ezra Pound's rendering of its literal, graphic meaning as a man standing by his word. That is what prophets do—they stand by their word—and I recommend Berry's prophetic words to anyone ready to learn about Confucianism and ecology, words from one, with his feet on the ground and standing firmly on his own soil, who knows firsthand what he is talking about. Like Berry's later work, *Home Economics*,[8] *The Unsettling of America* makes the Confucian point that the home and family are central, and we cannot hope to do anything about the environment that does not first reestablish the home—not just the self and family—as the home base of our efforts.

If we have to live in a much larger world, because ecological problems can only be managed on a global scale, the infrastructure between home locality and state (national or international) is also vital. But without home, we have nothing for the infrastructure, much less the superstructure, to rest on. This is the message of Wendell Berry; it is also the lesson of Confucian and Chinese history.

Notes

1. Tu Weiming, "Global Community as Lived Reality: Exploring Spiritual Resources for Social Development," *Social Policy and Social Progress* (New York: Secretariat of the United Nations) 1 (1995):40. Portions of this article are reprinted in this volume in Tu Weiming's essay, "Beyond the Enlightenment Mentality."

2. Ibid., 41.

3. Ibid., 42.

4. Ibid., 50.

5. Ibid.

6. Wendell Berry, *The Unsettling of America* (San Francisco: Sierra Club, 1996), 55–56, 70–71.

7. Ibid., 16, 26.

8. San Francisco: North Point Press, 1987.

The Context for Response

Companionship with the World:
Roots and Branches of a Confucian Ecology

Rodney L. Taylor

In his essay "Wild Wool," first published in the *Overland Monthly* in 1875 and later in his volume *Steep Trails*, John Muir, American naturalist and father of the conservation movement, set out the perimeters of what today would be described as an ecological or environmentalist view of the world and the place of humankind within it:

> No dogma taught by the present civilization seems to form so insuperable an obstacle in the way of a right understanding of the relations which culture sustains to wildness as that which regards the world as made especially for the uses of man. Every animal, plant, and crystal controverts it in the plainest terms. Yet it is taught from century to century as something ever new and precious, and in the resulting darkness the enormous conceit is allowed to go unchallenged.
>
> I have never yet happened upon a trace of evidence that seemed to show that any one animal was ever made for another as much as it was made for itself. Not that Nature manifests any such thing as selfish isolation. In the making of every animal the presence of every other animal has been recognized. Indeed, every atom in creation may be said to be acquainted with and married to every other.[1]

Muir, in many respects, was one of the first American authors to draw our attention to the need to view life on this planet as a complex and interrelated whole, not the privilege of one species to dominate and exploit. The essay quoted here, "Wild Wool," is a

significant statement of what might be called the American tran-
scendentalist point of view about wilderness,[2] what today would
come close to a position of deep ecology.

The argument of the essay is that wild wool, that is, wool from
undomesticated sheep, is of better quality than that from any
domesticated animal. This suggests to Muir that an animal left to
its own purposes is better than one that has been brought under the
control of humankind to serve the needs and ends of the human
population. The passage quoted reinforces this same point. The
world of nature stands as its own creation with its own value, not
as something that has been created for the express purpose of
serving humankind. What Muir suggests is radical change in the
orientation of humankind to themselves and their place in the
scheme of things by altering the view of nature as an extension of
humankind's own world.

The geocentric model that sees the earth at the center of the
universe may have been replaced by the discovery that the sun
actually was at the center of the solar system, but even with a
heliocentric world anthropocentrism has continued to dominate
much of humankind's reflection about their place in the order of
things and in particular their place in relation to other living things
on the earth. For Muir it is the anthropocentrism that must be struck
down. In its place, Muir argues, there must emerge a new view of
the world that recognizes the dignity of each living thing with a new
ethic that respects the life of each living thing.

In the late nineteenth and early twentieth century such a position
as Muir advocated was at best shared by only a small community
of like-minded people. The point of view did not, however,
disappear. Others have also followed in the wake of John Muir. In
a now classic statement of the early conservation movement, *A Sand
County Almanac*, Aldo Leopold states:

> Conservation is getting nowhere because it is incompatible with
> our Abrahamic concept of land. We abuse land because we regard
> it as a commodity belonging to us. When we see land as a com-
> munity to which we belong, we begin to use it with love and
> respect. . . . That land is a community is the basic concept of
> ecology, but that land is to be loved and respected is an extension
> of ethics.[3]

Leopold, like Muir, focuses upon the need to understand human-kind as a part of the ecological systems of the world, not a separate and *sui generis* category with unique privileges over animals and the earth itself. His suggestion of moving from land as a commodity to land as a shared community is the basis for the development of an environmental ethic, an attitude he characterizes as showing the earth love and respect. He argues against a background of use, misuse, and abuse of the environment, an attitude he sees directly tied to the principle of dominion over the earth stemming from the Judeo-Christian religious traditions.

Leopold suggests that any change in environmental ethic will be inexorably connected to one's philosophical and religious view and laments the failure of religion and philosophy generally to discuss environmental issues:

> No important change in ethics was ever accomplished without an internal change in our intellectual emphasis, loyalties, affections, and convictions. The proof that conservation has not yet touched these foundations of conduct lies in the fact that philosophy and religion have not yet heard of it. In our attempts to make conservation easy, we have made it trivial.[4]

Leopold, like Muir before him, expresses a frustration in his encounter with a worldview so anthropocentric that it has blinded itself to the organic wholeness of life and exercised an "ethic" of dominion that only sought to exploit and justify such exploitation for the benefit of humankind. As Muir and Leopold correctly deduced, such anthropocentrism was deeply rooted in religious and philosophical concerns, perhaps more unconscious than conscious, but difficult to change and transform when there appeared to be an authority behind such points of view that suggested "rights" assigned to one species from a still higher source.

Leopold was writing in the late 1940s, in a period in which there was little articulation of an environmentalist point of view. The ecological crisis that looms large before us today was little known or understood in Leopold's day except as a minority point of view. Today, as we are well aware, Leopold's observation that neither philosophy nor religion has heard of conservation is no longer the case. Environmental philosophy has developed as a form of

discourse within the field of philosophy. In turn, ecology has
developed as an interdisciplinary approach for work within the
sciences and social sciences. In addition, religion has begun to take
seriously the challenge to the lack of attention that seems to have
characterized much of the historical development of religious
traditions to matters of the environment.

There is now a religious response to the ecological crisis and a
role for the environment within the context of theological discourse.
It may still be the case that specific traditions are predisposed
toward a certain attitude about the environment and the place of
humankind within it. Some traditions simply seem more favorably
inclined than others to questions of the complex interconnectedness
of life-forms on planet earth, but even within those traditions where
humankind is viewed as *sui generis* and thus distinct and separate
from the organic world, there still appears to be a minority voice
calling for a revisiting of the theological questions that establish
such distinctiveness for the human species.

Only a change in the deepest layer of religious and philosophical
concern within the individual can change the way in which the
individual reacts to and relates with the larger organic context of
the world. This change can now be seen in the increasing role given
to environmental philosophy as well as in the serious responses of
religious traditions to the impending ecological crisis. The good
news is that the environment is now being taken seriously; the bad
news is that such serious concern for the environment is against a
backdrop of the continued history of use, misuse, and abuse. The
only question is whether any concern at this point is already too
late and always too little in the face of seemingly insurmountable
odds. The good news of interest and concern is where our hope lies
for our own species as well as the planet as a whole.

Asian Religious Traditions and the Environment

Environmental philosophy has come of age, as has an interest in
environmental issues related to the academic study of religion. I
want to focus particular attention upon the treatment of Eastern
religion and philosophy in discussions of the environment as well
as the question of the contribution such traditions might make to

the larger understanding of the history of environmental consciousness. Of major significance to the understanding of Eastern religious
and philosophical traditions is the recent work by J. Baird Callicott
and Roger T. Ames, *Nature in Asian Traditions of Thought*. Let me
begin with the agenda set out by Callicott and Ames:

> The complex of problems constituting the "environmental crisis"
> (in chronological order of their popular notice) include environ-
> mental pollution, the aesthetic degradation of nature, human
> overpopulation, resource depletion, ecological destruction, and, now
> emerging as the most pressing and desperate of problems, abrupt
> massive species extinction. These problems are largely Western in
> provenance, albeit global in scope. . . . And they all appear to be
> symptoms of a fundamental misunderstanding of the nature of
> nature and of a tendency to exclude nature from moral concern or
> consideration.[5]

Callicott and Ames provide a contemporary and comparative
philosophical perspective echoing the sentiments of Muir and
Leopold, articulating the necessity of conscious inclusion of nature
in moral discourse whether it be philosophical or religious. For
Callicott and Ames the objective is to introduce Eastern philosophical and religious traditions into the discussion of environmental
issues to broaden the perspectives represented. Certainly within our
own society it has become more and more difficult to represent an
American perspective on environmental issues by including only
Western philosophical and religious perspectives. We live in a
rapidly demographically changing society and any representation of
our society as a whole is in need of sources of information for
worldviews not readily understood and poorly accessed. Simply to
represent an American perspective or Western perspective, we must
be inclusive in the sources that are brought to bear upon the topic.
It is no longer adequate to represent only a Judeo-Christian view,
or even Abrahamic view, when discussing the West.

Callicott and Ames have also undertaken their project in part as
a corrective to those who are too ready to adopt that which appears
different. Much of environmental literature, highly critical of
Western philosophical and religious traditions as a cause of the
present environmental crisis, has chosen to search for different

paradigms as an intellectual support for environmental attitudes. The
need to enrich the discussion of environmental concerns cannot be
met by the adoption of any one view but by the clarification of as
many views as possible. Callicott and Ames do not intend the
adoption of Eastern paradigms but rather the benefit that a different
perspective can bring to the discussion of the issue. In this respect
they state:

> To try to see the world through an alternative frame of mind,
> however, can be very revealing of one's own. One clear way that
> the East can help the West to understand and value nature is,
> therefore, by revealing certain premises and assumptions—
> concerning the nature of nature and who we human beings are in
> relation to it, as well as the kind of knowledge of it that we seek to
> obtain—which lie so deep within or which so pervade the Western
> world view that they may not come to light any other way.[6]

The resonance with Eastern paradigms felt by many contemporary voices and authors for the environment is in part explained
by Callicott and Ames as a response to the shifting of Western
worldviews in the twentieth century, particularly with the transformation of scientific paradigms imperative, and the seeming
ability of Eastern traditions to express new paradigms.

> The emerging Western world view is nondualistic, nonreductive,
> integrative, systemic, holistic, and relational rather than substantive,
> and organic rather than mechanical. . . . Eastern modes of thought,
> in short, may resonate with and thus complement and enrich the
> concepts of nature and values in nature recently emergent in the
> historical dialectic of Western ideas.[7]

To date, most of the literature that has addressed Eastern
philosophical and religious paradigms and their relation to environmental issues has looked to Hinduism, Buddhism, and Taoism with
varying levels of sophistication as well as varying levels of success.
It is a sad fact that the examination of the history of ideas worldwide
for a broad understanding of what humanity has said about nature
and the relation between nature and humankind has been remarkably
limited both in terms of the few traditions covered as well as the at
times apologetic nature of the studies themselves. One such tradition

as yet little studied is Confucianism. A dominant tradition of China, Korea, and Japan for the past several thousand years, only a very small amount of work has even entertained the study of Confucianism as an untapped resource in an attempt to rethink the relationship between humankind and the earth as well as develop new models for the understanding of the interaction between the earth and its organic systems.

"The Continuity of Being" and Confucian Ecology

Prior to the present group of essays, several scholars of Confucianism have addressed the issue of a Confucian ecology. These include Tu Weiming, Mary Evelyn Tucker, and Okada Takehiko. All three scholars have focused their attention upon the later Confucian tradition, what is called Neo-Confucianism, rather than the early tradition of Classical Confucianism. The Classical Confucian tradition, though establishing an ethical basis for the interconnectedness of all living things, focuses almost all of its attention upon the relation of the individual to himself and to other human beings.[8] It is in the Neo-Confucian materials that we find the articulation of the relation between the individual and the cosmos. Tu Weiming, picking up the theme of interconnectedness between self and universe, has addressed the possibility of a Confucian ecology in his article "The Continuity of Being: Chinese visions of Nature."[9] Tu sees a Confucian universe as one of organic process, a spontaneously self-generating life force. This life force possesses continuity, wholeness, and dynamism.[10]

The critical issue for Confucians, according to Tu, is the degree to which humankind is a part of, rather than separate from, the life process. Tu sees Chinese thought as grounded in a harmony incorporating all things and interrelating humankind and everything else in the universe. In turn, it is the moral responsibility that is bestowed upon humankind as the highest embodiment of the moral content of the universe that draws the unique Confucian position on the relation of humankind and the universe. This moral nature becomes for Tu the defining character of what he calls "moral ecology."[11] Such a moral ecology suggests the interaction, for the Confucian, between the world and humankind based upon humankind's integral role in the universe. Humankind is seen as the embodiment of the highest moral reflection of the universe itself, or at least as an indication of what moral reflection is possible, though not necessarily daily manifest in human conduct. As Tu says: "It is true that we are consanguineous with nature. But as humans we must make ourselves worthy of such a relationship."[12] If the potential for moral cultivation is realized within the individual, then a moral ecology becomes a reality.

Mary Evelyn Tucker has also brought attention to the possible ecological dimensions of Neo-Confucianism. Tucker emphasizes both the natural cosmology and ethics of self-cultivation, or spiritual-cultivation, lying at the base of the Confucian vision of the universe. In an article entitled "The Relevance of Chinese Neo-Confucianism for the Reverence of Nature,"[13] Tucker argues that organic holism and dynamic vitalism characteristic of the Neo-Confucian vision of the universe is what creates a universe envisioned as unified, interconnected, and interpenetrating.[14]

Tucker also sees self-cultivation, or spiritual-cultivation, as a component of the ecological dimension of the tradition. She argues that self-cultivation focuses upon the development of the moral character of the individual, which in turn is what relates the individual to Heaven and Earth, or the universe—what is called in Confucian terminology the forming of one body with Heaven and Earth. Thus the act of self-cultivation becomes for the Confucian a way whereby the vision of forming one body with all things is realized. Using Tu's terminology, Tucker refers to this process as one of moving from an anthropocentric vision to an anthropocosmic worldview.[15]

In his essay "The Value of the Human in Classical Confucian Thought,"[16] Tu Weiming expresses the movement from anthropocentric to anthropocosmic in the following way:

> Confucian humanism is fundamentally different from anthropocentrism because it professes the unity of man and Heaven rather than the imposition of the human will upon nature. In fact the anthropocentric assumption that man is put on earth to pursue knowledge and, as knowledge expands, so does man's domain over earth is quite different from the Confucian perception of the pursuit of knowledge as an integral part of one's self-cultivation.[17]

Self-cultivation is directly connected to the larger ecological dimension of the Confucian tradition. Nowhere is this more plainly stated than in Tu's observation:

> The human transformation of nature, therefore, means as much an integrative effort to learn to live harmoniously in one's natural environment as a modest attempt to use the environment to sustain basic livelihood. The idea of exploiting nature is rejected because it is incompatible with the Confucian concern for moral self-development.[18]

Both Tucker and Tu suggest a metaphysical underpinning to Neo-Confucianism that can speak directly to issues of ecological concern. The principle of forming one body with all things is a statement that has direct ramifications for the understanding of the ecological dimensions of the Confucian tradition. Both have also argued that self-cultivation is not an activity removed from consideration in our attempt to understand the ecological foundations of the tradition. By defining humans as less anthropocentric than anthropocosmic, the development of humaneness as a characteristic of what is most human relates humans not just to other humans but to all other living things as well.

Okada Takehiko and Confucian Ecology

Okada Takehiko, a major contemporary Confucian scholar, has also addressed Confucian attitudes toward nature. My interviews with him, which appear in my book *The Confucian Way of Contemplation: Okada Takehiko and the Tradition of Quiet-Sitting*[19] and which are on-going in a joint project with Mary Evelyn Tucker compiling further dialogue with Okada, have touched upon environmental concerns. His responses have been based in large part upon his vast knowledge of the Confucian tradition as a whole, rather than on a previously articulated environmental concern or position by the tradition.

When dealing with the Confucian tradition, not unlike other historical traditions, one can point to a potential the Confucian tradition possesses for being a resource for environmental thinking but not to clear statements or a clear position articulating an

environmental awareness as we might define it. Since ecology and
environmental philosophy as technical fields and forms of discourse
are largely after the fact in terms of the history of the Confucian
tradition, one can only postulate what impact the historical tradition
may have chosen to have in the continuing discourse of environmental concerns.

Other historical traditions have become "modern," of course, and
their theological discourse is now routinely inclusive of environmental problems. With the Confucian tradition, as we set out to
define a Confucian agenda for the twenty-first century, its future is
being defined in terms of a small number of people. The tradition
lacks its historical contexts in a contemporary environment. It is a
tradition without institutions at this stage of its history. If the agenda
for the twenty-first century of Confucianism is to be created, then
we must look to those who espouse a contemporary Confucian
perspective for response and articulation of a Confucian form of
environmental philosophy—those such as Okada.

To Okada the ecological crisis of the world is a pressing concern,
and he sees the Confucian tradition as a potential resource to address
the crisis. The present problem is deeply rooted, from his perspective, in the technological society we have created. Such a society
is the product of the growth of the scientific worldview and its
application into the development of technology. For Okada it is
imperative that a new form of thinking, one that places humankind
in community with the natural world, begin to take place within the
science community.

Okada begins his discussion of ecology by describing the
development of science and the potential threat developments of
applied science might pose for life on this planet. He suggests that
the science community, from his perspective, needs to develop a
profound respect for life. The attitude of respect for life that he finds
a necessary component of science is the groundwork for a Confucian
position on environmental issues. He observes:

> I have a concern about the way in which science has developed.
> Its development has reached a point where it threatens the very
> existence of human life. . . . If we are going to make science totally
> responsive to the needs of the human community, we must let
> everyone—scientists and non-scientists alike—learn the importance

of human life. In speaking of the importance of human life, it is essential to realize the importance of one's own life as well as the lives of others. We live in the same world together and mutual respect for life is a prerequisite. From my point of view Confucianism provides a suitable basis for this perspective. At the center of this perspective lies the Confucian idea of being in community (forming one body) with others. In short, one can live only by living in the company of others. In order to do this it is essential to follow the rules of society. The basis of Confucian ethics is to have consideration for the other person's heart. If we extend this concept, we can include all of nature.[20]

One can see the focus that is placed upon human life. In turn, having articulated human life as the centerpiece of the Confucian worldview, Okada places human life within the context of the life of all things. This is the concept of forming one body with all things. I asked Okada whether he considered that we have ethical obligations to all forms of life. His answer is not only a statement about the status of animals but is in turn a statement with clear implications for a Confucian ecology:

Taylor: I wonder about the degree to which a Confucian can speculate on the importance of not just human life, but of *all* life. In brief, do we have ethical responsibilities to *all* forms of life, not just human life?

Okada: Yes I think we do, and such an ideal should be extended to all forms of life, animals and plants alike. The Confucian concept of being in community (forming one body) with other human beings can be extended to the community of life itself. . . . All humankind has a mind that cannot bear to see the suffering of others and this is something that should be applied to all life.

Taylor: From a Confucian perspective, humankind has the possibility of moral self-reflection and moral self-consciousness. The distinguishing mark of the human from the animal is moral self-consciousness and moral decision-making. Based upon the degree to which the human being is a moral decision-making individual, does the person have a moral responsibility for the safekeeping or stewardship of other forms of life?

Okada: Because the Confucian ideal of forming one community (forming one body) with other human beings should be extended to other forms of life, we do therefore have a moral responsibility for other forms of life. That all humankind has a heart of commiseration that cannot bear to see the suffering of others, such an idea should be applied to animals as well.[21]

Tu Weiming, Mary Evelyn Tucker, and Okada Takehiko have all focused upon and highlighted similar elements in the construction of a Confucian ecology. Such an ecology consists of a cosmology recognizing, in Tu's words, a "continuity of being." It is a universe with a unitary structure, that which forms a single body. For Okada it is expressed in the sayings of two prominent Neo-Confucians during the Sung dynasty: the saying of Ch'eng Hao (1032–1085), "The humane person forms one body with all things comprehensively";[22] and that of Ch'eng I (1033–1107), "The humane person regards Heaven and earth and all things as one body."[23] It is holistic, dynamic, and vitalistic, in Tucker's terms. The universe is ethically charged and humankind is given a priority in ethical consciousness and therefore potentially assigned a role of not only learning and self-cultivation but stewardship of all living things as well. One forms a single body with Heaven and Earth and all living things, as the Sung philosopher Chang Tsai (1020–1073) suggested in his writing, the *Western Inscription*:

Heaven is my father and earth is my mother, and even such a small creature as I finds an intimate place in their midst.

Therefore that which extends throughout the universe I regard as my body and that which directs the universe I consider as my nature.

All people are my brothers and sisters, and all things are my companions.[24]

As an ethical maxim, as central to the contemporary Confucian philosopher Okada as it was to the early Confucian Mencius, one cannot bear to witness the suffering of another.[25] This ethical stance has profound ramifications for the way a Confucian thinks about the individual, other persons, and the world as an organic unity fecund with life. Confucianism, particularly Neo-Confucianism, is thus a resource for ecological thinking, what Tu Weiming has described as moral ecology.

Confucian Ecology: A Methodological Inquiry

We have ample evidence that Confucianism can serve as a resource for environmental philosophy, but before employing these materials from historical sources to address issues affecting the late twentieth century, a certain caution must be exercised in thinking through the relation between historical context and contemporary crisis. Considering Neo-Confucianism as a potential resource for environmental philosophy raises certain methodological considerations. One must be concerned that the history of ideas is more than just history, that is, that ideas born out of historical context have a relevancy to a contemporary problem.

One can agree with Holmes Rolston, an important voice in the literature of environmental ethics, for using caution in the application of historical ideas to a contemporary problem. Rolston, in his article "Can the East Help the West to Value Nature?"[26] is certainly correct in calling our attention to the difference between the primarily religious intent of Eastern views and the ecological crisis whose roots lie principally in Western philosophical, scientific, and religious traditions. His concern is whether these two different elements can be brought together for any meaningful discourse. As he states, "We must inquire more particularly whether what the East believed before science helps the West to value nature after science."[27]

In addition to his concern about the ability to construct meaningful discourse across historical religious and contemporary scientific lines, Rolston expresses concern that "ideas" do not generate action. The question he is posing is whether historical religious ideas from another cultural context can be brought to bear upon a contemporary Western problem with any positive outcome in the resolution of the present environmental situation. For Rolston there must be more than simply a description of a religious worldview with possible correlations to a scientific worldview. To validate the capability of "valuing nature," there must be a prescription for action. The historical resource must demonstrate a prescription for action emanating from its ideas, that action which will then have a direct effect upon the present situation in which humankind finds itself.

Thus far the work we have summarized has primarily focused upon the "ideas" of a Confucian ecology, that is the metaphysics that lie at the base of the worldview. To all intents and purposes, these are primarily historical ideas, which functioned differently in the past. The tradition from which these ideas were developed is now in different historical circumstances. This clearly does not suggest the end of the tradition and most would argue that there has been a rekindling of interest. But it calls into question the ability of the tradition to act upon its ideas at present in a way sufficient to warrant a call to Confucian action. This is because Confucianism no longer has a broad contextual infrastructure to provide cultural leadership. While it may be useful as a historical source, and thus a resource, it is largely incapable of drawing attention to a cultural context. This is the reason that Okada, in discussing the future of Confucianism, referred to the need to move beyond the name Confucianism. From his point of view, as long as the teaching of respect for life is retained, then the Confucian agenda can proceed, even in a post-Confucian world.[28]

One might argue that these ideas, whether Confucian or post-Confucian, have implicit within them the act of valuing nature because an integrated and holistic universe will produce a better ecology than a description of a universe that is not holistic and integrated. Callicott and Ames grapple with this problem, suggesting that people's ecology is either affected by how they think about themselves in relation to the world, or there are glaring inconsistencies in the relationship.[29] Callicott and Ames side with the former position, suggesting that while there may be some inconsistencies, evidence supports a position that sees some correlation between what people think and how they act.

Rolston continues to argue, however, that no one particular philosophical construction of the world is necessarily better than another as a foundation for ecology, if there is no accompanying prescription for action. One can have a worldview of noble thoughts about the world and the place of humankind within it, but if there is no call to act on the basis of that worldview, then the ideas themselves may be of little value.

What intrigues me most about Rolston's argument is the question of the relevance of a particular worldview to changing not only the way in which one *thinks* about nature but, most importantly, the way one *acts* in relation to nature. The example he uses illustrates his concern. The question is one of valuing animals. Does it make a difference in the valuing of animals that one would accept a worldview predicated upon a belief in *karma* and rebirth where all forms of life would be drawn together by relating them to each other in mutual dependence across lifetimes on an ascending scale of evolutionary life-forms?

In other words, is the belief in *karma* and rebirth more pre-disposed to accept the value of animal life than a belief that rejects *karma* and rebirth, accepting instead naturalistic evolution? Is there anything within a naturalistic model which at the outset rejects the value of life or of particular species? As Rolston asks, isn't it possible to value the multiplicity of life-forms precisely because they are so different from each other, rather than emphasizing their mutual dependence? In turn, a valuing of the ecological world may stem as much from an appreciation of the diversity of life as from the unity of life.

What we need to see, following Rolston's concern, is more than a description of a philosophical worldview and the suggestion that a particular worldview is conducive to the development of an ecology. We must be able to draw a connection between description and the act of valuing. If this connection is not immediate as demonstrated by acts of valuing, then the ability of a given worldview to serve as a philosophical paradigm for an ecology is at best problematic. Or, put another way, the descriptive capacity of a worldview may be only as good as its ability to demonstrate a commitment to prescriptive action.

In his discussion of bipolar complementarity as a Chinese philosophical construct and its relation to the understanding of nature, Rolston asks how the *description* of the commonality of complementarity between Chinese philosophy and science becomes a *prescription* for human conduct in the valuing of nature.[30] Rolston implies that in the models he has posed of Eastern religious discourse and contemporary science, there might be ideas that appear to resemble one another, but there is no movement from the ideas to actual practice. That is, at the practical level one may discuss the "great ideas" and their potential for commonality, but they are just ideas, nothing more. Because they are just ideas and because their correlation to the Western setting is at best prob-lematic, there is, according to Rolston, little that such Eastern ideas can do in helping the West value nature. Rolston seems uninterested in the possibility, as suggested by Callicott and Ames, that the value of Eastern ideas is to act as a sounding board for self-reflection, not as a panacea for adoption.[31]

Valuing nature is more than establishing a set of propositions about the nature of reality and the nature of nature. The valuing of nature is a form of action. Rolston and I agree on this point. Where Rolston goes wrong in his critique of attempts to correlate Eastern historical religious ideas with contemporary scientific discourse is the limitations he has placed upon his set of "Eastern ideas." So-called Eastern ideas of the kind described are not just ideas. They are not in this sense pure philosophy. They are primarily, if not exclusively, religious in intent and are not isolated from practice. Description and prescription flow from the same mold.

For Rolston "Eastern ideas" can be described in the abstract because Western philosophy has so frequently focused primarily upon the act of thinking or thinking about the act but not the act itself. Because of his involvement in the Western model, he questions the movement from description to prescription, failing to recognize that in the examples he employs there is a continuum between description and prescription. Religion is both thought and practice or action. It is both "thought about" and "movement towards" an ultimate end.[32] Philosophy may well be thought alone, and therefore description, but religion is both description and prescription. Through illustrating the religious character of the tradition, we are demonstrating both description and prescription. A religious tradition's capacity for providing description of an ecological worldview is at the same time going to be descriptive of actions involved in the valuing of nature. And what of Confucianism? I am not going to discuss its capacity for the religious in this context,[33] but it is useful to demonstrate its articulation of the prescriptive act of valuing nature.

The Confucian Prescription for Environmental Action

Can Confucianism say of itself that it has articulated prescriptions for action built upon the descriptions of a universe regarded as a single body, the single unifying metaphysical structure found at the root of possible ecological concerns within the tradition? The answer for those of us who study the tradition is obvious. There are a series of examples, common literary references as we teach and conduct research in the tradition, that reference ecological concerns. What may be distinctive is the consideration of these references as examples of environmental impact or a potential resource for environmental consideration.

Chang Tsai's *Western Inscription*[34] is well known, but how many of us see in this writing a potential reference for environmental thought and action? The *Western Inscription* is not simply a description of the interrelatedness of all things; it is a call to act in a manner that recognizes such interrelatedness. Through the identification of the commonality of material force and the nature of all things as a description of the nature of the universe, there is a call to treat all people as brothers and sisters and a call to see all things as companions, a prescription to act upon the basis of the knowledge of the nature of things. Using Chang Tsai's *Western Inscription* as probably the most well known of such calls to action, one might well conclude that "companionship with all things" could be posed as the Confucian prescription for ethical action and the root definition of a Confucian ecology.

We have other well-known examples from the literature, such as Chou Tun-i (1017–1073) not cutting the grass in front of his window, stating that he and the grass share a common nature.[35] It is the recognition that the feeling of the grass and his own feelings are the same that restrains him from cutting the grass. By extension, the feeling of the trees and the animals are also the same. From a religious perception of the nature of the world as a unified body comes the explicit prescription for action that suggests a caring and respect, not just for other persons, but for all living things.

Wang Yang-ming (1472–1529) expresses in equally well-known passages the same form of moral action derived from the image of all things united as a single body throughout the universe:

> Therefore when he sees a child about to fall into a well, he cannot help a feeling of alarm and commiseration. This shows that his humanity forms one body with the child. It may be objected that the child belongs to the same species. Again, when he observes the pitiful cries and frightened appearance of birds and animals about to be slaughtered, he cannot help feeling an "inability to bear" their

suffering. This shows that his humanity forms one body with birds
and animals. It may be objected that birds and animals are sentient
beings as he is. But when he sees plants broken and destroyed, he
cannot help. . .feeling. . .pity. This shows that his humanity forms
one body with plants.[36]

What Wang has conveyed in this passage expresses concrete and
specific feelings for the full range of living things. Wang has
suggested ways in which humankind might act in relation to living
things through the expression of commiseration for their plight. The
connection of such feelings to the philosophical observation that all
things form a single body is made even more explicit in the
following passage:

> Everything from ruler, minister, husband, wife, and friends to
> mountains, rivers, spiritual beings, birds, animals, and plants should
> be truly loved in order to realize my humanity that forms one body
> with them, and then my clear character will be completely mani-
> fested, and I will really form one body with Heaven, Earth, and the
> myriad things.[37]

And during the Tokugawa period in Japan, Kaibara Ekken (1630–
1714) is also well known for a number of statements moving from
description to prescription of a moral consciousness that ultimately
found kinship with all forms of life. Kaibara bases himself philosophically upon the unified nature of the universe through the
commonality of material force and relies upon the image of the
universe as a single body derived from Chang Tsai. As Tucker has
demonstrated, the abiding image for Kaibara remains that of Heaven
and Earth as father and mother. As humans we are the sons and
daughters of Heaven and Earth; as such we share in the nature of
Heaven and Earth. This nature is humaneness itself.

For Kaibara, humans have a unique position in the hierarchy of
creation and as a result of this position also have certain specific
responsibilities. On this unique position, Kaibara says:

> The sages taught in the *Book of History* that heaven and earth
> are the parents of all things and that human beings are the spirit of
> the universe. This means that heaven and earth, being the source
> which gives birth to all things, are the great parents. Since humans

receive the purest material force of heaven and earth from birth, they surpass all other things and their mind-and-heart shines forth clearly. . . .

Heaven and earth give birth to and nourish all things, but the deep compassion with which they treat humans is different from [the way they nourish] birds and beasts, trees and plants. Therefore, among all things only humans are the children of the universe. Thus humans have heaven as their father and earth as their mother and receive their great kindness. Because of this, always to serve heaven and earth is the Human Way.[38]

Based upon this perception of the unity of all things and the special position of humans as the sons and daughters of Heaven and Earth, Kaibara stresses the sense of gratitude to Heaven and Earth as a central component of self-cultivation. One manifestation of this gratitude and indebtedness is a sensitivity to all life. Kaibara says:

The root of the practice of humaneness is, first, loving parents and brothers and sisters. . . . Next, we should love relatives, retainers, and friends, and all other people. Then we should love and not wantonly kill birds, beasts, insects, and fish. Finally, we should love and not recklessly cut down grass and trees. This is the order of showing compassion toward people and living things. . . .

. . . Thus even birds and animals, grasses and trees, are all made by nature—if we damage them recklessly, we should realize that it is a lack of filiality toward nature.[39]

With this statement Kaibara sets out an agenda for a Confucian ecology. It is similar to the other statements we have seen. There is a clear focus upon the common and shared nature of all things. All things are companions—they form a single body of the universe. In turn, however, humankind bears a special position in the order of all things. Because of this special position, they have special responsibilities and duties. Such duties suggest the focus of self-cultivation upon the fulfillment of humaneness, and humaneness is to be shown toward an ever-widening circle of living things.

From the beginning of the Confucian tradition, the priority of the tradition has remained human relations. It is no accident that the special moral relations articulated throughout the tradition, the Five Relations, do not mention animals, plants, or nature. In this respect Confucianism is no different from any of the major literary religious traditions of the world. Such traditions are first focused upon humankind. They are, after all, human religions. Having focused upon humankind, the question becomes how a religious tradition chooses to situate humankind in the cosmos and articulate humankind's interconnectedness with all things. Only from the later question will the basis emerge for measuring a tradition's capacity for entertaining an ecological foundation.

Confucianism is a human-centered tradition and is focused upon a special status given to humankind. Yet, in terms of its ability to demonstrate its focus upon viewing humankind as interconnected to the cosmos, it has been characterized as more anthropocosmic then anthropocentric. Human learning, human self-cultivation, and human relations form the foundation, but as humanity is realized, the humaneness which is at its center is found to be the center of the universe itself. Thus to become humane is to move beyond humankind and here is where its ecological roots lie. It is important not to move beyond humanity before humanity has been fully addressed, but the extension of humanity embraces all life. Ultimately, humaneness within the Confucian tradition is ecology because it is, in the words of Chang Tsai, companionship with the world.[40]

Notes

1. John Muir, *Steep Trails: California, Utah, Nevada, Washington, Oregon, The Grand Canyon* (Boston and New York: Houghton Mifflin, 1918), 18–19.

2. See Michael P. Cohen, *The Pathless Way: John Muir and American Wilderness* (Madison: University of Wisconsin Press, 1984), 178, for a discussion of the importance of the essay "Wild Wool" and its connection to American transcendentalism.

3. Aldo Leopold, *A Sand County Almanac and Sketches Here and There* (London: Oxford University Press, ca. 1949, 1974), viii.

4. Ibid., 209–10.

5. *Nature in Asian Traditions of Thought: Essays in Environmental Philosophy*, ed. J. Baird Callicott and Roger T. Ames (Albany: State University of New York Press, 1989), 3.

6. Ibid., 16.

7. Ibid., 17

8. For a discussion of the Classical Confucian attitudes toward nature as seen in their stance on animals, see R. L. Taylor, "Of Animals and Men: The Confucian Perspective," in *Animal Sacrifices: Religious Perspectives on the Use of Animals in Science*, ed. Tom Regan (Philadelphia: Temple University Press, 1986), 237–64.

9. Tu Wei-ming, "The Continuity of Being: Chinese Visions of Nature," in Tu Wei-ming, *Confucian Thought: Selfhood as Creative Transformation* (Albany: State University of New York Press, 1985), 35–50. This article is reprinted in the present volume; page references are to the original edition.

10. Ibid., 38.

11. Ibid., 43.

12. Ibid., 47.

13. Mary Evelyn Tucker, "The Relevance of Chinese Neo-Confucianism for the Reverence of Nature," *Environmental History Review* 15, no. 2 (summer 1991):55–67.

14. Ibid., 62.

15. Ibid., 65.

16. Tu Wei-ming, "The Value of the Human in Classical Confucian Thought," in Tu Wei-ming, *Confucian Thought: Selfhood as Creative Transformation* (Albany: State University of New York Press, 1985), 67–80.

17. Ibid., 75.

18. Ibid.

19. Rodney L. Taylor, *The Confucian Way of Contemplation: Okada Takehiko and the Tradition of Quiet-Sitting* (Columbia: University of South Carolina Press, 1988).

20. Ibid., 199, with modifications.

21. Ibid., 201, with modifications.

22. *Sources of Chinese Tradition*, comp. Wm. Theodore de Bary, Wing-tsit Chan, and Burton Watson (New York: Columbia University Press, 1960), 559.

23. Ibid., 530.

24. Ibid., 524.

25. *Mencius*, 2A.6.

26. Holmes Rolston, III, "Can the East Help the West to Value Nature?" *Philosophy East and West* 37, no. 2 (April 1987):172–90.

27. Ibid., 174.

28. Taylor, *The Confucian Way of Contemplation*, 212.

29. Callicott and Ames, *Nature in Asian Traditions of Thought*, 285.

30. Rolston, "Can the East Help the West to Value Nature?" 177.

31. Callicott and Ames, *Nature in Asian Traditions of Thought*, 16.

32. For a general discussion of the definition of religion as it is applied to Confucianism, see R. L. Taylor, *The Religious Dimensions of Confucianism* (Albany: State University of New York Press, 1990). The definition applied to the Confucian tradition is based upon the work of Frederick Streng and Joachim Wach. See Frederick Streng, *Understanding Religious Life*, 3rd ed. (Belmont, Calif.: Wadsworth, 1985), and Joachim Wach, *The Comparative Study of Religion* (New York: Columbia University Press, 1961).

33. I have written about this problem in a number of different contexts over the past twenty-five years. For my most recent attempt see R. L. Taylor, "The Religious Character of the Confucian Tradition," *Philosophy East and West* 48, no. 1 (January 1998):80–107, and R. L. Taylor, *The Illustrated Encyclopedia of Chinese Confucianism* (New York: Rosen Publishing Group, forthcoming).

34. de Bary, Chan, and Watson, *Sources of Chinese Tradition*, 524.

35. *Reflections on Things at Hand: The Neo-Confucian Anthology Compiled by Chu Hsi and Lü Tsu-ch'ien*, trans. Wing-tsit Chan (New York: Columbia University Press, 1967), 302–3.

36. Wang Yang-ming, *Instructions for Practical Living and Other Neo-Confucian Writings*, trans. Wing-tsit Chan (New York: Columbia University Press, 1963), 272.

37. Ibid., 273.

38. Mary Evelyn Tucker, *Moral and Spiritual Cultivation in Japanese Neo-Confucianism: The Life and Thought of Kaibara Ekken, 1630–1714* (Albany: State University of New York Press, 1989), 136.

39. Ibid., 186.

40. de Bary, Chan, and Watson, *Sources of Chinese Tradition*, 524.

Early Confucianism and Environmental Ethics

Philip J. Ivanhoe

Introduction

The aim of this essay is to explore some of the ways the Confucian tradition can serve as a resource for contemporary environmental ethics. I begin, in the first part, by presenting brief descriptions of four general types of environmental ethical theories; these represent a range of influential and important contemporary philosophical views. In the second part, I offer an analysis of two concepts, "oneness" and "anthropocentrism," that are central to many contemporary accounts of environmental ethics, including the present study. My intent is to be clear about significantly different senses of these terms, which I later draw upon in my analysis of Confucian thinkers. In the third part, I offer examples of environmental teachings from three early Confucian thinkers—Confucius, Mencius, and Hsün Tzu—and point out some of the ways their thought can be related to the four theories and two concepts described earlier. I will argue that while neither Confucius nor Mencius offer us an adequate environmental ethic, their teachings do contain or suggest valuable conceptual resources for building such theories. I will further argue that Hsün Tzu's writings do present us with an explicit and well-developed environmental ethic and one that is extremely valuable for contemporary philosophical work. I go on to explore some problematic aspects of Hsün Tzu's environmental view and suggest ways in which his position might be strengthened and improved. In the conclusion, I review the main lines of argument presented in this essay.

Four Types of Environmental Theory

Our first type of contemporary environment theory represents the various views arising from the Gaia hypothesis. Gaia is the name of an ancient Greek earth goddess who was the mother of the Titans. The original Gaia hypothesis was put forth in the late 1960s by the British atmospheric chemist James E. Lovelock.[1] Lovelock's original view concerned his observation that phenomena like mean global temperature and the salinity or alkalinity of the oceans are not fixed but rather move around a roving set point. That is, these phenomena are *regulated* over certain ranges by the combined interactions of the earth's air, water, surface soil, and living things (the biota). This resembles the kind of *self*-regulation we see in other organisms and that many regard as a central feature of any living organism. According to this view, all of the various constituents of the biota are part of a larger comprehensive system which operates more like a living organism than any mechanical system.

At times, Lovelock alternates between the more modest claim that the Gaia hypothesis is a useful model for thinking about global systems and the stronger claim that the earth itself *is* a single living organism. The latter, however, is his primary position. Because he accepts the fact that life on earth is continually evolving, this single organism, Gaia, keeps changing. No species, no particular part of Gaia is, in principle, indispensable to its health. In its ongoing effort to maintain the ideal conditions for life, Gaia occasionally destroys and sloughs off parts of itself. Human beings may in fact be on the way out, purged by Gaia in order to keep the conditions for life from being degraded to a dangerous point. Gaia will go on with or without us. This indifference to the value of any given species in the greater effort to maintain the conditions for life is a distinctive feature of Lovelock's view and distinguishes his position from the deep ecologists I will discuss below.

Later writers, inspired by Lovelock, embrace and develop stronger versions of the Gaia hypothesis. They argue that we all are parts of a large, cosmic organism that is conscious and acts intentionally (a view one might get from an uncharitable reading of Lovelock's works). Some go on to equate Gaia with God. Others argue that since as a species we arise from and have a long history of alternately drawing sustenance from and then returning to the biota, we are "one" with it in a strong though imprecise sense.² This purported "oneness" is stronger than the notion that we are "one" with the earth's biota, in the way that my arm is "one" with the rest of my body, for the claim is that we both are *part of* and *share* significant constituents with the earth.

The different positions grouped under the category of our second type of theory, deep ecology,³ vary considerably on the issue of the strength of the "oneness" they claim exists between humans and the rest of nature. In general, however, they tend not to hold anything quite as strong as the strongest sense of oneness one finds among proponents of the Gaia hypothesis. Deep ecologists do tend to regard ecosystems as very much like single bodies, but these are subentities within nature whose mutual influences generate the greater dynamic of the natural world.

The most significant and distinctive ethical claim deep ecologists make, or at least the deep ecologists I want to single out, is that each organism and ecosystem is of *equal* value and hence every one should be protected and preserved as it is. Since other organisms and ecosystems are actively being harmed, and in many cases irreparably damaged by current human behaviors, and their habitats continually invaded by excessive human populations, deep ecologists conclude that we must both dramatically alter our behavior and reduce our population. For the deep ecologist, human beings have reached the point of being a strongly destabilizing and often lethal *infestation* on the planet.⁴

While those who promote the third of our theories, the land ethic, see profound value in every species and appreciate the complex contributions each makes to the others within a given ecosystem, they do not claim a principled equality among species or ecosystems. Thus they avoid some of the more obvious problems inherent in the deep ecology view as I have described it. People like Aldo Leopold⁵ are dedicated to conserving nature; they bemoan the loss of any species and insist on the complex interdependence of all aspects of nature. But their guiding principle is *balance*, or *harmony*, among the various constituents of the natural realm. Moreover, they recognize that human beings play a prominent role as both *users* and *caretakers* of nature—for pleasure and personal development as well as for sustenance. Most deep ecologists would consider such uses of nature as examples of rank exploitation, and they would regard both the notion of "using nature" and the idea that we are "caretakers" of the natural realm as strongly paternalistic: cases of anthropocentric as opposed to biocentric thinking.

The fourth and final theory, social ecology, explains our ecological myopia in terms of the distorting and deforming influences of socially constructed categories such as gender, race, and class. Such influences are thought to generate warped beliefs about and perceptions of nature. For example, ecofeminists[6] argue that the deep cause of ecological degradation is the socially constructed nature of patriarchal society. Patriarchy instills and reinforces a set of beliefs, attitudes, and behaviors that objectify all that is "other" and exploit it for personal satisfaction. Patriarchal society regards nature in the same way as men within such a society regard women: as things to be used for selfish, private ends. As a result, men within such a society are encouraged to "rape" and exploit nature in the same way as they are encouraged to rape and exploit women. Like other forms of social ecology, ecofeminists argue that the result is not only the oppression and exploitation of women and nature but the profound alienation of men from themselves and from the world in which they live. Another example of this type of theory sees a disturbing similarity between false beliefs concerning racial superiority and its purported natural privileges and views about "higher" forms of life and their "natural right" to make use of "lower" life-forms.[7] A third and prominent line of reasoning within this type argues that capitalist views about property inform our conceptions of and attitudes toward other creatures and the rest of the nonhuman world and lead us to see these as our possessions, which we are at liberty to use or dispose of in any way we see fit.[8] Regardless of their specific form, social ecologists see our distorted view of nature as leading not only to profound exploitation of other creatures and things but also to a debilitating alienation on the part of those in positions of power, who must live within worldviews which futilely attempt to deny important and obvious truths about themselves and their relationship with the rest of the world.

All four of these general theories, with varying degrees of assent, agree that our present view of nature is much too anthropocentric, in the specific sense that only human *interests* are taken into consideration.[9] Social ecologists can be understood as claiming that our perception of nature is even more provincial, in that we take the narrower perspective of patriarchy, racial superiority, or class preference as authoritative in deciding what are legitimate interests. All four types also agree that we can attain a clearer and more accurate view of nature, and most see this end as requiring *both* removing certain epistemological blinders and coming to understand and be moved by real features of the world we presently fail to see or fully appreciate.

Oneness and Anthropocentrism

It turns out that there is more than one way to be "one." First there is the sense in which I can be "one" with a given organization or group, the way in which I might be "part of the same team" or "one of the gang." For example, I am a member of the University of Michigan's faculty and in this sense I am "one" with the university. But the university existed before I became a member of it and will almost certainly exist long after I am dead and gone. In the same way, human beings might be thought of as "one" with nature, and yet nature existed before they evolved into their present form and will likely exist long after they are extinct.

Even such a weak sense of "oneness" entails a greater concern on my part for Michigan and its well-being because of my association with it. I am more concerned with the well-being of Michigan than say Ohio State (or even Harvard). I wish these other institutions well, but my strongest and immediate concern is for the institution of which I am a part. Perhaps this is how we should think of ourselves and our relationship with nature.

We see a slightly stronger sense of "oneness" in the way a creature or thing can be part of a given ecosystem, for example, the way in which the crocodile is part of the ecosystem of the Nile River. This sense of oneness is stronger than the first in that the crocodile interacts and affects the rest of the system in extremely complex ways, both directly and indirectly. The University of Michigan could go on without professors of philosophy or Asian studies (though it would be a less interesting place), but it is not clear that the Nile River could go on without the crocodile. The loss of such an important and powerful predator would almost certainly have more dramatic and far-ranging repercussions.

The third sense of "oneness" is perhaps what people mean when they talk about "organismic" ecological views (though this is another term that is often used in a rather fast and loose fashion). For example, one might argue that we and the earth's biota constitute a single organism in the same way that my arm is "one" with the rest of my body. If you cut off my arm, you radically and directly affect the rest of my body. Without immediate, expert help, this will probably kill me. Cutting my arm off might seem like taking the crocodile, as a species, out of the Nile, and we sometimes talk metaphorically about a loss in such terms: a parent might say the death of a child was "like having my arm cut off." Taking crocodiles out of the Nile would surely have a profound effect on the ecosystem, but it would not have as direct and dramatic an effect as cutting off my arm would have on me. The former will certainly alter the ecosystem and might conceivably destroy it. But the effects are less direct and in many cases less dramatic, because the connection, while intimate and widespread, is not as close. While similar, the "one-body" or "organismic view" is stronger than the "one-ecosystem" view.

The best examples of the fourth sense of "oneness" are the stronger versions of the Gaia hypothesis mentioned earlier. These involve the claim that we both are part of nature and at the same time share significant constituents with the biota. Some proponents of the Gaia hypothesis speak not only as if they were part of a planetary-wide system (a large-scale ecological view), and not only as if this system were a single body (the "one-body" view), but as if they and the rest of the planet were in some deep sense co-extensive, as if they and the world were inseparably intertwined and able fluidly to pass into one another.[10]

Finally, the strongest sense in which two things can be "one" is by being identical, the way in which Bruce Wayne and Batman are one. More than a few people assert that we and nature are "one" in this extremely strong, logical, sense. Hua-Yen Buddhists and many Neo-Confucians hold something like this view: the former believing that in the deepest sense we are all *fo-hsing*, Buddha-nature, and the latter claiming that all things share the same *pen-hsing*, "original nature," or *li*, "principle" or "pattern." These folks seem to be saying something even stronger than the strongest versions of the Gaia hypothesis. Not only are we and the rest of the world inseparably intertwined, not only do we share significant constituents, we have *the same* fundamental nature.[11]

The second notion I would like to discuss is "anthropocentrism." Again, I find this term used in ways that are quite helpful in certain respects but which often end up being too vague to be of much value. The only characteristic that is consistent across the different senses of "anthropocentric" one finds in the literature is that it is bad. That is, "anthropocentric" tends to be used as a term of disapprobation. I would like to describe three types of anthropo-centrism—*epistemological, metaphysical,* and *ethical*—and I will argue that the first, while of considerable interest, is not necessarily bad at all. Nothing much of ethical significance follows from this kind of anthropocentrism and we should take note of this fact.

Epistemological anthropocentrism in its most simple form is the claim that we see things from the human point of view; we employ certain humanly evolved concepts and rely upon human perceptual faculties in perceiving and coming to understand the world. We can't find our way through the night using echolocation like the bat does. We lack this ability and such an experience, at least its subjective "feel," is not accessible to us. As Thomas Nagel[12] has argued, we don't know what it *is like* to be a bat (assuming that there *is* something like being a bat which a bat experiences). But this limitation is not in itself either good or bad. For one thing, while we can't get a complete feel for the subjective experiences of a creature like a bat, we share much more than one might at first think we do, and we can extend our understanding even beyond this. We share more than one might think in that we live in the same world and have access to much of the same information.[13] The bat might use echolocation to detect bug "A" above bug "B," moving to the right at a certain rate of speed. But if it is not too dark, I can *see* all of this and thereby possess the same information (at least in these respects). And if I learn how to read a radar screen of sufficient sensitivity, I can even receive this information in a way that is somewhere between the way the bat gets it and visually perceiving these bugs.

Some people seem to think that because I can't experience things *the way* other creatures do, I necessarily fail utterly to understand what they need. This may be true for certain subjective states—at least these might make things very difficult—but in most cases such a conclusion simply does not follow. I don't need to be able to track a scent like my dog in order to understand what he is doing. I smell well enough to avoid skunks or to follow my nose to the kitchen or to recall the fragrance of a former lover. The similarities between my dog's experiences and my own, together with other behavior the dog exhibits, lead me to infer with reasonable confidence that my dog *likes* tracking a scent. (Perhaps *this* is what Chuang Tzu meant when he said he could understand what fish enjoyed even though he was not a fish.[14])

It is often the case that I can have a more reliable understanding of what other creatures (and even plants) *need* than I can have of what my fellow human beings need. I know my plants need good soil, water, and sunshine and that the papyrus plants need much more sun than my asparagus fern does. I not only understand their different needs, I worry about them and work to satisfy them. In terms of their needs and what I can do about them, I think I am often more successful with them than I am with most people, even those I know well and care for, who try to *tell* me what they want. Epistemological anthropocentrism is an impediment but not a bar to my understanding of and concern for other creatures and things. In itself, it is neither good nor bad.

The second sense of anthropocentrism I would like to discuss concerns metaphysical views. Some have claimed, for a variety of reasons, that human beings are the natural "masters" of the rest of nature. In one version of this view, we are created apart from nature and stand above it, a separate, superior, and *sui generis* kind. A rather straightforward implication of such a view is that nature is there for us to use in whatever way we will.

Such strong traditional versions of metaphysical anthropocentrism lack scientific credibility. Many blame such views as the primary source for much of what is wrong with our conception of and behavior toward the environment. But it is important to note that these kinds of criticisms are equally valid against certain materialist views of nature, for example, those that take a crude and shortsighted instrumentalist approach toward nature. As we shall see, there are also less strong versions of metaphysical anthropocentrism that are much more plausible and considerably less objectionable.

Our third and final form of anthropocentrism involves ethics and particularly that part of ethics known as axiology, what things have value. This is the most important form of anthropocentrism for those interested in environmental ethics. For a view to be ethically anthropocentric in what I will call the strong sense, it would first have to be an *ethical* view, that is, a view about what things are *valuable*. For example, forms of ethical hedonism can be anthropocentric in this sense if they only value human well-being. But one can be an ethical hedonist and give equal value to the well-being of other creatures (as do many advocates for the equal ethical status of animals). This might still leave one ethically anthropocentric in regard to plants and inorganic things, but it would at least be a less strong form of such anthropocentrism. A view is ethically anthropocentric in the *strong* sense if it values *only* human well-being. For example, the traditional kind of metaphysical anthropocentrism described above has been used to justify absolute ethical anthropocentrism. According to such a view, only human needs and desires have value, and the rest of nature exists for our sake. As we shall see, others hold less strong versions of this view and some of these are much more interesting.

Early Confucian Teachings on the Environment

In both the *Analects* and the *Mencius* we find important themes and ideas that both influenced later Confucian views on the environment and that are of value in the contemporary effort to develop an adequate environmental ethic. Perhaps the most characteristic feature of the early Confucian views about nature to be found in these texts are their "human-nature analogues."[15] I mean by this the tendency to regard certain natural phenomena as emblematic of ethically good people or particular human excellences. For example, in *Analects*, 2:1, the ideal king, one who rules through the power of moral charisma, is likened to the polestar, which maintains its august position at the apex of the heavens while all the lesser stars pay homage by revolving around it in a stately and orderly fashion. In *Analects*, 6:23, we are told that those who are wise, being active, flexible, and wide-ranging, are thought to have a natural correspondence with and delight in flowing water, while those who are *jen*, "perfectly good," being still, stable, and immovable, are thought to have a natural correspondence with and delight in mountains. We are also told, in *Analects*, 9:17, that Confucius took special delight in watching the unceasing movement of a flowing stream, seeing it perhaps as a symbol of the unceasing operation of the Tao, or the steady and uninterrupted effort needed to master the Way. In these and other examples, we see Confucius's belief that nature exemplifies and provides us with models of important ethical virtues. At the same time, they show that Confucius also saw nature as a source of aesthetic pleasure and what, in other work, I have called "metaphysical comfort."[16] For him and other early Confucians, human beings are very much at home in nature; they find ethical inspiration, delight, and comfort in many of its features. While I am not certain that I fully understand Tu Weiming's use of Mircea Eliade's term "anthropocosmic," the characteristics I have described here seem consistent with what I take to be the basic sense of this term.[17]

We see these same characteristics and more in the *Mencius*. In one of the most memorable and moving passages in the text, the deforested Ox Mountain serves as one of Mencius's most important and informative illustrations. The image of the denuded mountain is used to show, among other things, that we cannot infer that human nature is without moral tendencies just because we encounter some who manifest no evidence of such tendencies. Human nature can be ground down and effaced just as Ox Mountain was systematically stripped of its once lush vegetation. The story also illustrates the tenaciousness of both our moral sprouts and the mountain's vegetation; both continue to put forth new growth—shoots and buds—despite the sustained harsh treatment each receives.[18]

The *Mencius* also contains a remarkable story about the origin of civilization which bears similarities and even more significant differences with the creation myth and other stories found in the book of Genesis. In *Mencius*, 3A.4, we are told of a time when "The Flood, still raged. . .plants grew thickly. . .the five grains did not ripen; birds and beasts encroached upon men. . . ."[19] A trio of sage heroes came forth and worked to realize a harmonious ordering of the world: driving off the beasts with fire, controlling the flood, and bringing the land under settled cultivation. Unlike the story in Genesis, in this primordial Confucian myth, the world is not created *ex nihilo*, nor are human beings given "dominion" over it (however one interprets this). Rather, human beings find themselves as things among things, buffeted about in a dangerous and unruly world until the civilizing work of a series of sagely heroes—not God—brings order to this chaos. A feature of this story worth noting, and to which I will later return, is that Mencius strongly implies that the world itself had to await these sages before it could become orderly.[20]

These early Confucian teachings concerning human beings and their relationship with the rest of nature offer many interesting ideas and suggestions. Among these is the view, mentioned earlier, that human beings live in an anthropocosmic universe, one that exemplifies ethical virtues and which offers both aesthetic pleasure and metaphysical comfort as well as sustenance. Another related idea concerns the way in which the sages brought order out of an originally chaotic universe. It was not simply a matter of imposing some humanly devised structure upon raw and unruly nature. As Mencius says in a later passage, what was remarkable about the sage-hero Yü was not simply that he was able to tame the flood but *the way* he controlled it: "Yü guided the water by imposing nothing on it that was against its natural tendency."[21] In fashioning the Tao, the sages were not simply imposing an ad hoc order of their own design, nor one revealed through scripture or communicated through a prophet; they were discovering as much as they were inventing. They recognized and worked to harmonize with the patterns and processes they found (and which we can find) in nature.

These general features of early Confucian thought are developed and find their most complete expression in the *Hsün tzu*. In other work,[22] I have argued that in this text we do find an explicit and very interesting environmental ethic, a view which I refer to as Hsün Tzu's "happy symmetry." Hsün Tzu believed that the form of life described by the ancient sages shows human beings the way to regulate and develop their own needs and desires and to harmonize these with the patterns and processes of nature. This is the meaning of his teaching that the cultivated person "forms a triad with heaven and earth." This is more than a call for prudence. Hsün Tzu is not just arguing for the need to preserve the source of the goods that satisfy us (though the Way accomplishes this goal as well). He is arguing that the Way enables us to take our proper place and fulfill our proper destiny in a universal scheme.

Since Hsün Tzu accords some value to other animals, plants, and inorganic things *qua* parts of the Tao, he is not ethically anthropocentric in the strong sense. But his view is anthropocentric in the weaker sense that even when he talks about the well-being of other creatures and things, he tends to describe their interests in terms of how they relate to human beings. This is seen clearly in his claim that there is some kind of inherent deficiency in all things in the world prior to the coming of the sages. Hsün Tzu says, "All creatures of the universe, all who belong to the species of man, must await the sage before they can attain their proper places."[23] As we have seen, on this issue Hsün Tzu agrees with Mencius, who strongly implies that the world needed the wisdom and efforts of the sages before it could attain order and balance. And so both Mencius and Hsün Tzu are ethically anthropocentric in the weak sense I have described.

Hsün Tzu's ethical anthropocentrism is a result of his more plausible and less destructive form of metaphysical anthropocentrism. He does not believe in creation *ex nihilo*, nor does he claim that human beings are created in the image of some world-transcending God. But he does assert that human beings have intellectual capacities that enable them to form communities and recognize social roles, norms, and obligations in unique and powerful ways, ways that set them both apart from and *above* other creatures. As he says, human beings possess not only energy, life, and intelligence but *i*, "proper roles and norms," and this makes them "the most noble creatures in the world."[24] This also is what enables them to subjugate and make use of other creatures, such as oxen and horses, which are physically superior to—stronger and faster than—human beings.

Hsün Tzu presents a weaker and more plausible form of metaphysical anthropocentrism than we find in Genesis, in that he simply reports facts about how things are in the world; because of their unique ability to organize themselves self-consciously into societies, humans are able to subjugate other, physically superior animals. Moreover, his form of metaphysical anthropocentrism is less arrogant and may tend to be less destructive. While it affords human beings a superior position in the world, it also 1) recognizes the inherent value of and our mutual interdependence with other creatures and things; 2) places limits on what humans can legitimately do with nature; and 3) advocates a deep sense of human *responsibility* as well as prerogative. In these respects, though in not all, Hsün Tzu's view resembles the land ethic described earlier.

There is a more charitable way to read Hsün Tzu's claim that the world must await the sages before it can attain order and harmony. This would be to understand him as saying that *given* the existence of precivilized human beings, with their powerful, unruly, and unlimited needs and desires, the world cannot possibly be orderly and harmonious without the wisdom and work of the sages. This would be to focus on the disorderly and disruptive tendencies of human beings (which Hsün Tzu of course does) rather than on some inherent disorderliness in the rest of nature. Such a reading is at least consistent with much of what Hsün Tzu says, and in any event, it represents an interesting view clearly inspired by his thought.

Some will object strongly to the idea, which I attribute to Hsün Tzu, that a world *without* human beings would be devoid of value. But I agree with at least one version of this claim. Contrary to what some maintain, it makes little sense to insist that there are any ethical or aesthetic values completely apart from the human perspective.[25] Of course, in the absence of human beings, other living creatures (though I doubt inanimate things) would still have *interests*, but without us around somewhere to entertain and judge among various options, it is difficult to see in what sense there would be ethical or aesthetic *values*. However, my basic point is that such a view does not entail the belief that only those parts of nature that have been *made orderly* by human beings have value to us. As others have argued, I believe informed and reflective human beings naturally tend to value nature apart from what they have touched and altered (that is at least part of *why* we value it). Those who fail to appreciate this aspect of nature are missing part of its value; they are like someone who is color-blind who fails to perceive the stunning beauty of a glorious sunset. In Hsün Tzu's work, we see no appreciation of the value of wilderness.[26]

An appreciation of wilderness is a central aspect of the third theory I introduced, the land ethic. A number of different arguments have been advanced for why we should preserve, or more accurately protect,[27] wilderness areas. Most convincing are arguments that combine appeals to prudence, aesthetic enjoyment, and the cultivation of epistemological virtues, such as wonder and humility. All of these strike me as reasons that Hsün Tzu could easily have embraced. Similar arguments can also be found in early Taoist writings, in specific images like the "unhewn wood" of the *Tao-te-ching*, in widespread Taoist criticisms of society and socialization, and in their advocacy of spontaneity and what is "so of itself." Thus the Taoist tradition offers another, indigenous, resource which one could draw upon in an effort to modify and strengthen Hsün Tzu's position.

Hsün Tzu does express what might at first seem like feelings of wonder and awe in the face of nature in his beautifully crafted and deeply moving paeans to the Way.[28] But upon closer examination, we see that he experiences these feelings, not when faced with the vastness, power, and beauty one finds in wild nature, but when he contemplates the scale, detail, and efficacy of the Tao.[29] Hsün Tzu marvels at the magnificent symmetry of the Tao—how it provides for and makes use of all things and brings them together in universal harmony. As moving and marvelous as this vision is, what we see here is nature tamed and harnessed—not nature in its original and unruly state. We can get a sense of this difference if we compare Confucius's stately admiration for the unceasing flow of the stream (mentioned earlier) with Chuang Tzu's overflowing delight and fascination for the wildly surging cascades of Lü Liang Waterfall.[30] In the passage from the *Chuang tzu*, the old man who is able to ride—not tame—the torrent, "going in with the swirls and out with the whirls," is held up as a paragon of the Taoist ideal.

Conclusion

The Confucian views about human beings and their relationship with the rest of nature that we have explored here and the Taoist views that I have only had occasion to mention are interesting in their own right and can be instructive and even inspirational. I am convinced that some of these views hold significant value beyond offering us knowledge about what others have believed and what some still do. I think many of these ideas can help us to see more clearly *how things really are*, and hence that they are important resources for contemporary environmental theory. I am quite dubious about views that require the strongest senses of "oneness" discussed above, because I do not see much of a case for these as plausible accounts of how things really are. Such views may still prove instructive in some ways and profoundly inspirational—like the first pictures of the earth taken from the moon—but they do not recommend themselves as a solid basis for contemporary philosophical justification. They rely upon metaphysical claims that are very difficult for many modern people to accept.

I have described four different types of environmental ethical theory and several different senses of the two notions of "oneness" and "anthropocentrism," which play important roles in many contemporary debates about environmental ethics. I have also described and explored the environmental views of three early Confucian thinkers, offering a more complete analysis and discussion of Hsün Tzu's environmental ethic. My hope is that these conceptual distinctions and the brief accounts of the views of Confucius, Mencius, and Hsün Tzu will add to the interesting and important work currently being done on Confucian environmental ethics by both enhancing the analysis of Confucian views and facilitating comparison and mutual exchange between this work and that being done in related areas in environmental philosophy.

Notes

*I thank Shari Ruei-Hua Epstein and Bryan W. Van Norden for very helpful comments and suggestions on earlier drafts of this essay. I also thank the participants at the "Confucianism and Ecology" consultation held at Harvard University, 30 May–1 June of 1996, for their comments. I especially want to thank Mary Evelyn Tucker and John Berthrong for inviting me to participate in this stimulating and edifying conversation.

1. See James E. Lovelock, *Gaia: A New Look at Life on Earth* (Oxford: Oxford University Press, 1979), and *The Ages of Gaia: A Biography of Our Living Earth*, reprint (New York: W. W. Norton, 1995).

2. Some combine this idea with a belief in multiple lives. For example, in her "Gaia Meditations" Joanna Macy says, "Think of your next death. Will your flesh and bones back into the cycle. Surrender. Love the plump worms you will become. Launder your being through the fountain of life." Quoted in Lawrence E. Joseph, *Gaia: The Growth of an Idea* (New York: St. Martin's Press, 1990), 243. For a discussion of Gaia as goddess, see pp. 66–73, 223–47.

3. The classic statement of this view is Arne Naess, "The Shallow and the Deep, Long-Range Ecology Movement: A Summary," *Inquiry* 16 (1973):95–100. See also his *Ecology, Community and Lifestyle: Outline of an Ecosophy*, translated and revised by David Rothenberg (Cambridge: Cambridge University Press, 1989).

4. Hence like any other creature that has attained such destabilizing proportions, human population and behavior need to be strictly managed.

5. Aldo Leopold, *A Sand County Almanac: With Essays on Conservation from Round River*, reprint (New York: Sierra Club/Ballantine Books, 1970).

6. See *Ecofeminism: Women, Animals, Nature*, ed. Greta Gaard (Philadelphia: Temple University Press, 1993).

7. See Robert D. Bullard, *Confronting Environmental Racism: Voices from the Grassroots* (Boston: South End Press, 1993).

8. See Murray Bookchin, *The Ecology of Freedom: The Emergence and Dissolution of Hierarchy* (Palo Alto, Calif.: Cheshire Books, 1982). Bookchin argues against all forms of hierarchy as impediments to a proper appreciation of the environment, but his central target is capitalism.

9. See the discussion of anthropocentrism below. For an insightful discussion of the difference between seeing things from the human point of view versus seeing only human interests as valuable, see Bernard Williams, "Must a Concern for the Environment Be Centred on Human Beings?" in *Reflecting on Nature: Readings in Environmental Philosophy*, ed. Lori Gruen and Dale Jamieson (New York: Oxford University Press, 1994), 46–52.

10. See, for example, the quote of Joanna Macy in n. 2 above.

11. Both Buddhists and Neo-Confucians employ the notion of our being *i-t'i* (lit., "one body") with the world to argue for their different ethical views (e.g.,

compassion). In texts like the *Platform Sūtra*, this image is used to illustrate cases where two things are only logically (not actually) separable. This implies a very strong sense of oneness. Their metaphysical position claims a profound identity between self and world. For a discussion of this idea, see Francis H. Cook, *Hua-Yen Buddhism: The Jewel Net of Indra* (University Park: Pennsylvania State University Press, 1977), and my *Ethics in the Confucian Tradition: The Thought of Mencius and Wang Yang-ming* (Atlanta, Ga.: Scholar's Press, 1990), 15–25. Some deep ecologists also espouse views approaching this strong sense of oneness. For example, the radical environmentalist John Seed says: "this change of perspective follows from actions on behalf of mother earth. 'I am protecting the rain forest' develops to 'I am part of the rain forest protecting myself. I am that part of the rain forest recently emerged into thinking.'" Quoted in an excerpt in Bill Devall, "Deep Ecology and Radical Environmentalism," in *Reflecting on Nature: Readings in Environmental Philosophy*, ed. Lori Gruen and Dale Jamieson (New York: Oxford University Press, 1994), 120.

12. See "What Is It Like to Be a Bat," in Thomas Nagel, *Mortal Questions* (Cambridge: Cambridge University Press, 1979), 165–80.

13. I have in mind here something like the general view described by Fred Dretske in his *Knowledge and the Flow of Information* (Cambridge, Mass.: MIT Press, 1981), and *Naturalizing the Mind* (Cambridge, Mass.: MIT Press, 1995). The following example was developed in a conversation with Dretske about Nagel's views.

14. For this story, see *The Complete Works of Chuang Tzu*, trans. Burton Watson (New York: Columbia University Press, 1968), 188–89.

15. See my "Human Beings and Nature in Traditional Chinese Thought," in *A Companion to World Philosophies*, ed. Eliot Deutsch and Ron Bontekoe (Cambridge, Mass.: Blackwell, 1997), 155–64.

16. See my "Nature, Awe and the Sublime," in *Midwest Studies in Philosophy*, vol. 21, *Philosophy of Religion*, ed. Peter A. French, Theodore E. Uehling, Jr., and Howard K. Wettstein, (Notre Dame, Ind.: University of Notre Dame Press, 1997), 98–117.

17. For the most complete description of Tu's sense of this term, see Tu Wei-ming, *Centrality and Commonality: An Essay on Confucian Religiousness* (Albany: State University of New York Press, 1989), 102–7,

18. There is a basic ambiguity, reflected in the commentarial tradition, about the issue of whether Ox Mountain has been damaged so badly and for so long that it can no longer regenerate itself. By analogy, this would determine whether or not people can be so damaged and deformed as to be beyond hope of moral regeneration. For an insightful discussion of these interpretations, see Bryan W. Van Norden, "Kwong-loi Shun on Moral Reasons in Mencius," *Journal of Chinese Philosophy* 18 (1991):358–59.

19. *Mencius*, 3A.4. For a translation, see *Mencius*, trans. D. C. Lau (London: Penguin Books, 1970), 102.

20. In this regard, Mencius agrees with Hsün Tzu who says explicitly that all things must await the coming of the sages in order to attain their "proper place." See the discussion below.

21. *Mencius*, 4B.26; Lau, *Mencius*, 133.

22. Philip J. Ivanhoe, "A Happy Symmetry: Xunzi's Ethical Thought," *Journal of the American Academy of Religion* 59, no. 2 (summer 1991):309–22.

23. See *Hsün Tzu: Basic Writings*, trans. Burton Watson (New York: Columbia University Press, 1963), 103. Cf. 44, "Therefore, Heaven and earth produce the gentleman and the gentleman brings order to Heaven and earth." For a discussion of this idea, see Ivanhoe, "A Happy Symmetry," especially 316.

24. Cf. Watson, *Hsün Tzu: Basic Writings*, 45, but note that he translates *i* as "sense of duty." I follow the as yet unpublished work of Eric Hutton, "On the Meaning of *Yi* for Xunzi," and translate *i* as "proper roles and norms."

25. This is by no means an uncontroversial view. For example, G. E. Moore, responding to Henry Sidgwick, argues that we would choose to bring into being a world that is "exceedingly beautiful" over one that is exceedingly ugly, even if no human being ever has or "*can*, live in either, can ever see and enjoy the beauty of the one or hate the foulness of the other." Now I agree that human beings might choose to do this, just as we might decide to set aside certain land as pristine forest, never to be disturbed (or appreciated) by human beings. But I disagree with Moore that this in any way establishes the mind independence of values. Everything that *makes* one of these worlds *beautiful* and hence *valuable* and the other foul depends on the particular needs, desires, and capacities of human beings. For Moore's view, see *Principia Ethica* (Cambridge: Cambridge University Press, 1903), 83–84. For the kind of view I am advocating here, see David Wiggins, "Truth, Invention and the Meaning of Life," or John McDowell, "Values and Secondary Qualities," both reprinted in Geoffrey Sayre-McCord, *Essays on Moral Realism* (Ithaca, N.Y.: Cornell University Press, 1988).

26. I mean by wilderness, nature that has been untouched, or at least unaltered, by human technological intervention.

27. For this distinction, see Holmes Rolston, III, "The Wilderness Idea Reaffirmed," *The Environmental Professional* 13, no. 4 (March 1992):370–77.

28. See, for example, Watson, *Hsün Tzu: Basic Writings*, 44–45, 94. For a discussion of this aspect of Hsün Tzu's views, see Ivanhoe, "A Happy Symmetry."

29. This is a critical difference and fully consistent with Hsün Tzu's general point of view as I understand it. Hsün Tzu (and Confucius before him) saw *human society*—not nature—as the ultimate source and center of value.

30. For this passage, see Watson, *The Complete Works of Chuang Tzu,* 204–5.

Extending the Neo-Confucian Tradition: Questions and Reconceptualization for the Twenty-First Century

Michael C. Kalton

Introduction

Before the twentieth century, Confucians used the classics, Chu Hsi, Yi T'oegye, Yi Yulgok, and the whole tradition as a resource from which to think as they addressed the problems and needs of their lives and times.[1] Since the arrival of modernity, however, these have become less a resource for new thinking by engaged intellectuals and more an object and end of study in themselves; they are now the preserve of specialists in East Asian intellectual history, philosophy, or comparative religion. The heritage of the Confucian tradition also continues to contribute greatly and constructively to forming the distinctive and vital cultures of modern East Asian societies. This is a vestigial vitality, however, a living off of past wealth. It is conservative in the best sense, preserving the excellence of the past and using it to inform and enrich the present. But preservationism does not challenge, stimulate, and attract the best talents of the times, nor is it an adequate response to new questions and problems of a sort that could not have been imagined even fifty years ago.

More than ever before, as we approach the twenty-first century the world requires meaningful and useful resources from which to think, to envision the meaning of our conduct, and to find guidance for action, policies, and decisions. I am convinced that of all the traditions I deal with as a teacher of comparative religion and philosophy, Confucians have fashioned over the centuries a resource uniquely apt to the present world situation. It deserves to be known, utilized for reflection and self-cultivation, and extended—not to fill the world with "Confucians" and glorify a tradition, but because it is a precious resource that can help us at a point where we sorely need help.

This essay grows out of my experience teaching in a completely interdisciplinary undergraduate program for the last six years. The program offers me the liberty of following my interests and forming courses around important issues, with little regard for the boundaries of conventional academic disciplines. Because of my background specialization in comparative religion, I am especially interested in worldviews, the most fundamental assumptions people make in order to make sense of the world and of their own existence. As an American, it has always been natural for me to use contemporary America as a comparative reference point in my reflection and teaching, and in the last few years my courses have come increasingly to deal with the changes and challenges confronting the fundamental assumptions of the modern Western worldview.

Developing such courses has put new kinds of books on my shelf: alongside books on Hinduism, Buddhism, and Confucianism, there is a section on quantum physics and cosmology for my course on God and the new physics. Next to those are books on the environment, biology, and ecology for my environmental ethics course. And finally there is a mixture of social, economic and political thought that go into a course entitled "The End of the Modern World."

These may sound like an odd assortment of courses to be taught by a scholar whose academic research and publication for over twenty years has been focused on the Neo-Confucian tradition. I have found, however, that time and again it is the Confucian shape of my mind that gives me an especially useful perspective as I deal with these new materials. Patterns of thought familiar to anyone who studies the Neo-Confucian tradition have an unexpected currency in the contemporary world: they disclose hidden implications in common assumptions, point to paths around basic conceptual difficulties, and open up promising new approaches.

I have in this respect used my Neo-Confucian background continually. At the same time I have also been acutely aware that I could not directly use the concepts in which Neo-Confucians crystallized these deep patterns of thought. Central concepts, such as *li* and *ch'i*, human nature, the original nature, the Tao, or the Five

Relations, in their conventional Confucian form, have remained the kind of thing I can really teach only in courses dealing with Confucianism or the East Asian tradition. Somehow, knowing these things gives me a unique resource for thinking and teaching about contemporary issues, but the concepts themselves do not easily enter into contemporary discourse; their shape is still premodern.

If the Confucian resource is again taken up by newly self-aware East Asian thinkers or discovered and utilized by probing minds in the West, it will surely be transformed, graced with a renewed conceptual vocabulary related to streams of thought and understanding unknown to the past. That is what happened in China's Han dynasty (206 B.C.E.–220 C.E.), when Confucius's best insights were put together with yin-yang and Five Agents cosmological thought to make a grand unified vision suitable to the scope of the newly unified world of imperial China. And again in the Sung dynasty (960–1279), minds accustomed to centuries of Buddhism discovered new ascetical theories for the cultivation of the mind-and-heart and replaced Buddhist enlightenment with the attainment of sagehood as the goal of their spiritual quest. This "Neo-Confucian" development was supported by the elaboration of a metaphysics of *li* and *ch'i*, a new intellectual framework for a tradition which had not previously felt the need for systematic metaphysical thinking. In each case, the renewed tradition became the place for the best minds and spirits of the age to do their thinking and pursue their cultivation.

This does not mean I would suggest accepting and valuing everything modern in a "we can be modern too" mode. It is precisely this Western modern vision, the outworn heritage of the Enlightenment, that needs challenging, sifting, and reformulating. But in order to be a useful resource in this task, Neo-Confucian thinking must come into realistic contact with contemporary understanding and adjust itself so that serious dialogue can take place. Especially for a tradition that frames its most serious understandings about human life and society in a cosmological and naturalistic system, contemporary cosmological, biological, evolutionary, and ecological thinking has a serious claim. Clearly, we have more information about the actual processes of the natural world than did the ancients: refusal to rethink Neo-Confucian concepts seriously in the light of the best contemporary information would amount to consigning them to the museum of intellectual history.

In a way, I know what the postmodern world looks like to a Neo-Confucian because I use Neo-Confucian patterns of thought almost unconsciously in framing my own understanding. But I do not yet know what postmodern Neo-Confucian concepts would look like. This is, then, an experimental essay, an attempt first to see what becomes of the traditional conceptual schema if it is put in complete interaction with contemporary understanding, and second, to see what kind of benefit to contemporary understanding might come from thinking from the Neo-Confucian tradition. It is offered as a tentative and exploratory first step, recognizing and hoping that others may develop this material in alternative and far better ways.

Li and *Ch'i*

Neo-Confucians spoke of the cosmos (all that exists) in terms of the Supreme Ultimate, the Tao, and *li* and *ch'i*; modern thinkers speak of space-time, singularities, the genetic code, and evolution. The interface between these systems has great potential. There is symmetry insofar as both conceptual systems presume an all-encompassing process of ongoing but patterned change and trans-formation. But the contemporary concepts belong to the putatively value-free world of descriptive science; as such, they suggest an open arena for manipulative intervention and control but offer little normative guidance for life. The Neo-Confucian concepts, on the other hand, were originally conceived precisely as a foundation and guide for human conduct and self-cultivation, although in order to achieve that they also had to offer a satisfactory account of the general framework of all existence. If the Neo-Confucian concepts could withstand the transformation and retain their Confucian character, a more modern, scientifically informed philosophy of *li* and *ch'i* might still show us how the processes of the natural world delineate a place and a way of life for human beings.

Ch'i

Ch'i, according to Neo-Confucian tradition, is the stuff of the universe. It is therefore impossible to think of it in a serious contemporary way and ignore Einstein's $E = mc^2$, the equation of energy and mass. Bringing together *ch'i* and modern notions of energy could benefit the modern notion in various ways. One of the most immediate might be an easing of the burden of the tendency toward a materialistic reduction of life which has characterized much modern thought. A major problem in the Western tradition is that ideas of energy have a materialistic, mechanistic background, matter itself being conceived of as fundamentally nonconscious and nonliving. Thus, when scientists begin to investigate life processes and consciousness in terms of the patterned transformation of energy, many people instinctively feel this is a degrading materialistic reduction and find it threatening. In contrast, the Confucian tradition conceives *ch'i* as vitalistic, naturally fit to be not only the stuff but the life-force of both body and mind. Energy thought of against the backdrop of *ch'i* makes it seem simply a matter of course that life emerges naturally from an energetic universe, and it is to be expected that our thinking and feeling can be studied in terms of neural networks and electromagnetic phenomena. In short, *ch'i* provides a path around many of the problems that have accompanied the increasingly dysfunctional conceptual dichotomy of spirit/matter which the West inherited from the Greeks.

But one cannot simply grant this largess of Confucian wisdom to contemporary thinkers without a price: *ch'i* must be able to bear their realistic scrutiny in order to offer anything to contemporary thinkers. High on the list of once plausible but outmoded notions associated with *ch'i* is its characterization in terms of varying degrees of turbidity and purity or coarseness and fineness. Dropping this aspect of the concept, of course, opens up a critical area for systematic rethinking in the Neo-Confucian framework, for the purity and turbidity of *ch'i* played a major role in accounting for different kinds or levels of creatures and, most importantly, it also accounted for human moral and intellectual shortcomings. *Ch'i*'s relative purity or turbidity thus explained the distortions of the mind-and-heart and played a vital role in the theory of self-cultivation: if these features must be given up, it might seem the concept is stripped of all true philosophic and spiritual significance, which would be too high a price to pay.

When it comes to explaining the distortions evident in human conduct, modern Western secular thought shares an intriguing similarity with pre-Neo-Confucian limitations: neither could get much beyond relatively adventitious social or psychological explanations for this fundamental human problem. Neo-Confucians made a significant contribution to the understanding of human imperfection and self-cultivation by describing the source of the problem in the very processes of *ch'i*. A modern disciple of Chu Hsi might well still scrutinize the universe's processes of transforming energy for a more profound insight into what goes "wrong" with us. The traditional explanation in terms of degrees of purity and turbidity might find a contemporary analogue in the notion of degrees of complexity, a new systems theory concept that knits together physics, biology, and social, economic, and political systems in ways Neo-Confucians would find novel but somehow familiar. Energy becomes complex in atoms and molecules, and more so in organic, living systems; these organic units in turn associate and develop in complex ecosystems, and finally human societies emerge as the most complex of all. A contemporary Neo-Confucian Chu Hsi might well look to this evolutionary process of increasing complexity in hopes of discovering some factor that might account for the distorting or disconnecting of appropriate, natural (*tzu-jan*) responsiveness and coherence that is built into these layers of complexity as they evolve. We will return to this question below in the section on the human problem.

Li

Whether one is looking at physics, biology, economics, or political science, every kind of energy process is also patterned. Here we find a place for the half of the Neo-Confucian dualistic-monism system enshrined in concepts such as the Supreme Ultimate, Tao, or *li*. These are variant terms for expressing the structural, normative, patterning aspect of the universe. Things must not only exist, they must be and act some way. On a holistic level there is but one pattern that includes all particular subpatterns, and that is the Supreme Ultimate. This pattern running through and governing all things was traditionally referred to as the Tao, and within the patterned whole one could likewise consider each individual thing as having its own Tao, somewhat like the organic differentiation within a single body. *Li* became the favored Neo-Confucian term; it could be used virtually interchangeably with Tao, but lent itself more to the discourse regarding moral principles[2] so central to Confucian concerns.

One of the major shifts in late-twentieth-century thought is the shift from mechanistic reductionism, a tendency to explain wholes in terms of parts, to a new holistic orientation. This shift has been brought about by the emergence of systems theory to center stage: computers and cybernetics, information and data systems, ecology and economics are but a few of the areas where thinking in terms of structure, pattern, or systems has taken control. The terminology of these disciplines is beginning to develop a shared core, and the underlying patterns of thought involved are familiar to anyone trained in Neo-Confucian philosophy. For example, chaos theory and complexity theory have discovered and investigated unsuspected ways in which systems organize themselves, so now the concept of "self-organization," very similar to the East Asian concept of "self-so" (*tzu-jan*) processes unfolding in accord with a deep inner pattern, replaces mechanistic notions to explain the origin of the cosmos and of life itself. Likewise, in biology and the life sciences traditional thinking of causation from part to whole is now complimented by attempts to understand causation from whole to part, from organism to cell, from ecosystem to participant, from globe to subsystem.

This serious holistic turn of thought is a recent departure that begs for a more profound, consistent philosophical interpretation, while the Neo-Confucian tradition provides an unmatched depth of experience in this kind of reflection. Contemporary thought points toward an understanding of the cosmos, the world, physical systems, biosystems, ecosystems, and social systems as patterned energy of many levels and modes: not just pattern and not just energy; not just multiple and not just one. The dualistic monism[3] of Chu Hsi's system is steeped in understanding the dynamics, tensions, and problem areas for this kind of thinking. In fact, arguments in this area and difficulties in explaining causality from pattern/system downward seem amusingly similar to the interminable arguments of traditional Neo-Confucians about *li* and *ch'i*.

In the Neo-Confucian tradition, concepts such as Tao or *li* were central because they carried normative content for life in society; this was the core of Confucian concern. On the other hand, the world of modern inquiry has found this an almost impossible task: the

West may have become more holistic, but it is not skilled in drawing moral meaning from value-free systems, nor in understanding how the values got there if the systems are not value-free. It is clear that the Neo-Confucian *li*, if it could retain its normative content, might offer what is urgently needed here.

Traditional Neo-Confucians established moral content in the cosmic pattern by the outright identification of *li* as a heaven-bestowed norm[4] which is pure and perfect goodness. But in a contemporary context this lacks plausibility, for it represents precisely what modern thinkers are unwilling to assume about the patterns of nature. Traditional thought gave *li* such content automatically and easily; in a serious contemporary Neo-Confucianism *li* would have to come by normative content in a new and much more arduous way. Anxious to get on with the real and primary task of humanizing humans, Neo-Confucians simply rooted ideal human qualities in the cosmos and the world of nature. The new challenge is to view humans as thoroughly belonging to the cosmos and world of nature and then carefully work out what this means for their humanity. This is the challenge posed initially by Darwinian evolution and now, even more urgently, by the need for a deeply grounded ecological ethics. Indeed, working out this question might be the most fundamental philosophical task for post-traditional Neo-Confucian thinkers.

To be suited for this task, a renewed concept of *li* or Tao would need to be much more deeply informed by an understanding of evolutionary processes. This is not that difficult, for there is significant convergence between Tao or *li* and the Darwinian notion of natural selection, the keystone of evolutionary process. As the fundamental criterion of selection in evolutionary processes, natural selection is a powerful normative patterning dimension controlling and shaping ecosystems and evident in the dynamics of every activity in the interrelated whole. The popular equation of natural selection with "survival of the fittest" interpreted it as an amoral interplay of pure power relationships, almost the antithesis of the kind of content Neo-Confucians might hope for. Now a deepened understanding of systems, however, has extensively modified the earlier ideas. In contemporary understanding, survival of the fittest is not so much a matter of the strongest and meanest surviving in brutal competition, but more a matter of truly fitting in successfully with everything else in the system. Strategies of fitting in are numerous, and "fit" is a more fundamental criterion than power or strength. Symbiosis, even among predator and prey, is essential, and life-taking must ultimately be life-giving or it cancels itself out. The most successful parasites, it turns out, benefit their hosts rather than destroy them.

Evolution, then, involves a myriad ways of fitting in, with creative adaptive strategies emerging with each new element of change and complexity in the system. All life exists in a web of responsive relationship with all other life, and with the physical system that supports the living system. Such patterned interdependence is not limited to only the systemic evolution of lifeforms; it also frames their daily existence in ecosystems and extends upward to include the human-made ecosystem called "culture" or "society" as well. The existing pattern of beings at every level, which includes the patterned interdependent relationships among the various levels, has a normative force: it is only in terms of this pattern that life is supported. The nature of this norm, of course, is pragmatic; evolution is above all a mighty process elaborating a more and more complex and interwoven system of what works to give and maintain life. This would be the meaning of *li* as evolutionary pattern.

The Neo-Confucian saying, "*li* is one but manifested diversely," arose when Ch'eng I was trying to explain Chang Tsai's *Western Inscription*, the document which put Confucian ethics on a new metaphysical footing. The same expression carries equal insight as we now try to put ethics on a cosmic/life evolutionary footing. Such a *li* is in fact far more appropriate to the evolutionary context than is the traditional Western notion of each kind of creature being endowed with a separate, distinctive "nature" of its own. The interdependent systemic process of evolving life insures both differentiation and that each thing develops its own distinctive specialization precisely in terms of everything else: one everchanging and developing pattern encompasses all, and each has its own particular pattern in terms of the whole. Human ethics must ultimately be framed in a more encompassing ecological ethics that considers the whole network of these patterned relationships.

Ethics

Western moral philosophers would be quick to note the pragmatic foundation of the normative *li* I have described, and would have probing questions about how one could derive a moral "ought" out of a practical "what works or what doesn't work." Western philosophy has generally treated morality as a completely distinctive realm based upon attributes considered uniquely human, such as rationality and free will. Kant brought this tradition to an especially sharp focus by describing the moral "ought" as a "categorical imperative," unlike any merely conditional "ought" relating to practical considerations. This but crystallized a common assumption that moral good/evil belongs to a realm apart from any other kind of good or evil. Confucians, working in the context of a nontheistic worldview, drew no such strict distinctions, somehow making the transition from natural fact to moral obligation, from is to ought, effortlessly, hardly pausing to notice or explain what to the trained Western philosophic mind is a huge question. Human morality was indeed their central concern, but they did not hesitate to see partial manifestations of the same moral characteristics in the birds and beasts or, on another level, in the cycle of the four seasons.

Much of the difference in these approaches to ethical or moral questions goes back to the most basic framework. Western thinkers have commonly framed the question as a matter of our use of freedom in choosing between good and evil, while Confucians have thought in terms of responding appropriately to a given situation. For those who think in terms of the exercise of freedom and choice, the most obvious conditions limiting proper conduct generally have to do with other humans and their exercise of their own freedom. This closes the circle of a morality which is not only practiced exclusively by humans but also views moral obligations as relating only to other humans. Confucians devoted their attention likewise almost entirely to the realm of human relationships and appropriate response or treatment of other humans, but in principle the question of appropriate responsiveness could apply to any situation. While both traditions have been in this respect anthropocentric, nothing about the Confucian framework systemically limits its applicability only to humans. This is the underlying reason it was so easy above to adapt *li* to the evolutionary process of the natural universe: the concept is not inherently anthropocentric, and such dimensions have been part of it all along.

In the contemporary world, and increasingly as one looks a few decades into the future, these frameworks and their differences become critically important. At the threshold of the twenty-first century, humankind—east, west, north, south—faces an era of unprecedented challenge. The organization, habits, and lifeways of industrial society are wiping out species, eroding soil, exhausting and polluting water, making air unbreathable, and the very light of the sun now becomes something we must avoid. No informed observer thinks what we are doing is sustainable, but masses choose to be uninformed rather than face problems and a future they do not understand. These are ethical questions of appropriate conduct that weigh as heavily or even more heavily than issues of how humans are treating other humans. The perspective, and the conduct of our lives, is badly distorted when we see both as "only pragmatic" and hence not on a par with the interhuman "moral" concerns. In fact, this very anthropocentrism is at the heart of the problem.

In this circumstance the relatively simple Confucian question of appropriate response is ethically far more powerful than exclusively human notions such as moral imperatives and obligations based on rights and duties or some kind of social contract. *Li* is a guide or norm to modes of conduct and ways of life that fit, that maximize life throughout the system. The investigation of this kind of *li* could offer flexible insight into the conduct of human relationships in various kinds of cultures or societies; at the same time it opens with equal weight the question of appropriate human relationship with the whole life system of the planet—and allows some new answers. It is of critical importance here that *li* not only includes but goes beyond the human sphere, demanding a fit that ultimately is appropriate to the whole earth. Such a view is often dismissed as hopelessly idealistic. But a careful investigation of *li*, I would argue, reveals that it is cold, hard, pragmatic realism; it is the only ethos that fits the dimensions and proportions human life has assumed at the end of the twentieth century.

The Emergence of Life and Consciousness and the Place of Humans

The systemic ethics I have been describing supposes in the very concept of *li* that human beings are part of the entire patterned world of nature. But, for the working out of ethics, a more precise consideration of just how and where we fit in this overall pattern is a matter of great importance. In the world of premodern anthropocentric thought, it was sufficient for Neo-Confucians simply to presume the superiority of human beings and substantiate it by a metaphysical theory that endowed us with the finest *ch'i*, and hence with the fullest participation in *li*. This wonderfully explains how humans seem to be flexibly and responsively engaged with virtually anything in existence (the whole pattern), compared to the more limited and specialized responsiveness of other creatures. But the meaning and implications of the emergence of these abilities in the broad evolving pattern of life must be carefully examined; the simple assumption that we are the crowning glory of evolution might carry a very misleading message about our real situation.

The question of the emergence of life is full of wonderful ambiguities. A review of theories on life/nonliving makes one thing clear: no one can draw a precise line between the two, though there is a wide acceptance of the intuitive feeling that there really is some difference. How one treats this question seems to depend to a large extent upon the conceptual resources one brings to it: it has no "scientific" answer.

In this context it is especially interesting that if, without knowing later philosophical developments, one were to seek a classical Western counterpart for the East Asian concept of *ch'i*, in Greek it would be *pneuma*, in Latin, *spiritus*. Both *pneuma* and *spiritus* originally had to do with wind, hence air, breath, the breath of life, the force of vitality, and the power of feelings. *Ch'i*, from a base meaning having to do with steam or vapor, developed almost exactly the same set of associations. But the Western terms eventuated in "spirit" as opposed to and contrasted with "matter," while *ch'i*, as the concretizing and energizing component, became paired with *li*, a role thinkers East and West have intuitively equated with the "matter" side of Western thought. In effect, much of what went into "spirit" in the West went into the physical in East Asia.

So it is that in traditional Western thought physical stuff (matter) needed animation, an *animus* or "soul" to become alive, and accordingly the evolutionary question of the emergence of life from a presumably nonliving material substrate has been a difficult one, the case of the "spiritual" soul of humans being the most difficult of all. By contrast, life is only to be expected in the case of *ch'i*, and the question rather becomes whether there is such a thing as nonliving. One could easily think of the difference as more a matter of complexity than of kind, and somewhat arbitrarily specify a degree of organized behavior as the cutoff line for practical purposes.

The emergence and evolution of life is an energetic (*ch'i*) thrust toward systemic complexity (*li*). The complex pattern of organism and ecosystem is emergent rather than preexisting. The process starts with self-organizing systems at a relatively simple level and transforms as adaptive strategies within the system lead to continually increasing levels of complexity. In a sense *li* continually gives birth to itself, emergent pattern leading to yet further pattern.

As I mentioned above, the boundaries of the distinctive pattern called "life" are virtually impossible to fix clearly: in somewhat circular fashion, we recognize life when we see things somehow "making a living." That is, things begin in an active way to maintain an existence in terms of something else: amino acids have no need for protozoa, but protozoa require amino acids. Life is thus distinguished by a qualitatively new level of relatedness.

This new form of relatedness is in some way a "presence" of one thing in another. Primitive life emerged in a soup of nutrients, amino acids, which were simply absorbed through semiporous membranes. But as soon as this system emerged, the single-cell creatures by their very structure "expected" certain nutrients, which in that respect were present even when physically absent. I would suggest that this present-while-absent quality inherent in the advent of "needs," even though it is only a matter of structure or pattern at this point, might be regarded as the seed of what we recognize at a far more complex level as consciousness.

To put it another way, the most elementary form of consciousness seems to emerge as creatures begin to live in terms of one another. The strategies for making a living, which fit an organism into the emergent and ever-transforming community of life ("survival of the fittest"), become more complex as we move from plants to herbivores to carnivores. Structural consciousness, the selective taking in of nutrients, takes on new and more active dimensions as more elaborate strategies for sustenance and reproduction come into play. The emergence of controlled mobility, accompanied by the development of the various forms of sensation that make mobility meaningful, is a decisive step in the direction of more familiar forms of consciousness.

In this framework, consciousness in its more and more progressive forms might be best regarded as a particular strategy in an overall process which is most fundamentally a matter of adaptation, literally "fitting in." As the range of consciousness increases, so do flexibility and the complexity of the fitting in. Mobility and sensation emerge as strategies that can detach the creature from strict dependence on immediate environment, and bring instead a new kind of dependence spread out over a much larger environment. A blade of grass grows in a few inches of soil, while a hawk soars over miles interacting with a wide range of creatures. The hawk interdepends more broadly and flexibly, but to describe this freedom as independence would be an illusion.

The meaning of consciousness as a particular evolutionary strategy is perhaps best considered in context with alternative strategies. If one thinks of intelligence as a matter of problem-solving, for example, one might broadly distinguish at least two basic forms: there is genetic intelligence and experiential intelligence. Some sentient, mobile life-forms specialize in genetic, rather than experiential, strategies for handling problems. Many insects, for example, are minimally individualized and flexible, live a short time, but reproduce massively. Instead of specializing in advancing along the consciousness and experiential learning line, their species have become in this way highly complex and diversified systems possessing a high ability to adaptively mutate around changed circumstances. This form of intelligence has at least held even and may be emerging victorious in the chemical warfare of pesticides and antibiotics waged against it by humans, who represent the crowning achievement of the alternative, experientially based line of evolved intelligence.

Life-forms that put the greatest weight on experience and on immediate (versus insect-like genetic) flexibility typically live longer and produce proportionally fewer young. In this line of development, a growth in the ability to accumulate and utilize experience is an important advantage: experience thus becomes learning. Herein we find the deep significance of increased brain size, which increases memory to store a broader and broader range of experience and enhances our flexible adaptability to make use of it. We humans have represented the foremost thrust of this development, getting such big heads for memory storage and experience processing that we have to be born early (about six to eight months prematurely from any ordinary mammalian development standard) so that our growing heads would not become a death warrant for our mothers. Thus our brains continue growing at fetal rates well after we are born, and they finally reach about quadruple the size they were at birth. Also, corresponding to our premature birth, we have a longer period after birth of intense dependency on our parents than any other creature, a factor that puts an especially heavy weight on sociability. When former Confucians noted social relationships, with a special emphasis on the qualities of the parent-child relationship, as primary human characteristics they were right on the evolutionary mark!

We humans have not only developed the biological capacity to accumulate personal experience, we also discovered language, a means by which experience is shared and accumulated in community over many generations rather than being quantized in single life units. Writing was another major step, allowing for a qualitatively new level of complexity and continuity in the transmission of accumulated information from generation to generation. And now the globe is electronically linked and computer memory banks put this whole process of information and learning accumulation into yet another mode. This is so much more powerful and rapid than anything that has gone before that we do not yet begin to understand its potentials and implications.

This process has taken place within human society, and at each stage human relationships have been transformed in important ways. There is much to be reflected upon and understood just in the human social dimension, but such reflection should also be extended to take in the larger picture. This whole process of maximizing experience began as one of a number of adaptive strategies in the complex evolution of life, and it is shared in various degrees by many other creatures. We have thrust ahead on a vector entirely natural in its direction, yet somehow this process has also become self-enclosed and distinct from nature in a uniquely human way. Experience became deliberate learning, and language (including writing and computers) empowered the learning thrust in a way that transformed our adaptation to the world into a matter of adapting the world to our needs and desires: "nature" and "culture" have become different categories. Again, other creatures do this as well; we only represent an extreme development of this life strategy.

At the same time the naturalness of this process should not blind us to risk: evolutionary strategies are attempts, probes, adaptive reachings that may not succeed or may even undercut themselves by their own success. In an anthropocentric world the relative permanence of our species could be simply assumed; in an evolutionary universe continued existence is an achievement that no creature can take for granted. When earlier Confucians observed that man, by possessing the fullness of *li*, is thus in a more universally responsive relationship with all things than any other creature, they were considering a very real consequence of this evolutionary pattern. But the anthropocentric habit of preferring human forms over all others foreshortened for them considerations that are now urgent. There is now, as never before, an awareness that the very capacities in which we most glory also are capacities that put us in peril. This, too, calls for interpretation and understanding.

The Human Problem

The question of how the kind of evolutionary process we have described could ever arrive at the kind of critical situation evident at present is initially perplexing. We have characterized the *li* of the cosmic evolutionary process as a self-organizing, emergent, ramifying, and interwoven systemic pattern. Since everything in this burgeoning pattern happens in terms of everything else, apart from major interventions from outside the immediate system (collisions with asteroids and the like), it would seem that things should go well. As in the case of the Tao, or perfect *li* of old, one imagines pure and perfect harmony and then must struggle to account for the sense of something amiss that most often, and especially now, is a feature of human experience. In particular, it seems that the rest of the natural world more or less of itself (*tzu-jan*) maintains a certain balance; how is it, then, that a similar balance is not evidenced in the human part of nature's pattern?

Some traditions have solved this question by removing human beings from the natural system and giving them unique powers (free will), along with unique problems to match (moral good and evil, sinfulness). However, in times such as we now confront, when human relations with the entire earth system are problematic and an object of grave concern, it is a particular strength of the Confucian tradition that they have avoided any such structural split. But assuming a basic continuity between humans and nature makes it difficult to describe what goes wrong. It is awkward to describe humans as evil if human nature is but part of an all-embracing and somehow normative pattern; on the other hand, saying humankind is good leaves nothing but adventitious circumstantial explanations of evil such as Mencius's appeal to social forces. The Neo-Confucians achieved a systematic explanation by introducing the turbidity of *ch'i*, a more powerful solution than that of Mencius, but still limited. In particular, the relative turbidity of their *ch'i* differentiated and fit the various species into their places in the patterned mosaic of life, but only in the case of humans does this differentiating function transform into a matter of a distortion of appropriate responsiveness. This seeming uniqueness of the human "moral problem" is more a question in proportion as humans have otherwise been framed in terms of a single, all-embracing natural system.

I have not found that traditional Neo-Confucians devoted much attention to this question. At most one finds passing reference to the fact that only humans have the capacity for self-cultivation. The implication is that the responsive scope of nonhuman creatures is so "blocked up" by the turbidity of their psychophysical *ch'i* that they have little latitude for further perfecting their fundamental endowment. Humans, endowed with a greater purity or fineness of *ch'i*, participate responsively in the fullness of the *li* which patterns all things. Endowed with the capacity to respond to all things, there is a wide range in which we may fall short in the exercise of our lofty constitution. Self-cultivation, in this perspective, is both a sign of a relatively high psychophysical endowment and also an urgent necessity.

In this account of the human situation there are implications regarding the human place in existence that reflect traditional anthropocentric assumptions. But there is assumed in this vision a fundamental continuity in the community of being which supports the naturalness of the human phenomenon. Further, assessing consciousness in terms of different scopes of responsiveness deals with observable differences and is much more secure than attempting to differentiate it in terms of the possession of unique spiritual powers. Turbid *ch'i* may no longer be much help in explaining the uncertain fittingness of our responses, but the general framework puts the question in a way that can easily be pursued through avenues opened by contemporary understandings of evolutionary processes.

Evolution is a process of developing complex adaptive strategies, each with its own rhythm but controlled by the necessity of meshing with the rhythms of the physical world and interdependent with other life-forms. Life on this planet began perhaps some 3.5 billion years ago, but for about 3 billion years it was mostly one long dynasty of single-celled blue-green algae. Evolution by random genetic mutation is a very slow process indeed. The much more rapid strategy of gene pooling and mixing through sexual reproduction after the emergence of eucaryotic cells really took off only about 550 million years ago; that process has been incredibly rapid and productive, filling that half-billion years with an estimated 4 billion species, of which perhaps 5 million remain. Short-lived bacteria that pack generations into our days can use this genetic strategy to mutate around our drugs in a matter of months or years, and insects do the same with our pesticides. The same mechanism cannot serve us in chemical warfare because we live too long and reproduce too modestly; thus, it took over 3 million years to accomplish the relatively modest alterations that separate the earliest homonids from modern homo sapiens sapiens, the form of modern humans which emerged about 100,000 years ago.

Our long lives and low reproduction are not a problem, however, because they are complemented by another adaptive strategy: we can adapt to chemical warfare or any other perilous situation by learning from experience, the fastest and most flexible of all evolved adaptive strategies. So dependent are we on this strategy that we are often inclined to think all our problems are really somehow a matter of our difficulty in sufficiently absorbing and learning from experience. We feel we learn too slowly, but human learning as an adaptive strategy is far more rapid than other natural processes of mutation: unlike genetic mutation which demands a new generation, this strategy operates in the momentary framework of lived individual experience, and it brings its power to bear upon goals that may be similarly framed in the context of immediate needs or wants. But in the broader pattern of nature, when the immediacy of flexible response to experience is developed with the power it has achieved in the human case (memory, learning, language, writing, computers, and so on), there is a new pressure on the whole system to move or harmonize with the newly dominant rhythm. That, however, is not possible.

There is, then, a serious question of systemic fit. Earth systems have a natural rate of production and absorption: being in harmony with that clock is the difference between clean or polluted rivers and groundwater, breathable or toxic air, life-giving or acid rain. Life-forms have likewise a varied genetic, reproductive, biological rhythm which must somehow mesh with the clock of the earth systems or forfeit survival. Experience-based adaptation is a far more rapid time framework, geared to enable sentient creatures to respond successfully to the vagaries of the passing moment, be it an opportunity for a meal or to avoid becoming a meal. We have specialized and elaborated this most rapid framework and achieved unprecedented mastery over our immediate circumstances, in the process detaching our responses from groundings in the slower processes of nature. We have become the fastest living creature on earth, producing more than the earth can absorb or sustain, changing entire ecosystems and environments faster than life-forms can adjust, and straining our own capacity to deal with our ever more dense, eventful, experience-packed lives in which the dominant feeling is that we never have enough time.

One can see that the question or problem of successfully harmonizing the temporal rhythms of energetic change and flow at various systemic levels is structural; it is neither intrinsically good nor intrinsically evil, but that does not prevent it from being problematic and giving rise to many of the phenomena at various levels that we identify as good and evil. By the development of increased memory and language, experience has been transformed into a process of cumulative learning and opened a new space for artifice: the world of humanly wrought culture comes to overlay the world of nature. Human activity is no longer directly shaped by the natural system, although it must ultimately harmonize with it. And if there is to be such harmony, it must be achieved deliberately through human knowledge, discipline, and self-cultivation (i.e., artifice)—or through the natural disaster which finally systematically corrects for adaptive misfits.

Self-Cultivation

Self-cultivation, the process of study and reflection coupled interdependently with practice in active life and meditative quiet, is certainly at the heart of the Neo-Confucian endeavor. It is also where renewed thinking from the Confucian tradition has much to offer in the coming decades. The major temptation of the modern era has been to believe that technical expertise is the essential and adequate foundation for proper activity, and this will remain as a temptation of the emerging postmodern world as well. But the above reflections on the nature of the human problem offer little hope that furthering the technological mastery that has rendered the globe increasingly subject to the fast clock and immediate framework of human responsive experience and desire can be expected to slow the clock or chasten the desires. Instead, in a typically Neo-Confucian way, we are returned to the central role of self-cultivation.

The scope and emphasis of concern in this readjusted, environmentally oriented framework have shifted somewhat from the traditional Confucian focus on human society. But the nature of the central problem to be addressed in cultivation changes little from the perennial Confucian insight: it is still the effects of inappropriate desires that are the basic source of distortion in the way we respond within our network of interrelated existence. Traditional analysis of what makes certain forms of desire "inappropriate," or a "distorted" form of response, generally looked to the way self-centeredness destroys the life-giving network of interdependent relationships within which individuals are constituted. Now, looking beyond the limits of human society to the question of the adaptive fit between human society and the rest of the natural world, the meshing of temporal rhythms emerges as a primary criterion of life-givingness or appropriateness. But as in the case of self-centeredness in social relations, on the level of psychological description the central problem comes down to a matter of the proper discipline and function of desire.

There is nothing wrong with desire. It is in fact the basic substrate of an experience-centered strategy for adaptation and survival: experience has meaning largely as a guide for desire and so for action, which is mediated by desire. But this means that the evolution of the experience-centered survival strategy into the world of human learning and adaptation by manipulation has brought about a world in which human desire plays an unprecedented role. In the contemporary world of technologically empowered desire, the enlarged task of self-cultivation is to harmonize the naturally immediate or relatively short temporal frame of reference, which is the original sphere of desires, with the very different rhythms of other sectors of the natural system. The traditional task of subordinating desire for immediate and personal self-gratification to larger considerations and self-identities in terms of family and society is not supplanted, only enlarged. We must now do not only that, but also finally transcend the anthropocentric limits of traditional self-identities. The need to adjust our desires to the rhythms of other life-forms and earth processes is different in scope, but not in kind, from the kind of thing Confucians have taken as a central task for thousands of years.

The means devised by Neo-Confucians for self-cultivation remain among the most sophisticated, powerful, and appropriate for this task. The purpose of the traditional "investigation of *li*" was ultimately the task of understanding one's complex relational reality and the conduct fitting such a reality: What does it mean to be a son, a father, a husband or wife, a brother or a minister to the king? What is the pattern of the seasons? How is it manifest in me? What does that mean for my conduct today, tomorrow? These questions remain valid, and a deep, reflective personal grasp of these matters is a means for profound transformation and growth.

But beyond such traditional concerns, a postmodern investigation of *li* would direct itself not only to the pattern of human social relatedness, but also to its embeddedness in the larger network of life and earth relationships as well. The simple facts that bear on our relational reality and the temporal rates of natural processes call for equally deep reflection and also have the power to transform our lives profoundly. How many humans are there on the globe? How many years will it take to double this at a 2 percent growth rate? How much uncultivated but arable land is left on earth? How much cultivated land is lost annually? What is the rate of deforestation, of water usage, of river siltation? How many chemicals do we produce, in what quantities, and where do they go? If we continue exterminating one hundred species each day (Harvard biologist Edward O. Wilson's estimate), how many years before we will drive into extinction 25 percent of the earth's life? How do bacteria, plants, insects, and animals (including humans) interdepend in the web of life? This is a small and arbitrary sample of matters for investigation and reflection relating to *li* as we now know it to be that have normative import and call for serious consideration. If the answers to such questions do not overshadow and outweigh our other more immediate concerns and change our desires, it is only because we do not bother to reflect on them profoundly: we do not investigate this *li*. For creatures who have elaborated an experience/ information-based adaptation strategy into such an instrument of power, perhaps nothing is more fundamental than the deep, reflective investigation of *li*. Just as former Confucians observed regarding matters such as filial piety, we need to know in our hearts and bones what we already know superficially with our intellects and read as numbers on a page.

Neo-Confucians knew this required some retreat from total immersion in the affairs of a busy life. Basing themselves on Mencius's reflections concerning the healing properties of a quiet night, they introduced quiet-sitting, a meditative practice aimed at cultivating a deep inner stillness and calm that could extend to active life as well. Quietness is not part of the typical rhythm of most modern human lives, but without inner quietness it is difficult to achieve the depth of reflection required to make learning a process of self-transformation. Human biology and psychology also have rates and limits for absorbing new information and experience. Even the human mind-and-heart, the most rapidly flexible adaptive system devised in life's three-billion-year evolution, threatens to be inundated by the artificial extensions we have devised to pack time more and more densely with more information, activity, and accomplishment. Quiet-sitting and similar forms of discipline open a space that can restore a responsiveness often numbed by the pace and demands of modern life.

The evolutionary line that has led from experience to learning and deliberate technique culminates in the entirely artificial speed of modern technological cultures. The traditional Neo-Confucian demand for a balanced process of learning and practice, reflection and direct cultivation, activity and quiet, is if anything more necessary under these conditions. As always, the two sides of this single self-cultivation process mutually inform and enhance one another. The investigation of *li* reveals the necessity of tuning the rhythm of our desires to fit appropriately in a life-supporting way with the patterned processes of society, biosphere, and the earth. Quiet is the direction of the needed adjustment as well as the condition that enables the required reflective investigation of these matters. Without attention to this sort of self-cultivation, it will be difficult to see clearly or walk responsively the paths that must be trod in the twenty-first century.

Conclusion

This paper assumes that a truly living philosophical/religious tradition is, at least for an intellectual, a place from which to think. The possible objects of thought are many. My own feeling is that real questions confronting the world, society, and one's own person are the most obvious and important matters for reflection; secondarily, there is the inward gaze with which a tradition keeps its own conceptual house in order. Buddhists, Christians, or Confucians must certainly spend some effort reflecting on doctrines and modes of understanding that are particularly Buddhist, Christian, or Confucian. But the real point is to understand life and the world, and to conduct oneself accordingly.

My first priority in this paper thus has been to exemplify what happens when one uses the Neo-Confucian tradition, not as an object of study, but as a place from which to think. I have done this almost unconsciously for years and it has shaped my thoughts in ways of which I was hardly aware. But until writing this paper I have not tried to do such thinking in a highly conscious and deliberately Neo-Confucian mode. The attempt has meant trying to push beyond the general holistic systemic fit, to see if the conceptual system itself would come to life when placed in serious interaction with contemporary knowledge about cosmic, earth, and life processes.

Somewhat to my surprise, *li* and *ch'i* and related understandings of consciousness and the mind-and-heart seem to enter the contemporary world without much difficulty. My personal test of how they survived the transition is whether they fit the new milieu in a way that generates new and important insight: did using them in a serious way lead to new ideas, or to seeing new connections, or to finding a new clarity of explanation in areas of familiar reflection? I found this indeed to be the case in a number of areas. Those that stand out most in my mind are the derivation of a meaning of morality and a foundation for normative content within a totally natural milieu, new ways of pursuing the mind/body problem, and a useful and practical description of the human problem in terms of our place and specialization within the whole evolutionary system.

I am under no illusion that my way of adapting *li* and *ch'i* to the contemporary world is the best or most appropriate. No one would be more pleased than I if a hot debate arose with a number of adaptations being proposed, critiqued, and refined over a period of years. But perhaps the more important part of my project here has been to exemplify the special fittingness of the Neo-Confucian tradition as a place from which to think in the contemporary world. Most of the ideas in this paper are not particularly "Neo-Confucian": they come from systems theory, quantum physics and cosmology, neo-Darwinism and ecology. In a Neo-Confucian context, however, these ideas take on a new kind of coherence, thematic structure, and pointedness. The normative dimension, the place of human consciousness, and the need for and application to self-cultivation are elements that come into play only at the interface of these materials and Neo-Confucian thought. Although the vision of the world, and humankind's place in it and the essential problem(s) as presented here, does not pretend to be a new Neo-Confucianism, I would hope that anyone deeply familiar with the tradition might be able to recognize it as a typically Neo-Confucian way of thinking that is appropriate to the questions and needs of the twenty-first century.

Notes

1. This is a reworked version of a paper first presented at and published in the proceedings of the Eighth International Conference on Korean Studies, held in Korea at the Academy of Korean Studies in 1994.

2. Moral principles in this view are simply a level of manifestation of the pattern, not a unique and distinctive realm apart from what the Western tradition refers to as "Nature." The same *li* that is the pattern whereby life arises abundantly in spring, for example, is manifested in human nature as the life-giving character of humane feeling and commiseration with the lot of our fellow beings.

3. Although it makes use of two fundamental concepts, *li* and *ch'i*, in proportion as there is emphasis on their complementary roles and absolute interdependence and inseparability, the system is in a deeper sense monistic. Depending on the emphasis of individual thinkers, either the more dualistic or more monistic potentials of this situation could be emphasized.

4. "Heaven" in such Neo-Confucian usage simply points to the ultimate normative agency in existence. By the fourth century B.C.E. the understanding of this agency had already evolved from the idea of a personal supreme being to the non-personal inherent norm, or Tao.

Conceptual Resources from
China, Korea, and Japan

The Continuity of Being:
Chinese Visions of Nature

Tu Weiming

The Chinese belief in the continuity of being, a basic motif in Chinese ontology, has far-reaching implications in Chinese philosophy, religion, epistemology, aesthetics, and ethics. F. W. Mote comments that

> the basic point which outsiders have found so hard to detect is that the Chinese, among all peoples ancient and recent, primitive and modern, are apparently unique in having no creation myth; that is, they have regarded the world and man as uncreated, as constituting the central features of a spontaneously self-generating cosmos having no creator, god, ultimate cause, or will external to itself.[1]

This strong assertion has understandably generated controversy among Sinologists. Mote has identified a distinctive feature of the Chinese mode of thought. In his words, "the genuine Chinese cosmogony is that of organismic process, meaning that all of the parts of the entire cosmos belong to one organic whole and that they all interact as participants in one spontaneously self-generating life process."[2]

However, despite Mote's insightfulness in singling out this particular dimension of Chinese cosmogony for focused investigation, his characterization of its uniqueness is problematic. For one thing, the apparent lack of a creation myth in Chinese cultural history is predicated on a more fundamental assumption about reality; namely, that all modalities of being are organically connected. Ancient Chinese thinkers were intensely interested in the creation of the world. Some of them, notably the Taoists, even speculated on the creator (*tsao-wu che*) and the process by which the universe came into being.[3] Presumably, indigenous creation myths existed, although the written records transmitted by even the most culturally sophisticated historians do not contain enough information to reconstruct them.[4] The real issue is not the presence or absence of creation myths but the underlying assumption of the cosmos: whether it is continuous or discontinuous with its creator. Suppose the cosmos as we know it was created by a Big Bang; the ancient Chinese thinkers would have no problem with this theory. What they would not have accepted was a further claim that there was an external intelligence, beyond human comprehension, who willed that it be so. Of course, the Chinese are not unique in this regard. Many peoples, ancient and recent, primitive and modern, would feel uncomfortable with the idea of a willful God who created the world out of nothing. It was not a creation myth as such but the Judeo-Christian version of it that is absent in Chinese mythology. But the Chinese, like numerous peoples throughout human history, subscribe to the continuity of being as self-evidently true.[5]

An obvious consequence of this basic belief is the all-embracing nature of the so-called spontaneously self-generating life process. Strictly speaking, it is not because the Chinese have no idea of God external to the created cosmos that they have no choice but to accept the cosmogony as an organismic process. Rather, it is precisely because they perceive the cosmos as the unfolding of continuous creativity that it cannot entertain "conceptions of creation *ex nihilo* by the hand of God, or through the will of God, and all other such mechanistic, teleological, and theistic cosmologies."[6] The Chinese commitment to the continuity of being, rather than the absence of a creation myth, prompts them to see nature as "the all-enfolding harmony of impersonal cosmic functions."[7]

The Chinese model of the world, "a decidedly psychophysical structure" in the Jungian sense,[8] is characterized by Joseph Needham as "an ordered harmony of wills without an ordainer."[9] What Needham describes as the organismic Chinese cosmos consists of dynamic energy fields rather than static matter-like entities. Indeed, the dichotomy of spirit and matter is not at all applicable to this psychophysical structure. The most basic stuff that makes the cosmos is neither solely spiritual nor material but both. It is a vital force. This vital force must not be conceived of either as disembodied spirit or as pure matter.[10] Wing-tsit Chan, in his influential *Source Book in Chinese Philosophy*, notes that the distinction between energy and matter is not made in Chinese philosophy. He further notes that H. H. Dubs's rendering of the indigenous term for this basic stuff, *ch'i*, as "matter-energy" is "essentially sound but awkward and lacks an adjective form."[11] Although Chan translates *ch'i* as "material force," he cautions that since *ch'i*, before the advent of Neo-Confucianism in the eleventh century, originally "denotes the psychophysiological power associated with blood and breath," it should be rendered as "vital force" or "vital power."[12]

The unusual difficulty in making *ch'i* intelligible in modern Western philosophy suggests that the underlying Chinese metaphysical assumption is significantly different from the Cartesian dichotomy between spirit and matter. However, it would be misleading to categorize the Chinese mode of thinking as a sort of pre-Cartesian naïveté lacking differentiation between mind and body and, by implication, between subject and object. Analytically, Chinese thinkers have clearly distinguished spirit from matter. They fully recognize that spirit is not reducible to matter, that spirit is of more enduring value than matter. There are, of course, notable exceptions. But these so-called materialist thinkers are not only rare but also too few and far between to constitute a noticeable tradition in Chinese philosophy. Recent attempts to reconstruct the genealogy of materialist thinkers in China have been painful and, in some cases, far-fetched.[13] Indeed, to characterize the two great Confucian thinkers, Chang Tsai (1020–1077) and Wang Fu-chih (1619–1692), as paradigmatic examples of Chinese materialism is predicated on the false assumption that *ch'i* is materialistic. Both of them did subscribe to what may be called philosophy of *ch'i* as a critique of speculative thought, but, to them, *ch'i* was not simply matter but vital force endowed with all-pervasive spirituality.[14]

The continuous presence in Chinese philosophy of the idea of *ch'i* as a way of conceptualizing the basic structure and function of the cosmos, despite the availability of symbolic resources to make an analytical distinction between spirit and matter, signifies a conscious refusal to abandon a mode of thought that synthesizes spirit and matter as an undifferentiated whole. The loss of analytical clarity is compensated by the reward of imaginative richness. The fruitful ambiguity of *ch'i* allows philosophers to explore realms of being which are inconceivable to people constricted by a Cartesian dichotomy. To be sure, the theory of the different modalities of *ch'i* cannot engender ideas such as the naked object, raw data, or the value-free fact, and this cannot create a world out there, naked, raw, and value-free, for the disinterested scientist to study, analyze, manipulate, and control. *Ch'i*, in short, seems inadequate to provide a philosophical background for the development of empirical science as understood in the positivistic sense. What it does provide, however, is a metaphorical mode of knowing, an epistemological attempt to address the multidimensional nature of reality by comparison, allusion, and suggestion.

Whether it is the metaphorical mode of knowing that directs the Chinese to perceive the cosmos as an organismic process or it is the ontological vision of the continuity of being that informs Chinese epistemology is a highly intriguing question. Our main concern here, however, is to understand how the idea of the undifferentiated *ch'i* serves as a basis for a unified cosmological theory. We want to know in what sense the least intelligent being, such as a rock, and the highest manifestation of spirituality, such as heaven, both consist of *ch'i*. The way the Chinese perceive reality and the sense of reality which defines the Chinese way of seeing the world are equally important in our inquiry, even though we do not intend to specify any causal relationship between them.

The organismic process as a spontaneously self-generating life process exhibits three basic motifs: continuity, wholeness, and dynamism.[15] All modalities of being, from a rock to Heaven, are integral parts of a continuum which is often referred to as the "great transformation" (*ta-hua*).[16] Since nothing is outside of this continuum, the chain of being is never broken. A linkage will always be found between any given pair of things in the universe. We may have to probe deeply to find some of the linkages, but they are there to be discovered. These are not figments of our imagination but solid foundations upon which the cosmos and our lived world therein are constructed. *Ch'i*, the psychophysiological stuff, is everywhere. It suffuses even the "great void" (*t'ai-hsü*) which is the source of all beings in Chang Tsai's philosophy.[17] The continuous presence of *ch'i* in all modalities of being makes everything flow together as the unfolding of a single process. Nothing, not even an almighty creator, is external to this process.

This motif of wholeness is directly derived from the idea of continuity as all-encompassing. If the world were created by an intelligence higher than and external to the great transformation, it would, by definition, fall short of a manifestation of holism. Similarly, if the world were merely a partial or distorted manifestation of the Platonic Idea, it would never achieve the perfection of the original reality. On the contrary, if genuine creativity is not the creation of something out of nothing, but a continuous transformation of that which is already there, the world as it now exists is the authentic manifestation of the cosmic process in its all-embracing fullness. Indeed, if the Idea for its own completion entails that it realize itself through the organismic process, the world is in every sense the concrete embodiment of the Idea. Traditional Chinese thinkers, of course, did not philosophize in those terms. They used different conceptual apparatuses to convey their thought. To them, the appropriate metaphor for understanding the universe was biology rather than physics. At issue was not the eternal, static structure but the dynamic process of growth and transformation. To say that the cosmos is a continuum and that all of its components are internally connected is also to say that it is an organismic unity, holistically integrated at each level of complexity.

It is important to note that continuity and wholeness in Chinese cosmological thinking must be accompanied in the third motif, dynamism, lest the idea of organismic unity imply a closed system. While Chinese thinkers are critically aware of the inertia in human culture which may eventually lead to stagnation, they perceive the "course of Heaven" (*t'ien-hsing*) as "vigorous" (*chien*) and instruct people to model themselves on the ceaseless vitality of the cosmic process.[18] What they envision in the spontaneously self-generating life process is not only inner connectedness and interdependence but also infinite potential for development. Many historians have remarked that the traditional Chinese notion of cyclic change, like the recurrence of the seasonal pattern, is incompatible with the modern Western idea of progress. To be sure, the traditional Chinese conception of history lacks the idea of unilinear development, such as Marxian modes of production depicting a form of historical inevitability. It is misleading, however, to describe Chinese history as chronicling a number of related events happening in a regularly repeated order.[19] Chinese historiography is not a reflection of a cyclic worldview. The Chinese worldview is neither cyclic nor spiral. It is transformational. The specific curve around which it transforms at a given period of time is indeterminate, however, for numerous human and nonhuman factors are involved in shaping its form and direction.

The organismic life process, which Mote contends is the genuine Chinese cosmogony, is an open system. As there is no temporal beginning to specify, no closure is ever contemplated. The cosmos is forever expanding; the great transformation is unceasing. The idea of unilinear development, in this perspective, is one-sided because it fails to account for the whole range of possibility in which progress constitutes but one of several dominant configurations. By analogy, neither cyclic nor spiral movements can fully depict the varieties of cosmic transformation. Since it is open rather than closed and dynamic rather than static, no geometric design can do justice to its complex morphology.

Earlier, I followed Mote in characterizing the Chinese vision of nature as the "all-enfolding harmony of impersonal cosmic function" and remarked that this particular vision was prompted by the Chinese commitment to the continuity of being. Having discussed the three basic motifs of Chinese cosmology—wholeness, dynamism, and continuity—I can elaborate on Mote's characterization by discussing some of its implications. The idea of all-enfolding harmony involves two interrelated meanings. It means that nature is all-inclusive, the spontaneously self-generating life process which excludes nothing. The Taoist idea of *tzu-jan* ("self-so"),[20] which is used in modern Chinese to translate the English word *nature*, aptly captures this spirit. To say that *self-so* is all-inclusive is to posit a nondiscriminatory and nonjudgmental position, to allow all modalities of being to display themselves as they are. This is possible, however, only if competitiveness, domination, and aggression are thoroughly transformed. Thus, all-enfolding harmony also means that internal resonance underlies the order of things in the universe. Despite conflict and tension, which are like waves of the ocean, the deep structure of nature is always tranquil. The great transformation of which nature is the concrete manifestation is the result of concord rather than discord and convergence rather than divergence.

This vision of nature may suggest an unbridled romantic assertion about peace and love, the opposite of what Charles Darwin realistically portrayed as the rules of nature. Chinese thinkers, however, did not take the all-enfolding harmony to be the original naïveté of the innocent. Nor did they take it to be an idealist utopia attainable in a distant future. They were acutely aware that the world we live in, far from being the "great unity" (*ta-t'ung*) recommended in the *Evolution of the Rites*,[21] is laden with disruptive forces, including humanly caused calamities and natural catastrophes. They also knew well that history is littered with internecine warfare, oppression, injustice, and numerous other forms of cruelty. It was not naïve romanticism that prompted them to assert that harmony is a defining characteristic of the organismic process. They believed that it is an accurate description of what the cosmos really is and how it actually works.

One advantage of rendering *ch'i* as "vital force," bearing in mind its original association with blood and breath, is its emphasis on the life process. To Chinese thinkers, nature is vital force in display. It is continuous, holistic, and dynamic. Yet, in an attempt to understand the blood and breath of nature's vitality, Chinese thinkers discovered that its enduring pattern is union rather than disunion, integration rather than disintegration, and synthesis rather than separation. The eternal flow of nature is characterized by the concord and convergence of numerous streams of vital force. It is in this sense that the organismic process is considered harmonious.

Chang Tsai, in his celebrated metaphysical treatise, "Correcting Youthful Ignorance," defines the cosmos as the "Great Harmony":

> The Great Harmony is called the Way (Tao, Moral Law). It embraces the nature which underlies all counter processes of floating and sinking, rising and falling, and motion and rest. It is the origin of the process of fusion and intermingling, of overcoming and being overcome, and of expansion and contraction. At the commencement, these processes are incipient, subtle, obscure, easy, and simple, but at the end they are extensive, great, strong and firm. It is *ch'ien* (Heaven) that begins with the knowledge of Change, and *k'un* (Earth) that models after simplicity. That which is dispersed, differentiated, and capable of assuming form becomes material force (*ch'i*), and that which is pure, penetrating, and not capable of assuming form becomes spirit. Unless the whole universe is in the process of fusion and intermingling like fleeting forces moving in all directions, it may not be called Great Harmony.[22]

In his vision, nature is the result of the fusion and intermingling of the vital forces that assume tangible forms. Mountains, rivers, rocks, trees, animals, and human beings are all modalities of energy-matter, symbolizing that the creative transformation of the Tao is forever present. Needham's idea of the Chinese cosmos as an ordered harmony of wills without an ordainer is, however, not entirely appropriate. Wills, no matter how broadly defined, do not feature prominently here. The idea that Heaven and Earth complete the transformation with no mind of their own clearly indicates that the harmonious state of the organismic process is not achieved by ordering divergent wills.[23] Harmony will be attained through spontaneity. In what sense is this what Mote calls "impersonal cosmic function"? Let us return to Chang Tsai's metaphysical treatise:

> [*Ch'i*] moves and flows in all directions and in all manners. Its two elements [yin and yang] unite and give rise to the concrete. Thus the multiplicity of things and human beings is produced. In their ceaseless successions the two elements of yin and yang constitute the great principles of the universe.[24]

This inner logic of *ch'i*, which is singularly responsible for the production of the myriad things, leads to a naturalistic description of the impersonal cosmic function. Wang Fu-chih, who developed Chang Tsai's metaphysics of *ch'i* with great persuasive power, continues with this line of thinking:

> The fact that the things of the world, whether rivers or mountains, plants or animals, those with or without intelligence, and those yielding blossoms or bearing fruits, provide beneficial support for all things is the result of the natural influence of the moving power of [*ch'i*]. It fills the universe. And as it completely provides for the flourish and transformation of all things, it is all the more spatially unrestricted. As it is not spatially restricted, it operates in time and proceeds with time. From morning to evening, from spring to summer, and from the present tracing back to the past, there is no time at which it does not operate, and there is no time at which it does not produce. Consequently, as one sprout bursts forth it becomes a tree with a thousand big branches, and as one egg evolves, it progressively becomes a fish capable of swallowing a ship. . . .[25]

The underlying message, however, is not the impersonality of the cosmic function, even though the idea of the moving power of *ch'i* indicates that no anthropomorphic god, animal, or object is really behind the great transformation. The naturalness of the cosmic function, despite human wishes and desires, is impersonal but not inhuman. It is impartial to all modalities of being and not merely anthropocentric. We humans, therefore, do not find the impersonal cosmic function cold, alien, or distant, although we know that it is, by and large, indifferent to and disinterested in our private thoughts and whims. Actually, we are an integral part of this function; we are ourselves the result of this moving power of *ch'i*. Like mountains and rivers, we are legitimate beings in this great transformation. The opening lines in Chang Tsai's *Western Inscription* are not only his article of faith but also his ontological view of the human.

> Heaven is my father and Earth is my mother, and even such a small creature as I find an intimate place in their midst.
>
> Therefore that which fills the universe I regard as my body and that which directs the universe I consider as my nature.
>
> All people are my brothers and sisters, and all things are my companions.[26]

The sense of intimacy with which Chang Tsai, as a single person, relates himself to the universe as a whole reflects his profound awareness of moral ecology. Humanity is the respectful son or daughter of the cosmic process. This humanistic vision is distinctively Confucian in character. It contrasts sharply with the Taoist idea of noninterference on the one hand and the Buddhist concept of detachment on the other. Yet the notion of humanity as forming one body with the universe has been so widely accepted by the Chinese, in popular as well as elite culture, that it can very well be characterized as a general Chinese worldview.

Forming one body with the universe can literally mean that since all modalities of being are made of *ch'i*, human life is part of a continuous flow of the blood and breath that constitutes the cosmic process. Human beings are thus organically connected with rocks, trees, and animals. Understandably, the interplay and interchange between discrete species feature prominently in Chinese literature, notably popular novels. The monkey in the *Journey to the West* came into being by metamorphosis from an agate;[27] the hero in the *Dream of the Red Chamber* or the *Story of the Stone*, Pao Yü, is said to have been transformed from a piece of precious jade;[28] and the heroine of the *Romance of the White Snake* has not completely succeeded in transfiguring herself into a beautiful woman.[29] These are well-known stories. They have evoked strong sympathetic responses from Chinese audiences young and old for centuries, not merely as fantasies but as great human drama. It is not at all difficult for the Chinese to imagine that an agate or a piece of jade can have enough potential spirituality to transform itself into a human being. Part of the pathos of the White Snake lies in her inability to fight against the spell cast by a ruthless monk so that she can retain her human form and be united with her lover. The fascinating element in this romance is that she manages to acquire the power to transfigure herself into a woman through several hundred years of self-cultivation.

Presumably, from the cosmic vantage point, nothing is totally fixed. It need not be forever the identity it now assumes. In the perceptive eye of the Chinese painter Tao Chi (1641–1717), mountains flow like rivers. The proper way of looking at mountains, for him, is to see them as ocean waves frozen in time.[30] By the same token, rocks are not static objects but dynamic processes with their particular configuration of the energy-matter. It may not be far-fetched to suggest that, with this vision of nature, we can actually talk about the different degrees of spirituality of rocks. Agate is certainly more spiritual than an ordinary hard stone and perhaps jade is more spiritual than agate. Jade is honored as the "finest essence of mountain and river" (*shan-ch'uan ching-ying*).[31] By analogy, we can also talk about degrees of spirituality in the entire chain of being. Rocks, trees, animals, humans, and gods represent different levels of spirituality based on the varying compositions of *ch'i*. However, despite the principle of differentiation, all modalities of being are organically connected. They are integral parts of a continuous process of cosmic transformation. It is in this metaphysical sense that "all things are my companions."

The uniqueness of being human cannot be explained in terms of a preconceived design by a creator. Human beings, like all other beings, are the results of the integration of the two basic vital forces of yin and yang. Chou Tun-i (1017–1073) says, "the interaction of these two *ch'i* engenders and transforms the myriad things. The myriad things produce and reproduce, resulting in an unending transformation."[32] In a strict sense, then, human beings are not the rulers of creation; if they intend to become guardians of the universe, they must earn this distinction through self-cultivation. There is no preordained reason for them to think otherwise. Nevertheless, the human being—in the Chinese sense of *jen*, which is gender neutral—is unique. Chou Tun-i offers the following explanation:

> It is human beings alone who receive [the Five Agents] in their highest excellence, and therefore they are most intelligent. Their physical form appears, and their spirit develops consciousness. The five moral principles of their nature (humanity or *jen*, righteousness, propriety, wisdom, and faithfulness) are aroused by, and react to, the external world and engage in activity; good and evil are distinguished; and human affairs take place.[33]

The theory of the Five Agents or the Five Phases (*wu-hsing*) need not concern us here. Since Chou makes it clear that "by the transformation of yang and its union with yin, the Five Agents of Water, Fire, Wood, Metal, and Earth arise" and that since "the Five Agents constitute one system of yin and yang,"[34] they can be conceived as specific forms of *ch'i*.

That humankind receives *ch'i* in its highest excellence is not only manifested in intelligence but also in sensitivity. The idea that humans are the most sentient beings in the universe features prominently in Chinese thought. A vivid description of human sensitivity is found in the "recorded sayings" (*yü-lu*) of Ch'eng Hao (1032–1085):

> A book on medicine describes paralysis of the four limbs as absence of [humanity (*pu-jen*)]. This is an excellent description. The person of [humanity] regards Heaven and Earth and all things as one body. To him there is nothing that is not himself. Since he has recognized all things as himself, can there be any limit to his humanity? If things are not part of the self, naturally they have nothing to do with it. As in the case of paralysis of the four limbs, the vital force [*ch'i*] no longer penetrates them, and therefore they are no longer parts of the self.[35]

This idea of forming one body with the universe is predicated
on the assumption that since all modalities of being are made of
ch'i, all things cosmologically share the same consanguinity with
us and are thus our companions. This vision enabled an original
thinker of the Ming dynasty, Wang Ken (1483–1540), to remark that
if we came into being through transformation (*hua-sheng*), then
heaven and earth are our father and mother to us; if we came into
being through reproduction (*hsing-sheng*), then our father and
mother are Heaven and Earth to us.[36] The image of the human that
emerges here, far from being the lord of creation, is the filial son
and daughter of the universe. Filial piety connotes a profound
feeling, an all-pervasive care for the world around us.

This literal meaning of forming one body with the universe must
be augmented by a metaphorical reading of the same text. It is true
that the body clearly conveys the sense of *ch'i* as the blood and
breath of the vital force that underlies all beings. The uniqueness
of being human, however, is not simply that we are made of the
same psychophysiological stuff that rocks, trees, and animals are
also made of. It is our consciousness of being human that enables
and impels us to probe the transcendental anchorage of our nature.
Surely the motif of the continuity of being prevents us from positing
a creator totally external to the cosmic organismic process, but what
is the relationship between human nature and Heaven which serves
as the source of all things? Indeed, how are we to understand the
ontological assertion in the first chapter of the *Doctrine of the Mean*
that our nature is decreed by Heaven?[37] Is the Mandate of Heaven
a one-time operation or a continuous presence? Wang Fu-chih's
general response to these questions is suggestive.

> By nature is meant the principle of growth. As one daily grows,
> one daily achieves completion. Thus by the Mandate of Heaven is
> not meant that Heaven gives the decree (*ming*, mandate) only at the
> moment of one's birth. . . . In the production of things by Heaven,
> the process of transformation never ceases.[38]

In the metaphorical sense, then, forming one body with the
universe requires continuous effort to grow and to refine oneself.
We can embody the whole universe in our sensitivity because we
have enlarged and deepened our feeling and care to the fullest
extent. However, there is no guarantee at the symbolic or at the

experiential level that the universe is automatically embodied in us. Unless we see to it that the Mandate of Heaven is fully realized in our nature, we may not live up to the expectation that "all things are complete in us."[39] Wang Fu-chih's refusal to follow a purely naturalistic line of thinking on this is evident in the following observation: "The [profound person] acts naturally as if nothing happens, but. . .he acts so as to make the best choices and remain firm in holding to the Mean."[40] To act naturally without letting things take their own course means, in Neo-Confucian terminology, to follow the "heavenly principle" (*t'ien-li*) without being overcome by "selfish desires" (*ssu-yü*).[41] Selfish desires are forms of self-centeredness that belittle the authentic human capacity to take part in the transformative process of Heaven and Earth. In commenting on the *Book of Changes*, Ch'eng Hao observes:

> The most impressive aspect of things is their spirit of life. This is what is meant by origination being the chief quality of goodness. . . . Humans and Heaven and Earth are one thing. Why should man purposely belittle himself?[42]

Forming a trinity with Heaven and Earth, which is tantamount to forming one body with the myriad things, enjoins us from applying the subject-object dichotomy to nature. To see nature as an external object out there is to create an artificial barrier which obstructs our true vision and undermines our human capacity to experience nature from within. The internal resonance of the vital forces is such that the mind, as the most refined and subtle *ch'i* of the human body, is constantly in sympathetic accord with the myriad things in nature. The function of "affect and response" (*kan-ying*) characterizes nature as a great harmony and so informs the mind.[43] The mind forms a union with nature by extending itself metonymically. Its aesthetic appreciation of nature is neither an appropriation of the object by the subject nor an imposition of the subject on the object, but the merging of the self into an expanded reality through transformation and participation. This creative process, in Roman Jakobson's terminology, is "contiguous," because rupture between us and nature never occurs.[44]

Chuang Tzu recommends that we listen with our minds rather than with our ears; with *ch'i* rather than with our minds.[45] If listening with our minds involves consciousness unaffected by sensory perceptions, what does listening to *ch'i* entail? Could it mean that we are so much a part of the internal resonance of the vital forces themselves that we can listen to the sound of nature or, in Chuang Tzu's expression, the "music of Heaven" (*t'ien-lai*)[46] as our inner voice? Or could it mean that the all-embracing *ch'i* enables the total transposition of humankind and nature? As a result, the aesthetic delight that one experiences is no longer the private sensation of the individual but the "harmonious blending of inner feelings and outer scenes,"[47] as the traditional Chinese artist would have it. It seems that in either case we do not detach ourselves from nature and study it in a disinterested manner. What we do is to suspend not only our sensory perceptions but also our conceptual apparatus so that we can embody nature in our sensitivity and allow nature to embrace us in its affinity.

I must caution, however, that the aesthetic experience of mutuality and immediacy with nature is often the result of strenuous and continual effort at self-cultivation. Despite our superior intelligence, we do not have privileged access to the great harmony. As social and cultural beings, we can never get outside ourselves to study nature from neutral ground. The process of returning to nature involves unlearning and forgetting as well as remembering. The precondition for us to participate in the internal resonance of the vital forces in nature is our own inner transformation. Unless we can first harmonize our own feelings and thoughts, we are not prepared for nature, let alone for an "interflow with the spirit of Heaven and Earth."[48] It is true that we are consanguineous with nature. But as humans, we must make ourselves worthy of such a relationship.

Notes

1. Frederick W. Mote, *Intellectual Foundations of China* (New York: Alfred A. Knopf, 1971), 17–18.

2. Ibid., 19.

3. For a thought-provoking discussion on this issue, see N. J. Girardot, *Myth and Meaning in Early Taoism* (Berkeley: University of California Press, 1983), 275–310.

4. For a suggestive methodological essay, see William G. Boltz, "Kung Kung and the Flood: Reverse Euphemerism in the *Yao Tien*," *T'oung Pao* 67 (1981):141–53. Professor Boltz's effort to reconstruct the Kung Kung myth indicates the possibility of an indigenous creation myth.

5. Tu Wei-ming, "Shih-t'an Chung-kuo che-hsüeh chung te san-ko chi-tiao" (A preliminary discussion on the three basic motifs in Chinese philosophy), *Chung-kuo che-hsüeh shih yen-chiu* (Studies on the history of Chinese philosophy) (Peking: Society for the Study of the History of Chinese Philosophy) 2 (March 1981):19–21.

6. Mote, *Intellectual Foundations of China*, 20.

7. Ibid.

8. See Jung's foreword to the *I ching (Book of Changes)*, translated into English by Cary F. Baynes from the German translation of Richard Wilhelm, Bollingen Series, 19 (Princeton: Princeton University Press, 1967), xxiv.

9. Needham's full statement reads as follows: "It was an ordered harmony of wills without an ordainer; it was like the spontaneous yet ordered, in the sense of patterned, movements of dancers in a country dance of figures, none of whom are bound by law to do what they do, nor yet pushed by others coming behind, but cooperate in a voluntary harmony of wills." See Joseph Needham and Wang Ling, *Science and Civilisation in China*, 2 (Cambridge: Cambridge University Press, 1969), 287.

10. Actually, the dichotomy of spirit and matter does not feature prominently in Chinese thought; see Tu, "Shih-t'an Chung-kuo che-hsüeh," 21–22.

11. *A Source Book in Chinese Philosophy*, trans. and comp. Wing-tsit Chan (Princeton: Princeton University Press, 1963), 784.

12. Ibid.

13. For a notable exception to this general interpretive situation in the People's Republic of China, see Chang Tai-nien, *Chung kuo che hsüeh fa wei* (Exploring some of the delicate issues in Chinese philosophy) (T'ai-yuan, Shansi: People's Publishing Co., 1981), 11–38, 275–306.

14. For a general discussion on this vital issue from a medical viewpoint, see Manfred Porkert, *The Theoretical Foundations of Chinese Medicine: Systems of Correspondence* (Cambridge, Mass.: MIT Press, 1974).

15. Tu, "Shih-t'an Chung-kuo che-hsüeh," 19–24.

16. A paradigmatic discussion on this is to be found in the *Commentaries on the Book of Changes*. See Chan, *Source Book in Chinese Philosophy*, 264.

17. See Chang Tsai's "Correcting Youthful Ignorance," in Chan, *Source Book in Chinese Philosophy*, 501–14.

18. For this reference in the *Chou i*, see *A Concordance to Yi Ching*, Harvard-Yenching Institute Sinological Index Series, Supplement no. 10 (reprint; Tapei: Chinese Materials and Research Aids Service Center, Inc., 1966), 1/1.

19. The idea of the "dynastic cycle" may give one the impression that Chinese history is nondevelopmental. See Edwin O. Reischauer and John K. Fairbank, *East Asia: The Great Tradition* (Boston: Houghton Mifflin Co., 1960), 114–18.

20. *Chuang tzu*, chap. 7. See the Harvard-Yenching Index on the *Chuang tzu*, 20/7/11.

21. See *Sources of Chinese Tradition*, comp. Wm. Theodore de Bary, Wing-tsit Chan, and Burton Watson (New York: Columbia University Press, 1960), 191–92.

22. Chan, *Source Book in Chinese Philosophy*, 500–501.

23. Ibid., 262–66. This idea underlies the philosophy of change.

24. Ibid., 505, § 14. In this translation, *ch'i* is rendered "material force." The words *yin* and *yang* in brackets are my additions.

25. Ibid., 698–99.

26. Ibid., 497.

27. Wu Ch'eng-en, *Hsi-yu chi*, trans. and ed. Anthony C. Yü as *Journey to the West*, 4 vols. (Chicago: University of Chicago Press, 1977–83), 1:67–78.

28. Ts'ao Hsüeh-ch'in (Cao Xuequin), *Hung-lou meng* (Dream of the Red Chamber), trans. David Hawkes as *The Story of the Stone*, 5 vols. (Harmondsworth, England: Penguin Books, 1973–86), 1:47–49.

29. For two useful discussions on the story, see Fu Hsi-hua, *Pai-she-chuan chi* (An anthology of the White Snake story) (Shanghai: Shanghai Publishing Co., 1955), and P'an Chiang-tung, *Pai-she ku-shih yen-chiu* (A study of the White Snake story) (Tapei: Students' Publishers, 1981).

30. P. Ryckmans, "Les propos sur la peinture de Shi Tao traduction et commentaire," *Arts Asiatique* 14 (1966):123–24.

31. Teng Shu-p'in, "Shang-ch'uan ching-ying-yü te i-shu" (The finest essence of mountain and river—the art of jade), in *Chung-kuo wen-hua hsin-lun* (New views on Chinese culture) (Taipei: Lien-ching, 1983), section on arts, 253–304.

32. Chan, *Source Book in Chinese Philosophy*, 463. Again, this translation renders *ch'i* as "material force."

33. Ibid.

34. Ibid.

35. Ibid., 530, § 11.

36. Wang Ken, "Yü Nan-tu chu-yu" (Letter to friends of Nan-tu), in *Wang Hsin-chai hsien-sheng ch'üan-chi* (The complete works of Wang Ken) (1507 edition, Harvard-Yenching Library), 4.16b.

37. Chan, *Source Book in Chinese Philosophy*, 98.

38. Ibid., 699.

39. *Mencius*, 7A.4.

40. Chan, *Source Book in Chinese Philosophy*, 699–700.

41. For example, in Chu Hsi's discussion of moral cultivation, the Heavenly Principle is clearly contrasted with selfish desires. See Chan, *Source Book in Chinese Philosophy*, 605–6.

42. Ibid., 539.

43. For a suggestive essay on this, see R. G. H. Siu, *Ch'i: A Neo-Taoist Approach to Life* (Cambridge, Mass.: MIT Press, 1974).

44. Roman Jakobson, "Two Aspects of Language and Two Types of Aphasic Disturbances," in Roman Jakobson and Morris Halle, *Fundamentals of Language* ('s-Gravenhage: Mouton, 1956), 55–82. I am grateful to Professor Yu-kung Kao for this reference.

45. *Chuang tzu*, chap. 4. The precise quotation can be found in *Chuang tzu ying-te* (Peking: Harvard-Yenching Institute, 1947), 9/4/27.

46. *Chuang tzu*, chap. 2, *Chuang tzu ying-te*, 3/2/8.

47. For a systematic discussion of this, see Yu-kung Kao and Kang-i Sun Chang, "Chinese 'Lyric Criticism' in the Six Dynasties," American Council of Learned Societies Conference on Theories of the Arts in China (June 1979), published as *Theories of the Arts in China*, ed. Susan Bush and Christian Murck (Princeton: Princeton University Press, 1983).

48. See *Mencius*, 7A.13.

Response and Responsibility:
Chou Tun-i and Confucian Resources
for Environmental Ethics

Joseph A. Adler

Introduction

Issues in environmental ethics can be grouped broadly under two headings: questions of human nature and destiny and questions of moral responsibility. Under the first, for example, are such questions as: What is the place of human beings in the natural order? What is the relationship of human nature to the nature of animals, plants, and nonliving matter? Is human nature (or destiny) fulfilled in shaping, developing, perfecting the nonhuman natural world? Or is it fulfilled by adapting and conforming to nature? Should we—and if so, how can we—strike a balance between the anthropocentric and ecocentric (or biocentric) perspectives?

Questions of moral responsibility include: To what extent (if any) are human beings morally responsible for the fate of the earth? For the spotted owl? The snail darter? Is a concern with the natural environment merely prudential, as a way of protecting human health and life? This would imply that ecological concern is a matter of our responsiblity to human interests but not to the environment per se. If, on the other hand, we accept some level of responsibility to the natural world, how then do we balance it with our responsibility to the human, social world?

In this paper I shall argue that the Neo-Confucian concept of "moral responsiveness" (ying)[1] plays a role functionally equivalent to that of moral responsibility to the natural world, and that this concept is particularly well suited to serve as a basis for an environmental ethic—despite the fact that environmental concerns never figured prominently enough in traditional Confucian agendas for this to be developed. Moreover, by focusing on the thought of Chou Tun-i (1017–1073),[2] we shall see how the concept of moral responsiveness is linked to the concept of authenticity (*ch'eng*), the moral-metaphysical basis of sagehood. This complex of ideas, therefore, addresses both sets of questions in environmental ethics in an integrated, systematic fashion. It also establishes a basis for mediation of the tension between anthropocentric and ecocentric perspectives on environmental issues.

Response and Responsibility

The concept of moral responsibility in Western theology and philosophy has generally been expressed in terms of questions of *justice* and *free will*.[3] The "response" implied by the term "responsibility" is the proper or just *reward or punishment* for voluntary actions. To act responsibly is to act in such a way as to deserve reward or approval (whether or not an actual reward or response is likely to occur in the given situation). The root metaphor here is that of *judgment*, whether legal, soteriological, or moral; that is, the judgment of either a representative of a sovereign state (king or judge) meting out reward or punishment, or a personal deity deciding one's fate, or simply a moral observer approving or disapproving of the behavior in question.

While in Chinese philosophy the metaphor of judgment by a semipersonalistic Heaven is sometimes invoked, in general the functional equivalent of the concept of moral responsibility occurs in a different discursive context.[4] In Classical Confucianism, the most pertinent term in this connection is *reciprocity* (*shu*). Reciprocity is defined against a background of social or kinship relations between individuals as members of a family or a wider social group modeled on the family. The root metaphor here is *kinship*, not judgment.[5] An act that embodies the virtue of reciprocity is one that is correct (*cheng*) in terms of the established norms of ritual propriety (*li*) and appropriate (*i*) to the specific social relationship in question.

The functional equivalent of "moral responsibility" in this context is therefore twofold. First, it is the act's "correspondence" with the normative patterns of social behavior.[6] Second, it is the appropriateness of the act in "response" (so to speak) to the given social circumstances, defined in terms of the personal relationships obtaining between the subjects involved.

Reciprocity, as a functional equivalent of moral responsibility, thus presupposes a relationship of conscious moral subjects. Although these subjects can be either human or spiritual (ancestors and deities also have relations of mutual reciprocity with living people), reciprocity in Classical Confucianism does not apply directly to human relations with the nonhuman natural world.

From the beginning of the Neo-Confucian revival in the Sung Dynasty (960–1279), the term *ying* ("response") entered the Confucian ethical lexicon in such a way as to extend the concept of reciprocity to the natural world. The term was employed by such Northern Sung Confucians as Chou Tun-i and Ch'eng Hao (1032–1085) to refer to a crucial aspect of sagehood. The sage is the "authentic" (*ch'eng*) human being whose thoughts, intentions, desires, and behavior naturally and spontaneously respond in an active sense to the natural/moral order (*t'ien-li/tao-li*) in which he is embedded.[7] Thus, the sage responds morally, not only to other moral subjects, but also to the myriad things of Heaven and Earth. What the *Chung yung* (Centrality and Commonality) had called "assist[ing] [*ts'an*] in the transforming and nourishing process of Heaven and Earth"[8] was reformulated by the Ch'eng-Chu Neo-Confucians in terms of the metaphysics of *li* (order, principle) and an epistemology in which mind was considered to be a natural organ (or substance) that followed the same principles as nonhuman things.

"Moral responsiveness," under this model, is not conceived as a just reward or punishment meted out by a king or judge to a freely acting subject; rather, it is the subject's own proper response to his or her environment. What is "proper" or "right" is determined, not by an abstract or divinely decreed standard of justice, but rather by the actual conditions defining the subject's relationship with the object; by the interrelationship and interdependence of the moral subject with his or her environment. In Neo-Confucian terms, then, moral responsiveness, rather than moral responsibility, provides a framework for the discussion of environmental ethics.

Both reciprocity and moral responsiveness imply a network of concrete relations as the context in which actions can be morally evaluated. Kinship relations are, of course, the fundamental model of all human relations in Confucian discourse. The extension of kinship to the nonhuman natural world is seen most eloquently in Chang Tsai's (1020–1077) *Western Inscription*, which begins:

> Heaven is my father and Earth is my mother, and even such a small creature as I find an intimate place in their midst.
>
> Therefore that which fills the universe I regard as my body and that which directs the universe I consider as my nature.
>
> All people are my brothers and sisters, and all things are my companions.[9]

It is instructive to compare and contrast this notion of kinship with the etymology of the word "ecology," which was coined by Ernst Haeckel in 1866[10] from the Greek roots *oikos*, "house," and *logia*, "discoursing." "Ecology" thus means the science of the household.[11] The closely related word "economy" comes from *oikos*, "house," and *nemein*, "to manage"; an *oikonomos* was a person who managed a household, that is, a steward.[12] The notion of stewardship is commonly used by Jewish and Christian theologians to provide a foundation for a biblically based environmental ethic. In the stewardship model, it should be noted, the "owner" of the house is God; human beings are merely caretakers.

Given the connection of the word "ecology" with the concept of the household, Chang Tsai's use of the family as the model for an authentic relationship with the natural world is a perfectly appropriate starting point for an environmental ethic. In fact, it suggests the potential for a deeper relationship than that implied by the Jewish and Christian concept of "stewardship," for a steward is one who is appointed to care for the household but is not a family member.

However, the kinship model begs the question: What precisely is the common nature shared by the human being and the natural object? Members of a family share a common genotypic and phenotypic inheritance; what do human beings and rocks share?

On one level it is *ch'i* (vital energy or psycho-physical stuff) that is the philosophical basis for human beings' kinship with the natural world, as expressed in Chang Tsai's *Western Inscription* and in Ch'eng Hao's statement that "The person of *jen* [humanity] forms one body with all things without any differentiation."[13] Let us call this the *organic* level of commonality.[14] As Tu Weiming puts it:

> Forming one body with the universe can literally mean that since all modalities of being are made of *ch'i*, human life is part of a continuous flow of the blood and breath that constitutes the cosmic process. Human beings are thus organically connected with rocks, trees, and animals.[15]

Parallel to this organic commonality there is also, in Neo-Confucian thought, the *metaphysical* continuity described in terms of *li*, "order/principle."[16] This concept rose to prominence in the school of the Ch'eng brothers during the Northern Sung (960–1126) and was later codified by Chu Hsi (1130–1200), through whose influence this school (referred to here as the Ch'eng-Chu school) became the dominant school of Confucian thought.[17]

Linking the metaphysical and organic levels of Neo-Confucian discourse is the concept of "authenticity" (*ch'eng*), a term that is most prominent in the Classical Confucian text *Chung yung* (Centrality and Commonality)[18] and in Chou Tun-i's *T'ung shu* (Penetrating the *Book of Changes*).[19] In Chu Hsi's formulation, *ch'eng* means "actualized order" (*shih-li*),[20] that is, the metaphysical order instantiated in a concrete thing or activity; hence its mediating role between the metaphysical and organic levels of discourse. It is closely related in the *T'ung shu* to the terms *ying*, "responsive," and *t'ung*, "penetrating, circulating, comprehensive." The dynamism of these concepts reflects both the organic process implied by the term *ch'i* and the developmental (yet atemporal) order implied by *li*. By pursuing this functional, dynamic sense of commonality, or "kin ship," in Neo-Confucian discourse we can show that the concept of responsiveness functions, not only as the equivalent of moral responsibility, but also as an authentic expression of the meta physical ground of human nature. Moral responsiveness in Neo-Confucian thought therefore constitutes, at least in part, both the goal and the basis of a proper and healthy relationship with the natural world.

Responsiveness (*Ying*) in Early Chinese Thought

Like such notions as harmony, unity, and order, the concepts of reciprocity and responsiveness, broadly conceived, have been characteristic of Chinese thought since the beginning of the written record.
For example, the relationship between the Shang king and his
ancestors, as evidenced in the oracle bone inscriptions, can clearly
be understood as the same type of reciprocity or interdependence
that still characterizes the relationship between the living and the
dead (as well as deities) in Chinese popular religion. Likewise, the
early Confucian concept of *t'ien-ming*, or Mandate of Heaven, can
be seen as the responsiveness of Heaven to the moral character of
the ruling family. Conversely, the term "responding to Heaven"
(*ying-t'ien*) was used to mean being attentive to Heaven's decree.[21]
Both reciprocity (in the case of relations between conscious
subjects) and responsiveness (as a more general concept operative
in the natural as well as the social realms) can be conceived as
corollaries of the holistic, organic tendencies in traditional Chinese
thought, according to which particulars are defined in terms of their
functional relationships with larger wholes.[22]

Philosophical use of the term *ying* probably goes back to the Yin-
Yang school of the late Warring States period, whose chief exponent
was Tsou Yen (third century B.C.E.), since the term emerges as an
important concept in texts influenced by yin-yang thought. It is
found, for example, in the *Lü-shih ch'un-ch'iu* (Mr. Lü's *Spring and
Autumn Annals*) and in Tung Chung-shu's *Ch'un-ch'iu fan-lu*
(Luxuriant gems of the *Spring and Autumn Annals*). In chapter 57
of the latter text we read that "things of the same kind arise in
response to each other" (*lei chih hsiang-ying erh ch'i yeh*).[23] The
"kinds" (*lei*) referred to here are chiefly the categories of yin and
yang and the Five Phases (*wu-hsing*). The nearly contemporaneous
Huai-nan tzu (139 B.C.E.), one of the central texts of Huang-Lao
Taoism, says in a similar vein, "The mutual response [*hsiang-ying*]
of things belonging to the same category [*lei*] is darkly mysterious
and extremely subtle [*shen-wei*]."[24]

Acccording to Charles Le Blanc, the concept of "resonance," or
"stimulus-response" (*kan-ying*), is the central conception of the
Huai-nan tzu, where it is used to explain the classical Taoist concept
of "non-action" (*wu-wei*) and is a hallmark of the "True Man" (*chen-*

jen), or perfect ruler.[25] This True Man, or sage, is "merged with Grand Harmony [*t'ai-ho*] and holds fast to the Responses of the Natural [*tzu-jan chih ying*]";[26] he therefore "is like a mirror, neither sending [things] away nor welcoming [things], responding [*ying*] but not storing."[27] People can become sages

> by concentrating their essences (*ching*) and disciplining their thoughts, discarding all concerns and gathering together their spirits (*shen*). . . .[28]

And,

> when the Sage rules, he treasures *Tao* and does not speak; yet his kindness [*tse*] reaches the Ten Thousand People. [But] when ruler and minister distrust each other in their heart, concave and convex halos appear in the sky [on each side of the sun]. These are indeed evidences of the mutual influence [*hsiang-ying*] of the marvellous *ch'i* (*shen-ch'i*)[29]. . .because *Yin* and *Yang* share a common *ch'i* and move [*tung*] each other.[30]

Under the rule of a sage,

> the Son of Heaven reigns supreme, sustaining [all] with *Tao* and *Te*, assisting [all] with human-heartedness (*jen*) and equity [*i*].[31]

This fusion of cosmology, self-cultivation, and ethics, although distinctly Taoist (the Confucian concepts *jen* and *i* are subsumed under Taoist ones[32]), foreshadows in significant ways certain features of Neo-Confucian thought, especially that of Chou Tun-i, who was strongly influenced by Taoism. (Chou, of course, subsumed his Taoist concepts under a Confucian framework.) Le Blanc's account of the epistemological basis of the Taoist sage's capacity to respond to all things is also worth quoting here, for it bears on the topic of environmental ethics:

> [T]he human mind [according to the *Huai-nan tzu*], being itself in continuity with nature, has the capacity 'to know', 'to become' and 'to reproduce' the cosmic process, not through divinely granted revelation, reflection or contemplation, but on the affective and participative level of being. In this sense true knowledge (*chen-chih*) is not a mirror-image—neither a representation of 'what's out there'

nor a focal or peripheral vision of the intellect—but rather a direct and immediate *affectus* of things themselves, an affinitive correspondence and union that precedes any reflected awareness of it. It is this ontological relation of an affinitive rather than causal type that actualizes in the discrete world of space, time, species and individuals the primal unity of the cosmos.[33]

The organic basis of the human mind's "continuity with nature," in both Huang-Lao Taoism and Neo-Confucianism, is the immanence of *ch'i*. Neo-Confucianism adds to this the metaphysical commonality of *li*. The Confucian sage realizes or instantiates the perfection of the natural/moral order in his or her thought and action. Thus, in Chou Tun-i's thought we shall find the same kind of "affinitive correspondence" of the sage and the natural world as we see in the *Huai-nan tzu*, but worked out in Confucian terms (with a substantial Taoist flavor).

Chou Tun-i and the Conceptual Framework of Sagehood[34]

The word "responsive" occurs only once in the *T'ung shu* and not at all in the *T'ai-chi t'u shuo* (Explanation of the Supreme Polarity Diagram). But in the *T'ung shu* it is situated in a conceptual framework that enables us to say more about it than we could by reading only the passage in which it occurs. That passage is chapter 4, which reads (in its entirety):

4.   The Sage (*sheng*)[35]

(a)   That which is "silent and inactive" (*chi-jan pu-tung*)[36] is authentic (*ch'eng*). That which is "penetrating when stimulated" (*kan erh sui t'ung*)[37] is spiritual (*shen*). That which is active but not yet formed, between existence and nonexistence, is incipient (*chi*).

(b)   Authenticity is essential (*ching*), and therefore clear. Spirit is responsive (*ying*), and therefore mysterious. Incipience is subtle (*wei*), and therefore obscure.

(c)   One who is authentic, spiritual, and incipient is called a sage.[38]

Here we have a definition of sagehood in terms taken from three of Chou Tun-i's most important sources. The concept of "authenticity" (*ch'eng*) is most prominently discussed in the *Chung yung* (Centrality and Commonality). The concepts of activity and stillness (*tung-ching*), spirit (*shen*), penetration (*t'ung*), and incipience (*chi*) together form an important theoretical unit in the "Appended Remarks" (*Hsi tz'u*) wing of the *I ching*.[39] And the concept of "responsiveness" (*ying*), as we have seen above, is associated with "spirit," "essence" (*ching*), and the "subtle" (*wei*) in the Taoist *Huai-nan tzu*.[40] Overall, there are eight key terms in the chapter:

1. Authenticity (*ch'eng*)
2. Spirit (*shen*)
3. Incipience (*chi*)
4. Activity-stillness (*tung-ching*)[41]
5. Penetrating (*t'ung*)
6. Responsive (*ying*)
7. Essential (*ching*)
8. Subtle (*wei*)

By examining other chapters of the *T'ung shu* that contain these terms (mainly chapters 1, 2, 3, 9, 16, and 20), we can construct a conceptual framework in which the significance of responsiveness can be elucidated.

"Authenticity" is the central topic of the first four chapters of the *T'ung shu*. The major textual source of this term is the *Chung yung*, which, in chapter 22, contains the classic Confucian statement of a moral relationship with the natural world:

> Only those who are absolutely authentic [*ch'eng*] can fully develop their nature. If they can fully develop their nature, they can then fully develop the nature of others. If they can fully develop the nature of others, they can then fully develop the nature of things. If they can fully develop the nature of things, they can then assist in the transforming and nourishing process of Heaven and Earth. If they can assist in the transforming and nourishing process of Heaven and Earth, they can thus form a trinity with Heaven and Earth.[42]

Ch'eng, in Tu Weiming's words, is "the most genuine manifestation of human virtue" and "the truth and reality of human's
heavenly endowed nature."[43] This alludes to the first two lines of
the *Chung yung*, which make the claim that human nature is
endowed by Heaven and that its natural course of development is
the Way (*tao*), which is to say that it is good.[44] The connection with
Heaven—what Tu calls the "transcendent anchorage" of Confucian
morality[45]—suggests "a strong belief in the organismic unity of human and nature,"[46] which of course is quite explicit in the last two
lines of *Chung yung*, 22 (quoted above). In these lines we have what
Tu calls a "covenant" with Heaven (in which the concept of "moral
duty" is not entirely out of place),[47] and an attitude of "reverence"
(*ching*) toward Heaven that is the counterpart of "filial piety" (*hsiao*)
in the social realm. These two are, in this context, "ecological
principles humanly designed but heavenly inspired for the primary
purpose of bringing peace and harmony to the universe."[48] Note that
reverence and filial piety are forms of reciprocity; they are dyadic
relationships in which mutual obligations are understood. But in
Chung yung, 22, the implied dyadic relationships (self and others,
self and things) are subsumed under the concept of *ch'eng*, which
does not easily lend itself to a dyadic, personalistic model. *Ch'eng*,
understood as "authenticity," is in fact the link between the
personalistic concept of reciprocity and the naturalistic concept of
moral responsiveness.

   Chu Hsi, in his commentary on the *T'ung shu*, defines *ch'eng*
as "being perfectly actualized (*chih-shih*),"[49] or "actualized
principle/order" (*shih-li*).[50] *Ch'eng* in this sense is the actualization
in moral activity (or function, *yung*) of the true nature (*hsing*), or
fundamental substance (*pen-t'i*), of a thing. Only human beings can
fail to be *ch'eng*—a rock is a rock, but not every human is humane
(*jen*).[51] As Tu puts it in reference to human beings, "*Ch'eng* as a
state of being signifies the ultimate reality of human nature and, as
a process of becoming, the necessary way of actualizing that reality
in concrete, ordinary human affairs."[52] It is manifested in a human
being when one is truly being or actively manifesting what one truly
is by nature; when one is a morally actualized agent.[53]

   Chapter 1 of the *T'ung shu* primarily concerns the metaphysical
foundation or substance of authenticity, framed in terms of the "Way

of Ch'ien" (hexagram 1 of the *I ching*), creativity and transformation. It begins:

> Being authentic is the foundation of the Sage. "Great indeed is the
> originating [power] (*yüan*) of Ch'ien! The myriad things rely on it
> for their beginnings."[54] It is the source of being authentic. "The Way
> of Ch'ien is transformation, each [thing] receiving its correct nature
> and endowment."[55] In this way authenticity is established.

Here the substance or source of authenticity is identified with the
order or principle underlying the ceaseless transformation of the
cosmic process of "life and growth" (*sheng-sheng*).[56] From the
perspective of *ch'eng* as "actualized order," this underscores the
notion that the ultimate cosmic order (*t'ien-li*), while atemporal
itself, is the pattern of change, mutual response, and creativity.

Chapters 2, 3, 4, and 9 contain the core of the conceptual matrix
of responsiveness. They are reproduced below (with chapter 4
repeated for the convenience of the reader). Following the texts is
a table of the key terms of these chapters, intended as a helpful
interpretive device. (Chinese words in the texts indicate terms
included in the table.) Chapters 16 and 20 will be included in the
discussion following the table.

2.   Being Authentic (*ch'eng*) (B)[57]

(a)   Sagehood (*sheng*) is nothing more than being authentic
(*ch'eng*).

(b)   Being authentic is the foundation (*pen*) of the Five Constant
[Virtues] (*wu-ch'ang*) and the source of the Hundred Practices
(*pai-hsing*).

(c)   It is imperceptible when still (*ching-wu*) and perceptible when
active (*tung-yu*),[58] perfectly correct and clearly pervading.

(d–h)   When the Five Constants and Hundred Practices are not
authentic, they are wrong; blocked by depravity and confusion.
Therefore one who is authentic has no [need for] undertakings.
It is perfectly easy, yet difficult to practice; when one is determined and precise, there is no difficulty with it. Therefore
[Confucius said], "If in one day one could subdue the self and
return to propriety, then all under Heaven would recover their
humanity."[59]

3.   Authenticity, Incipience, and Virtue (*ch'eng chi te*)

(a)   In being authentic there is no [intentional] acting (*ch'eng wu-wei*).

(b)   In incipience there is good and evil (*chi shan-wu*).

(c–f)   As for the [Five Constant] Virtues (*te*), loving is called humanity, being right is called appropriateness, being principled is called propriety, being penetrating is called wisdom, and preserving is called faithfulness. One who is by nature like this, at ease like this, is called a sage. One who recovers it and holds onto it is called a worthy. One whose subtle signs of expression are imperceptible, and whose fullness is inexhaustible, is called spiritual.

4.   The Sage (*sheng*)

(a)   That which is "silent and inactive" (*chi-jan pu-tung*) is authentic (*ch'eng*). That which is "penetrating when stimulated" (*kan erh sui t'ung*) is spiritual (*shen*). That which is active but not yet formed, between existence and nonexistence, is incipient (*chi*).

(b)   Authenticity is essential (*ching*), and therefore clear. Spirit is responsive (*ying*), and therefore mysterious. Incipience is subtle (*wei*), and therefore obscure.

(c)   One who is authentic, spiritual, and incipient is called a sage.

9.   Thinking (*ssu*)

(a)   The *Hung-fan* [Great Plan] says: "[The virtue of] thinking is called perspicacity. . . . Perspicacity makes one a sage."[60] To be without thinking (*wu-ssu*) is the foundation (*pen*). When thinking is penetrating (*t'ung*), this is its function (*yung*). When there is incipient activity (*chi-tung*) on the one hand and authentic activity (*ch'eng-tung*) on the other, with no thinking and yet penetrating everything (*wu-ssu erh wu pu-t'ung*),[61] one is a sage.

(b–e)   If one does not think, then one cannot penetrate subtleties. If one is not perspicacious, then one cannot penetrate everything. Thus, [the ability] to penetrate everything arises from penetrating subtleties, and [the ability] to penetrate subtleties arises from thinking. Therefore thinking is the foundation of the sage's achievement and the opportunity for good fortune or misfortune.

The *I* says, "The superior person perceives incipience and acts, without waiting all day."[62] It also says, "Knowing incipience is his spirituality."[63]

In the *T'ung shu* Chou Tun-i refers to *ch'eng* mainly in the cosmological terminology of the *I ching*, not in terms of *li*. But by applying Chu Hsi's interpretation of *ch'eng* to this text (as the later tradition invariably did), we can flesh out Chou's often cryptic pronouncements.

As the congruence of activity with the natural/moral order, authenticity per se is not activity (chaps. 3 and 4); yet it is imperceptible in the absence of activity (chap. 2). It becomes perceptible when a stimulus *(kan)* produces a response *(ying)* that "penetrates" like a spirit (chap. 4)—when incipient activity emerges or develops without the intervention of deliberate thought and is expressed as authentic activity (chaps. 3 and 9), that is, activity that is perfectly consonant with the natural/moral order (chap. 2). (While it may seem surprising to find the *absence* of thought valorized in a Confucian text, the point here is not that thinking is misleading but that the responsiveness of a sage is *spontaneously* correct.[64]) "Penetrating" *(t'ung)* here refers to activity that, because of its consonance with *li*, resonates with, responds to, and pervades the entire natural/moral order, beyond the empirically immediate and observable situation. Hence, it is like a spirit *(shen)*, which is not limited to empirical cause-effect conditions.

Further light may be shed on the key terms of the *T'ung shu* by extracting them and placing them under the major categories found in the *Explanation of the Supreme Polarity Diagram (T'ai-chi t'u shuo)*. In Table 1, the numbers on the left side correspond to the chapters and sections of the *T'ung shu* given above.

The two outer columns of the table correspond on the most general level to the yin-yang polarity (manifested as stillness and activity) discussed by Chou in the *T'ai-chi t'u shuo*, which outlines the Taoist-influenced cosmogonic scheme that became a standard element in the Neo-Confucian synthesis:

Non-polar *(wu-chi)* and yet Supreme Polarity *(t'ai-chi)*! The Supreme Polarity in activity *(tung)* generates yang; yet at the limit of activity it is still *(ching)*. In stillness it generates yin; yet at the

TABLE 1

	Supreme Polarity *T'ai-chi*		
	Yin/stillness		Yang/activity
4 (c)	Sage: authentic *ch'eng*	incipient *chi*	spiritual *shen*
(a)	silent and inactive *chi-jan pu-tung*	stimulated and *kan erh*	then penetrating *sui t'ung*
(b)	essential *ching*	subtle *wei*	responsive *ying*
2 (c)	Authenticity: imperceptible when still (*ching-wu*)		perceptible when active (*tung-yu*)
	perfectly correct *chih-cheng*		clearly pervading *ming-ta*
(b)	the foundation *pen*		of the Five Constants and Hundred Practices *wu-ch'ang pai-hsing*
3 (a)	Authenticity: no [intentional] acting (*ch'eng wu-wei*)		
(b)		Incipience: good and evil *chi shan-wu*	
(c)			[Five Constant] Virtues *te* (*jen, i, li, chih, hsin*)
9 (a)	without thinking: *wu-ssu*		thinking penetrates: *ssu-t'ung*
	foundation *pen* (=*t'i*)		function *yung*
		incipient activity *chi-tung*	authentic activity *ch'eng-tung*

limit of stillness it is also active. Activity and stillness alternate; each is the basis of the other. In distinguishing yin and yang, the Two Modes are thereby established.[65]

The relationship between stillness and activity here is primarily a temporal one: the two are different phases of the cosmic process. But in chapter 16 ("Activity and Stillness") of the *T'ung shu*, Chou implies that the two modes interpenetrate one another:

(a–d)   Activity as the absence of stillness and stillness as the absence of activity characterize things (*wu*). Activity that is not [empirically] active and stillness that is not [empirically] still characterize spirit (*shen*). Being active and yet not active, still and yet not still, does not mean that [spirit] is neither active nor still. For while things do not [inter-]penetrate (*t'ung*),[66] spirit subtly [penetrates/ pervades] the myriad things.

(e–h)   The *yin* of water is based in *yang*; the *yang* of fire is based in *yin*. The Five Phases are *yin* and *yang*; *yin* and *yang* are the Supreme Polarity. The Four Seasons revolve; the myriad things end and begin [again]. How undifferentiated! How extensive! And how inexhaustible!

Here Chou is speaking of the metaphysical foundation of stillness and activity. On this level they are interpenetrating, not mutually exclusive, categories. This underlying unity became the basis, in Chu Hsi's system, for access to the ultimate reality by the mind in its ordinary activity.[67]

In the terminology of the Ch'eng-Chu school, the two outer columns of the table correspond to the substance (*t'i*) and function (*yung*) of the human mind, or human nature (*hsing*) and dispositions (*ch'ing*), or order (*li*) and psycho-physical stuff (*ch'i*).[68] Note that "authenticity" occurs in both outer columns: under "stillness" in lines 4c and 2c, and under "activity" in 9a and (by implication) 2c. This reflects the notion that authenticity is the condition in which the metaphysical substance is fully realized in function.

The center column corresponds to the crucial moment of incipient (*chi*) change or response, when a stimulus has been received but the response has not yet become manifest. I have discussed this phase of change elsewhere,[69] so here I will be brief; it will suffice

to quote some of Chu Hsi's comments on Chou's treatment of
incipience in chapter 3 of the *T'ung shu*. Chu says:

> Incipience is the imperceptible beginning of activity. It is that
> according to which good and evil are distinguished. With the first
> sign of activity in the human mind, the Heavenly/natural order
> (*t'ien-li*) will certainly appear there; yet human desires (*jen-yü*) have
> already sprouted amidst it.[70]

And:

> Incipiencies, or the subtle indications of activity, lie between
> deciding to act and imminent activity, where there is both good and
> evil. One must understand them at this point. If they reach the point
> of becoming manifest, then one cannot help anything. . . . The point
> of subtle incipience is extremely important.[71]

Thus, according to Chu Hsi, the incipient phase of mind is the
critical point at which either evil human desires or the original
goodness of human nature and the natural order can become
actualized in the world; hence its importance in the task of moral
cultivation.

Equally significant to Chu is moral responsiveness, which in our
table falls under the right column as an aspect of moral activity.
Commenting on chapter 4, Chu says:

> The primary and unmanifest [ground] is the substance of the
> actualized order (*shih-li*, i.e., *ch'eng*). Good (*shan*) yet unfathom-
> able response is the function of the actualized order. Between activ-
> ity and stillness, substance and function, suddenly in the space of
> an instant there is the beginning of the actualized order and the aus-
> picious and inauspicious omens of the multitudinous phenomena.[72]

"Good yet unfathomable response" refers to the "spiritual" (*shen*)
characteristic of the sage, which, as we have seen above, Chou Tun-i
defines as "penetrating" (*t'ung*) and "responsive" (*ying*).

The overall picture we have here is that of a mind that is perfectly
still and therefore perfectly good (since good and evil arise first in
incipient activity, according to line 3b). When stimulated, this sagely
mind immediately and without deliberation responds to and penetrates, or comprehends, the external object. In line 9a we have a

similar scenario: "With no thinking and yet penetrating everything, one is a Sage."

Thus the sage is one who effortlessly, spontaneously, and properly responds to external stimuli. The significance of this spontaneously moral response to things was widely acknowledged in the Ch'eng-Chu tradition of *Tao-hsüeh* (Learning of the Way). For example, in Ch'eng Hao's "Letter on Stabilizing Human Nature" (written to his uncle, Chang Tsai), he says:

> The constant principle of Heaven-and-Earth is that its mind pervades all things, yet it has no [personal] mind. The constant principle of the sage is that his dispositions accord with all phenomena, yet he has no [private, selfish] dispositions. Therefore, in the education of the *chün-tzu* (gentleman or superior person), there is nothing like being completely broad and impartial, and responding in accordance with things as they come (*wu-lai erh hsün-ying*).[73]

The significance of moral responsiveness was also frequently noted by Chu Hsi. In his commentary on *Mencius*, 7A.1, he says:

> Mind is human being's spiritual clarity (*shen-ming*). It is that by which one embodies (*chü*) the various principles and responds to the myriad phenomena.[74]

And in his "Treatise on the Examination of the Mind," Chu says:

> The learning of the sages is to base one's mind on fully investigating principle, and to accord with principle by responding to things.[75]

The sage responds to things, not only with clear understanding, but also with moral activity. This we see in *T'ung shu* 2b and 3a–c, where Chou describes the response of the still substance of the mind as the Five Constant Virtues and the Hundred Practices, referring to "moral activity" (*te-hsing*).[76] In chapter 11, Chou suggests that this moral activity applies as much to the nonhuman world as to the human:

> Heaven gives birth to the myriad things through yang, and completes the myriad things through yin. Giving birth is humanity. Completion is appropriateness. Therefore when a sage is above [on

the throne], he nourishes (*yü*) the myriad things with humanity and corrects the myriad people with appropriateness.

Here we are reminded again of *Chung yung*, 22: "If they can assist in the transforming (*hua*) and nourishing (*yü*) [process] of Heaven and Earth, they can thus form a trinity with Heaven and Earth." Responding to the nonhuman world is not just a matter of passively fitting into the flow of nature, nor is it merely a cognitive understanding of the natural order for the benefit of the social order. The Confucian sage actively "transforms" the world around him by "nourishing the myriad things with humanity/humaneness (*jen*)." This is not limited to the social world and it does not mean manipulating the natural world to suit human purposes. As Ch'eng Hao said (above), "The constant principle of the Sage is that his dispositions accord with all phenomena, yet he has no [private, selfish] dispositions." By "according" with things, or "responding in accordance with things as they come," the sage does not impose his own will on nature. According to Shao Yung (1011–1077), the sage

> reflects the universal character of the feelings [dispositions] of all things. The sage can do so because he views things as things view themselves; that is, not subjectively but from the viewpoint of things.[77]
>   . . .The sage benefits things and forgets his own ego.[78]

Thus it is the sage's identification with things and his active, nourishing, life-giving response to things (including but not limited to human beings) that constitutes his transforming influence on the world. In Chou Tun-i's terms, this is what it means to be an authentic human being.

Responsiveness as Authenticity

We have seen that Chou Tun-i defines sagehood in terms of 1) authenticity, 2) the capacity to perceive incipient change, and 3) the spiritual capacity to penetrate (or comprehend) and to respond spontaneously to things, without deliberate mental activity or thought. Adding to these propositions Chu Hsi's interpretation of authenticity as "actualized order" (*shih-li*), we find that moral responsiveness is a defining characteristic of the sage (one of several—i.e., a necessary but not sufficient condition) because responsiveness and interpenetration are essential characteristics of the natural world. The sage is responsive because he or she fully manifests the natural principles (*t'ien-li*) of yin-yang, stillness-activity (*tung-ching*), and stimulus-penetration (*kan-t'ung*) or stimulus-response (*kan-ying*). As Chu Hsi describes the responsiveness of the sage:

> When there is nothing happening then his mind is silent (*chi-jan*), and no one can see it. When there is something happening then the operation of his spiritual understanding (*shen-chih*) responds when stimulated (*sui kan erh ying*).[79]

In chapter 20 of the *T'ung shu*, Chou explicitly links sagehood to stillness and activity (as also in chapter 4); the chapter title is "Learning to be a Sage":

> [Someone asked:] "Can Sagehood be learned?"
> Reply: It can.
> "Are there essentials?"
> Reply: There are.
> "I beg to hear them."
> Reply: To be unified (*i*)[80] is essential. To be unified is to have no desire. Without desire one is vacuous when still (*ching-hsü*) and direct in activity (*tung-chih*). Being vacuous when still, one will be clear (*ming*); being clear one will be penetrating (*t'ung*). Being direct in activity one will be impartial (*kung*); being impartial one will be all-embracing (*p'u*).[81] Being clear and penetrating, impartial and all-embracing, one is almost [a Sage].

Thus we can conclude that the Neo-Confucian sage, who symbolizes the perfection of human virtue and fulfillment, is attuned to the conditions and changes in the environment, even in their incipient (*chi*) stages, with no intervening egoistic or prudential considerations. He responds to the environment spontaneously and directly, that is, as a direct expression of his essential nature, with "penetrating thought," "spiritual clarity," and "authentic activity," which includes "nourishing things." Confucian spirituality is therefore not just interiority, as it is sometimes conceived; it involves contact, sensitivity, and interpenetration with *external* things.[82] In fact, "spirit" (*shen*) in Neo-Confucian discourse is a characteristic of *ch'i* itself: it refers to the underlying continuity and interpenetration (*kuan-t'ung*) of natural processes, whether empirically observable or not.[83] For the mind of the sage, such spiritual interpenetration is based on and enabled by authentic contact with and expression of the ultimate reality within.

Furthermore, in Neo-Confucian theory at least, the distinction between ecocentric and anthropocentric interests is a false one. A situation that seemed to demand a choice between them from this perspective would not have been fully understood; it would be necessary to dig deeper to discover the level of order/principle on which human and natural interests coincided. In practice, of course, this would be extremely challenging; it would require the subject to confront a bedrock article of faith on which the Confucian world-view rests: the claim that the underlying order of things (*li*), or the Way (*Tao*), comprehends both the natural order and the moral order.

Authentic selfhood, according to this way of thinking, manifests itself (among other ways) by nourishing, creative responsiveness with the environment. The authentic human being fully manifests his or her inherent nature and moral potential by actualizing in practice the natural/moral order, which includes the principles of creativity, life, and growth. One completes oneself by participating in the completion of Heaven, Earth, and humanity. Thus, nourishing, moral responsiveness to the natural environment, in Neo-Confucian terms, is a *necessary* expression of an authentic or genuine human life.

Notes

1. *Ying* is more literally translated simply as "response" or "responsiveness." But since the Confucian use of the word clearly means "moral responsiveness," I shall use this term where appropriate.

2. Chou Tun-i (or Chou Lien-hsi) lived during the period of the revival of Confucianism that has come to be known in the West as Neo-Confucianism. He was for a short time the teacher of the Ch'eng brothers, Ch'eng Hao (1032–1085) and Ch'eng I (1033–1107), who were instrumental in this revival. Although he did not play a prominent role in intellectual circles during his lifetime, he was posthumously declared by Chu Hsi (1130–1200)—the real architect of what became the orthodox version of the tradition—to be the founder of the revival and the first true Confucian sage since Mencius in the fourth century B.C.E. His two major works are the *Explanation of the Supreme Polarity Diagram* (*T'ai-chi t'u shuo*) and a longer text called *T'ung shu* (Penetrating the *Book of Changes*). For the translation of *t'ai-chi* as "supreme polarity," see note 65.

3. See Arnold S. Kaufman, "Responsibility, Moral and Legal," in *The Encyclopedia of Philosophy*, ed. Paul Edwards (New York: Macmillan and The Free Press, 1967).

4. In Chinese popular religion the picture is quite different. There, judgment is quite explicitly an important role of the Ten Kings of Hell to whom the recently deceased must report. See Stephen F. Teiser, *The Scripture on the Ten Kings and the Making of Purgatory in Medieval Chinese Buddhism* (Honolulu: University of Hawaii Press, 1994).

5. It is also worth noting that the etymology of the word *shu* suggests similarity or likeness (*ju*).

6. One could add the further point that by fitting with the general patterns or principles of ritual propriety (*li*), the act also matches (*p'ei*) the natural principles upon which the *li* are based (e.g., according to the *Li chi* [Book of rites], chap. 17; see Fung Yu-lan, *A History of Chinese Philosophy*, trans. Derk Bodde [Cambridge, Mass.: Harvard University Press, 1952], 1:343–44). But this correspondence with natural principle is more explicit in Neo-Confucian discourse and will be discussed below.

7. I translate *li* here as "order," in the sense of the natural order and the moral order, because the conception of *li* in the Ch'eng-Chu school of Neo-Confucianism is precisely the sum or confluence or congruence of these two concepts. The common terms *t'ien-li* and *tao-li* correspond roughly to these two aspects of order: the former connotes more the natural order and the latter the moral order. While in most cases I find the word "principle" too vague as a translation of *li*, in some cases it is appropriate—for example, when a particular principle is meant, such as the principle of yin-yang bipolarity.

8. *Chung yung* (also translated as "Doctrine of the Mean"), 22; *A Source Book in Chinese Philosophy*, trans. Wing-tsit Chan (Princeton: Princeton University Press, 1963), 108.

9. Chan, *A Source Book in Chinese Philosophy*, 497.

10. Donald Worster, *Nature's Economy: The Roots of Ecology* (Garden City, N.Y.: Anchor Books, 1979), 192; cited in David Kinsley, *Ecology and Religion: Ecological Spirituality in Cross-Cultural Perspective* (Englewood Cliffs, N.J.: Prentice-Hall, 1995), xv.

11. This is the reason for the title of Gary Snyder's book of poems and essays, *Earth House Hold* (New York: New Directions, 1969). *The Oxford English Dictionary* (1971 reprint of 1933 ed.) defines "œcology" as "The science of the economy of animals and plants; that branch of biology which deals with the relations of living organisms to their surroundings, their habits and modes of life, etc."

12. *The Oxford English Dictionary*.

13. *Ho-nan Ch'eng-shih i-shu*, in *Erh Ch'eng chi* (Beijing: Chung-hua shu-chu, 1981), 2A, p. 15; trans. Chan, *A Source Book in Chinese Philosophy*, 523.

14. I take "organic" to mean "having parts arranged and subordinated as instruments (*organa*) towards the end of keeping the whole being alive and enabling it to perform its function" (W. K. C. Guthrie, *A History of Greek Philosophy* [Cambridge: Cambridge University Press, 1962], 1:207). Regarding the "instrumental" sense of "organic," cf. the well-known passage from the *Book of Changes* (*I ching*), "What is above form is called the Way; what is below [and within] form is called an instrument (*ch'i*)." *Hsi tz'u* (Appended remarks), A.12.4; in Chu Hsi, *Chou-i pen-i* (Original meaning of the *Book of Changes*) (1177; reprint, Taipei: Hua-lien, 1978), 3:16a.

15. Tu Weiming, "The Continuity of Being: Chinese Visions of Nature," included in this volume; originally published in *Nature in Asian Traditions of Thought: Essays in Environmental Philosophy*, ed. J. Baird Callicott and Roger T. Ames (Albany: State University of New York Press, 1989), 74. It should be added that there is clearly another level to Ch'eng Hao's remark, since "one body" (*i-t'i*) also means "one substance," referring to the metaphysical ground, or principle (*li*), which the man of humanity fully expresses in his moral activity. Without taking account of this level, it would be difficult to explain the implication that *only* the man of humanity, or the humane person, is continuous with the natural world.

16. The precise relationship between *li* and *ch'i* has been the subject of vigorous debate at least since the twelfth century, but we shall conveniently sidestep it here.

17. After the twelfth century, the term *tao-hsüeh*, or "Learning of the Way," came to be used primarily in reference to this school—although during the Northern Sung it had included a much wider variety of thinkers. See Hoyt

Cleveland Tillman, *Confucian Discourse and Chu Hsi's Ascendancy* (Honolulu: University of Hawaii Press, 1992).

18. See Chan, *A Source Book in Chinese Philosophy*, 95–114, and Tu Wei-ming, *Centrality and Commonality: An Essay on Confucian Religiousness* (Albany: State University of New York Press, 1989).

19. Chan, *A Source Book in Chinese Philosophy*, 465–80.

20. See Chu's comments on *T'ung shu*, chaps. 2–4, in Chang Po-hsing, comp., *Chou Lien-hsi hsien-sheng ch'üan-chi* (Complete collection of Master Chou Lien-hsi; 1708), in *Cheng-i t'ang ch'üan-shu* (Pai-pu ts'ung-shu chi-ch'eng ed.), 5:9a–11a, 17b. Hereafter cited as *Chou Lien-hsi chi*.

21. The traditional adage "Heaven and man are one" (*t'ien jen ho i*) expresses this dyadic relationship subsumed under a more fundamental unity.

22. See Joseph Needham, *Science and Civilisation in China* (Cambridge: Cambridge University Press, 1956), 2:281. By "holistic" I mean both 1) that the whole is more than the sum of its parts and 2) that the whole is reflected in each of its parts. For "organic," see note 14 above.

23. Tung Chung-shu, *Ch'un-ch'iu fan-lu* (Shanghai: Ku-chi Publishers, 1989), 75; trans. Chan, *A Source Book in Chinese Philosophy*, 283.

24. *Huai-nan tzu*, 6:3a. *Huai-nan Tzu: Philosophical Synthesis in Early Han Thought*, trans. Charles Le Blanc (Hong Kong: Hong Kong University Press, 1985), 116. For the claim that the *Huai-nan tzu* is a major Huang-Lao Taoist text, see ibid., 6–7, 37, and Harold D. Roth, "Psychology and Self-Cultivation in Early Taoistic Thought," *Harvard Journal of Asiatic Studies* 51, no. 2 (1991):599–650.

25. Le Blanc, *Huai-nan Tzu*, 8–9. *Chen-jen* is Chuang Tzu's term for the fully realized person. This same concept of resonance (*kan-ying*) is discussed in Robert Weller and Peter Bol, "From Heaven-and-Earth to Nature," included in this volume.

26. *Huai-nan tzu*, 6:6a; trans. Le Blanc, 133.

27. Ibid., 6:6b; trans. Le Blanc, 135, again echoing Chuang Tzu (chap. 7).

28. Ibid., 6:1b; trans. Le Blanc, 104.

29. Ibid., 6:4a; trans. Le Blanc, 118.

30. Ibid., 6:4b; trans. Le Blanc, 121.

31. Ibid., 6:15a; trans. Le Blanc, 180–81.

32. See Le Blanc, *Huai-nan Tzu*, 186. Note that these passages refer to the three fundamental "substances" of the human body understood as a microcosm of the universe: *ch'i* (psycho-physical stuff, or vital energy), *ching* (vital essence), and *shen* (spirit). See Livia Kohn, "Guarding the One: Concentrative Meditation in Taoism," in *Taoist Meditation and Longevity Techniques*, ed. Livia Kohn (Ann Arbor, Mich.: Center for Chinese Studies, 1989), 130. See also Kristofer Schipper, *The Taoist Body* (Berkeley: University of California Press, 1993).

33. Le Blanc, *Huai-nan Tzu*, 207–8.

34. Here I will be examining only those aspects of Chou's concept of sagehood

that are most directly related to our topic. And since I am not primarily concerned here with isolating Chou's own ideas as distinct from their interpretation and use in the later tradition, I shall freely make use of Chu Hsi's interpretations, identifying them as such in cases where they go beyond what Chou might have intended. Where there are differences, it is clear that Chu Hsi's interpretations were the more historically influential, as it was his commentaries that became the "orthodox" basis of the civil service examinations. Chu's interpretations are in any case much more accessible to us, since he not only wrote commentaries but also discussed Chou's texts extensively with his students. And Chou's texts are epigrammatic at best and in some places probably corrupt (fragmentary).

35. The chapter titles are those of Chu Hsi. The divisions into sections simply indicate where Chu Hsi divided the text for his commentary; they are used here to facilitate reference to Table 1 below.

36. *Chou-i, Hsi tz'u*, A.10.4 (*Chou-i pen-i*, 3:12b).

37. Ibid.

38. *Chou Lien-hsi chi*, 5:17b–18a.

39. I have elsewhere discussed the significance of responsiveness, spirit, and incipience in relation to Chu Hsi's understanding of divination and self-cultivation. See Kidder Smith, Jr., Peter K. Bol, Joseph A. Adler, and Don J. Wyatt, *Sung Dynasty Uses of the* I Ching (Princeton: Princeton University Press, 1990), 190–99.

40. It should be noted, however, that Chou apparently does not use the term "essence" (*ching*) in its standard Taoist meaning, which is a concentrated form of vital *ch'i*, such as semen. See *T'ung shu*, 30, for his use of *ching* in a way that is clearly different from this.

41. Although *ching*, "stillness," does not occur literally in the chapter, "silent and inactive" (*chi-jan pu-tung*) is clearly synonymous with it, and *ching* is paired with *tung* in chapter 16.

42. Trans. Chan, *A Source Book in Chinese Philosophy*, 107–8, with "authentic" substituted for "sincere."

43. Tu, *Centrality and Commonality*, 77.

44. "What Heaven. . .imparts to man is called human nature. To follow our nature is called the Way (Tao)." Trans. Chan, *A Source Book in Chinese Philosophy*, 98.

45. Tu, *Centrality and Commonality*, 69.

46. Ibid., 78.

47. Ibid., 98–99.

48. Ibid., 107.

49. *Chou Lien-hsi chi*, 5:2b.

50. Ibid., 5:9b, 5:11b, etc.

51. In the Mencian tradition of Confucianism, which by the Sung dynasty had become normative, humanity or humaneness (*jen*) is the hallmark of human nature

(*hsing*); human nature is the principle (*li*) of being human and is thus continuous with the natural/moral order (*t'ien-li/tao-li*).

52. Tu, *Centrality and Commonality*, 80.

53. Given this interpretation of *ch'eng*, I think it is clear that "authenticity" is a better translation than "sincerity" (the usual translation), as "authenticity" connotes the reality and genuineness of one's moral subjectivity, agency, or "authorship."

54. *Chou-i, T'uan* commentary on hexagram 1 (*Chou-i pen-i*, 1:3a).

55. Ibid.

56. See *Hsi tz'u*, A.5.6 (*Chou-i pen-i*, 3:6a).

57. This is a continuation of the first chapter.

58. I take *wu* and *yu* here to mean "without characteristics" and "having characteristics"; hence, "imperceptible" and "perceptible."

59. *Analects*, 12:1, referring to the ruler.

60. *Hung fan* chapter of the *Shu ching*. See James Legge, trans., *The Chinese Classics*, 2nd ed. (1893; reprint, Hong Kong: Hong Kong University Press, 1960), 3:327.

61. This is undoubtedly a pun on *Lao tzu*, 37, "No doing and yet nothing undone" (*wu wei erh wu pu wei*).

62. *Hsi tz'u*, B.5.11 (*Chou-i pen-i*, 3:22b).

63. Ibid.

64. The terms "without thinking" and "without acting" (*wu-ssu, wu-wei*), which we have here in chapters 3 and 9, are both taken from the "Appended Remarks" wing of the *I ching*: "*Change* [both the book as an oracle and, by extension, the universal cosmic process] is without thinking and without acting. Silent and unmoving, when stimulated it penetrates all situations under Heaven" (*Hsi tz'u*, A.10.4; *Chou-i pen-i*, 3:12b). It should also be noted that, despite Chu Hsi's enshrinement of Chou Tun-i as the first true sage since Mencius, Chou's Confucian credentials were not entirely beyond reproach. Lu Hsiang-shan (1139–1193), in a famous exchange of letters with Chu Hsi, argued strongly that Chou's ideas were too Taoist to include in the Confucian tradition (see Tillman, *Confucian Discourse and Chu Hsi's Ascendancy*, chap. 9). In fact, Chou's *T'ai-chi t'u shuo* (but not the *T'ung shu*) was included in the Taoist Canon (*Tao tsang*).

65. For a complete translation of the *T'ai-chi t'u shuo*, see Chan, *A Source Book in Chinese Philosophy*, 463–64; and Joseph A. Adler, "Zhou Dunyi: The Metaphysics and Practice of Sagehood," in *Sources of Chinese Tradition*, ed. Wm. Theodore de Bary and Irene Bloom, 2nd ed. (New York: Columbia University Press, forthcoming).

T'ai-chi is usually translated as "Supreme Ultimate," which in my view fails to convey a clear idea of what the term means to Chou Tun-i and Chu Hsi (although it is justifiable). The clearest support for translating *t'ai-chi* as "Supreme Polarity" comes from Chu Hsi. According to him, the most fundamental ordering principle (*li*) is the yin-yang polarity; it is this pattern, or principle, of interaction, not yin and yang themselves, that is *t'ai-chi*. Commenting on the line from the *I ching* (*Hsi tz'u*, A.11.5), "In change there is the Supreme Polarity," he says: "Change is the alternation of yin and yang. The Supreme Polarity is this principle (*li*)" (*Chou-i pen-i*, 3:14b). Also: "[The sentence] 'The alternation of yin and yang are called the Way' (*T'ung shu*, 1, quoted from *Hsi tz'u*, A.5.1) refers to the Supreme Polarity" (*Chou Lien-hsi chi*, 5:5b).

In other words, *t'ai-chi* is the name for the most fundamental, all-embracing pattern of the natural/moral order (*li*), and this pattern is the principle of yin-yang bipolarity. Hence the translation "Supreme Polarity" for *t'ai-chi*, and "Non-Polar" for *wu-chi*.

66. I.e., they are limited by their physical forms.

67. See Joseph A. Adler, "Divination and Philosophy: Chu Hsi's Understanding of the I-ching" (Ph.D. diss.; University of California at Santa Barbara, 1984), chap. 4.

68. Although this is not precisely consistent with the system of the Ch'eng-Chu school, it clearly constitutes a logical precursor. The major discrepancy is that in Chu Hsi's system, only *t'ai-chi*, or *li*, is classified as metaphysical substance; yin and yang are cosmological function. Also, Chou's claim that the Supreme Polarity *acts* was a problem for Chu Hsi because he defines *t'ai-chi* as *li*, and *li* as order itself is atemporal. Chu's solution was to say that *t'ai-chi* does not act but contains the principle of activity. Of course, if this were what Chou Tun-i had really meant to say he could have expressed it quite easily, rather than saying "*T'ai-chi tung. . .*" (literally, "The Supreme Polarity acts. . .").

69. Smith, Bol, Adler, and Wyatt, *Sung Dynasty Uses of the* I Ching, 190–92.

70. *Chou Lien-hsi chi*, 5:10b.

71. Ibid., 5:12b.

72. Ibid., 5:17b.

73. *Ming-tao wen-chi*, in *Erh Ch'eng chi*, 1:460. Cf. Chan, *A Source Book in Chinese Philosophy*, 525–26.

74. Chu Hsi, *Ssu-shu chi-chu* (Collected commentaries on the Four Books) (Ssu-pu pei-yao ed.), 7:1a.

75. *Chu Wen-kung wen-chi* (Ssu-pu pei-yao ed., entitled *Chu Tzu ta-ch'üan*), 67:19b. Cf. Chan, *A Source Book in Chinese Philosophy*, 604.

76. There is another slight discrepancy here with Chu Hsi's system: for Chu, the "virtues" (*te*) are principles (*li*) of moral activity, and so would properly belong in the left column of this diagram. But for Chou, the virtues clearly refer to moral activity.

77. Shao Yung, *Kuan wu* (Contemplating things), *Nei p'ien*, 12, in *Huang-chi ching-shih shu* (Book on supreme principles governing the world) (Ssu-pu pei-yao ed.), 6:26b. Trans. Chan, *A Source Book in Chinese Philosophy*, 488.

78. Shao Yung, *Hsin hsüeh* (Learning of the mind), in ibid., 8B:27b. Trans. Chan, *A Source Book in Chinese Philosophy*, 494, slightly modified.

79. *Chou-i pen-i*, 3:13b.

80. This means to focus the mind on fundamentals, to be composed and reverently attentive (*ching*) to the seriousness of the task.

81. Cf. Ch'eng Hao's "Letter on Stabilizing the Nature," quoted above.

82. Note the importance of the term "investigating things" (*ko-wu*), or "contacting things" (*chi-wu*), in Chu Hsi's program of self-cultivation. See Chu Hsi's commentary on the *Great Learning*, especially his "supplement" to chapter 5, in *Ssu-shu chi-chu* (Ssu-pu pei-yao ed.), *Ta hsüeh*, 4b–5a.

83. According to Chu Hsi (quoting Chang Tsai), "*Ch'i* has [the two modes] yin and yang. When it proceeds slowly, it is transformation (*hua*). When it is unified and unfathomable, it is *shen*" (*Chou-i pen-i*, 3:21a). For a more extended discussion, see Smith, Bol, Adler, and Wyatt, *Sung Dynasty Uses of the I Ching*, 190–94. See also Joseph A. Adler, "Varieties of Spiritual Experience: *Shen* in Neo-Confucian Discourse," in *Confucian Spirituality*, ed. Tu Weiming and Mary Evelyn Tucker (New York: Crossroad Press, forthcoming).

The Philosophy of Environmental Correlation in Chu Hsi

Toshio Kuwako

Introduction

When Ch'eng Hao asked his master, Chou Tun-i, "Why don't you weed the grass in front of your window?" Chou Tun-i answered, "The will to live that is in the grass is the same as mine." Impressed by these words, Ch'eng Hao stated, "Observe the disposition of all living things within Heaven and Earth."[1] This episode suggests what was the main concern of the philosophers of the Sung dynasty: that weeds are not planted by human beings but are grown by the activities of Heaven and Earth; that the will to live found in all living beings should be regarded as identical to that of humans; and that we must be conscious of this identity, or continuity, between humans and nature. In other words, the humaneness, or *jen*, in humans reflects the life force in nature: "The most impressive aspect of things is their spirit of life (*sheng-i*). This is what is meant by origination being the chief quality of goodness. This is humanity [*jen*]."[2]

The idea, manifest in Chou Tun-i's attitude toward nature, that there is a fundamental parallelism between the life system of grass and that of a human being led the philosophers of the Sung dynasty to observe how humans are related to their environmental universe. Chu Hsi (1130–1200) tried to integrate the thoughts of such philosophers into a consistent system, supposing that the universe is full of living things sustained by the harmonious movements of Heaven and Earth. This integration resulted not only in the explanation of the structure that the environmental universe displays but also in the inquiry into a difficult problem, that of where we can locate the most basic values in terms of which we evaluate human actions.

The circumstances in which Chu Hsi and other philosophers were living when they tried to clarify the relation between nature and humans are, admittedly, very different from our present environmental crisis, but we, too, must attempt to understand our situation and deal with the issues of value underlying the crisis. What we need today is a theory of value and action in which actions toward nature as well as actions toward humans can be approached properly. The aim of this essay is to propose how Chu Hsi's philosophy might contribute to such a theory.

Chou Tun-i's *T'ai-chi t'u* (Diagram of the Great Ultimate) and *T'ai-chi t'u shuo* (Explanation of the Diagram of the Great Ultimate)

In dealing with the ethical problems underlying environmental issues, we sometimes compare Eastern views of nature to Western understandings of nature. Nature in the former tradition is characterized as a self-contained process rather than as the creation of a supreme entity. Thus, it often happens that we concentrate our attention too much on the word "nature" itself and are then misled into conceiving of nature only as some abstract process. To avoid this, it is better to see how the phrases "Heaven and Earth" and "Heaven, Earth and the four seasons" are used, since these expressions imply the features of environmental space and time. In order to have a picture of this space and time, I will first examine the most important works of Chou Tun-i, namely, the *T'ai-chi t'u* and the *T'ai-chi t'u shuo*. These texts had a significant impact upon philosophers and initiated a new wave of philosophical thinking. They can be characterized as the first step toward a new tradition of attempts to understand the correlation between humans and nature.

These works contain both Chinese traditional views of nature and Chou Tun-i's original interpretation. One of the traditional views is the so-called yin-yang and the Five Agents (Phases) theory, which says that the whole universe consists of the gaseous substance called *ch'i*. It is perhaps important here to see *ch'i* as vital force or energy rather than as material substance, but this is misleading as it implies that the philosophy of Neo-Confucianism is simply naïve or primitive animism. One of the primary goals of this essay is to remove such misapprehensions.

The interpretation I advocate here puts more stress upon the material side than on the vital side. The activities of *ch'i* are the source of vitality in the universe, yet in the *T'ai-chi t'u shuo*, at least, there is no assumption that *ch'i* itself is such vital force. *Ch'i*, which without doubt contains vital force in a sense, is viewed as yin or yang according to the amount of deviation from thermal equilibrium. It is *ch'i*'s energetic condition that determines whether it is described as yin or yang, but this condition must be regarded only as relative. The deviation from equilibrium causes the flow and circulation of the gaseous substance, resulting in an exchange of nature between them. The *T'ai-chi t'u shuo* tries to trace the two features (yin and yang) of *ch'i* to its very origin, called *t'ai-chi* (the Great Ultimate) and *wu-chi* (the Ultimate of Nonbeing). Together, these are the basis for and ground of the processes in the universe. It is important here to see that all physical processes are regarded as based upon heat distribution, and, after that, the description of movements—motion and tranquillity—appears. The loss of equilibrium causes motions resulting in so-called phase transitions, which is a physical or chemical explanation of *ch'i*. Accordingly, it is improper to say that this philosophy is naïve animism, at least as expounded in the *T'ai-chi t'u shuo*.[3]

The movements of *ch'i* cause interactions and phase transitions, from which the Five Agents of wood, fire, water, metal, and earth arise. These agents interact, circulate, liquefy, and solidify. Thus, the most philosophically significant aspect of the philosophy of *ch'i* is its insight that the basic processes of nature involve this physical process called phase transitions and that the most basic phase of all is that of gases. I see here a fundamental difference between Neo-Confucianism and Western ways of thinking, since the Western philosophical tradition is based mainly upon the solid phase of things rather than the gaseous or liquid phase. It is this solid phase that gives a metaphysical basis for the individuation and differentiation of things and persons, which, in turn, is the requisite for constructing any modern ethical theory of person and rights.[4]

In the theory of the Five Agents, the agents arise in order: wood generates fire; fire generates earth; earth generates metal; metal generates water. This relationship of generation is contrasted with that of overcoming: wood overcomes earth; earth overcomes water; water overcomes fire; fire overcomes metal. These two interrelations of the Five Agents also constitute a symbolic system in which the structures of the environmental universe, human nature, and the correlation between them are interpreted and explained. The concept of space and time is also explicated with regard to the Five Agents. Thus, though various systems of signification are composed of the Five Agents, it is important to see that the *T'ai-chi t'u shuo* tells us that they are originally only two features (yin and yang) of *ch'i*.

After introducing the theory of the Five Agents, Chou Tun-i tries to explain the production of the myriad things in terms of the interaction between the male principle, *ch'ien*, and the female principle, *k'un*. This restless process of interaction is called *sheng sheng*, namely, producing and reproducing. In his use of this idea, Chou Tun-i intends both to describe the universe in physical terms and to characterize the status of humans with the words for evaluation. When Chou Tun-i explains the phenomena in the universe on the basis of the material principle of *ch'i*, he tries to grasp the very point that connects physical and objective explanations with the notion of the endless process of producing lives, that is, the interaction of the male and female principles. This consideration of life-producing processes enables him to open the gate to the evaluation of human nature and human actions.

When we consider Chou Tun-i's explanation that after the human body is shaped the functions of the mind begin to work, we can see his nondualistic conception of the mind. It is regulated by the essential material qualities of the Five Agents. Various emotions occur and actions are performed when the five qualitative natures, which have their origins in the Five Agents, are acted on from the outside. Chou Tun-i says that all human affairs take place in the interaction between humans and their environment and that an ideal state of mind for humans is to maintain tranquillity in spite of stimuli from outside. This state, with respect to mental activities, is said to be achieved by the principles of the Mean, correctness, benevolence, and righteousness. (Here I translate *jen*, not as humanity or humaneness, but as benevolence, which might seem awkward to those who know that the original meaning of the word has reference to being human.[5])

One of the main points I would like to make in this essay is that the most important contribution made by Neo-Confucianism to the history of Chinese philosophy is the interpretive turn of *jen* from humanity or humaneness to the most basic structure correlated to both humans and their environmental universe. Thus, if we continue to adopt the translation "humanity" or "humaneness," we would overlook that turn—the turn from traditional Chinese humanism to the position that I would call "antianthropocentrism" or "counter-anthropocentrism." Moreover, insofar as the humanism of Western traditions is understood as a system of beliefs and standards derived only from the consideration of human factors, not from such external or transcendent entities as nature or God, I would dare to say that Chu Hsi's philosophy can be seen not only as antianthropocentrism but also as antihumanism.[6]

I believe that the key that enabled the meaning of *jen* to turn from morality to the metaphysical basis of morality is "the endless process of transformation with producing and reproducing lives." Various living things are produced and kept alive by *ch'i*'s restless motion. Heaven and Earth constitute the environmental space and time containing all forms of life sustained by this process of *sheng sheng* (producing and reproducing). Given that both the weeds in Chou Tun-i's garden and human beings are produced and sustained in this environmental space, we can understand why he did not weed his garden: the will of the weeds to live was identical to his own.

Chu Hsi's Interpretation of the *T'ai-chi t'u shuo*

Chu Hsi's commentary on the *T'ai-chi t'u shuo* does not aim at explaining the genetic processes of the world. It is said that Chu Hsi deleted "from" from the text in order to deny any interpretation suggesting that the *t'ai-chi* is generated from *wu-chi*. Here Chu Hsi intended to exclude any hint of Taoism that might be read as suggesting that the universe developed from nonbeing. *Wu-chi, t'ai-chi*, yin and yang, and the Five Agents do not explain the stages in the development of the universe in time; rather, they explicate the actual process by referring to different layers that can be described from these points of view. This interpretive strategy may be called "multiple description" of the environmental universe.

It is important to observe that, in this multiple description, Chu Hsi takes a negative attitude toward substantializing the explanatory principles, as seen, for example, in Plato's theory of Forms. Chu Hsi thinks that it is certainly possible to search out the basic structures that explain the activities of the endless process of producing and reproducing lives, but to him these structures are not separable or independent from these activities. We can see, therefore, that Chu Hsi's search for the principles of explanation and his refusal to substantialize them stand in a strained relationship. We understand the world in which our lives are sustained by giving fundamental structures to the world, but the principles of these structures do not exist independently from them in some separate region.

The above consideration leads us to appreciate Chu Hsi's understanding of the order found between Heaven and Earth, such as the orderly cycle of life, in contrast to the cosmic order in the Western tradition. The order conceived in Classical Greece, for example, is that which is actualized in the movements of stars and planets, in the mathematical regularities that these movements show. This Pythagorean and Platonic view had a great influence over Western civilization. The mathematical and deterministic physical laws were the objects of inquiry in modern sciences as well. It is very suggestive that Kant, who tried to give an epistemological foundation for Newtonian mechanics, wanted to maintain universal moral laws as being in the realm of freedom, regarding the moral laws and the sky with its twinkling stars as having the highest value.[7] This tradition (of which Kant is but one representative) is related to the attitude toward idealized regularities and laws separated from the world of living things, which has complexity, multiplicity, and alteration. In contrast, the tradition of Neo-Confucianism sees as typical the order in the environment, that is, the region between Heaven and Earth where phase transitions occur incessantly, causing meteorological phenomena and producing and reproducing lives.

In addition, as I suggested earlier, we find another significant difference between the traditions in the concept of material substance. This is because *ch'i* contains, as is often suggested, a kind of vital force or vital energy, whereas Western traditions have attempted to see the phenomena of life from the material principles that lack such vital force completely. The objection might be made that Aristotle inquired into nature, observing natural life as the most important phenomena and trying to explain them in terms of biological principles. This path of inquiry, however, was criticized mainly on the basis of celestial movements in modern times as well as in ancient times. It should be noted that the method of modern physical science takes as its starting point principles of a nonvital sort.

If we put too much emphasis, however, on the vitality of *ch'i*, we risk overlooking the crucial point that the strategy of the *T'ai-chi t'u shuo* is taken from the gaseous phase of material substance and thus mystifying the doctrine of Neo-Confucianism. If we do not assume that *ch'i* is vital force but recognize that vitality is formed in the process of the interaction of yin and yang, we will be able to appreciate the philosophical significance of Chou Tun-i's philosophy.

Another characteristic of the *T'ai-chi t'u shuo* is that it states that the five principles of human nature engage in activity, aroused by, and reacting to, the external environment. Here, with good and evil being diverted, human affairs take place. Chu Hsi states explicitly that these five principles of nature are the five moral principles, benevolence, righteousness, propriety, wisdom, and faithfulness. It is surprising, surely, to see that the qualitative natures are characterized by ethical terms. From this, it would appear that Neo-Confucianism contains a naïve, probably false, assumption that we can make judgments of evaluation from factual descriptions of the world.[8] It is crucial, therefore, to understand why Chou Tun-i and Chu Hsi used such moral terms to describe the qualities, since it would be utterly inconceivable for those who take as their basic philosophical position the dualism of mind and body. How can Chou Tun-i and Chu Hsi deal with the recognition of nature and value at the same time? Do they naïvely assume, as is often suggested, that there is a continuity between facts and values?

Description and Evaluation

The difficulty that confronts us is how Chou Tun-i and Chu Hsi are justified in making use of terms of evaluation in the multiple description. To answer this question, let us briefly examine the history of the five moral principles.

Chu Hsi finds his position in the Confucian tradition, the tradition that began with Confucius and was continued by Tseng Ts'an, Tse Sze, and Mencius. Confucius stressed the importance of *jen* and *li* as compared with righteousness, wisdom, and faithfulness. Tseng Ts'an understood his master's *jen* as "being true to our nature and benevolent to others." Mencius tried to systematize the four virtues in his ethical thought and explained the concept of *jen* as the mind that cannot bear to see the suffering of others (*Mencius*, 6A.6). Admittedly, here the word *jen* is justifiably rendered as humanity; neither Confucius nor Mencius extended the meaning beyond the range of human affairs. How, then, are Chou Tun-i and Chu Hsi able to introduce these moral concepts into the explanation of the world?

Chou Tun-i expresses his appraisal of the *Book of Changes* (*I ching*) in the last paragraph of the *T'ai-chi t'u shuo*. The *Book of Changes* is not only a work for divination but also a book for explicating the structure of human actions and the environmental world in which they are performed. The origin of the theory of yin and yang in the *T'ai-chi t'u shuo* can be traced to this book, and the term *t'ai-chi* is also cited from the *Great Appendix of the Book of Changes*. It is this book that inquires into the unchanging truths in the changing phenomena in which nature manifests itself and the worth of human actions is evaluated. Indeed, the *Great Appendix* tries to explain all the phenomena, including human affairs, starting from the Supreme Ultimate down to the complex and multiple forms of living.

The symbols for Heaven, *ch'ien*, written with six strokes of yang, and for Earth, *k'un*, with six strokes of yin, represent the purest activity of Heaven and of Earth, respectively. Both activities act upon each other and this interaction produces things in the world. The hexagram of *ch'ien* has four characters that are understood as the judgment of the divination that "the creative works sublime success, furthering through perseverance." They can also be interpreted differently, however. Another interpretation of the *Commentary on the Decision* is to take the four characters apart and attribute to each the virtues of Heaven, to the effect that the fourfold work of Heaven is to cause meteorological phenomena (such as rainfall and sunshine) and to produce lives. Undisturbed change and transformation, it is said, come into permanent accord with the Great Harmony, which the holy person has the power to maintain. Here it is important to see that when the *Book of Changes* recognizes that various processes in nature are sustained by the Great Harmony, it implies also that humans can accord, or fail to accord, with this Harmony. Another commentary, the *Commentary on the Works of the Text*, states explicitly that the fourfold activities of Heaven and Earth are characterized by, and correspond to, the four qualities of morality. The above considerations suggest that the *Book of Changes* sees the basis of value in the life-producing processes of yin and yang.

The Structure of Environmental Correlation

We must not overlook the point in Chu Hsi's argument at which he distinguishes the process of forming sensible things from the orderly structure embodied in them. This orderly structure is the pattern in which *ch'i* manifests itself when condensed and solidified. *Ch'i* gathers, forming some patterns, and, without this process of gathering, there is no place in which the patterns show themselves. The specific nature of a living thing—the essential pattern of birth and growth—has its own seed, from which it develops its potentialities. In other words, the essence of a seed is the pattern in which it shows its nature. However, these patterns do not exist, Chu Hsi asserts, apart from *ch'i*, and it is not the pattern but material substance that generates things. While it is *ch'i* that is this material substance, being in the process of producing and reproducing lives, the pattern for the sake of which *ch'i* gathers to form them is called *li*.[9]

In the *Chu Tzu yü-lei* (Classified conversations of Chu Hsi), Chu Hsi understands *jen* as the mind with which Heaven and Earth generate things in the universe. He says that *jen* encompasses all the things in the world and resides in human minds, too. Here Chu Hsi stresses the point that it is not sufficient to know only the fact of this comprehensive feature of *jen*; it is necessary to know why it is characterized as such. Trying to explain Mencius's notion of *jen*, which is a virtue of the human mind, Chu Hsi explicitly refers to the mind of Heaven and Earth that produces all beings in the world. The impressive comparison that he employs is a steamer, in which boiling water thrusts vapor upward and circulates steam rapidly. As rice is steamed, so do Heaven and Earth contain vast quantities of gaseous matter.[10] Chu Hsi says that there is no activity in Heaven and Earth other than those which are compared to the boiling matter that forms things. He calls this activity "the mind of Heaven and Earth."

The analogy of a steamer suggests that Chu Hsi is trying to grasp the physical process caused by heat, and that he sees the process of phase transition from the gaseous phase to the liquid and solid phases as basic movements of the material *ch'i*. In this case it is observed that *ch'i* in its gaseous phase is not in equilibrium but in rapid circulation and flow, and that it is this process of circulation and flow that produces things.

It might seem that the circulation of *ch'i* is a physical process which can be described only in physical terms, but Chu Hsi sees here the mind of Heaven and Earth. When he says that in one sense Heaven and Earth have no mind but that in another it is possible to say they do, he is very conscious of his use of the steamer analogy. Heaven and Earth have no deliberation and prudence, but there is an orderly circulation of the four seasons, and this circulation is the cause of the generation of things. It should be noted here that when Chu Hsi asserts that Heaven and Earth have a mind, he is saying more than that the orderly motion of *ch'i* produces the order in the universe. His intention is to say that the orderly circulation causes *the continuation of the identities of species*. If there were no mind in Heaven and Earth, a cow would beget a horse and a peach would have plum flowers. It proves, then, that the mind of Heaven and Earth is an activity to preserve the identities of species. This is why Chu Hsi refers not only to *li* but to the mind of Heaven and Earth.

Chu Hsi also asserts that the circulation and flux of *ch'i* not only produce the order in a life system but also keep and maintain its structure. If the circulation ceases to work, the structure itself collapses. This means that the circulation is the necessary condition for the maintenance of a system. When the grand circulation of *ch'i* brings an appropriate amount of rain and sunshine, life systems maintain their lives and the continuity of species. Accordingly, meteorological circulation must be in accordance with the order within a life system. A human being, as a living being, is also generated by this activity of *ch'i* and is maintained in accordance with the environmental order. We must note here that it is not possible for humans to exist outside this environmental universe. They are mixed inseparably with Heaven and Earth, as Chang Tsai indicated.[11]

Both a life system and its surrounding environmental system maintain their existence in the process of the circulation. The order that is common to both the environment and to living beings is not a permanent one in the way that Aristotle, for example, understands the order of celestial movements. Rather, it is one which always encompasses the possibility of collapse and destruction, even by humans. The environmental order can be affected by human activities due to the physical continuity between them. The doctrine of penetration between Heaven and humans is the natural development of such a way of thinking. According to this doctrine, human activities can help or disturb the process of producing and reproducing in Heaven and Earth.

The notion of order sustained by the harmonious movements of gaseous matter can be clearly understood when it is compared to the geometrical order conceived in ancient Greece or to the mechanical laws considered in modern European science. In Europe, the object of scientific inquiry has been to discover the permanent order hidden behind the complex and phenomenal world. This kind of order is regarded only as the object of pure contemplation. It is a necessary order with a regularity that humans, by their activities, can never alter. Such an order, therefore, has not been incorporated into the theory of human action, since no matter what humans do, the order is in no way affected. In contrast, the order viewed by the theory of the gaseous phase is the object of both inquiry and action. The rationale behind this theory is not only that a human life system is maintained by the environmental order, but also that the order itself can be the direct object of human actions.

Correlation as the Basis of Value

As we saw in the example of a steamer, the recognition of order that appears in the circulation of *ch'i* has a deep connection with the physical phenomena of heat. The original meanings of yin and yang referred to the sunny side and the shaded side of a hill and expressed an uneven distribution of heat. In the *Book of Changes*, the concepts of "hard" and "soft" in the original text are replaced by those of yin and yang, and, here, we see the shift of viewpoint regarding the nature of the symbolic system. Apparent reference to yin and yang shows how the circulation of *ch'i* occurs, since circulation and flux need the heat that causes movement.

It is interesting to know that an uneven distribution occurs both in space and time. For instance, space is grasped as an azimuth, for which there are two tables. The older one shows that south and north indicate Heaven and Earth, respectively, but in the new one south and north are fire and water. This shows that the interpretation of the azimuth became closer to notions concerning the phenomena of heat. Thus, space is interpreted in thermal terms, and time is also characterized by notions related to heat. When the progression of time causes the uneven distribution of heat and circulation of *ch'i*, four modes of time appear in its activities to produce and grow living things among Heaven and Earth. This is because the circulation of heat causes changes between warmth and coldness and, consequently, the distinction of four seasons. These four modes of time correspond to the four functions of time in regard to life.

Chu Hsi's grasp of the common ground for the recognition both of nature and value is that it is the circulation of yin and yang, warmth and coldness, and the four seasons which produces and sustains the order of life. The order in the environmental system is found in time as well as in space. Chu Hsi says that hours, days, months, and years are nothing other than the Five Agents, meaning that time is also characterized as a circulation of the Five Agents. Here, we can see how this concept of time differs from the concept of linear time in modern science. It is, so to speak, functional time with regard to the aspects of life.

As I have already stated, this order is not the eternal one, such as that grasped by Greek philosophers, nor is it the mechanical order seen from the perspective of modern physical science. It is, rather, the order that manifests itself in such regularity as that of peach trees blossoming at almost the same time every year. Trees produce flowers in correspondence to the exchange of warmth and coldness, but this correspondence is not determined by rigid necessity. The time of flowering changes every year according to the conditions of the environment. Thus, the environmental system and life systems maintain their existence, having a pattern of correlation in common.

Such patterns as the regularity of the peach trees flowering are the four aspects of life. Spring, Chu Hsi says, is the generation of the will to live; summer is the growth of the will; autumn is the completion of the will; winter is the storage of the will. These aspects of the will to live correspond to the functions of time which circulate continuously. The circulation of gaseous matter is, in a sense, that of the four seasons as functions of time and that of the four aspects of those which maintain their lives in the environment. A life system maintains its identity by correlating itself to the circulation of its outer environment. This constant circulation of the four aspects of life should not be regarded only as a factual state but also as the necessary state to maintain life itself. The collapse and destruction of the circulation in a life means that the four aspects of generation, growth, completion, and storage cannot work to sustain lives.

This circulation of the four aspects of life can work when the functions of the environmental system are not disturbed. Any given life system depends on the process of *sheng sheng* (producing and reproducing) in the circulation of *ch'i* and therefore cannot maintain its existence if the circulation loses its balance and harmony. For instance, when the circulation is disturbed, lives are not generated in spring. There is no growth in summer, and we cannot harvest in autumn. Here the four aspects of life, the four seasons, are characterized in terms of ethical evaluation.

It is this correlation between any life system and its environment that is the basis of value. Chu Hsi refers to the disposition of a living thing to maintain its existence with regard to this correlation as the "will to live." This is the same will to live that Chou Tun-i described. Ch'eng Hao says that the will to live in all things can be seen in the time of birth, and that this is the primary and supreme good (*jen*) of all good. According to Ch'eng Hao, we can locate the ground of the good in the process of circulation of the four aspects of life.

Return to the Ground of the Good

It is interesting to compare the notion of the Way, which I understand as the fundamental pattern of circulation in space and time, with that of natural law in the Western traditions, since following the Way does not mean being necessarily determined. The Way has width, so to speak, and it is possible for those who follow it to deviate from the path. The existence of functional space and time depends upon the balanced and harmonious movements of *ch'i*, and the entire process is called the Way. Humans can disturb, or even destroy, this great harmony. The supreme good is, therefore, the maintenance of this harmony. Chu Hsi has no intention of searching for a new value that is not yet known. Rather, he requires us to trace back to the basic state according to which the fundamental correlation between humans and nature is sustained. This state is regarded as the ground of the good. The correlation can be understood as that aspect of life which encompasses the most basic value for all living beings.

If these considerations are correct, then we can contrast Chu Hsi's way of thinking and the concept of value in Western thought, characterized in terms of progress and evolution. Progress is based on the human desire for what has not previously existed, or on what is better than that which exists when a life system is produced. Greek philosophers pursued this kind of goodness. Socrates, for example, asserted that it is more important to live well than to live simply. Plato, succeeding Socrates, sought after the universal and unchanging good in the realm outside this changing world. Aristotle, regarding the object of pursuit as the good, located the supreme good in the regularity found in the celestial motions.

Modern philosophy and science also sought after the natural laws in phenomena, such as celestial motions, and the moral laws found in human inner intelligence. It is possible to say that there is no concept, in the Western tradition, of seeing the ground of value in the very structure of the correlation between lives and the environment that enables living beings to maintain their lives. In that tradition, nature, both in the sense of external nature and in the sense of internal nature, is rather that which should be conquered, controlled, and improved by the notion of value conceived from human reason or desires. Following this argument, those which are *conceived as good* are better than those which exist in nature. Inventions of science and technology are products that did not exist before humans began to search for them. The ground of this good originated, not in the correlation between humans and nature, but in intelligence separated from nature in the sense of the inner nature of the human mind.

Of those environmental issues that require us to reexamine the fundamental relationship between nature and value, the most critical is pollution and its consequences. In particular, we need to be concerned about the pollution of the environment by chemical or nuclear materials that are in liquid or gaseous phases and about the abnormality of genes caused by such pollution, since it jeopardizes the generation of life and the continuity of production and reproduction. The manufacture, consumption, and abandonment of artificial goods are human activities to actualize a good that is seen as better than that which exists in nature. Human beings have produced such goods, choosing values set by themselves. These artificial things threaten the basis of the creation of those things, since they bring on negative results to the creators themselves. This situation can be characterized, not as the collision between humans and their external environment, but as the collision of values in humans themselves. It is clear that environmental issues are not simply problems of the environment as our external surroundings. Rather, they are conflicts of values with regard to the correlation between humans and their environment.

If we see our own situation in the eyes of Chu Hsi, the things that seem better than that which exists in nature have value only on the condition that humans maintain their lives as life systems correlated to their environment. The ground on which life systems depend has the origin of all values, including human good. Chu Hsi recommends that we trace back to this basis, which is called *jen*. *Jen* in this sense, therefore, should not be rendered simply as "humanity" or "humaneness." The greatest achievement of Neo-Confucianism is this interpretive turn of the meaning of *jen*. Its original meaning, humanity or humaneness, is changed to signify the function and activity of the correlation between living beings and nature.[12]

Conclusion

It is often asserted in so-called environmental ethics that we should shift the point of view from anthropocentrism to ecocentrism. The claim is also made that this shift may be achieved by enlarging the use of such notions as "person" or "rights." However, such notions were originally used only for humans, who are individuated and differentiated from each other. This means that such a scheme of ethical inquiry is based upon the solid phase of things. If one extends the use of these notions even to land, water, and air, we must realize that this scheme involves an artificial and unjustifiable manipulation of concepts. This is because the large part of the environment is composed of gaseous and liquid matter that cannot be individuated and differentiated. Environmental issues, therefore, threaten this very scheme. If the philosophy of Neo-Confucianism has any contribution to make to environmental philosophy, it is that it provides us with a methodology for incorporating the idea of "the correlation between living beings and nature as the basis of value" into the theory of value and human action.[13]

Notes

1. Chu Hsi and Lu Tsu-ch'ien, *Chin-ssu lu*, 1:22, in *Reflections on Things at Hand: The Neo-Confucian Anthology*, trans. Wing-tsit Chan (New York: Columbia University Press, 1967), 21. The commentary on this quote is as follows: "In the creative process, all things grow and flourish. The process is all-prevalent and the principle is orderly and penetrates everything. When one sees this, one's originally good mind grows abundantly." *Chin-ssu lu chi-chieh*, in Chan, *Reflections on Things at Hand*, 21.

2. This saying is attributed to Ch'eng I in the *Chu Tzu yü-lei*, 95:19a. See Chan, *Reflections on Things at Hand*, 21.

3. I emphasize the material side of *ch'i* for two reasons. On the one hand, we can see that Chang Tsai's conception of *ch'i*, which is characterized in materialistic terms, is the most important development of the *T'ai-chi t'u shuo*. See Chang Tsai, *Cheng Meng, Chang Tzu ch'ü'an-shu* (Taipei: Chung Hwa Book Company, 1976), vols. 2–3. On the other hand, although I do not deny the vitalistic character of *ch'i*, this aspect has been so exaggerated that *ch'i* has appeared to be the origin of life and value by itself. Such an understanding of *ch'i* would make the notion of *li* superfluous. Consider Chu Hsi's subtle expressions in his answers to his pupils' questions concerning the priority of *ch'i* and *li* in the *Chu Tzu yü-lei*, the *Classified Conversations of Chu Hsi* (Beijing: Chung Hwa Book Company, 1986), 1:3.

4. See John Locke, *Two Treatises of Government*, ed. Peter Laslett (Cambridge: Cambridge University Press, 1960), 285–89. Locke asserts that God has given to humans the world in common and reason to make use of it to the best advantage of life and convenience. To justify the use of that which is common to all, Locke says that every human has a property in his own person. His body and the work of his hands are his properties. Here, of course, the properties are individuated and separated from other things. Locke says, interestingly, "Though the water running in the fountain be every ones, yet who can doubt, but that in the pitcher is his only who drew it out?" He implies that to be property, water must be individuated in a pitcher. The notion of property contains the relationship between individual persons and individuated things. See also Hegel's discussion of the ideas of property and individuation. G. E. F. Hegel, *Grundlinien der Philosophie des Rechts* (Frankfurt am Main: Suhrkamp Verlag, 1970), 115–57.

5. I am not completely satisfied with "benevolence." As I shall argue, it must be meaningful to say "the *jen* of the environmental universe." To speak of "humanity in Heaven and Earth" seems not only awkward but also contradictory. It might be better to say "the benevolence of Heaven and Earth." This is why I adopt "benevolence," but for a more detailed explication, see *A Source Book in Chinese Philosophy*, trans. Wing-tsit Chan (Princeton: Princeton University Press, 1963), 788–89. See also Wing-tsit Chan, "The Evolution of the Confucian Concept of *Jen*," in *Neo-Confucianism, Etc.: Essays by Wing-tsit Chan*, ed. Wing-tsit Chan (Hanover, N.H.: Oriental Society, 1969).

6. As an instance of such humanism, Aristotle tries to understand the nature of human action and to construct a theory of evaluation of actions in terms of inner factors of human mind, that is, desire and belief. See Aristotle, *Nicomachean Ethics*, books 1, 2, 6, 7, and 10 (Oxford: Oxford Classical Texts, 1894).

7. Immanuel Kant, *Grundlegung zur Metaphysik der Sitten*, in *Schriften zur Ethik und Religionsphilosophie, Kant Werke*, vol. 4 (Wiesbaden: Insel-Verlag, 1956), 385–463. It should be noted that the spirit of enlightenment lies both in the universal laws embodied in the celestial motions of stars in external nature and in the universal moral laws as the objects of practical reason.

8. The problem of the relationship between the factual description of information and evaluative judgment can be rephrased as the connection between description and prescription. Since the notion of prescription usually implies the order to give medicine or treatment, the use of the notion points to the location of the problem of evaluation in environmental issues, that is, to the health of our own bodies and the environment around them.

9. To say that *li* is the pattern for *ch'i* might seem to give a static image to the concept. However, I mean by "pattern" "some dynamic pattern of movement." *Li* is, therefore, not simply the pattern of things but the pattern of changes.

10. *Chu Tzu yü-lei*, 4:1281. See also 1:4.

11. Chang Tsai, *Hsi ming* (Western Inscription), *Chang Tzu ch'üan-shu* (Taipei: Chung Hwa Book Company, 1976), vol. 1.

12. It should be noted that we are not studying Chu Hsi's environmental philosophy *apart*, or *independent*, *from* the context of Western thought. Rather, we are inquiring into the East Asian context *in view of* Western thought, since environmental issues require us to inquire into human attitudes toward nature by reexamining the worldviews that we have taken for granted in the course of modernization.

13. One of the most crucial questions to ask is why no original environmental ethics or philosophy has been offered in Japan, Korea, or China in spite of the fact that we find traces of Neo-Confucian tradition in their cultures. In the case of Japan, an answer to the question might be that in the 1950s and 1960s, while Japan was experiencing bitter environmental pollution, Neo-Confucianism was criticized as an optimistic, premodern philosophy that did not distinguish between nature and society, i.e., between fact and value. It is ironic that in those days land was regarded as an economical resource and was developed and destroyed for the sake of human benefit.

Ecological Implications of
Yi Yulgok's Cosmology

Young-chan Ro

Scholars of Confucian studies are relative latecomers to the ecological scene compared with their counterparts in Taoist and Buddhist studies. Even Christian theologians who have felt that Christianity bears some responsibility for the ecological crisis are now busy reinterpreting scripture, especially the Genesis creation narrative, in order to be "environmentally correct." In spite of attempts by Christians to modify the meaning of "dominion" over nature, some theologians acknowledge that the Christian tradition may have contributed to the ecological crisis.

Confucianism, unlike Taoism and its interpreters, for example, has not directly concerned itself with environmental issues and thus cannot pretend to have the answer to the earth's ecological problems. In Confucianism, however, we may well be able to find some significant philosophical and spiritual "resources" for ecological concern. Our task is not just to find some "justification" in order that Confucianism can be a viable or relevant tradition in this area; the challenge that we face is unique in comparison with other religious traditions.

The Christian approach has mostly been "repentant," "redemptive," and "reconstructive." Taoism, on the other hand, has been termed "instructive" and "indicative."[1] The Confucian approach must be neither "repentant" nor "reconstructive" but "explorative"— expounding an ecological *implication* of Confucian, and especially Neo-Confucian, cosmology.

Ecology and Confucian Cosmology

From a methodological point of view, one of the most fruitful ways to develop an ecology is to discover an ecological dimension to cosmology. The ecological concern has to do with perspective, or "worldview"[2]—a unitary vision or an integrated view of reality. Ecology is concerned with the idea of the Greek *oikos*, or "house," as in *oikumene*, "inhabited world." A house is a "dwelling" in a broad sense: an individual, social, and cosmic sense of house is *oikos*. *Eco-logy* has a double meaning: *logos* of *oikos* (the logical system of the universe) and *oikos* of *logos* (the house that embraces human logic, or the intellectual system). The former assumes a human rational and logical imposition on the universe, while the latter suggests human acceptance of the universe as the way it operates. We need a critical examination of the role of *logos*, or the human intellectual and rational system, when applied to *oikos*. The fundamental question is whether or not ecology is in the domain of the *logos*: Is ecology our human logical or ideological analysis of the cosmos and, thus, an exercise of human *logos* on the cosmos? If so, the nature and characteristics of this *logos* are the same as that *logos* which created the very problems and crisis in the first place. The concept of *logos*, as formulated and developed in Western civilization, has an unmistakable anthropocentric thrust. There is a common thread in this anthropocentric and Christian cosmology which has been the underlying assumption (or *logos*) of scientific and technological enhancement in Western civilization (*civitas*):

> Our science and technology have grown out of Christian attitudes toward man's relation to nature which are almost universally held not only by Christians and neo-Christians but also by those who fondly regard themselves as post-Christians. Despite Copernicus, all the cosmos rotates around our little globe. Despite Darwin, we are *not*, in our hearts, part of the natural process. We are superior to nature, contemptuous of it, willing to use it for our slightest whim.[3]

In the course of Neo-Confucian cosmological development, human beings and Heaven and Earth were placed within the proper context of the universe. Confucian ecology must concentrate not only on the earth but, more importantly, on the universe. In order to develop an ecology which will truly take care of the earth, we have to shift our perspective from an "anthropocentric," or even a "geocentric," view of the earth to a "cosmocentric" one. The earth has to be understood in relation to the universe. Ecology, in this sense, has to be situated within the proper context of cosmology: we cannot develop a proper ecology without a relevant cosmology. Ecology without cosmology is incomplete, and it may become yet another form of anthropocentric ecology that will make the earth subservient to human beings. Inadequate cosmological and *scientific* attitudes or mentalities toward the earth have alienated human beings from their "dwelling."

Developing a proper cosmology is a prerequisite for ecological concern. I will attempt here to explore a Neo-Confucian cosmology, in particular that of Yi I (known as Yi Yulgok; 1536–1584), a Korean Neo-Confucian thinker who developed a comprehensive view of the universe and human beings. Some methodological clarification is in order. First, my understanding of ecology is not one whereby the entire spectrum of the ecosystem is reduced to a logical, scientific formula nor one calling for an explanation of the ecosystem in terms of *nomos*, or rules and laws. My concern in an exploration of our cosmic dwelling is that we not seek the *nomos* of *oikos* nor that we reduce the mystery of our *oikos*, or house, into the realm of *nomos*. Instead, we are seeking a certain way to *appropriate*, not to *apprehend*, the "oikos." Second, the meaning of cosmology here, again, denotes an open system, not a rational or logical analysis of the cosmos (cosmos-logos). This open system allows for the irreducible, inexhaustible, and unexplainable aspects of cosmic phenomena that retain the mystery of the universe.

Confucian Cosmology

Unitary Vision in Confucian Cosmology

Neo-Confucian cosmology as expounded by Yi Yulgok implies the significance of a "cosmoanthropic" view of the universe and the world. I use the term "cosmoanthropic" rather than "anthropo-cosmic" because the term "anthropocosmic" still implies that human beings, rather than the cosmos, are the center. At the source of the ecological crisis is a "scientific" and "humanistic" worldview: "man is the measure of all things" (Protagoras). While this indicates that human beings are not only at the *center* of everything but are also the *measure* of everything, the "cosmoanthropic" worldview begins with the cosmos, not with humans. One of the significant transformations found in the Neo-Confucian tradition was not only the Neo-Confucian interest in cosmology but, more importantly, the shift of emphasis from "anthropocosmic" cosmology to "cosmoanthropic" cosmology: ideas such as *t'ai-chi*, yin-yang, *wu-hsing*, and *li* and *ch'i* all started with cosmological concepts and ontological principles before they were applied to human beings and became anthropological concepts. Even before the full development of Neo-Confucian cosmology, Confucianism had already established the foundation for an "cosmoanthropic" vision of the unity between the cosmos and human beings:

> Only those who are absolutely sincere can fully develop their nature. If they can fully develop their nature, they can then fully develop the nature of others. If they can fully develop the nature of others, they can then fully develop the nature of things. If they can fully develop the nature of things, they can then assist in the transforming and nourishing process of Heaven and Earth. If they can assist in the transforming and nourishing process of Heaven and Earth, they can thus form a trinity with Heaven and Earth.[4]

This statement demonstrates the unity and interaction between the cosmos and human beings. Furthermore, the idea of "sincerity" (*ch'eng*) plays a central role in connecting human beings to Heaven and Earth. However, it was during the Neo-Confucian period that the most comprehensive and elaborate cosmology was developed. For example, the concept of "sincerity" contained within it an important metaphysical, even spiritual, notion that went beyond mere moral or ethical significance.[5] The cosmological assertion in the *Doctrine of the Mean* was clearly "anthropocosmic" in stating that the development of "sincerity" from human beings to Heaven and Earth centered around the idea of the extension of human beings to Heaven and Earth. Some Neo-Confucian thinkers, however, developed a Neo-Confucian cosmology based on cosmological and ontological concepts. The Great Ultimate (*t'ai-chi*), for example, became one of the most fundamental cosmological ideas running through the whole Neo-Confucian cosmology and a unifying concept penetrating the universe, nature, and human beings. In this respect, *t'ai-chi* is the foundation of a "cosmoanthropic" vision.

Unlike Classical Confucianism, including Confucius himself who stated, "It is man that can make the Way great, and not the Way that can make man great,"[6] Neo-Confucianism explicitly explored the intrinsic unity of the way of human beings and the way of Heaven. The Neo-Confucian idea of the sage is of one who relates the way of Heaven and the way of human beings. Although the *Doctrine of the Mean* gave expression to the trinity of Heaven, Earth, and human beings, it was Neo-Confucianism that fully developed the cosmological significance of this insight in relating human beings to the universe. The well-known Neo-Confucian dual concepts of "principle" (*li*) and "material force" (*ch'i*), for example, were developed as cosmological and ontological concepts but also became anthropological concepts. The concept of "principle" (*li*) was not only a cosmological notion but was also an important anthropological and moral concept in relation to "human nature" (*hsing*). Neo-Confucianism was thus often referred to as the school of "human nature and principle" (*hsing-li-hsüeh*).

The idea of "material force" (*ch'i*) was also developed around the relationship of the universe, nature, and human beings. Neo-Confucian scholars, such as Chou Tun-i and Chang Tsai, and some Korean Neo-Confucian thinkers, including Sŏ Kyŏngdŏk, or Hwadam (1489–1546), and Yi Yulgok, developed a Neo-Confucian cosmology with the concept of *ch'i* in relation to origin and the dynamic process of the cosmos in relation to the dimension of human feelings and activities. It was another great Korean Neo-Confucian thinker, Yi Hwang (known by his pen name, T'oegye; 1501–1570), however, who further elaborated the moral and ethical implications of the cosmological concept of *li*. Both T'oegye and Yulgok tried to develop a coherent Neo-Confucian cosmology based on the concepts of principle and material force. T'oegye articulated an "anthropological cosmology" based on a dualistic understanding of principle and material force: principle has a moral quality, while material force has no moral implications. For T'oegye, principle has an inherent moral implication of "good," and this moral implication was based on his anthropological idea of principle. For him, human nature and principle are the same and thus principle must be good. Yulgok, however, developed his cosmology based on a nondualistic understanding of principle and material force. For Yulgok, neither principle nor material force has any intrinsic moral implication; rather, they are cosmological concepts that gain moral significance when applied to human beings, since human beings are not free of a moral dimension. We see here a contrast between two cosmological models: T'oegye formulated his cosmology based on an anthropological assumption of principle and material force, while Yulgok developed his cosmology without any presupposed anthropological assumptions: principle and material force are fundamentally and originally value-free cosmological concepts or ontological notions. In other words, T'oegye's approach was anthropologically oriented in its interpretation of the Neo-Confucian concepts of principle and material force, whereas Yulgok's was cosmologically oriented in formulating the two concepts. These two different approaches have enormous significance in understanding the controversy regarding the "Four-Seven" debate as well as the debate of the "moral mind" (*tao-hsin*) vs. the "human mind" (*jen-hsin*).[7] The first debate centered upon the Four Beginnings (found in the *Mencius*), or the moral qualities of human beings, and the Seven Emotions (mentioned in the *Doctrine of the Mean*), or human feelings. At issue were whether the Four Beginnings and the Seven Emotions were feelings and how they related to principle and material force. The discussions on the moral mind and human mind refer to the understanding in Confucianism that the human mind is seen as wavering, while the Way mind is not easily perceptible. Thus, proper moral discernment is frequently extremely difficult.

Another significant discussion relevant to our examination of a Confucian ecological cosmology was the "*horak*" debate, which concerned the question of how human beings and every other being could share the same principle and human beings could still be different.[8] The main issue involved the question of "universality" and "particularity." Yulgok understood that principle is universal, so that human beings and all other beings share the same principle, but, at the same time, this principle also becomes a specific principle in individual beings due to material force. Yulgok formulated his own theory of the relationship between principle and material force: "'principle' penetrates and 'material force' delimits."[9] For Yulgok, principle is universal, while material force makes this universal principle specific and particular. His theory influenced the "*horak*" debate regarding the relationship between human beings and all other beings in terms of their commonality and particularity. For Yulgok, as for many other Neo-Confucian scholars, principle is the Great Ultimate (*t'ai-chi*). The Great Ultimate is not only the cosmic and universal principle but also the principle of individual being.

T'ai-chi *Is One Yet Many*

T'ai-chi is a unifying principle and also a diversifying or multiplying principle. Paradoxically, *t'ai-chi* is the most universal and yet the most concrete. For Yulgok, *t'ai-chi* is a general principle in the universe and a specific principle in every being, including human beings. This *t'ai-chi* resides in the very transmutation of yin and yang. Yin-yang is the symbol of this *t'ai-chi*. In other words, the house of *t'ai-chi* is yin and yang. *T'ai-chi* cannot exist by itself without yin-yang. *T'ai-chi* manifests itself only through the inter-action of yin and yang. Yin-yang is a cosmic and a dynamic process of *being* and *becoming*. The form of existence, the way of manifes-tation, the mode of expression of *t'ai-chi* are all found in the yin-yang interaction. Comprehension and understanding of *t'ai-chi* is possible only through this interaction of yin-yang. For this reason, in my view, the idea of yin-yang is not to be termed a "concept" or a "notion"; it should be understood, rather, as a profound *symbol*. A symbol has the power to express reality without reducing it to mere logical formula or rational or "scientific" system. The implication of yin-yang symbolism is critical in understanding Neo-Confucian cosmology. Neo-Confucian cosmology, and especially Yulgok's cosmology, is based on this yin-yang symbol.[10] In my view, while *li* and *ch'i* are *conceptually* structured, *t'ai-chi* and yin-yang are *symbolic* manifestations of Neo-Confucian cosmology. It is interesting that the yin-yang symbol is one of the most well-known, popular symbols, not only in East Asia but also in America. Historically, the yin-yang symbol and *t'ai-chi* were favorite subjects

for diagraming, especially by Neo-Confucian thinkers, who used
them in their cosmological diagrams. Functionally, yin-yang and
t'ai-chi are often combined in one symbol, as seen in the national
flag of Korea.

Although most of us recognize the yin-yang and *t'ai-chi* symbols,
many of us do not fully appreciate the true significance of these
symbols. We have to make an attempt to understand Neo-Confucian
cosmology on two different levels: a conceptual level and a
symbolic level. Here, "symbolic" does not mean a mere formality,
but rather it means a holistic approach, beyond concept, to the
reality. The complexity and the richness of the Neo-Confucian
worldview lie exactly in this intricate relationship between the
cosmological symbols of *t'ai-chi* and yin-yang and the conceptual
framework of *li* and *ch'i*. Epistemologically speaking, the concept
is created for *apprehending* the rational structure of the reality, while
the symbol is used in *appreciating* beyond rationality, the mystery
of the reality. Concept is an *active* process while symbol is a *passive*
aspect of the understanding of reality. For example, the trigrams and
hexagrams, including the Sixty-four Hexagrams found in the *I ching*,
are *symbolic* manifestations, not mechanical representations, of the
reality of the universe. These symbols, however, are open to human
interpretation. The numbers and images in the *I ching* are symbols,
and each number, image, or trigram denotes certain corresponding
realities. Neo-Confucian arguments of *li* and *chi*, however, are
largely conceptually structured.

The Neo-Confucian fascination with cosmology grew out of the
rediscovery and reinterpretation of the *I ching*. As we will see in
the case of Yi Yulgok, Neo-Confucian interest in cosmology,
ontology, and anthropology was much influenced by the *I ching*.

What was the reason for Yulgok's interest in the *I ching* and his
fascination with the interpretation of the *I ching*? Yulgok studied
the *I ching* carefully and understood not only its cosmological structure but also its symbolic system. Influenced by the numerical cosmology of Shao Yung (1011–1077), Yulgok attempted to relate the
most prominent Neo-Confucian conceptual system of *li* and *ch'i* to
the most profound cosmological symbols of yin-yang and *t'ai-chi*.
Yulgok employed the Neo-Confucian conceptual tools *li* and *ch'i*
to analyze the ontological reality of the universe, but he employed
the symbols of yin-yang and *t'ai-chi* in the *I ching* in order to

comprehend the wonders of the universe. Yulgok wrote two well-known treatises, as part of the series of civil service examinations he took: the "Treatise on Changes and Numbers" (*Yŏksuch'aek*) and the "Treatise on the Way of Heaven" (*Ch'ŏndoch'aek*). The former explicates the symbolic structure of the universe manifested in numbers and images. The latter analyzes the rational structure of *li* and *ch'i* and their mutual relationship in understanding each and every being in the universe: *ch'i* causes what it is, *li* is the reason why it is[11] (a Neo-Confucian "ontological argument," so to speak). Yulgok combined the symbolic structure and conceptual framework in order to understand the state of *being* in the universe and the universe itself. This is Yulgok's unique contribution to the development of Neo-Confucian cosmology and ontology. For Yulgok, the cosmos was not just an *object* of human analysis but a *subject* to be appreciated, observed, or even encountered by humans. Yulgok thus developed a comprehensive way of understanding, and a proper way to relate to, the universe.

In his *Yŏksuch'aek*, or "Treatise on Changes and Numbers," Yulgok tried to establish the three fundamental frameworks for understanding and relating to the cosmos or the universe. These were as follows:

1. The symbolic structure as shown in the *I ching* and the numbers employed in it indicate that the universe is neither a fixed physical object nor a mere mechanical entity; rather, it is a living, dynamic, and changing reality.

2. The universe is not a mere physical reality but, more importantly, a *hermeneutical* reality: human understanding and interpretation of the universe, through the images, numbers, and hexagrams, play a critical role in the comprehensive process of the universe. For this reason, we may even say that human interpretation and understanding of the universe becomes a part of *being* the universe.

This is the case especially in Yulgok's cosmological construction. Although we have the inherent symbolic structure of the universe as illustrated in the *I ching*, the three sages, Wen, the first king of the early Chou period, the duke of Chou, and Confucius, clarified the significance of the numbers and images of the *I ching* and passed this knowledge on to later generations.[12] The human being is an active agent in the interpretive process of understanding the symbolic structure of the universe. The sage as a true human being is able to listen to the sound of the universe and interacts with, interprets, and communicates with the universe:

> Heaven and Earth wait for sages, with numbers, to show [the meaning of the universe] to the world. Sages wait for the clue of written characters to show the principle to the world. Heaven has to beget sages and sages have to produce the clue of the written characters to show to the world. This is the response of nature and the mutual interaction and mysteries of Heaven and human beings.[13]

It was also crucial for a sage to interact with the universe:

> The virtue of a sage is to coincide with Heaven and Earth. Their brilliance is like the sun and the moon. Their order coincides with the four seasons.[14]

3. The universe is an open system with a certain principle and regularity. The Sixty-four Hexagrams, for example, appear to be a limited number of variations, but when taken in symbolic form, they can provide unlimited possibilities of being in the universe: "In general, we know the limited variations of the Sixty-four Hexagrams but we do not know the inexhaustible functions of the Sixty-four Hexagrams."[15] These possibilities and variations, however, are governed by inherent patterns, norms, and principle (*li*). The principle and patterns of this dynamic process are called the Way (*Tao*). Thus, every being in the universe, and the universe itself, is governed by a certain principle (*li*). In this sense, the universe for Yulgok is an open system, not total *chaos* but a *cosmos*: it is an orderly universe but not a closed system.

The Sanctity and Mystery of the Universe

Yulgok believed that the universe could not be completely comprehended by human intelligence or through human thought processes. He believed that the universe is a "mystery" not to be reduced to the rational or conceptual framework of a human intellectual system. This dimension of mystery causes us to feel that the universe is sacred; hence, we have a sense of awe toward the universe. The universe "manifests" itself to us as much as it "conceals" itself from us. This is the power of symbol, which *reveals* without *defining*, or delimiting, itself. The universe reveals and the humans (sages) decipher the meaning of the universe or try to understand the working of the universe. A Confucian sage may not necessarily be an astrologer but must be able to understand Confucian cosmological assumptions and to discern their human implications. For this reason, even sage kings made use of sorcery or divination, not because of their blind trust in the practice but because of the acceptance of their intellectual limitations and their willingness to listen to the mysteries of the universe.[16] This attitude depicts the universe as a sacred vessel which generates a sense of awe as we observe it. As such, the Neo-Confucian understanding of divination or sorcery was not, in any sense, intended as an acceptance of a fatalistic or deterministic view of the universe and human beings but as recognition of the interrelationship of human beings and the universe. The universe, for Yulgok, was not an object to be mastered but a subject to be understood. This, however, does not imply that we subjugate our subjectivity to the universe nor reduce the subjectivity of the universe to the object of our knowledge. Rather, Yulgok's Neo-Confucian understanding of the human relationship with the universe was not a "subject to object" relationship but one of "subject to subject." We may approach the universe as a subject without reducing ourselves to the level of an object: human beings are not to be subordinated to the universe and likewise are not to treat the universe as an object and so dominate the universe. This intersubjectivity reflects the Confucian sage's relationship with the universe.

Yulgok's Approach to T'ai-chi *and Yin-Yang*

It would be useful to compare Yulgok's approach to *t'ai-chi* with that of Chou Tun-i (1017–1073). Chou Tun-i was another great scholar who developed Neo-Confucian cosmology in terms of an orderly emanation of the universe. For Chou Tun-i, *t'ai-chi* was a first cause of being:

> The Great Ultimate [*t'ai-chi*] through movement generates yang. When its activity reaches its limit, it becomes tranquil. Through tranquillity the Great Ultimate generates yin. When tranquillity reaches its limit, activity begins again.[17]

Here we see that *t'ai-chi*, as the source, or origin, of all beings, generates yin and yang, which means that *t'ai-chi* is a primary source of yin and yang. Such an explanation is highly logical, conceptual, and hierarchical. This sort of cosmology reflects a human, rational conception imposed on the universe. Shao Yung and Yulgok, however, understood *t'ai-chi*, not logically, but symbolically. Yulgok, for example, was more interested in *observing* the mystery of the universe than in *analyzing, conceptualizing,* and *rationalizing* the universe. "Observation" has the significant implication of being "passive": positioning human beings *under* the universe for *under*-standing. "Analysis" has an "active" connotation: placing human beings *over* the universe in order to conceptualize it. We may belong to or be a part of a symbol, but we cannot own a symbol; we may invent or create a concept, but we may not belong to it.

Yulgok understood *t'ai-chi*, not as an origin in terms of a physical entity, but as a phenomenon, or manifestation, of the yin-yang movement. *T'ai-chi* is nothing but the movement of yin and yang, and he therefore believed *t'ai-chi* to exist equally in yin as well as yang. The alternation and the transmutation of yin and yang is the most profoundly symbolic way to understand and to experience our cosmic dwelling (house, or *oikos*). In this way, the universe does not become the object of my "study" or "analysis" but is the mystery which we all observe.

If *t'ai-chi* does not have any independent substance apart from being in the interaction of yin and yang, why do we need the idea of *t'ai-chi* at all? How does *t'ai-chi* function in the universe and in all beings? Yulgok made the following statement on *t'ai-chi*:

> The myriad things are one: [this one is] the Five Forces and the Five Forces are one; [this one is] yin and yang, and yin and yang are one; [this one is] t'ai chi. T'ai chi is nothing but a *name* (or *symbol*) when we are forced to name it. Its substance [t'i] is change [i], its principle [li] is called way [Tao], its function [yung] is called spirit [shen].[18] (Italic mine)

The phenomena of the universe is not an object of our logical, rational, analytical, hierarchical, and scientific investigation but a subject to appreciate, to observe, to listen to and to learn from.

Yulgok treated nature and the universe as a subject requiring a holistic approach because the universe is "one" integrated reality. We may use concepts and the processes of analysis when we investigate an object (subject-object relation), but when we confront a subject (subject-subject relation), we need a holistic, comprehensive, immediate, and intuitive approach—what I would call a symbolic approach. Yulgok accepted the universe as "one," and then he observed the intricate workings of yin-yang, the Five Forces (Agents), without losing the sense of "one." Also, Yulgok saw the nature of *t'ai-chi* in the unity and alternation of the yin-yang symbol. In Yulgok's vision, *t'ai-chi* is a unity of "substance," "change," and "manifestation." This holistic and comprehensive understanding of *t'ai-chi* was well expressed in the trinitarian formula of Yulgok's thinking regarding "substance," "principle," and "function" of *t'ai-chi*. In contrast to Chou Tun-i, Yulgok saw the "substance" of *t'ai-chi* as "change." *T'ai-chi* is not a static "concept" but a dynamic and living "symbol"; thus, the substance of *t'ai-chi* is change. Yulgok was neither an essentialist nor a substantialist but a keen observer who was able to see change as substance.

The principle (*li*) governing this change is the Way (*Tao*). The Way, here, means the subtle alternation of yin and yang. The function, or manifestation, of *t'ai-chi* is "spirit," which is neither comprehensible nor explainable, but its presence is in all beings. It is interesting to note that Yulgok used the *t'i* (substance) and *yung* (function) conceptual scheme well known in Hua-yen Buddhism to show his understanding of *t'ai-chi*. Yulgok saw this substance and function of *t'ai-chi*, not in a dialectical dichotomy, but as a subtle movement of interaction: substance is substanceless change, so function is incomprehensible mystery. Or, we can state that the working, or function, of *t'ai-chi* is incomprehensible mystery, and its substance must be change. Here, "spirit," unlike a ghost which is detached from matter, is the inherent part of being and becoming matter that reflects Confucian spirituality.

Yulgok's approach in his "Treatise on Changes and Numbers" (*Yŏksuch'aek*) was holistic, comprehensive, even mystic, emphasizing the mystery and delicacy of the function of *t'ai-chi*. In his "Treatise on the Way of Heaven" (*Ch'ŏndoch'aek*), Yulgok becomes much more analytical and specific in explaining the concrete phenomenon of the universe. As we have seen, Yulgok explains all phenomena of the universe in terms of yin and yang, but in his *Ch'ŏndoch'aek* he introduces the paired concept, *li* (principle) and *ch'i* (material force), to explain how yin and yang become possible:

> When *ch'i* becomes active it is yang, when passive, yin; thus yang and yin are not two different elements but rather two different appearances or phenomena of *ch'i*. Yet while *ch'i* is the source of yin and yang—that is, the stuff that becomes either yin or yang— the law which governs its mutation is *li*.[19]

Furthermore, Yulgok also relates the *li* and *ch'i* of the universe to human beings:

> The human mind and the mind of Heaven are the same. When the human mind is right, the mind of Heaven is also right. When the *ch'i* of humans is in order, the *ch'i* of Heaven and Earth is also in order.[20]

Yulgok's idea of *ch'i* also reflects his idea of cosmology. Yulgok should not be defined as either a *li*-oriented or a *ch'i*-oriented thinker. Rather, he should be seen as a nondualistic thinker. He was not terribly concerned about the metaphysical or conceptual structure of the universe in terms of *li*, nor did he abandon *li* and plunge into *ch'i* alone. He rejected any preconceived idea of *li* without the concrete shape and form of *ch'i* manifestation. The working of *ch'i* is always so subtle and mysterious that we cannot comprehend it with the prestructured rational system or logical process of *li*. Instead, whenever and wherever the concrete form or shape of *ch'i* manifestation occurs, *li* is there. "*Ch'i* arises" and "*li* rides" was Yulgok's formula. For this reason, he may be considered a *ch'i* philosopher. But Yulgok was not a *ch'i* monist. Yulgok was quite reluctant to formulate or develop a coherent cosmology consistent with *li* (principle) because the cosmos cannot be comprehended through any system or structure of *li*. Rather, Yulgok's approach was to observe, appreciate, and marvel at the working of *ch'i* in multiplicity, after which he could humbly explore and learn how *li* is inherent in all beings without ever imposing a universal formula or rational structure.

Toward Cosmological Ecology

Our concern here has been to find an ecological significance implied in Yulgok's cosmological approach but not to formulate Yulgok's cosmology per se. Neo-Confucian cosmology can be a good resource for us to use in exploring the ecological dimensions of Neo-Confucianism before we move on to investigate the ecological and environmental ethics of the Confucian and Neo-Confucian tradition. We should not rush headlong into the establishment of a Confucian environmental ethics based solely on fragments of Confucian and Neo-Confucian teachings. What we need to do, rather, is to reflect on Confucianism as a whole from the perspective of an ecosystem. Neo-Confucian cosmology does certainly provide a foundation for this reflection in terms of relating human beings and the earth to the universe. However, we have to acknowledge that some of the predominant Neo-Confucian scholars, including Chu Hsi and T'oegye, who became the foremost authority on Chu Hsi in Korea, inclined toward an anthropological cosmology, an understanding of the universe from a human standpoint. Yulgok, however, developed his cosmology from a cosmic point of view independent of human values—that is, Yulgok's understanding of Neo-Confucian concepts, such as *li* and *ch'i*, was not necessarily solely associated with moral significance or human values.

In order to develop a Confucian ecology, we must first make an attempt to liberate ecology from anthropocentrism. Confucian humanism must not be understood as anthropocentrism. Confucian humanism is a unique kind of humanism that goes beyond human interest, extending to a realm that relates human beings to Heaven and Earth. Confucian humanism understands human beings, not only from a "human" point of view, but also from a cosmic point of view. The full significance of a human being is found in the relationship to Heaven and Earth, realizing the Heavenly endowed potential in the human. The sage is the person who fully realizes his or her Heavenly endowed potential.

The Confucian sage is the person who truly practices "reciprocity" (*shu*)—"Do not do to others what you do not want them to do to you"[21]—not only in human, social contexts but in the context of nature and the universe. In this respect, Confucian humanism is based on a reciprocal relationship with Heaven and Earth, nature and the universe. Reciprocity can be achieved when we become receptive. In this sense, a Confucian sage is a receptive person who is able to discern the signs of Heaven and Earth. Observation and discernment can be achieved through receptivity.

Ecology, thus, must be based on a reciprocal receptivity with nature and the universe, by "seeing" and "listening" to the wonder, mystery, and pain of the universe. Passive and receptive aspects are important elements in developing a cosmological anthropology rather than an anthropological cosmology: human beings must be understood in light of the universe rather than the human rationality or *logos* being imposed on the universe. Ecology based on anthro-pological cosmology will become anthropological ecology, which is but another form of anthropocentrism. The term *eco-logy* may not be the right one for the direction I have been exploring in this chapter. What we need to develop, instead, is a cosmological ecology that will help us open up to the universe and learn from the cosmos. Since the term ecology holds within it misleading concepts, it may be worthwhile to look for a better word to express the approach that reflects a receptive attitude toward nature and the universe.[22]

Cosmological ecology is neither a logic nor a system but an awareness of the universe. The sage is the person who has developed the wisdom and art of seeing and listening in order to feel and be able to respond to Heaven and Earth.

Notes

1. Huston Smith's claim, "Tao Now," clearly illustrates this attitude. See his "Tao Now: An Ecological Testament," in *Earth Might Be Fair: Reflections on Ethics, Religion, and Ecology*, ed. Ian G. Barbour (Englewood Cliffs, N.J.: Prentice-Hall, 1972), 62–81.

2. I use the term "worldview" in the way Ninian Smart uses it when he speaks of "worldview analysis." See Ninian Smart, *Worldviews: Crosscultural Explorations of Human Beliefs* (New York: Scribner's, 1983).

3. Lynn White, Jr., "The Historical Roots of Our Ecologic Crisis," in *Western Man and Environmental Ethics: Attitudes toward Nature and Technology*, ed. Ian G. Barbour (Reading, Mass.: Addison-Wesley, 1973), 27–28. Originally published in *Science* 155 (March 1967):1203–7.

4. *A Source Book in Chinese Philosophy*, trans. Wing-tsit Chan (Princeton: Princeton University Press, 1963), 107–8.

5. For a comprehensive understanding of "sincerity" (*ch'eng*), see Young-chan Ro, *The Korean Neo-Confucianism of Yi Yulgok* (Albany: State University of New York Press, 1989), 75–110.

6. *Analects*, 15:28, in Chan, *A Source Book in Chinese Philosophy*, 44.

7. The "Four-Seven" debate was the most famous Korean Neo-Confucian achievement. The issues involved in this debate were discussed in detail in the following three books: Michael Kalton et al., *The Four-Seven Debate* (Albany: State University of New York Press, 1994); Edward Y. J. Chung, *The Korean Neo-Confucianism of Yi T'oegye and Yi Yulgok* (Albany: State University of New York Press, 1995); and Ro, *The Korean Neo-Confucianism of Yi Yulgok*.

8. The "*horak*" debate, another Korean Neo-Confucian scholarly debate, came after the "Four-Seven" debate. This debate is of ecological significance because it deals with issues of human nature and the nature of other beings. For more information, see Hyun Sang-yun, *Chosŏn Yuhaksa* (History of Korean Confucianism) (Seoul: Minjungsŏkwan, 1949), 284–87. See also Bae Chong-ho, *Hanguk Yuhaksa* (History of Korean Confucianism) (Seoul: Yonsei University Press, 1974), 210–40.

9. This is Yulgok's famous theory, "*it'ong kiguk/li-t'ung ch'i-chu*," *Yulgok chŏnsŏ*, 10:26a (vol. 1, 209), cited in Chung, *The Korean Neo-Confucianism*, 114; see also 252, note 186.

10. By "symbol" I mean a way of knowing that is comprehensive, holistic, intuitive, and immediate. A symbol has the unique power of grasping a reality without going through a "rational" or "conceptual" process. I would like to argue, in this respect, that yin-yang and *t'ai-chi* belong in the category of symbol rather than concept. This is evident when we look at other significant religious symbols, such as the star of David or the cross, which represent the reality as understood in Judaism or in Christianity. Although Yulgok never used the term "symbol" in

his explanation of *t'ai-chi* and yin-yang, his way of exploring the significance of the *I ching*, however, was "symbolically" oriented. Some modern thinkers, including Paul Tillich, Paul Ricoeur, and Raimon Panikkar, have expounded the meaning of symbol in a way that may help in understanding Yulgok's approach to the symbolic structure of the *I ching* in general and to its cosmological ideas, *t'ai-chi* and yin-yang.

11. *Yulgok chŏnsŏ*, vol. 1 (Seoul: Songgyungwon University Press, 1971), 308 (kwon 14:55b).

12. Ibid., 14:48b.

13. Ibid., 14:49a.

14. Ibid., 14:50b.

15. Ibid.

16. Ibid., 14:51a.

17. Chou Tun-i, in Chan, *A Source Book in Chinese Philosophy*, 463.

18. Ro, *The Korean Neo-Confucianism of Yi Yulgok*, 30.

19. *Yulgok chŏnsŏ*, kwon 14:55.

20. Ibid., 14:55b.

21. *Analects*, 15:23, in Chan, *A Source Book in Chinese Philosophy*, 44.

22. Raimon Panikkar, for example, suggests the term "ecosophy." For more discussion on ecosophy, see Raimon Panikkar, "Ecosophy," *The New Gaia: The World as Sanctuary* (Gregory, Miss.: Eco-Philosophy Center) 4, no. 1 (winter 1995):2–7.

The Philosophy of *Ch'i* as an Ecological Cosmology

Mary Evelyn Tucker

Introduction

The ecological crisis of the late twentieth century reflects a profound alienation from nature and indeed from matter itself.[1] In trying to resituate ourselves in relation to the earth, it has become apparent that we have lost our understanding of the nature of matter and materiality.[2] Our feeling of alienation in the modern period has extended beyond the human community and its patterns of material exchanges to our interaction with nature itself. Thomas Berry has suggested that we have become autistic in our interactions with the natural world and that we need a new cosmology and cultural coding to overcome this deprivation.[3]

The reexamination of other worldviews, philosophies, and religions may be critical to our recovery of a sufficiently comprehensive cosmology for the twenty-first century. Clearly, within the Confucian tradition of East Asia there are rich resources for understanding how others have viewed nature and the role of the human in nature. From the early integration of the human into the great triad with Heaven and Earth, to seeing the dynamic interactions of nature as expressed in the *Book of Changes (I ching)*, to the more complex metaphysical discussions of the relationship of principle (*li*) and material force (*ch'i*), the Confucian worldview provides a wealth of suggestive resources for rethinking our contemporary situation. This essay will focus, in particular, on the philosophy of material force (*ch'i*) in Confucianism as a means of contributing to larger contemporary discussions on the relationship of matter and spirit so vital to new perspectives in the current ecological crisis.

The idea of *ch'i* emerges in the early classical Confucian period in China and suggests a unified vision of reality as composed of matter and energy. In the Neo-Confucian era the philosophy of *ch'i* develops metaphysically this essential understanding of the profound interconnection of matter and spirit. It also gives us a worldview which affirms the significance of materiality in such a way as to have important implications for both ethics and empiricism. Ethically, the idea of *ch'i* provides a basis for a this-worldly spirituality which reveres humans and nature as part of a single continuum of *ch'i*. Empirically, it suggests a rationale for affirming the importance of matter, of sense knowledge, and of the investigation of things in this world. The philosophy of *ch'i*, then, provides a nondualistic cosmology for going beyond the conventional Western separations of matter and spirit, mind and body.

The Philosophy of *Ch'i*

It is against the broader background of the Neo-Confucian concern for the importance of cultivating the individual, of understanding moral principles, and of affirming the connection of humans to a dynamic, changing natural order that the philosophy of *ch'i* arose. The Neo-Confucians were interested in developing a clear metaphysical understanding of the relationship of humans to nature through *ch'i* so as to "assist in the transforming and nourishing process of Heaven and Earth"[4] more effectively. While these discussions at times appeared somewhat abstract and theoretical, they had practical implications for metaphysics, ethics, and empiricism. They helped to provide the cosmological basis for a profoundly this-worldly spirituality which affirmed the importance of matter, of the body, of human emotions, of change, and of investigation of the natural world.

The philosophy of *ch'i* arose as a result of certain ambiguities regarding the relationship between *li* (principle) and *ch'i* (material force) in the thought of the great Neo-Confucian synthesizer, Chu Hsi (1130–1200). A debate emerged between those who supported Chu Hsi's apparent dualism of *li* and *ch'i* and those who advocated a monism of *ch'i*, also known as a philosophy of *ch'i*. It is the aim of this paper to trace the emergence of the philosophy of *ch'i* from the classical period in Mencius's thought to the Neo-Confucianism of Chang Tsai (1020–1077). I will then discuss the evolution of the philosophy of *ch'i* in two principal East Asian thinkers in China and Japan, namely, Lo Ch'in-shun (1465–1547) and Kaibara Ekken (1630–1714). Let me first review why this topic is of importance in relation to new ecological perspectives.

The Significance of *Ch'i* as an Ecological Cosmology

One of the contemporary legacies of the eighteenth-century French Enlightenment is the separation of matter and spirit and the devaluing in religious circles of the former over the latter. Because nature has become largely identified as matter which can be manipulated, the sense of reverence for nature has been removed and the grounds for exploitation set in place. Nature is seen as a "resource" to be used rather than a "source" of all life to be respected. We need new understandings, from a variety of traditions, of material reality as not simply a dead inanimate thing, but as something infused with life, dynamism, energy, and transformative possibilities.

This sense that matter and energy are not just mechanical processes but also spiritual processes is beginning to be recovered.[5] That sensibility regarding matter is what has been removed from modern consciousness and has given rise to a crisis of culture, a crisis of the environment, and a crisis of the spirit. We have lost a sense of reciprocity with and relatedness to nature, the cosmos, and other species and forms of life in part because we have privileged the spiritual as a transcendent entity and have drained it from the world of matter.

The philosophy of *ch'i* has several rich potential contributions to make in this regard:

1. It shows the continuance of a substratum of a nature-based, interconnected worldview of the indigenous religions, which is still present in the later religious traditions. In other words, *ch'i* reflects a synthesis of earlier religious worldviews of indigenous traditions in their closeness to nature within that of the later religious traditions, which tend to emphasize transcendence over nature. This synthesis represents in Confucianism a distinctive interweaving of immanence and transcendence.

2. It provides a cosmological basis for understanding the identity and difference of various life-forms. Namely, it asserts a common

ground for all living things by recognizing that while *ch'i* runs through everything, it provides the basis for making distinctions.

3. It encourages an understanding of the connection of the human mind-and-heart to nature and thus provides a basis for reciprocity and relationship with all life-forms. Indeed, it establishes an important grounding for a comprehensive environmental ethics.

4. It suggests a way of accounting for change and transformation in the cosmos which recognizes the vitality and dynamism of the universe and the special relation of humans to this process.

5. It affirms the role of the human in the unfolding, transforming universe. The human is seen as "assist[ing] in the transforming and nourishing processes of Heaven and Earth."[6] Indeed, the human completes the triad of Heaven and Earth and thus is an essential component of it. In light of this, a philosophy of *ch'i* becomes the grounds for avoiding quietism and for affirming action in the world.

6. The implications for social and political ethics are significant because all of life is made up of *ch'i*, and *ch'i* provides a context for identifying with other humans and with other communities. Through such identification, social and political participation, especially by the educated scholar-official class, was regarded by Confucians as essential to the creation of benevolent governments and humane societies.

7. The philosophy of *ch'i* also has implications for a kind of "empiricism" known as "practical learning" (Chinese, *shih-hsüeh*; Japanese, *jitsugaku*). It helped to encourage the "investigation of things" through the study of such subjects as history, agriculture, natural history, medicine, and astronomy.

The Term *Ch'i*

Wing-tsit Chan has translated *ch'i* as "material force," namely, something which consists of both matter and energy. Chan notes that before the notion of *li* developed in the Neo-Confucian tradition, *ch'i* referred to the "psychophysiological power associated with blood and breath."[7] He suggests that the terms "matter" and "ether" are not adequate translations for *ch'i* because they only convey one aspect of the term.[8]

The term *ch'i* is present in early Chinese thought in the *I ching*, along with the cosmological concepts of yin and yang and the Five Phases.

It is also found in the *Tso chuan,* the *Kuo yu,* and the *Kuan tzu.*

The term *ch'i* appears in the Classical period in Mencius, where he refers to *ch'i* as "that which fills the body."[9] In this context, *ch'i* can be translated as "vital force," or "vital power."[10] Mencius notes that the *ch'i* which fills one's body is directed by the will. He observes that it is important not to abuse or block one's *ch'i* but to allow it to flow with appropriate direction. If one does this and nourishes one's *ch'i,* it will fill the space between Heaven and Earth. A famous reference in *Mencius* speaks of a "flood-like *ch'i,*" sometimes translated as a "strong, moving power."[11] Mencius says that this "flood-like *ch'i*" is difficult to explain. He comments, none-theless, on the importance of nourishing it for he says that *ch'i* is:

> . . .in the highest degree, vast and unyielding. Nourish it with integrity and place no obstacle in its path and it will fill the space between Heaven and Earth. It is a *ch'i* which unites rightness and the Way. Deprive it of these and it will collapse. It is born of accumulated rightness and cannot be appropriated by anyone through a sporadic show of rightness. Whenever one acts in a way that falls below the standard set in one's heart, it will collapse.[12]

It is clear that this psychophysical energy must be cultivated carefully, for it is that which links us to all other living things. In other words, in humans *ch'i* is a special form of material energy which can be nurtured by self-cultivation. This contributes to our moral and physical well-being and provides a basis for respecting other humans. The whole universe is, likewise, filled with the matter-energy of *ch'i.* By nourishing not only our own *ch'i* but also the consciousness of our connection to this energy in nature, we become full participants in the dynamic, transformative processes of the universe. That is because *ch'i* is the underlying unity of life that is simultaneously moral and physical, spiritual and material. These ideas are further developed by Chang Tsai, Chu Hsi, and the other Neo-Confucians.

Chang Tsai's Development of *Ch'i*

Chang Tsai's great contribution to Neo-Confucian thought was his explanation of *ch'i* as the vital material force which runs throughout creation. *Ch'i* is in a constant process of transformation that is self-generating. This change, however, is not simply random, illusory, or purposeless. Underlying the dynamic movement of *ch'i* is the pattern of the alteration of the yin and yang. Thus all change, he asserts, occurs by means of principles (*li*). These principles, or patterns of change, are not simply repetitious or static entities. Each event, thing, or person is unique and hence of moral value in the continually unfolding process of *ch'i*. "In what has been created through stages of formation and transformation, no single thing (in the universe) is exactly like another."[13] The constantly changing quality of *ch'i*, then, is its dynamic force, which reveals both pattern and uniqueness as inherent in the universe.

Chang Tsai took an important step for Neo-Confucian metaphysics when he proceeded to identify *ch'i* with the void or the Great Vacuity (*t'ai-hsü*). T'ang Chun-i sees this as an attempt to synthesize the notion of *ch'i* developed by the scholars of the Ch'in and the Han with the emptiness of the Taoists and the Buddhists.[14] There are two extremely significant consequences of this synthesis which T'ang Chun-i characterizes as the vertical aspect and the horizontal aspect. By the vertical aspect Chang essentially provides a basis for asserting the unity of being and nonbeing, thus challenging what he perceived to be the Buddhist and Taoist positions on emptiness and nonbeing. In the horizontal aspect Chang provided a metaphysical explanation for intercommunion and change by means of the voidness of *ch'i*. Both these dimensions—the vertical and horizontal—laid the groundwork for Chang Tsai's theory of mind. Essentially, he was aiming to show the intrinsic connection between the human mind and the cosmic order through the principle of *ch'i*. Humans have the potential for understanding the underlying unity of *ch'i* behind all forms of change. Furthermore, humans have the capacity for intersubjective empathy with all of creation through comprehending the constant fusion and diffusion of *ch'i*.

The Vertical Aspect of Chang Tsai's Synthesis: Metaphysical Implications

In developing the concept of *ch'i*, Chang Tsai, like the other Neo-Confucians before him, drew on the *Book of Changes* as one of his chief sources of inspiration. Chang Tsai's cosmology is distinctive, however, in that he identifies material force (*ch'i*) with the Great

Ultimate (*t'ai-chi*). He describes the two aspects of *ch'i* as its substance and its function. As substance it is known as the Great Vacuity (*t'ai-hsü*), which is the primal undifferentiated material force, while as function it is the Great Harmony (*t'ai-ho*), which is the continual process of integration and disintegration. The significance of differentiating this dual aspect of *ch'i* is to affirm the underlying unity of being and nonbeing, of the seen and the unseen. Thus, both inner spirit and external transformation are understood as part of a whole that is the constant appearance and disappearance of *ch'i*. Comprehending this reality brings one to "penetrate the secret of change,"[15] namely, the understanding that material force is never destroyed, only transformed. While the forms of things are constantly changing there is, nonetheless, a "constant unity of being and non-being."[16]

The significance of Chang Tsai's metaphysical position is that it provided a comprehensive explanation of change that could then be related to the dynamics of spiritual growth in human beings. Change is affirmed as purposive process, and humans are called upon to identify with change and participate in the transformation of things.

Chang Tsai emphasizes his position in contrast to the Taoist belief that being arises from nonbeing and in contrast to the Buddhist tendency to emphasize our illusory perception of reality. Instead, he affirms the phenomenal world as a manifestation of *ch'i*. Moreover, he does not see nonbeing as a void into which phenomena disappear and are annihilated. Rather, he sees it in more positive terms as the source, not only of life, but of generation and transformation because material force is transforming through "fusion and intermingling."[17] He writes: "the integration and disintegration of material force is to the Great Vacuity as the freezing and melting of ice is to water. If we realize that the Great Vacuity is identical with material force, we know that there is no such thing as nonbeing."[18] Thus, the Great Vacuity is the unmanifested aspect of the creativity and fecundity of the universe. The Great Harmony is the manifested aspect. They are not two separate things.

Ultimately, Chang Tsai's identification of *ch'i* with the Great Vacuity is to overcome any duality between that which produces and that which is produced, between substance (*t'i*) and function (*yung*). "If one says that the Great Vacuity can produce *ch'i* (i.e., is itself distinct from *ch'i*)," he writes, "then this means that the Void is infinite whereas *ch'i* is finite and that the noumenal (*t'i*) is distinct from the phenomenal (yung). This leads. . .to. . .failure to understand the constant principle of unity between being and non-being."[19] Apprehension of this essential unity is what T'ang Chun-i calls the vertical aspect of Chang Tsai's identification of *ch'i* with the void.

The Horizontal Aspect of Chang Tsai's Synthesis: Ethical Implications

T'ang Chun-i says the horizontal aspect is the voidness of *ch'i* itself, which accounts for the fact of the constant intercourse—and, hence, generation—of things. Transformation depends on the inter-penetration and "mutual prehension"[20] of things. This could not occur unless the *ch'i* of all things was empty, for the emptiness becomes the matrix of intersubjectivity. Thus, things and persons can become uniquely present to one another through the mutual resonance of the voidness of *ch'i*. As T'ang writes, "whenever a thing is in intercourse with another it is always that the thing by means of its void contains the other and prehends it."[21] Spatiality, or emptiness, is the means by which communion occurs, and hence change becomes possible. Generation and transformation arise because through the void things can "diffuse their ether (*ch'i*) and extend themselves to other objects."[22] This fusion and diffusion of *ch'i* is expressed by Chang Tsai as extension (*shen*) and trans-formation (*hua*). Through these two principles, change in *ch'i* has both continuity and discontinuity, both the power to produce and be produced. Creativity and communion are possible, then, by the very nature of *ch'i* itself.

The whole universe can be seen as in a process of generation and evolution which are themselves regarded as positive qualities exhibiting moral characteristics.[23] Chang Tsai expresses this as:

Spirituality or extension is the virtue of Heaven
Transformation is the way of Heaven
Its virtue is its substance, its way its function
Both become one in the ether (*ch'i*).[24]

In an analogous manner, the human has a moral nature which is exhibited in the virtues of righteousness and humaneness. Righ-teousness in the human corresponds to transformation and differentiation in the natural order, for it brings things to completion. Similarly, humaneness corresponds to generation and extension, for it means sharing the same feeling. The fecundity of the cosmological order has its counterpart in the activation of virtue in the human order.

Central to Chang Tsai's cosmology is his assertion that the task of the human is to understand and identify with the transformation of things, which he sees as essentially a spiritual process. He writes, "All molds and forms are but dregs of this spiritual transformation."[25] The person who knows the principles of transformation will be able to "forward the undertakings of Heaven and Earth."[26] His comprehensive affirmation of the role of the human in the universe can be seen in the *Western Inscription*, where he identifies the human with the whole cosmic order:

> Heaven is my father and Earth is my mother, and even such a small creature as I find an intimate place in their midst.
>
> Therefore that which fills the universe I regard as my body and that which directs the universe I consider as my nature.
>
> All people are my brothers and sisters, and all things are my companions. . . .
>
> In life I follow and serve [Heaven and Earth]. In death I will be at peace.[27]

Chang Tsai's ethical, "mystical humanism"[28] is the necessary corollary to his understanding of the dynamics of change in the physical order. He sees the same process of fusion and intermingling as acting in the human through the operation of humaneness (*jen*). Change holds a great creative potential for growth and fulfillment. Yet, he realizes that there is also a mystery of interaction which is impossible to grasp fully. "This is the wonder that lies in all things."[29]

For Chang Tsai the key for harmonizing human nature and the Way of Heaven is through the practice of sincerity. As the *Doctrine of the Mean* says:

> Sincerity is the Way of Heaven. To think how to be sincere is the way of humans. One who is sincere is one who hits upon what is right without effort and apprehends without thinking. One is naturally and easily in harmony with the Way. Such a person is a sage. One who tries to be sincere is one who sees the good and holds fast to it.[30]

Sincerity and enlightenment are the two poles of a spiritual practice that consists of the cultivation of one's nature and the investigation of things. In this process of balancing inner and outer wisdom, Chang Tsai distinguishes between nature and destiny, saying that the nature is endowed by Heaven and is not obscured by material force. Destiny he defines as what is decreed by Heaven and permeates one's nature. One of the goals of achieving sagehood is to develop one's nature and thus fulfill one's destiny. In this way a person can form one body with all things.

The significance of these distinctions in Chang Tsai's thought is that he maintains (in the tradition of Mencius) that human nature is originally good. To account for evil he does, however, posit two natures, an original one and a physical one. Evil arises because of imbalances in our physical nature due to the mingling of our physical nature with *ch'i*. Material force (*ch'i*) emerges from its undifferentiated state in the Great Vacuity and differentiation arises in its phenomenal appearances. Because of this inevitable process, conflict and opposition are bound to arise and hence the existence of evil. He recognizes that the physical nature, while not evil in itself, has the potential for giving rise to evil in human actions. It is possible, however, to recover one's original nature through moral cultivation. Indeed, one can overcome any incipient tendencies toward evil by enlarging one's mind to embrace all things through intensive study. Chang Tsai notes that "the great benefit of learning is to enable oneself to transform his own physical nature."[31] Chang Tsai also observes that it is the mind which can harmonize human nature and feelings. This doctrine of mind, however, is left for later Neo-Confucians to develop more fully.

In summary, then, Chang Tsai's doctrine of the Great Vacuity provides a metaphysical basis on which to explain the unity and the constant interaction and penetration of things. This also gives an ethical grounding for the understanding of the interactions between people. Through both the fecundity of the natural order and the activation of virtue in the human order, change and transformation can be understood as possible because of spatiality and emptiness. As Wing-tsit Chan points out, it is precisely this condition which allows all things to realize their authenticity and full being. For "only when reality is a vacuity can the material force operate and only with the operation of the material force can things mutually influence, mutually penetrate and mutually be identified."[32] Identification and communion of humans with nature and with each other is possible because of the emptiness of *ch'i*.

Lo Ch'in-shun and the Philosophy of *Ch'i*

Lo Ch'in-shun, the most eminent Neo-Confucian in the mid-Ming period, compiled his philosophy of *ch'i* toward the end of his life and published it in 1528 under the title *K'un-chih chi* (Knowledge Painfully Acquired).[33] In this work of remarkable scholarship and careful thought, Lo, following Chang Tsai, lays out his argument for the importance of *ch'i* as the unitary basis of reality and of the source of changes in the natural world. He argues forcefully against Chu Hsi's dualism of *li* and *ch'i* because he wants to preserve the importance of the vital material force within the world. He hoped to avoid either a potential transcendentalism of the Chu Hsi school of Neo-Confucianism or a subjective idealism of the Ch'an school of Buddhism or the Wang Yang-ming school of Neo-Confucianism. Instead, he emphasized viewing the world of humans as part of a single unified reality of *ch'i*. Acquiring knowledge of this world and of the human mind was part of the moral cultivation of the individual. Thus, Lo hoped to preserve both unity and diversity and to establish a metaphysics whereby the natural world and the human mind are identified yet distinct. These are surely perennial problems in philosophy, but the subtle agonizing discussions of Lo had a powerful influence on the evolution of Neo-Confucian thought in China and influenced the development of both Korean and Japanese Neo-Confucianism. The implications for metaphysics, ethics, epistemology, and empiricism are once again significant.

Metaphysics: Monism of *Ch'i*

Lo, in seeking to explain the evolution of the universe and its constant changes over time, speaks of the unitary force of *ch'i*.

> That which penetrates heaven and earth and connects past and present is nothing other than material force (*ch'i*), which is unitary. This material force, while originally one, revolves through endless

cycles of movement and tranquillity, going and coming, opening and
closing, rising and falling. Having become increasingly obscure, it
then becomes manifest; having become manifest, it once again
reverts to obscurity.[34]

This *ch'i* has its manifestations in the seasons and in natural growth,
as well as in moral relations in human life. Yet Lo insists that in
the midst of this transformation and variety there is a "detailed
order" and "an elaborate coherence which cannot ultimately be
disturbed."[35] This order is what is called principle (*li*), but it is not
something separate from material force. Lo states repeatedly that *li*
and *ch'i* are not different things. Indeed, he notes that he hopes to
recover the original unity of *li* and *ch'i*.[36]

    Ch'i operates throughout the universe in a process of continual
disintegration and integration, like the waxing and waning of yin
and yang. Lo describes this process relying on Chang Tsai's text
Cheng meng (Correcting Youthful Ignorance):

> In its disintegrated state, *ch'i* is scattered and diffuse. Through
> integration, it forms matter, thereby giving rise to the manifold
> diversity of persons and things.[37]

In another passage Lo acknowledges the subtlety of the kind of
distinctions he is trying to make in the relationship of *li* and *ch'i*.
He writes:

> *Li* must be identified as an aspect of *ch'i*, and yet to identify *ch'i*
> with *li* would be incorrect. The distinction between the two is very
> slight, and hence it is extremely difficult to explain. Rather we must
> perceive it within ourselves and comprehend it in silence.[38]

Ethics: One Nature in Humans

The implications of Lo's monism is that he does not accept the
distinction of two natures in the human, namely, an original nature
and a physical nature. This dual nature had often been posited by
the Sung Neo-Confucians, such as Chang Tsai, as a means of
explaining the origin of evil.

    Lo maintains that in the classical Confucian tradition human
nature is one. He believes that "Human beings are fundamentally

alike at birth in sharing the unitary *ch'i* and the compassionate mind."[39] Humans are united with all living things because of their *ch'i*. "The *ch'i* involved in human breathing is the *ch'i* of the universe. . . . Heaven (or nature) and humans are basically not two. There is no need to speak of combining them."[40] He accounts for diversity through Ch'eng I's phrase, "Principle is one, its particularizations are diverse." Lo observes: "At the inception of life when they are first endowed with *ch'i*, the principle of human beings and things is just one. After having attained physical form, their particularizations are diverse."[41]

Along with a rejection of a dualism of an original nature and a physical nature comes a denial of an antagonism between the principles of nature and human desires. Thus, human emotions and desires are affirmed as a valid part of human nature and they deserve to be cultivated and expressed appropriately.

Epistemology and Empiricism: Investigating Things

In terms of knowledge, Lo's emphasis on *ch'i* gives rise to his strong affirmation of the importance of sensory knowledge and experience. He does not see this as less valid than the kind of moral knowledge derived from texts or history. He thus affirms the necessity of "investigating things" and "plumbing principles" in the world as a means of acquiring knowledge. While the idea of investigating things originates with Classical Confucians in the *Great Learning* (*Ta hsüeh*), it became a central doctrine of the Ch'eng-Chu Neo-Confucians. However, with Lo, the grounds for the extension of Confucianism into an empirical area are clearly laid. This is precisely what happens in the thought of Kaibara Ekken in seventeenth-century Japan.

Kaibara Ekken and the Monism of *Ch'i*

For Lo Ch'in-shun and for Kaibara Ekken a monism of *ch'i* was an articulation of a naturalism which helped to explain the dynamics of change in the universe. This became a basis for a unified doctrine of human nature, an affirmation of human emotions, and a rationale for the investigation of the natural world.[42] In contrast to Chu Hsi's rationalistic formalism, both Lo and Ekken attempted to penetrate patterns in the midst of process and to articulate the quality of renewal and regeneration in nature and in human life. They wished to avoid the subjective position of Wang Yang-ming, who emphasized principles in the mind. They each affirmed that principles within material force in nature ought to be investigated. Precisely because *li* was the principle of material force, Ekken believed it contained within it both constancy and transformation (*rinojohen*) and thus was neither prior nor absolute. His desire to articulate a clear understanding of the constancy and transformation of principle is an underlying theme of his important treatise called the *Taigiroku*, or *Record of Great Doubts*.

Ekken felt the need to articulate a cosmology that was vital, dynamic, and naturalistic, thus reflecting the actual state of fecundity and generation in the universe. When the great source and operation of this productivity was effectively understood, humans could begin to be in harmony with the ongoing processes of life. They would be able to realize their fundamental continuity with the cosmos and, consequently, activate the dynamic potential of human nature for moral action. Just as Heaven and Earth generate the myriad things, so human beings, through their efforts at moral and spiritual cultivation and through their investigation of nature, might come to realize their essentially life-inducing capacity.

Ekken's Metaphysics: *Li* and *Ch'i* Are One

Ekken argued for a naturalism which sees the universe as emerging and continuing solely due to the operations of the primal energy of *ch'i*. This primal energy above physical forms is the configuration of yin and yang while within physical forms it becomes concrete objects. This ceaseless process of generation and transformation was seen as a unified, organic whole. Bifurcation or dualism did not adequately describe the process for Ekken or provide a satisfactory basis for an understanding of human nature and action in the midst of change.

In the *Record of Great Doubts* Ekken wrote of his disagreements with Chu Hsi regarding the relationship of *li* and *ch'i*. In this treatise he identifies two forms of *ch'i* as constituting the Great Ultimate (*t'ai-chi*). One is the primal material force before it divides into yin and yang and the other is after it divides into yin and yang. The flow of yin and yang is principle and is called the Way. Nonetheless, the Great Ultimate as the primal *ch'i* and yin and yang as the Way are two aspects of the same dynamic material force. It is this primal *ch'i* which constitutes the origin, growth, and transformation of life. This means that the Way is one of constant productivity and does not arise from emptiness.

Ekken wanted to make a clear distinction between any associations with Buddhist or Taoist ideas of emptiness in the cosmology of the *t'ai-chi* because he feared this could lead to quietude and passivity instead of ethical involvement in the world. Thus, Ekken, following Chang Tsai, identified the *t'ai-chi* with the primal material force. This was in contrast to Chu Hsi who identified it with principle, which Chu claimed was prior to material force. Ekken felt that Chu saw *li* and *ch'i* as two distinct entities, whereby *li* was identified with the Way above forms (noumenal order) and *ch'i* was identified with yin and yang within the realm of forms (phenomenal order). Ekken feared this could lead to an abstraction of the Way as separate from concrete reality and a bifurcation of principle (*li*) apart from material force (*ch'i*). Ekken hoped to avoid this kind of dualism because he felt it could result in an idealism that either undervalued this world or focused on life-denying rather than life-affirming ethical practices.

Ekken used the same arguments against dualism as had Lo Ch'in-shun in *K'un-chih chi*. These were Cheng I's phrase, "Principle is one, its particularizations are diverse," and Lo's formulation, "Principle is the principle of material force." Ekken used these to assert the essentially unified, dynamic, and creative nature of reality, which consisted of both unity and multiplicity. Thus, he felt *li* should not be seen as separate from or prior to material force.

Ekken summarized his argument for the Way as the dynamic operation of the yin and yang, which is the root of the generation and transformation of life:

> Ancient sages regarded yin and yang as the Way and they didn't speak of the Way outside of yin and yang. Sung Confucians regarded the Way as separate from yin and yang and as something empty and void of oneness and without vitality and power. They regarded the root of all things to be the marvel of the Great Ultimate

but it was not the "Way of the sages." The "Way of the sages" is
the principle of life and growth of heaven and earth; the original
ch'i harmonizing the yin and yang is ceaseless fecundity.[43]

Ekken felt he was returning to the basic inspiration of Classical
Confucian thought in its concern to express the intimate relation of
the human to the cosmos. The primacy of the life process is
emphasized by Ekken, for it is understanding and harmonizing with
this vital operation which becomes the basis for moral and spiritual
cultivation. His efforts to return to a simple and naturalistic
metaphysical formulation of the monism of *ch'i* is paralleled by his
concern with spontaneity and sincerity in ethical practices as well.

Ethics: Human Nature Is One

The consequences of Ekken's monistic and naturalistic position can
be seen in his doctrine of human nature. Following Lo Ch'in-shun,
he claimed that because *li* and *ch'i* are one, there should be no
distinction between an ideal nature and a physical one such as Chang
Tsai and other Sung Neo-Confucians had made. Ekken felt that one
could not argue that a heavenly conferred original nature was
separate from physical nature. Like Mencius, he maintained that all
people were potentially good because they received the four seeds
which could be cultivated into virtues. Differences arose due to the
varied nature of *ch'i* as it mingled in each person.

The implications of Ekken's doctrine of human nature is most
clearly seen in his efforts to affirm rather than deny or suppress the
emotions. His discussions of spiritual discipline frequently focused
on ways to achieve a balanced means of expressing the emotions.

Ekken emphasized in particular the virtue of "sincerity" (*makoto*)
rather than "seriousness" (*kei*). He felt that overemphasis on
seriousness by the Sung Neo-Confucians had sometimes led to
austere and artificial practices which missed the creativity of an
ethical path connected to a dynamic metaphysical basis of *ch'i*. He
criticized the Sung Neo-Confucians as concentrating on abstract
ideas at the expense of what was essential, dynamic, and close at
hand. He felt they tended to become too rigid and narrow-minded
and thus withered, dried up, and without harmony or compassion
in human relations. Self-cultivation was intended to eliminate the

separation between oneself and others so that one's heart-and-mind could embrace all things.

This ultimate identification of the human with all life-forms reflects the dynamic process of the flow of *ch'i*. Just as *ch'i* is the life-inducing material force in the natural order, so is humaneness the creative principle of the moral order. He wrote that the principle of life and the principle of humaneness are intimately connected:

> What is the heart of heaven and earth? It is nothing but birth (*sei*). The great virtue of heaven and earth is [nourishing] life (*sei*). What is birth and life? Chu Hsi said, "Heaven and earth does nothing else but give birth to all things." This is birth. The Way to obey and not hinder this [process] is only through humaneness. In other words, heaven and earth are the heart of living things. Humans receive this heart and it becomes their own. This is humaneness. Nourishing life and [practicing] humaneness are not two different things. Nourishing life belongs to heaven and humaneness belongs to humans.[44]

It is this understanding of the generative power of material force (*ch'i*) and humaneness (*jen*) which informs all of Ekken's ethical treatises and is the underlying theme of moral and spiritual cultivation. It is also the basis for his interest in investigating things in the natural world.

Empiricism: The Investigation of Things

Ekken believed that until one began to understand the processes of nature, one could not fully comprehend the human Way. Observing and recording various aspects of nature can be a foundation for a more fully human life. His empiricism was thus linked to his ethics.

Although Ekken did not himself clearly explicate the relationship of his empirical studies to his cosmology of *ch'i*, it seems apparent that his affirmation of the absolute within the phenomenal world (the *li* within the *ch'i*) provided a theoretical basis for investigating principle within material force. In this sense his desire to catalogue and describe various species of plants, fish, and shells can be seen as a drive to understand the unifying forms and underlying principles within reality itself. To investigate things came to mean seeking the patterns within change, uncovering the principles behind flux. While this understanding can be interpreted as being within the Chu Hsi tradition, investigation was more often directed by Neo-Confucian scholars toward illuminating the moral significance of texts, especially the classics. In Ekken this impetus for investigation shifted toward the natural world. All things were seen as within its province: botany, topography, agriculture, medicine, arithmetic, and astronomy. The physical sciences and the pure sciences, theoretical speculation and pragmatic observation came under this broadened concept of investigating things in order to determine their principle. This was part of Ekken's practical learning (*jitsugaku*).

In content and in method Ekken's interest in practical learning had significant implications. Indeed, he saw this investigation as another aspect of self-cultivation and as a means of relating to the vital force in the cosmos. To examine plant or agricultural methods, for example, was a way of understanding nature's life-giving capacity. Similarly, studying or practicing medicine was meaningless without the recognition that a person was nourishing life and encouraging humaneness.

Ekken's empiricism and his affirmation of the material world was rooted in his metaphysics of *ch'i* and was a further expression of his ethics. To see the interrelationship of these various components was to recognize the connecting thread of the monism of *ch'i* underlying his holistic thought and practice.

Conclusion

From the early articulation of *ch'i* in *Mencius* to the later metaphysical elaboration of it by Chang Tsai, the philosophy of *ch'i* had an important history in Confucian and Neo-Confucian thought in China. With its fuller elaboration as a monism of *ch'i* by Lo Ch'in-shun in sixteenth-century China and Kaibara Ekken in seventeenth-century Japan, it provided a rich metaphysical, ethical, and empirical basis for a this-worldly spirituality remarkable for its holistic and comprehensive qualities. As we seek new perspectives on matter and on our relation to it, this fruitful and complex philosophy of material force may be as useful in our own time as it was in Ming China or Tokugawa Japan because it provides a cosmological basis for understanding the inherent unity of matter and energy.

Notes

1. This essay is an adaptation of my article "An Ecological Cosmology: The Confucian Philosophy of Material Force," in *Ecological Practice*, ed. Christopher Key Chapple (Albany: State University of New York Press, 1994).

2. The historian of religion Charles Long has written on this. See his article "Matter and Spirit: A Reorientation," in *Local Knowledge, Ancient Wisdom*, ed. Steven Freisen (Honolulu: Institute for Culture and Communications, East-West Center, 1991).

3. See Thomas Berry's collection of essays called *The Dream of the Earth* (San Francisco: Sierra Club, 1988). He also has a book written with Brian Swimme called *The Universe Story: From the Primordial Flaring Forth to the Ecozoic Era* (San Francisco: Harper San Francisco, 1992).

4. *Doctrine of the Mean*, chap. 22, in *A Source Book in Chinese Philosophy*, trans. Wing-tsit Chan (Princeton: Princeton University Press, 1963), 108.

5. As Pierre Teilhard deChardin understood it, spirit and matter are intrinsically related. For him, matter radiates interiority and intelligibility. Human reflexivity is not simply an addendum to the evolutionary process but rather something that arises from the process itself. Thus, the psychic and physical are dimensions of one another and are evolving together. In this respect, with the evolution of greater complexity there emerges greater consciousness. See his *The Phenomenon of Man* (New York: Harper & Row, 1959).

For Thomas Berry, who follows in the Teilhardian tradition, the three principles which govern the universe are differentiation, subjectivity, and communion. Subjectivity is that which defines the interiority of matter, and it is the life force and organizing principle of each living being (see Berry, *Dream of the Earth*). Likewise, for Brian Swimme the hidden heart of the cosmos is this radiating energy from the "big bang" to the present, which illumines matter: *The Hidden Heart of the Cosmos: Humanity and the New Story* (Maryknoll, N.Y.: Orbis Books, 1996).

6. *Doctrine of the Mean*, chap. 22, in Chan, *A Source Book in Chinese Philosophy*, 108.

7. Chan, *A Source Book in Chinese Philosophy*, 784.

8. Ibid.

9. *Mencius*, 2A.2.

10. Chan, *A Source Book In Chinese Philosophy*, 784.

11. Ibid.

12. *Mencius*, 2A.2.

13. Quoted in Huang Siu-chi, "Chang Tsai's Concept of *Ch'i*," *Philosophy East and West* 18 (October 1968):251. For some of the ideas in this first paragraph, I am indebted to Huang's article.

14. T'ang Chun-i, "Chang Tsai's Theory of Mind," *Philosophy East and West* 6 (July 1956):121. T'ang Chun-i's ideas of vertical and horizontal synthesis comprise the main thrust of this article.

15. Chang Tsai, "Great Harmony," in *Sources of Chinese Tradition*, comp. Wm. Theodore de Bary, Wing-tsit Chan, and Burton Watson (New York: Columbia University Press, 1960), 467.

16. T'ang, "Chang Tsai's Theory of Mind," 123.

17. Chang Tsai, "Correcting Youthful Ignorance," in *A Source Book in Chinese Philosophy*, trans. Wing-tsit Chan (Princeton: Princeton University Press, 1963), 503.

18. Ibid.

19. Quoted in Huang, "Chang Tsai's Concept of *Ch'i*," 253.

20. T'ang is using Alfred North Whitehead's term here. See T'ang, "Chang Tsai's Theory of Mind," 123–25.

21. Ibid., 124.

22. Ibid., 125.

23. Ibid., 127.

24. Ibid., 126.

25. Chang Tsai, "Correcting Youthful Ignorance," 505.

26. Ibid., 497.

27. Ibid., 497–98.

28. This is a phrase used by Thomas Berry to describe the spiritual dimension of the Confucian tradition.

29. Chang Tsai, "Correcting Youthful Ignorance," 507.

30. *Doctrine of the Mean*, chap. 20, in Chan, *A Source Book in Chinese Philosophy*, 107.

31. Chang Tsai, "Correcting Youthful Ignorance," 516. For a clarification of Chang Tsai's doctrine of evil, I am indebted to Chan's comments in his *Source Book in Chinese Philosophy* and in his article, "The Neo-Confucian Solution to the Problem of Evil," in *Neo-Confucianism, Etc.: Essays by Wing-tsit Chan*, comp. Charles K. H. Chen (Hanover, N.H.: Oriental Society, 1969).

32. Chan, "The Neo-Confucian Solution to the Problem of Evil," 102.

33. This has been translated by Irene Bloom, *Knowledge Painfully Acquired* (New York: Columbia University Press, 1987).

34. Ibid., 58.

35. Ibid.

36. Ibid., 109

37. Ibid., 127

38. Ibid., 134

39. Ibid., 84.

40. Ibid., 161–62.

41. Ibid., 65.

42. Much of this section draws on my book, *Moral and Spiritual Cultivation in Japanese Neo-Confucianism: The Life and Thought of Kaibara Ekken (1630–1714)* (Albany: State University of New York Press, 1989), and on an unpublished translation I have done of Ekken's treatise, *Record of Great Doubts* (*Taigiroku*).

43. Kaibara Ekken, "Taigiroku," in *Kaibara Ekken, Muro Kyuso. Nihon shiso taikei*, vol. 34 (Tokyo: Iwanami shoten, 1970), 54.

44. *Jigoshu, Ekken Zenshu*, 3:182–83.

Philosophical Reflections

The Trinity of Cosmology, Ecology, and Ethics in the Confucian Personhood

Chung-ying Cheng

There exists, in recent philosophical literature, a quest for an environmental ethics, no doubt generated by a heightened awareness of the ecological crisis. Philosophers and ethicists have been quite outspoken regarding the harmful consequences for the environment of Western humanism or humanistic ethics.[1] Some critics simply see humanism, or personalism, as embodying a human-centered rationalism, as a form of "anthropological egoism" or "human chauvinism" that seeks what is good and of value in satisfying human interests and concerns and that confines morality to activities engaged in by humans alone.[2] There is no denying that humanism can be either deontological or utilitarian in orientation and goal-setting, but the ultimate goal for a utilitarian or deontological ethics in humanism is human goodness and human satisfaction, individually or collectively. Humanism thus is seen as a device for the exercise of "group selfishness" by or on behalf of humankind in the world of nature. It could be pointed out that, since a humanistic ethics might incorporate the Golden Rule, the Kantian "categorical imperative," and some law of comprehensive love as part of its content, humanism need not be considered exclusively human-centered. The ethics of humanism can be extended to all living sentient beings who are capable of pleasure and suffering in light of these moral principles.[3] It could even be specified that one might imagine oneself to be a wriggling worm in order to decide what one should do with regard to the worm. Or, one might require oneself to act in such a way as to treat other life-forms as ends, not as means. Or, one could simply decide to love all animals in order to protect their natural life activities and processes. This would constitute a humane-society approach to the ethics of the treatment of birds and beasts, but it does not answer the question of the human-centeredness aspect of humanistic ethics. Nor does it answer the question why a human must extend those universal principles of morality to the animal kingdom.

Clearly, when humanistic principles of morality were developed, they were intended to apply to the human world. In extending humanistic ethics to the animal kingdom and on to other life-forms, it is obviously, yet implicitly, assumed that this extension is necessary, if not sufficient, to ward off the ill effects of a human-centered morality and thus prevent humanity from causing an ecological breakdown. Though this justification for a humanistic ethics is, on reflection, more holistic and totalistic than other such considerations based on an awareness of the ecological crisis, it is still derived from implicit utilitarian considerations of human welfare.

Uncovering the underlying utilitarian considerations of the extension of humanism or humanistic ethics means undermining the ethical or moral validity of such an extension. One might imagine that, if circumstances require us humans to forfeit or rescind this extension for even more sophisticated reflective utilitarian considerations, we would still end up being human-centered in our ethical thinking and moral actions, which could either benefit or harm the world of nature and our environment as a consequence.

In view of this, three very basic questions must be raised: Is there a different formulation or understanding of humanism which might moderate its human-centeredness? Are there criteria according to which things in nature and in the human world can be equally and properly treated, based on considerations of the world of nature and humanity together rather than merely on considerations of a single human being or on the human world alone? If any such criteria exist, how might a human apply such criteria so that he or she might act morally within the world of nature and develop an ethical attitude or habits that would preserve such criteria? I intend, in this article, to explore these three questions from a philosophically deepened Confucian/Neo-Confucian point of view.

Inclusive Humanism as Cosmo-Ethics and Eco-Cosmology

In the intellectual journey humankind has made in the last twenty-five hundred years, two types of humanism can be distinguished: an "exclusive humanism," which exalts the human species, placing it in a position of mastery of and domination over the universe; and an "inclusive humanism," which stresses the coordinating powers of humanity as the very reason for its existence. The West has for the most part followed an "exclusive humanism" since the beginning of the modern age. Although we need not regard Descartes's rationalism as the very prototype of "exclusive humanism," his rationalistic philosophy no doubt provided a solid foundation for this type of humanism in the modern West.

Descartes developed the notion of an essentially deistic God who provided the single foundation for our knowledge of the external world. To have this knowledge also means using it to conquer nature, and there exist, then, no ethical restrictions on how we explore and use nature on the basis of our knowledge of the external world. Descartes's dualism of matter and mind or body and soul in fact further develops a logical basis for the domination of mind over matter and soul over body. The traditional Creator-God reigns in Heaven but also relegates his power of dominion to man on Earth. The modern rational man, unlike the artistic Renaissance man, is a free spirit liberated from the shackles of the Dark Ages (or Cage), able to taste the sweet fruits of power and relish the sense of domination by displaying his intelligence through invention and employing his cunning in industry. To use Nietzsche's metaphor, the modern man is like a young lion set free after being transformed from a camel. Thus, modern science and modern capitalism as the lion's claws arose at the same time to provide modern man with weapons for both play and prey. These two were linked through the Cartesian vision of knowledge as power or domination. In this sense, humanism in the modern West is nothing more than a secular will for power or a striving for domination, with rationalistic science at its disposal. In fact, the fascination with power leads to a Faustian trade-off of knowledge and power (pleasure and self-glorification) for value and truth, a trade-off which can lead to the final destruction of the meaning of the human self and human freedom.

It is in this development of the human being where the natural
world loses its enchantment and its inherent moral worth for
humans. Rather than as a natural abode for the soul of modern man,
the natural world becomes instead a hunting ground on which a
skilled marksman may pursue and collect his fortunes. Hence, it is
not science and rationality that deprived nature of its moral worth
or of its intrinsic significance to humankind. The post-medieval
human will, as a surrogate for the authority of a Creator-God,
accomplished this. Unlike God, however, modern humanity is
devoid of the goodness of God. This humanism is thus human-
centered and exclusive of any real connection or intrinsic link with
anything else in the world. This dominant exclusiveness results in
an increased control over natural resources as well as in an
accelerated development of technology and is a demonstration of
the ability and talent inherent in an invincible human urge for power
supported by the successful functioning of human instrumental
rationality. Humanism in this exclusive sense is a disguise for the
individualistic entrepreneurship of modern man armed with science
and technology as tools of conquest and devastation.

There is, however, a second kind of humanism, an "inclusive
humanism."[4] As the term suggests, humanism in this sense focuses
on the human person as an agency of both self-transformation and
transformation of reality at large. As the self-transformation of a
person is rooted in reality and the transformation of reality is rooted
in the person, there is no dichotomy or bifurcation between the
human and reality. There is always an underlying connection
between the two. How to conceive of and configure this underlying
connection is a metaphysical task to be carried out, not only in terms
of the imagination, but in light of a deep sense and wide experience
of the organic connection defining both what the real as the human
is and what the human as the real is. With regard to this connection,
there is no essential opposition or conflict between the human as a
subject and the world of nature as an object, nor is there any
opposition or conflict between the human as an entity and nature
as another entity. In fact, both the human and nature belong to each
other in a continuum of the whole reality. Since this whole reality
(to which both the human and nature belong as parts) must be
conceived as a dynamic and creative process of change and
transformation in order to allow the mutual transformation of the

human and nature, it should be clear that the very actuality and creativity of the transformation provide the required underlying link. We can see, then, that inclusive humanism is a view of the human as a creative process of self-fulfillment of reality, in reality, for reality, and from reality.

What needs to be addressed immediately in inclusive humanism is the basic recognition or understanding that nature, or even the whole of reality, whether in the form of a moving universe or in the form of the totality of things, has an interconnecting or interlinking context of being as value. This implies, not only that a single reality is a common source or common ground for human beings and all things, but because of this reality-source or reality-ground, each and every thing has intrinsic value, value in the sense of being able to form a mutually enriching or mutually strengthening relationship among things contributing to the total unity and harmony of things in reality. This amounts to saying that an ideal projection of harmony among things must always be a basic consideration for human action. This will always cause a natural strain in the development of a relationship among things. There is no transcendent God separate from the world and there is no delegation of power to humankind as the representative body of God in the world of nature, because God needs no such delegation. Humans have, from the beginning of their existence, participated in the sharing of the power of transformation with other things in the world.

Humans and nature are already intrinsically related when a human individual comes to know his or her role and station, and this is realized as an innate sense of being in the human individual, forgotten, perhaps, in transition but never eliminated. Although, under some historical circumstances, an emergent desire for power, in its quest for self-assertion, self-aggrandizement, or self-glorification, could lead to an inner split of the human self and a loss of the sense of the common source of being, and although this loss would inevitably result in the restlessness of strife and struggle for conquest and possession, this innate sense of being can always be cultivated and restored or reinstated. This reemergence of an ever-present sense of being is the transformation from an exclusive humanism to an inclusive humanism, a form that does not make the human the center of the world but instead makes the between-ness, or among-ness, of the human and things in the world the center of the world. We thus come to see that for inclusive humanism the defining spirit is the will for harmony—the transformation of the will for power into a spirit of friendly love and support. The human being thus stands for the way of creative transformation, inter-relating, coordination, and integration or mutual identification among things in the world. The whole process of the creative change of the human is meshed with the process of the creative change of the world. There is no permanent gain or permanent loss but a dynamic balance of the best efforts of the human for the dynamic balance of the possible and the actual, the positive and the negative, in a conscientious exertion of heart-and-mind. Inclusive humanism might also be called "cultivational humanism" or a "humanism for cultivation," based on the metaphor of the cultivation of the land so that it yields fruits that both benefit humankind and enrich the land at the same time. Exclusive humanism, by contrast, would be a human striving for domination of the land and possession of territorial rights out of a sense of alienation from an objectified world, perhaps best described as a nomadic tribe engaged in a perpetual hunt.

Since the basis of inclusive humanism calls for the inclusion of nature for there to be harmony, the object of moral action is not limited to the human world, nor is it derived solely from human concern. Anything in the world, animate or inanimate, can take on this role, for anything can be an integral part of the best possible harmony that may be achieved, considering both time and place, humans and nature, present and future, here and there. The human world and human concern are seen as presentations of the larger and deeper reality in the creative making. In this light, the entailed ethics cannot but be an ethics of the cosmos and an ethics of the creative change of the cosmos. This means that, as humans, we must think, act, plan, and decide with this vision of present and future harmony of nature always in mind. Thus, this cosmo-ethics is also an ecological cosmology that incorporates the values of being as creativity, creativity as harmony, and harmony as transformation.

I have called this cosmology of the life of the whole "ontocos-mology" in my earlier study of the metaphysical foundation of the *I ching* as a way to suggest the harmony and unity of change and reality, or process and reality.[5] As reality contains resources of human values, which must be recognized as intrinsic values in the universe, the ontocosmology of life-creativity is at the same time ecological, insofar as it presents itself in the natural environments of life processes and life-forms in the world and is also a basis for human ethical considerations and moral action. Hence, the onto-cosmology also becomes a matter of cosmo-ethics, or ethics based on the recognition and consideration of the nature of the reality as creative change.

It is evident that inclusive humanism marks a starting point in the axiological transformation of cosmological reality due to human participation, reflection, innovation, and renovation in humankind's ceaseless efforts to overcome obstruction and misunderstanding and find the way to achieving a dynamic equilibrium and harmonization of being, becoming, and nonbeing.

If Descartes can be singled out as the founding father of exclusive humanism in the West, Alfred North Whitehead may be considered the spokesman for inclusive humanism in the West. Because Confucianism was founded on the same principles of inclusive humanism, we can see how the Confucian works, in a partnership with all things in the universe, to establish not just a humane society but a harmonious universe.

Ontocosmology as the Inner Core of the Confucian Trinity

Confucianism is humanism in the inclusive sense. Often, Confucianism is perceived only as human-centered or human relations-centered. It is often perceived as merely a philosophy of morality and ethics. Its ethics of *jen* (benevolence/humanity) is seen as lacking a rational and transcendental foundation, whereas its ethics of *li* (rites/propriety) is looked upon as polished conventions governing social relations or rules of behavior intended for optimizing social utility. Even its ethics of *i* (righteousness/rightness) is taken to be merely a matter of doing right in a human and social context. I would not dismiss these perceptions simply as naïve misconceptions, but they are nevertheless misleading because they are based on incomplete and superficial understanding. Such misunderstanding arises from a failure to appreciate the underlying discourse of ontocosmology as the basis for Confucian ethics. Even though the Classical Confucianism of the *Analects* appears to consist primarily of virtue ethics and its political application, one cannot ignore the broad underlying ontocosmological discourse that gives vitality and spirit to the values and ideals of Confucius and his followers. As made amply clear in the works of Neo-Confucians of the Sung and Ming periods, Classical Confucian philosophy presents itself—and should therefore be seen—as a comprehensive unity comprising every single aspect of reality and humankind. This is particularly evident if we realize that the relevance of the ontocosmological view is implicit in the symbolism and texts of the *Chou i* and becomes explicit in the *I ch'uan* of the *Chou i*. I suggest, therefore, that we should not base our understanding of Confucianism on Confucius's *Analects* alone, nor even on the Four Books. It is important to relate Confucian morality and ethics to its ontocosmology in the commentaries of the *Chou i*, among other works.[6]

Aside from the need for acquiring a comprehensive and balanced understanding of Confucianism, there is another critical reason to examine these works: unless and until we read Confucian ethics and morality as practicality (praxis) and practical reason, we will not fully understand this ethics and morality as a discourse unified with, and thus requiring, a metaphysical and ontocosmological source and grounding. Many terms suggest the presence of such an ontocosmological grounding and reference: *t'ien* (Heaven) is the center of moral concern for value; *tao* (the Way) is the basis for *te* (inner power/virtue) and *jen*; *hsing* (nature/naturality) and *ming* (command/destiny) reveal the experience of the polarity of the reality of the human individual as a moral being. The discourse becomes even more complete and more structured when we take into account the *Ta hsüeh*, the *Chung yung*, the *Mencius*, and the *Hsün tzu*. Once we encounter the *Chung yung*, there is every reason to turn back to the *I ch'uan*, which gives a full disclosure of the ontocosmology of the Confucian Way presented in forms other than morality and ethics. But one must still heed the subtle difference between the *Chung yung* (and together with the *Mencius*) and the *I ch'uan*: whereas the *Chung yung* focuses on the practical and moral activation of the Way in a human being, and even in human society, one sees that the *I ch'uan* evokes very powerfully a heightened description of how the Way operates, how the world unfolds, and how the human being emerges with his moral destiny and creative mission. What I wish to stress, in light of this discourse, is that we not only see a fuller picture of Confucian ethics as praxis focused on the *I ch'uan* ontocosmology, but that we also realize that, unless we have such an ontocosmological worldview, we will not be able to effect real changes and transformations in the conditions of our existence and being through ethics and morality.

The ontocosmological worldview in the *I ch'uan* consists of the following basic points. First, there is an inexhaustible source of creativity, which is one and undifferentiated but which is always ready to be differentiated into concrete and individual things. This notion of *t'ai-chi* (the Great Ultimate) represents a reflective insight into the dynamic unity of the reality of things: it combines the elements of unity and multiplicity and their dynamic connections in a process of development and involution. The most important thing about *t'ai-chi* is that it is the constant fountainhead amidst all things and provides the integrative and purposive unity of any type or any individual token while, at the same time, it also serves as the impetus for the diversity of things as types or tokens. In other words, it is both the starting point and the ending point of all things and it always sustains connections among all things rooted in it as the origin.

We may thus see in *t'ai-chi* an intrinsic power of initiation leading to an intrinsic power of completion and fulfillment that gives reality and value to whatever is evolved or created. Furthermore, *t'ai-chi* can be seen as the state of equilibrium of nondifferentiation before or after any concretion of things; therefore, it subsists as an ultimate level for all things. Apart from being the creative source, it is the source of harmonization among things and provides the basis for harmonization of the differentiations among all things whatsoever. Harmony, or harmonization, here means that all things mutually support and complement one another; harmony is conducive to fostering a renewed creativity and future development. In this respect, *t'ai-chi* can be said to be also the Tao (the Way) and, together with the Tao, signifies both a process and world qua the totality of things in which there is a profound equilibrium from the beginning and a pervasive accord or harmony among all things at any time. Humans, like everything else, are founded on this profound equilibrium and are included in this pervasive harmony.

But, unlike everything else, the human being rises above everything to embody *t'ai-chi* and the Tao in his potential ability to create higher orders of equilibrium and harmony through culture and art. We come now to the second observation on the nature of creativity as a process.

It is said in the *I ch'uan*: "The alternation of one yin (the shady) and one yang (the bright) is called the Tao. What succeeds is the good and what completes is nature."[7] This statement underlines the polar nature of creativity during the process of producing all things in the world through *t'ai-chi*. What, then, is yin? What is yang? Clearly, the phenomenologically defined yin/yang can be realistically understood in a world of things and ontologically understood in the process of the creative production of things. The phenomenal paradigm of yin/yang presents a unity of contrast, a wholeness of complementarity, as well as a natural process of mutual transformation. It is the completion and return (one might call it creative circulation and recycling) illustrated in our aesthetic feelings and the felt qualities of things. Similarly, one may also see things which are congregations of qualities and dispositions exhibiting the same relationship and dynamic as the yin/yang interaction and integration. Not only things are created out of the interaction of yin/yang. All differentiation and unification of things, which then give rise to new things, can also be explained in terms of yin/yang, such that yin/yang could be ramified on different levels of being. An understanding of the relativity and multiplicity of yin/yang is, therefore, the basis for a reflective explanation of the natural processes of things. And, yin/yang is also an ontocosmological principle suggesting the unity and mutuality of the ontological and the cosmological. The yang is the visible, bright, changing, or moving cosmological process, whereas the yin is the invisible, hidden, and constant ontological reality. The interdependence and interpenetration of both give rise to the phenomenal reality of nature. We can, therefore, regard yin and yang as two inseparable and mutually transformable momenta of the ultimate reality (*t'ai-chi*), which, by being the ultimate and unlimited source, gives rise to the two moments of creative concretion of things. This process, in turn, completes the creative concretion of things in the fold of the oneness of *t'ai-chi* as the source.

This dialectics of the creative transformation of the ontological into the cosmological, and vice versa, assures the ceaseless creative activity of the Tao as the underlying process/reality revealed in a description of the dynamics of the yin/yang interaction. Chang Tsai provided an apt characterization of this process of interaction in terms of *t'ai-chi*, embracing both the oneness of the yin/yang polarity and the yin/yang differentiation of *t'ai-chi* oneness: "Being one, it is creative; being two, it is transformative."[8]

We need to illustrate, in this connection, the important proposition that all things in reality are things generated as value, for value, and toward value. What is realized is real and the real is value. A value is value, not just because it is created real, but because it has an intrinsic position in the scheme of things and is capable of being related and developed and intensified. Value also has a special relationship to the human mind; value is embodied in a feeling as well as in the felt qualities of things; it is an object of enjoyment, recognition, affirmation or negation, exploration, and development or reconstruction. Every thing has value because it arises from a creative source and is achieved in a creative process. Hence the statement, "What is accomplished is nature and what succeeds is good." Good is a presentation of nature and can thus be a basis for understanding the holistic nature of the world or can be an ideal form of value. Given this understanding of value, it is up to the human being to discover the real value of things and situations so that he or she can be engaged in a creative construction and reconstruction of values.

In light of this polaristic process of the creative initiation and completion of things, we can see how Heaven and Earth must be formed in the creative process of Tao or in the creative realization of the oneness of *t'ai-chi*. In the *Chou i*, Heaven and Earth are the most basic cosmological concretions of the yin/yang from which other cosmological concretions are derived, as indicated in the *pa-kua* (Eight Triagrams) system or in the *wu-hsing* (Five Phases) system. We may, in fact, conceive of Heaven and Earth in the whole symbolism of the *Chou i* as the basis for the creative evolution of the natural universe and as the basis for the further creative evolution of the human world. One can see how Heaven must be correlated with Earth in presenting the primordial creativity of *t'ai-chi* oneness via its polaristic momenta of yin/yang. This is how the creative power of Heaven (*ch'ien*) and the receptive power of the earth (*k'un*) work, where *ch'ien* and *k'un* are simply cosmic designations of yin/yang. It is interesting to note that in the symbolic text of the *Chou i*, the names of *ch'ien/k'un* are given to the icon-indexical symbols of Heaven and Earth, indicating the original oneness of *t'ai-chi* and its creative structuring of its momenta into the polarity of yin/yang. Therefore, the way to reach *t'ai-chi* cosmology, which I call the ontocosmology of *t'ai-chi* and the Tao in the *Hsi tz'u*, and which later was further elaborated in the *T'ai-chi t'u shuo* (Explanation of the Diagram of the Great Ultimate) of Chou Tun-i, is not arbitrary but logical.

When the Taoist philosopher Lao Tzu speaks of the one generating the two, the two generating the three, and the three generating the ten thousand things,[9] he clearly has in mind the scheme of *t'ai-chi* producing the polarity of yin/yang.[10] But the *Lao tzu* also says, "The Tao generates the one"; this underlines the dynamic creativity of the ultimate reality which, nevertheless, has the form of oneness.[11] If we see *t'ai-chi* as the source of the world, the Tao would be the same as *t'ai-chi* in generating the world of things as a whole system. But when Lao Tzu says that the three generates the ten thousand things, the three is also seen as the third, that is, the resulting offspring of the interaction of the two. We may see the whole world of things and life-forms springing from the yin/yang interaction of Heaven and Earth. But we might also see the two as any two forces or things and hence see the three as any three forces or as a third force or as things derived from the two forces or things.

In this context it is clear that the human being is the most unique and outstanding third in the production of Heaven and Earth. Together with Heaven and Earth the human being forms a ternion, or triad, with the whole universe. The interesting thing about this ternion is that a human is capable of doing what Heaven and Earth do, namely, nourishing life and helping things to grow. But a human is not exactly Heaven or Earth, although he or she possesses the virtues of Heaven and Earth in order to achieve higher orders of value. It is in this sense that the human creations, such as culture and art, should be treasured as products of human creativity. But what humankind creates has to be conducive to the continuation of the natural course of Heaven and Earth, not detrimental to it. Therefore, it is in this spirit of preserving our heavenly and earthly virtues that we should at no time act against such virtues that are not endowed in our human selves by nature but that are primarily exemplified in Heaven and Earth. In this way an ecological ethics can be constructed, as I shall explain in the next section.

What, then, is the position of the human being in this ontocosmological process of creative production? In the *I ch'uan* it is said:

> [The sage, namely, a human who has attained the highest stage,] is similar to Heaven and Earth and therefore his conduct would not violate Heaven and Earth. His knowledge is comprehensive of all ten thousand things and his way will save all under Heaven. Even in acting in terms of special considerations, he does not deviate from rectitude (*cheng*). He enjoys the principles of Heaven and knows the limitations of destiny (*ming*). Therefore he has no anxiety. He is settled on the land (*ti*) and devotes himself to the sincere practice of benevolence (*jen*) and therefore he is capable of love.[12]

Chu Hsi, in his commentary on this passage, says that this is a statement about fulfilling nature (*ching-hsing*). But *ching-hsing* means to practice *jen*, the way of Heaven and Earth, deeply and widely. Chu Hsi even comments on the comprehensive knowledge of the sage as a matter of Heaven and on the saving grace to the world as a matter of Earth.[13] In this sense the sage is an apt representative of Heaven and Earth as benign rulers, not just an offspring of Heaven and Earth as parents.[14]

As a representative of Heaven-Earth, the human is not to conquer and exploit nature for his own comfort and private enjoyment because he has knowledge. It is, rather, this comprehensive knowledge that enables the human to care for other life-forms and to appreciate and protect nature. In like manner, a human is able to institute ways of governing in accord with what Mencius called a "government of benevolence" (*jen-cheng*).[15] As a child of Heaven and Earth, the human should have even more empathy with and sympathy for other living things in the world and so cannot bear to see, for example, the suffering of an ox or a sheep.[16] It is in this sense that the notion of *ching-hsing* applies. *Ching-hsing* is a

complex notion, which in a narrow sense involves fulfilling one's
own nature but in a broad sense involves fulfilling the natures of
others and the natures of all things in the world apart from fulfilling
one's own nature. Thus:

> Only the most sincere under Heaven are capable of fulfilling their
> own natures. Once capable of fulfilling their natures, they are
> capable of fulfilling the natures of others. If they are capable of
> fulfilling the natures of others, they are capable of fulfilling the
> natures of things. If they are capable of fulfilling the natures of
> things, they are capable of supporting the transformation and
> nourishment of Heaven and Earth. If they are capable of supporting
> the transformation and nourishment of Heaven and Earth, they are
> capable of forming a triad with Heaven and Earth.[17]

Who is this most sincere person? It is the person able to preserve
and reveal the genuine virtues of Heaven and Earth so that he or
she is not only able to realize and complete him- or herself but is
able to realize and complete others. As the following quote from
the *Chung yung* notes, sincerity involves both *jen* and *chih* (comprehensive knowledge as wisdom):

> To accomplish oneself is *jen*, to accomplish things is *chih*. Both are
> virtues of the nature. Sincerity (*ch'eng*) is the union of outer and
> inner ways (meaning *chih* and *jen*). It is the fitness of timely
> action.[18]

It is also in this sense that Confucius says: "It is the human being
who is capable of enlarging the Tao and not the Tao that enlarges
the human."[19]

It is clear, then, that the human being is related to Heaven and
Earth in origination. If Heaven embodies the spirit of incessant
creativity and the development of life and Earth the everlasting
receptivity and consistency of love, then the human must embody
their combination in a harmonious fusion and should apply both in
appropriate measure in thought, emotion, and conduct. Heaven is a
symbol of the cosmology of creativity and development; Earth is a
symbol of an ecology of comprehension and harmonization; and,
finally, the human being is a symbol of the combination of the two,
thus producing the ethics of integration and fulfillment of values.

Hence, we see in the Confucian sage the trinity of Heaven, Earth, and human that embodies the unity of cosmology, ecology, and ethics. It is important to see that the unity of the three is based on and unified in the ontocosmology of the Tao and *t'ai-chi*. The relationship of the elements in the trinity may be diagramed as follows:

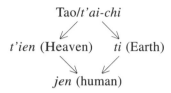

The concept of the trinity is derived from Christian theology, in which God the Father, God the Son, and God the Holy Spirit form a triad and yet are considered one, though as three positions within one.[20] As this trinity is historically soteriological, the question of how a trinity may be applied to cosmology, ecology, and ethics is a subtle and challenging question. In the *Chou i* interpretation of the trinity, explained above, we might see God the Son as the ideal human, God the Father would be Heaven (the creative spirit), and God the Holy Spirit the earth (the receptive co-spirit), or agent of the world which testifies to the accomplishment of the divinity. As I noted above, unless the transcendent notion of God is an immanent notion (immanent on Earth, immanent in humans, even immanent in Heaven), humankind's dominion of the earth becomes the domination of the earth in the name of God. Humankind then is enslaved by its own separate freedom and becomes the victim of its free will in isolation.

Finally, I now turn to an interpretation of the ontocosmological base of Confucian cosmo-ethics and ecological ethics in terms of the organismic cosmology of Whitehead. First, the open creativity and continuity of creativity of Whitehead is well suited to the principle of ceaseless creativity in the ontocosmology of the *I ch'uan*. The very way in which creativity takes place, which Whitehead describes as "Many are one and increases by one," signifies the unity and harmonious integration of differences into an emergent whole as a realization of novelty and value. As an open process of creative advance, the integration of the many in one is both an increase by one and a decrease by the many regarded as an intrinsic characteristic of the dynamic balance and harmony of the process of *i* in terms of the *T'ai-chi t'u* (Diagram of the Great Ultimate). In the *T'ai-chi t'u* a creative and correlative process displays the comprehensive harmony and dynamic transformation of the *i* in terms of the ontogenesis of the many, which can be described as "One are many and increase by many." This is the process of division and multiple divisions of yin and yang in the generation of sixty-four hexagrams and beyond. We may see this as a process of differentiation of novelty and value forming the Whiteheadian ingression of possibilities into concrete reality of actual occasions. What needs to be noted also is that, whereas many are one and increase by one, they are one and decrease by many as well. Similarly, whereas one are many and increase by many, they are many and decrease by one as well. This internal balance of "give and take," "come and go," "increase and decrease" exhibits the rich texture of harmony and balance of the reality as a creative process of novelty and value.

Second, Whiteheadian cosmic creativity is ultimately conceived in terms of the polarity of the primordial and consequent natures of God as two modes of the ultimate creative force. This suggests, no doubt, a strong analogy with the yin/yang polarity of the Great Ultimate in terms of its movement/rest and firmness/softness in which the concretion and individuation of things arise. Although one may note in Whitehead a certain transcendence of the primordial nature of God relative to its consequent nature, it may also be said to be a form of immanence with regard to the whole open process of the creative advance. The very inception of movement from the state of rest of the Great Ultimate can be seen as representing such a transcendent, yet immanent, power of the Great Ultimate and is therefore both an eternal source and an open process. The very fact that identity could negate itself to give rise to difference and difference could negate itself to give rise to identity, so that we have both difference of identity and identity of difference, shows how immanence can become transcendence and transcendence can become immanence and how, in the very action of creative change, both transcendence and immanence exist simultaneously. This must be the dialectical element in any effort of the mind to think about creativity and is conspicuously present in both the *I ch'uan* and

Whitehead. Hence, dialectically, the primordial nature of God as *t'ien* and the consequent nature of God as *ti* not only cannot be separated but are equally required for the evolution of all things in the world, including humans. That the human being can reflect on this creative process reveals the internal relationship existing between the human and the creative process of the world and indicates the source of human creativity.

Finally, we can see how a potential ecological ethics congenial with the *I ch'uan* can be developed from Whitehead, although Whitehead did not specifically address this issue. In his *Adventures of Ideas* (1933), Whitehead spoke of five values of culture that serve as a benchmark of the achievement of human civilization: truth, beauty, adventure, art, and peace.[21] It is obvious that these five marks of a civilized society are both descriptive and normative, applied to our thinking and conduct as both a standard and as a goal of our valuation. What is important is that they cannot be regarded in isolation but must be appreciated in conjunction, so that each will be reinforced and restricted by the others to form a truly harmonious and intense unity of values in a concrete sense. This harmonious unity of values can be called the *supreme goodness*, which ultimately defines human creativity as well as cosmic creativity. This is precisely the original goodness of the source of reality that is enlarged by the creative efforts of the successive stages of development—what is referred to as *chi-chih-che shan-yeh* (what is being succeeded is goodness) in the *I ch'uan*. For action with regard to ourselves, to others, and to the whole environment, there is simply no other goal or standard than this integration of values addressed to the whole of reality and to the future development of the whole reality. This is the essence of the cosmological-ecological-ethical imperative of *jen* and *chih* expressed by both the *I ch'uan* and Whitehead.

Cosmo-Eco Ethics and Moral Decision-Making

With the place of the human in the ontocosmological framework of the *I ch'uan* understood, one may draw distinctions in the approach to environment and nature between the Confucian sage and the traditional Taoist, on the one hand, and between the Confucianist and a modern technologist, on the other.

The Taoist believes in the natural and spontaneous action of nature and reality and advocates following a course of natural spontaneity as the ethical way of a good life. In order to reach the state of "doing nothing," or "doing nothing unnatural," that defines or is regarded as a method for following natural spontaneity, a common version of understanding implies, however, that one has to be cut off from both desire and knowledge so that one will not be stirred by desire or knowledge and thus act in ways detrimental to the equilibrium in which humankind and nature exist. On reflection, not only is this an unrealistic goal to attain, it is also not the principle according to which the Tao creates and moves in the world. The Tao is a creative impulse that finds intrinsic joy in the creation of the world. There is no creation if there is no vitality of life, and from the vitality of life come life-forms, with their naturally endowed desires and instinctive zest for learning and experience.

The human being, like any other life-form, belongs to the creativity of the Tao; but unlike other life-forms, the human is endowed with a far greater capacity for knowledge and a far greater ability for action. Thus, what is natural for a human is not that he or she should lead the life of a plant or a simple animal; rather, the human should accomplish a state of value befitting his or her capacity for knowledge and ability for action, but without twisting, damaging, losing sight of, or violating the larger harmony and equilibrium between him- or herself and nature, on the one hand, and among things in nature, on the other. The human being should have the wisdom to accomplish this and should strive always to develop such wisdom. This wisdom is an integrative wisdom composed of both a reflective reason—knowing and understanding the relationship between humankind and the environment—and a practical reason—acting to maintain the relationship between humankind and the larger world of nature. Insofar as humans are able to do this, they will also be able to extend their knowledge and preserve their vital desires.[22]

On many occasions in the *Tao-te-ching*, Lao Tzu has envisioned this more enlightened version of following natural spontaneity (*tzu-jan*). He speaks of the "nonselfishness" (*wu-shih*) of the sage that leads to his self-realization by way of the realization of others.[23] He also speaks of the Taoist principle of non-action (*wu-wei*) as that of "creating without possessing, doing without being arrogant, and growing without dominating."[24] This principle of non-action constitutes a new approach to natural spontaneity that could be broadly applied to human creativity generally and to environmental ethics specifically. Its general application is important and necessary for humans in order that they reflect on the extension (scope) and intension (meaning) of their thinking and knowing and on the motivation and consequences of their actions.

This first type of reflection could be called Questioning the Adequacy and Depth of Knowledge and the second type, Questioning the Adequacy and Depth of Action. It is only when questions on the adequacy and depth of knowledge and action are raised that we can gain a critical assessment of our knowledge and action according to value. Such considerations demand an understanding of the nature of things and the world of nature from a holistic and long-term point of view. They demand, especially, an intense critique of the inner self and the final good of human life. It is with such considerations in mind that any scientific knowledge must be examined from the perspective of a system of reality and value that transcends knowledge; and similarly, any action must be evaluated from a perspective taking into account the interaction, reversal, equilibrium, and harmonization of things in a whole system or process which necessarily transcends the action. Keeping this understanding in mind, it is clear that the ontocosmology of the Tao and *t'ai-chi* provides a meaningful and fundamental model for such assessment and reflection.

On the one hand, the cosmology of Heaven should provide a model for human creativity in which cultural and scientific activities must be conducive to the preservation of life, not only of the human species, but of the whole of nature. For human life would be cut short were it not to be sustained on the basis of the continuing creativity of nature. On the other hand, the ecology of the earth should provide a model for human non-action and natural spontaneity in which one must contemplate and reflect on one's creative activity so that it matures to a real fulfillment of value at large. As a final requirement, human ethics must combine the wisdom of Heaven and the wisdom of Earth in order to incorporate knowledge and action in a holistic context of equilibrium and harmony. Whether knowledge warrants action and whether action verifies knowledge are not considerations on the level of simple knowledge or on the level of simple action: they require the reflection and insight of the cosmology of Heaven and the ecology of the earth. It is on the basis of the synthetic wisdom of a cosmo-eco-ethics that we are able to fulfill our lives as human beings by fulfilling the values of our lives as the fusion of Heaven and Earth. On this point the Taoist of the Tao and the Confucianist of *t'ai-chi* coincide and reinforce each other in mutual support. The conceptual scheme of reflection for human creativity may be summarized as follows:

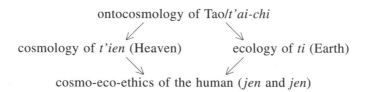

ontocosmology of Tao/*t'ai-chi*

cosmology of *t'ien* (Heaven)   ecology of *ti* (Earth)

cosmo-eco-ethics of the human (*jen* and *jen*)

I turn now to the issue of scientific and technological development. The evolution of science and technology makes a difference to human knowledge and human action. Modern science sheds light on humankind's place in nature, but it need not determine humanity's destiny or define what the good life ought to be. It is technology that actually changes human life and human society to an unpredictable degree. It is also technology based on industry that leads to environmental crisis. The question inevitably arises: Should we regard technology as a harmful activity of human culture that should be abolished from the start? It seems clear how Taoists would answer this question: Lao Tzu regarded modern technology as a "weapon of harm" (*hsiung-ch'i*) in the sense that, not only could it be applied to further war and destruction, but it could lead to "galloping and hunting which makes people crazy at heart."[25] Chuang-tzu also expresses his disapproval of technology as a means to promote the "skillful mind" (*chi-hsin*), which should be stopped before it takes root. The Taoist perspective on technology is that it does more harm than good, because it destroys the purity and innocence of the human self, leading then to a vicious cycle of the pursuit of desires following upon the pursuit of knowledge, and so on. Although Heidegger may not share exactly this same stance, his critique of technology could be construed as one concerning the ontological alienation of human from Being. It is not, therefore, simply that technology could be damaging to humankind's environment; it may actually obstruct the ontological integrity and authenticity of the human being.

According to the ontocosmology of the Tao and *t'ai-chi*, human creativity is not limited to one level of activity but is founded instead on the basis of both cosmological and ecological creativity. In this sense, both the world of nature and the world of culture form a continuum and a hierarchy of both embeddedness and ascendence. Insofar as human creativity functions in view of the cosmological creativity and takes into consideration the values of equilibrium, sustainability, harmonization, and a healthy constructive reversible cycling, there is no limitation on human creativity. This means that any technological development must be assessed and understood within a framework allowing for the interplay of knowledge and value, part and whole, past and future, and human individual and the world of nature. It is because of these considerations that we may state that the Confucian who thinks and acts according to the imperatives of cosmo-eco-ethics by using his or her abilities and capacities preserves the human value as a whole. It is with this understanding that the *I ch'uan* speaks of "opening things and forming new affairs of culture" (*k'ai-wu ch'eng-wu*), of "preparing things for extending functions, establishing utensils for the benefits of the world" (*pi-wu chih-yung li-ch'eng-ch'i i-wei-t'ien-hsia-li*)— statements that can be understood as technologically oriented and pro-technological.[26] It is with the same understanding of the actuality of both human and nature that Whitehead's organismic philosophy likewise allows for the development of technology in an open and creative context of interchange between the possible and the actual, with human self-reflection on the fulfillment of important values in a prospective course of time.[27]

In the *Chuang tzu* it is suggested that there must be a true man (*chen-jen*) before there is true knowledge (*chen-chih*). But what is a true man? What is true knowledge? The *Chuang tzu* considers true knowledge as knowing both the function of Heaven and the function of man. How, then, could one have knowledge of Heaven and of man if one does not establish in one's own mind a creative vision and a creative attitude? In fact, the *Chuang tzu* describes the true man as one who does not harm the Way with his mind and does not assist Heaven by being a human being. Furthermore, the true man is one who sees Heaven and man as a unity in which there is no opposition between Heaven and man (*t'ien-jen pu-hsiang-sheng*).[28] This emphasizes the fact that true man and true knowledge mutually ground and presuppose each other, and there is no separation between the two. But a different sense of knowledge and a different sense of the human being may be intended here. It also means that, in order to change knowledge and its use, one need change the person who has the knowledge. Similarly, in order to change the person, one needs to change the knowledge that person might have. Given the danger of environmental ruin and the urgency of the current environmental crisis, it is certainly not too great a demand to advance true knowledge and to cultivate the true person. My analysis here has demonstrated the need to raise up both the true person and true knowledge. An understanding of the trinity of cosmology, ecology, and ethics is such knowledge, and the cosmo-eco-ethical combination of the three in the accomplished Confucian personhood is such a true person. For the true person who holds true knowledge has a practical wisdom that may be mediated by technological reason but will remain rooted in the reflective and meditative reason of ontology and cosmology.[29]

Notes

1. Since 1979, many publications on environmental ethics have been published. *Ethics and Problems of the Twenty-first Century*, ed. K. E. Goodpaster and K. M. Sayre (Notre Dame, Ind.: University of Notre Dame Press, 1979), seems to set the tone for the exploration of the interface between ethical theory and certain practical problems of an environmental and social nature.

2. See R. and V. Routley, "Against the Inevitability of Human Chauvinism," in ibid., 36–59.

3. Cf. W. K. Frankena, "Ethics and the Environment," in ibid., 3–20.

4. I have, in earlier articles, used the term "intrinsic humanism" for what I mean here by "inclusive humanism" and the term "extrinsic humanism" for what I mean here by "exclusive humanism."

5. See my article "Chinese Metaphysics as Non-metaphysics: Confucian and Daoist Insights into the Nature of Reality," in *Understanding the Chinese Mind: The Philosophical Roots*, ed. Robert Allinson (Hong Kong and New York: Oxford University Press, 1989), 167–208.

6. Although a few scholars have argued for the Taoistic influence of Lao Tzu on *I ch'uan*, it is likely that both Taoism and Confucianism shared a common ontocosmological worldview that is derived from the time-worn tradition of the *I* view of its world and its use in divination. For more on this, refer to my article "On Ontohermeneutics of *Quan*: Comprehensive/Contemplative Observation," *International Journal for Yijing Studies* 1 (1995):156–203. Even though Taoism and Confucianism share the same philosophical origin in an ontocosmological worldview, this does not imply that their ethical, moral, and political attitudes must be the same. In fact, many factors influence the ways in which Taoists and Confucianists interpret the same ontocosmology and thus give rise to their specific approaches to life and politics. Besides, it could be the internal "ontological difference" in the *I* text which leads to the difference in Taoist ethics and politics and Confucian ethics and politics.

7. *Chou-i pen-i* of Chu Hsi, *Hsi-tz'u-shang*, sec. 5.

8. Chang Tsai, *Cheng meng*, chap. 2. I translate "*sheng*" in "*i ku sheng*" as being creative, because oneness is the source of creation and the motivating force behind the transformation of things. I translate "*hua*" in "*erh ku hua*" as being transformative, because it is through the interaction of the yin/yang that things are formed and transformed. In the *Hsi tz'u*, the term "*sheng*" in the statement "*sheng wu fang erh i wu t'i*" also suggests being creative. Hence, the statement means that creativity is without confinement and change is without forms, suggesting how profound and vast creative change could be.

9. See *Tao-te-ching* (Yen Ling-feng edition), sec. 42.

10. Lao Tzu said, "The ten thousand things hold the yin on the back and embrace the yang, reaching the harmony by stirring and fusing the vital energy." Ibid., sec. 42.

11. Whether this Tao is equal to the notion of *wuji* (the ultimateless) is an open question. In light of Lao Tzu's saying that the being (*yu*) and nonbeing (*wu*) mutually generate, it is better to see the Tao as combining the two as two functions of the Tao.

12. Ibid., *Hsi tz'u*, sec. 4; my translation.

13. See Chu Hsi's *Chou-i pen-i*, written after his essay on *jen* in which he explains *jen* as the virtue of heart/mind and the principle of love, which differs slightly from what he says in the *Pen-i*: "*jen* is the principle of love and love is the function of *jen*."

14. Chang Tsai, in his famous *Hsi ming*, precisely developed this parental relationship paradigm leading to the image of the universe as a large family.

15. Actually, this is the spirit of Chinese landscape painting, in which nature is represented as a place for joyful and peaceful wandering in the company of friendly birds and reposeful flowers or plants. This is a Taoist attitude derived, in fact, from the *Chou i* world outlook.

16. See Mencius's argument for the government of benevolence in the Liang-hui-wang chapter of the *Mencius*.

17. *Chung yung* (Doctrine of the Mean), 22; my translation.

18. Ibid., 25; my translation.

19. *Analects*, 15:29.

20. On the notion of positions (*wei*), see my recent article, "Philosophy of Positions in the *Chou-i*," *Orient Extreme, Occident Extreme* 18 (1996):181–98. In a recent publication in Chinese, Professor Pang Pu reiterated his philosophy of "one divided into three," which he names Confucian dialectics. His book *Ju chia pien cheng fa yen chiu* (originally published in Beijing in 1984 and reissued in Shen-chen under the title *I fen wei san: Chung-kuo chuan tung ssu hsiang kao shih* [Shen-chen: Hai tien chu pan she, 1995]) explores the formation of two from base one and the unity of two on the basis of one or toward the development of one. He has stressed the division of one into three more than the union of three into one or their subsistence. In my view, we need to stress both instead of relying on one.

21. Alfred North Whitehead, *Adventures of Ideas* (London: Macmillan, 1933).

22. A human being might also lose sight of the creative source and the holistic balance of the cosmos and act, therefore, with no consideration of the source and the interrelations among things. This creates a state of "unnatural" discord and disturbance that is bound to a cycle of self-defeating and self-destructing action. Hence, the question of human creativity is not a matter of simply following nature but a matter of participating in the natural course of creativity. It is a matter of exploring nature free from disturbing the fundamental equilibrium of nature and free from preventing the natural functioning of nature.

23. See *Tao-te-ching*, sec. 7.

24. See ibid., sec. 10 and sec. 51.

25. See ibid., sec. 12.

26. See *Chou i, I ch'uan, Hsi-tz'u-shang*, 11.

27. Cf. Joseph Grange, "Whitehead and Heidegger on Technological Goodness," *Research in Philosophy and Technology: Technology and Everyday Life* (Greenwich, Conn.) 14 (1994):161–73.

28. See *Chuang tzu*, Inner Chapters, Chapter on the Great Master (*Ta-chung-shih*), San Min version, Taipei: San Min Book Co., 1974. English translation mine.

29. Apart from Confucianism, even Aristotle can be interpreted as treating "theoretical reason" (contemplating eternal objects) as a part of human life rooted in practical reason (without, however, touching on the technological use of the theoretical). It is obvious that, for Aristotle, the human being must combine the theoretical or the philosophical with the practical in order to do the right thing. See Richard Kraut, *Aristotle on the Human Good* (Princeton: Princeton University Press, 1989), chaps. 2 and 5.

Motifs for a New Confucian Ecological Vision

John Berthrong

Introduction

It has been a hard century for Confucians. While it now seems a world lost, Wm. Theodore de Bary has reminded us that in China at the beginning of the twentieth century the Confucian tradition still dominated the educational system, the imperial civil service, and family rituals.[1] This overt Confucian domination of Chinese elite culture has since been swept away. By 1949, when Mao Tse-tung proclaimed that the Chinese people had stood up to the challenge of the West, Confucianism appeared to be one of the things that the Chinese people were going to leave behind in their rush toward Maoist modernization. Even the great intellectual historian Joseph Levenson in the mid-1960s agreed sadly with Mao that the only place Confucianism would have in modern China was in the museum of intellectual relics. It is now evidently the case that both Mao and Levenson were wrong; Levenson would be delighted, even if Mao would be disappointed, in the failure of the revolution to root out all remaining vestiges of the Confucian Way. The Confucian tradition shows new signs of life throughout East Asia; in its renewal, however, it likewise faces new challenges, one of the most striking being the ecological crisis of the late twentieth century.

The renewing Confucian tradition—now called New Confucianism in order to distinguish the modern movement from the Classical Confucianism of Confucius, Mencius, and Hsün Tzu and the great Sung-Yüan-Ming-Ch'ing Neo-Confucian scholars—faces a whole series of new challenges originating from its confrontation

with Western modernity. As is the case with so many of the historic
ethico-religious movements of the world, Confucians must come to
terms with new roles and intellectual challenges in modern East Asia
caused by what the sociologist of knowledge Peter Berger calls the
second great industrial and scientific revolution. A large part of the
renewal is directed toward figuring out just what role Confucians
will need to play in the modernization of East Asian societies and
then deciding what the tradition will want to share globally with
other cultures and philosophical traditions. To do this, the New
Confucianism will have to review, as such thinkers as Ch'ien Mu,
T'ang Chün-i, Liang Shu-ming, and Mou Tsung-san have already
done, what must be revived internally, what needs to be added to
the tradition from outside resources, and what must be rejected or
discarded from the historical inventory of the tradition as inappropriate in the modern world. For instance, the New Confucians
have uniformly rejected traditional restrictive views of the role of
women in the formation of a modern culture. The first generation
of New Confucians (from the 1920s to the 1990s) have mostly
carried out this revivification in terms of the reordering and
supplementing of a philosophic revival of the best of the entire range
of the Sung-Ming-Ch'ing Neo-Confucian heritage.

But the world has not stood still during the century in which
Confucians watched their traditional world being destroyed and then
revived. New issues have emerged, and one of the most pressing
concerns is the question of the ecological crisis. This was not
something even on the agenda of the late imperial Confucian
tradition, save as the persistent Confucian concern for economic
policies that recognized the need for the conservation of natural
resources. Here, traditional Confucians could approvingly cite
Mencius's and Hsün Tzu's reflections on the obligation to pay
attention to the human cultivation of the natural world. However,
if Confucianism is to play an active role in Chinese and global
intellectual life, it must learn how to address new as well as
traditional issues. While it is hard to conceive of a New Confucianism that does not take personal self-cultivation and social ethics
seriously, it is also now impossible to envision a New Confucianism
that does not deal with questions of international human rights, the
changing roles of women, and the ecological crisis. The crux of the
matter is that, whereas (along with many other of the global axial

age religions) the primary concern of the tradition was focused on human life and its salvation, the basis of the present intellectual and moral crisis is to discover how to preserve the best of Confucian self-cultivation and social ethics and expand it into the new area of concern for nature as the arena for ecological reflection.

This essay is a modest attempt to begin to think through what is an appropriate Confucian philosophical response to the ecological crisis of the modern world. New Confucians need to ask: What are the resources for ecological thinking within the tradition and how can they be related to the ecological crisis? How can Confucian insights into the relational sociality of human beings be expanded to include a positive view of the preservation of nature? Furthermore, New Confucians are aware that they need to think these issues through in light of global philosophy. Just as the great Sung Neo-Confucian revival was stimulated by the immense impact of Buddhist thought on Chinese culture, so too will the New Confucian movement be influenced by its dialogue with modern Western philosophy. What is intriguing about this new encounter is the joint perception that all human beings need to work together in order to address the profound question for human survival raised by the ecological crisis of the day. What this essay will try to do is to look at those major themes of the Confucian tradition that will play a role in its response to the ecological situation.

This essay will deal with the question of the nature of the Confucian cumulative tradition and will inquire how the New Confucians might address the ecological crisis. However these two historical and philosophical questions are answered, any future Confucian ecology must be based on acceptable elements or motifs of the tradition, ideal types that are amenable to searching for a Confucian method for constructing a responsible ecology. Such an ecological vision must be securely situated within the main body of the tradition and must not merely be some kind of ad hoc manipulation of items taken at random from the history of Confucian thought.

Comparison

Philosophy and religious studies are becoming more global in scope and, therefore, projects constructing comparative philosophy and theology are emerging as thinkers from the historic cultural regions of the North Atlantic world and West, South, and East Asia become aware of each others' histories and concerns.[2] Of course, most great philosophers and theologians have always assumed that their philosophies were world-encompassing in terms of truth, coherence, and adequacy. However, the statement that philosophy and theology are becoming world-encompassing emphasizes the historical fact that at the end of the second millennium Confucians are studying Plato, Aristotle, Aquinas, Kant, Hegel, and Tillich, and process, pragmatic, continental, and analytic philosophers and deconstructionists are studying Hinduism, Confucianism, Taoism, and Buddhism. Some pluralists like Walter Watson and David Dilworth have even sketched a hermeneutics based on Aristotle's four causes that takes into account as many world philosophies as they can fit into a standard-sized academic monograph.[3]

This embrace of the truly global reach of world philosophy and theology makes comparison even more difficult than it was before. Gone are the days when one could state with clarity the essence of any theoretical position simply because of the purportedly easy recognition of commonalities and differences that comes from working within one large philosophic tradition, such as what was called Western philosophy or the Confucian tradition in East Asia. At least these vast sets of interlocking Eurasian traditions did separately control their own internal canons and forms of discourse, allowing for a comparison based on common philosophic vocabularies to be made between thinkers. Essences or tight systems as stable forms of life have a way of shifting out of focus when the scope of philosophy and theology is expanded to include Western, Indian, Islamic, and East Asian forms of thought. While we are no longer able serenely to present the timeless essence of a tradition, we can still articulate synopses of prototypical positions that present the outlines of philosophies as collective intellectual narratives sharing some common features between generations. There are enough family resemblances that we can still tell a typical passage from Chu Hsi apart from Aquinas if we have a modicum of global philosophical competence.

In another essay I have outlined a view of Confucian self-understanding that does not rely on any particular philosophic affiliation but rather focuses on Confucian self-identity as a function of embracing one definitive canon as a central concern for what it

means to be Confucian.[4] This is the canon that was finally fixed
during the Sung dynasty (960–1279) as the thirteen official classics.
By centering on the notion of canon as one constitutive feature of
Confucian identity, I offer a working hypothesis that would include
thinkers as diverse as Confucius, Mencius, Hsün Tzu, Tung Chung-
shu, the great T'ang exegetes, Sung philosophers such as Chang Tsai
and Chu Hsi, poets like Su Shih, Ming activist intellectuals like
Wang Yang-ming and Liu Tsung-chou, and great Ch'ing evidential
intellectuals like Tai Chen. However, at least during the Sung
dynasty, the moral philosophers themselves, as much as they
disagreed on the total collection and organization of their concerns,
did have a selected range of themes or a medley of philosophic traits
that gave their form of discourse its particular flavor. By this I
simply mean that any educated person would be able to recognize
the difference in genre, substance, and style when reading Chu Hsi
and St. Thomas: certain themes, such as the nature of God, would
inform Aquinas, whereas Chu Hsi would be concerned with explaining the role of principle and the mind-heart. While I believe that
Confucianism is not a systematically doctrinal tradition, qua some
West Asian theological traditions, or even some Chinese Buddhist
schools like Hua-yen or T'ien-t'ai, there is most patently a series
of traits that serves to define how a group of Sung Confucian moral
philosophers read their much larger classical canon.

While I hold that all Confucians orient their thought in terms of
their understanding of the common canon as a necessary condition
for membership in the Confucian fellowship, this is not always a
sufficient reason to establish Confucian identity.[5] Modern scholars
of the tradition, such as Chang Hao, Liu Shu-hsien, Tu Weiming,
and Wm. Theodore de Bary, have noted that there is yet another
dimension to the Confucian tradition that must be acknowledged
as giving it its characteristic appeal as a philosophy, a form of
cultural discourse, and even a way of life. This is the element of
the Confucian Way's intrinsic value as something unique in the
intellectual, moral, social, technological, artistic, and religious life
of humanity. In short, this is what Confucians have recognized that
makes the whole tradition as an embodied way of life something
of more than merely instrumental value. It is the referent of worth
or excellence that can be commended to anyone seeking a moral,
intellectual, or spiritual orientation to life. It is that certain

something that, if properly understood, literally transforms the person who embraces or appropriates its message. The what and how of this axiological process is the ebb and flow of Confucian discourse as a way of self-cultivation. Furthermore, this ultimate source and process of supreme value has been called the religious dimension of the tradition or a transcendental faith in the ultimate connections of Heaven, Earth, and humanity. Chang Hao writes that ". . .Confucianism is not the secular humanism that some modern scholars take it to be, for its inner-worldly character was anchored in a transcendental belief that centered on the idea of Heaven (*t'ien*) or 'the way of Heaven' (*t'ien-tao*)."[6]

Chang Hao's interpretation of the issue is especially pertinent because he has never been identified as a partisan of the New Confucian philosophic revival that seeks to distinguish a unique Confucian sense of religiosity. Nonetheless, Chang clearly states what to him is the obvious transcendent reference of the tradition. "The overriding concern of Confucianism may be how to realize humanity in this world, but this concern was transcendentally ordained."[7] At its most basic reality, the value of the tradition lies in the ultimate as the human appropriation of *t'ien-tao*. But as Mencius recognized so long ago, this appropriation of the ultimate does not happen without human effort, defined as the Confucian task of self-cultivation. Nor, as Mencius also recognized, was this human effort to realize full humanity set within nature as a whole. For both Mencius and Hsün Tzu this recognition of human embeddedness in nature gave rise to what can aptly be called the Confucian conservationist view of human interaction with nature. Hence, to ask, why bother reading the canon, is to receive the answer that it preserves the message of the sages; yet this message remains mere words unless a person is transformed by its depth meaning. Philosophies and religions often both describe reality and commend a certain approach to it based on their description of what really is.

Tu Weiming, in a number of recent lectures, has pointed out that one cannot confine the tradition to the texts, even if the texts are crucial for a historical understanding of the development of the tradition. As Tu notes, there is a school within the Confucian tradition, rather like the Ch'an Buddhists, that would argue for a transmission of the Tao outside of the texts, a teaching that goes from mind-heart to mind-heart without the necessity of a scholarly rendition of all the texts per se. This is what Tu calls the extra-linguistic referent of the tradition. It is this extralinguistic referent, which others call the transcendent dimension of the tradition, that must be realized in the mind-heart and not merely recognized by the rationality of the mind-heart, even if there is nothing wrong with the union of reason and realization. In fact, it is precisely this fusion of reason and realization of the Tao that Chu Hsi argues is the essence of the learning of the Way.

Mou Tsung-san (1909–1995), the most systematic New Confucian philosopher writing within the circle of the moral philosophy tradition of Sung-Ming-Ch'ing thought, argued that any form of thought touched by the Confucian hand would have at least one common root metaphor as part of its interpretive matrix. Mou chose to call this root metaphor "concern-consciousness." Because of this sensibility of concern-consciousness, Confucianism has always been viewed by Western scholars as at least a social ethic, a way of helping human beings live in civility with other human beings. In terms of modern Western speculative philosophy, Mou's ideal type of concern-consciousness is a form of fundamental axiology. At the root of all being—or even the not-yet-come-to-be—is a concern for values as expressions of thought, action, and passion. Anything that is, is a value as a pattern of action, thought, and emotion; this is what is called the object-event, the subject of Confucian discourse about the creation of human relational values. As we shall see, because of this axiological view of reality, the New Confucians can expand their root metaphor of concern-consciousness to include a profound concern for nature as well as humanity.

Mou Tsung-san has himself proposed a list of four traits as a synopsis of the kinds of perennial themes he deemed essential to any fiduciary reading of the Confucian Way as a cumulative tradition and as an expression of ultimate concern-consciousness. It is perhaps better to think of these traits as ideal types, flexible constructions of sets of meaning that extend through the history of the development of the Confucian tradition. For instance, the trait of human nature has been differently understood from century to century though it has remained a perennial topic of analysis and debate within the tradition. The Confucian tradition was highly adept at adding new wine to old wineskins; in fact, the wineskins were so modified and repaired over time that it is sometimes difficult to see how they remain the same. Yet they are still wineskins and hence are useful for containing the new wine of thought.

Because Mou identified his own constructive thought more with the schools of Mencius, Ch'eng Hao, Hu Wu-feng, Wang Yang-ming, and Liu Tsung-chou, I have chosen to supplement his list with four additional traits, three from the common store of the Classical and Sung-Ming Confucian tradition as a whole and one, more specific, trait drawn from Hsün Tzu and Chu Hsi. Such a list is at least inclusive of the major trends in post-Sung philosophy, including the modern New Confucian intellectuals.[8] As we shall see, some of these key Confucian motifs relate directly to New Confucian discourse on ecology. In summary, the eight elements are:

1. *T'ien-ming* (Mandate of Heaven) as creativity itself, the ceaseless generativity of the Tao as the symbol for all that is or could be.

2. *Jen* (humaneness) as the embodiment of creativity itself as a primordial concern for others, as the Tao as manifested and made concrete in proper human ethical and social conduct.

3. *Hsin* as the mind-heart functioning as the locus of the experiential unity of concern-consciousness within any living human being.

4. *Hsing* as the formal structure of human nature, including the cultivation of the mind-heart, so that it actively creates and participates in the cosmic generativity of the Tao.

5. *Tao wen-hsüeh* as "pursuing inquiry and study" in order to exhaust principle (*ch'iung-li*) as a means for critical reason to discern the conformity of human conduct with the proper patterns of the Tao.[9] This is what the *Book of Changes* calls the "broad observation" of things and events and what the *Great Learning* calls the investigation of things.

6. *Li* as ritual action or civility as the methods and agreements human beings propose to deal with each other in a humane manner.

7. *Ch'i* as matter-energy, the dynamic force/matrix from which all objects and events are manifested and to which they return.

8. *Chih shan* or *ho* as the highest good or harmony, the peace and perfection of human nature that comes from the measured realization of the ethical life.

Mou argues—and here he is in agreement with our thesis that at least part of what defines the tradition is its canon—that each one of these traits is related to a specific canonical text or texts. Therefore, the trait of creativity, thematized as *t'ien-ming*, is best articulated in the *I ching* (Book of Changes) and the *Chung yung* (Doctrine of the Mean). It is suggestive that Mou employs *t'ien-ming*, or the Mandate of Heaven, as the primordial trait for creativity rather than Tao or *t'ien-tao*. This illustrates the point that Wang Yang-ming ceaselessly argued, namely, that principles must also be norms and that action without knowledge and knowledge without action are states empty of any true Confucian import. Or in other words, creativity as random motion without a purpose guided by moral concern is vacuous; creativity is a mandate for the good. A strong claim can be made on the basis of *t'ien-ming* that all Confucian thought can be characterized as a fundamental axiology as embodied in the art of the contextual and timely.

Jen, or humaneness as the specific way in which creativity ought to be normatively manifested in human life, is found as the central thread of the *Analects*. As for the mind-heart, the obvious canonical text from Mou's point of view is the *Mencius*. Furthermore, the patron text of *hsing* is again the *Mencius*, though I would supplement Mou's suggestions by adding the *Great Learning* because it provides many of the details about how human nature is to be structured as a process of self-cultivation. While Mou never privileges the *Great Learning* because of its associations, in his mind, with Hsün Tzu and then Chu Hsi, we need to remember that in his very last public lecture Mou himself noted that modern Confucians need to find a way to reintegrate Hsün Tzu's critical and rational approach to the tradition into its modern reformation.

The fifth trait of pursuing inquiry and study in order to exhaust principle is focused on the ideal of the investigation of things (*ko-wu*) according to Chu Hsi's interpretation of both the *Doctrine of*

the Mean and the *Great Learning*. While Mou Tsung-san believed
that Chu Hsi misread the Mencian mainline, including the *Doctrine
of the Mean*, Chu did read both texts with great piety and held that
they included the affirmation of the role of the critical use of reason
and reflection within the Confucian Way. Following a suggestion
of Cheng Chung-ying, the *I ching*'s characterization of broad
observation is yet another place where the Confucian tradition finds
a use for critical reason. Broad observation and critical reason as
reflection on the cultivation of the self through study and inquiry
neatly frame the Confucian understanding of reason per se.

As for the sixth trait, ritual action/civility, the various ritual texts
such as the *Chou li* serve to define how humaneness is understood
as ritual conduct and general social civility. It is hard to think of
Confucianism without some recourse to ritual action and social
ethics in very specific terms. In many respects, the domain of ritual
action came to be identified by many as the core of Confucian social
action and personal life when compared and contrasted to Taoist and
then Buddhist forms of self-cultivation. However much a Sung,
Ming, or Ch'ing literatus might practice Confucian quiet-sitting as
a form of meditation, when he (or sometimes even she in the late
Ming) arose from such personal cultivation, he was expected to be
a master of Confucian ritual. Of course, in the Classical period, it
was Hsün Tzu who most forcefully argued for the centrality of ritual
as a means of correcting our human propensity for inordinate self-
interest. In the Ch'ing dynasty scholars of the evidential research
school revived an interest in Hsün Tzu and ritual scholarship as the
most appropriate way to embody the Confucian Way without
recourse to Taoist or Buddhist accretions.

It is a bit more difficult to specify which pre-Han Confucian
canonical text best thematizes *ch'i* in its role as matter-energy. Of
course, the many layers of the *I ching* become the philosophic
foundation for Confucian discourse on *ch'i*, yin-yang, and the Five
Phases. The *I ching* is often the patron text not only of Confucian
thought but of all Chinese thought about these issues. Chang Li-
wen and his colleagues, in their monograph devoted to *ch'i*, begin
the pre-Ch'in period with selections from the *Tso chuan* and the *Kuo
yu*, both major historical texts for the Confucian tradition. They end
the chapter with a longer section on the *Kuan tzu* and its extensive
use of *ch'i*.[10] In the *Tso chuan* we find a list of six *ch'i*, all of which

indicate natural elements that represent the vital, life-giving nature of matter-energy; in the *Kuo yü* we read about the *ch'i* of Heaven and Earth, further expanding the role of *ch'i* as a crucial philosophic concept. It is perhaps appropriate that the trait of matter-energy is first found concretely in the historical sections of the canon, as well as in an eclectic text, because the cumulative Confucian tradition was always at pains to point out how important history becomes: it is only *in* history that the pragmatics of Confucian theory finds its moral ends.

There are at least two general reasons why it is difficult to find one patron text for *ch'i*. The first is that, of all Chinese philosophic concepts, *ch'i* is perhaps the most "metaphysical" in the sense that Alfred North Whitehead defined metaphysical concepts as those general ideas that are never absent from our consciousness. Or as Whitehead put it rhetorically, these are concepts so foundational to any cosmic epoch that they are never absent from any conceivable world. Because of the generality of true metaphysical concepts, Whitehead was loath to claim that he could identify just what these ideas really were from the limited perspective of human thought. He often said that dogmatism as to first principles was a sure sign of intellectual failure. The best that we can probably do is to approach these general ideas asymptotically and retain a healthy dose of skepticism about their finality for even this cosmic epoch.[11] Philosophy and science, Whitehead noted, are littered with failed attempts to capture the absolute.

Whitehead's point is that we normally learn about the world through the method of difference, save for metaphysical concepts that cannot be known through our normal way of learning about the world. Whitehead's own example is that of an elephant: sometimes we see an elephant and sometimes we do not, but given its size, we notice both its presence and its absence; we then make a comparison between the present elephant and its absence and generate the notion of elephant and non-elephant. Contrary to elephants, metaphysical concepts, according to Whitehead, never take a holiday from the backgrounds or foregrounds of our consciousness as elephants are wont to do. True metaphysical concepts are always there and hence we can never contrast presence and absence for metaphysical concepts for all possible worlds. Our normal ways of knowing and imagining simply do not work very well for these kinds of all-encompassing ideals. That is why Whitehead believed that we should be very nervous about proclaiming that we have actually discovered metaphysical ideas.

Ch'i plays this kind of role in Confucian thought; it is always there even when it is not the focus of conversation or concern. This was especially the case for the Neo-Confucian cosmologies of the Sung. Of course, Confucians can and do talk about *ch'i* when they frame their cosmologies, but even then they take for granted a great deal of generality for *ch'i* that needs no explanation simply because it is assumed to be obvious or clear and distinct or turbid or dense, as the particular allotment of *ch'i* under discussion may be.

The second reason why *ch'i* is not always mentioned in the short list of Confucian defining traits is historical. Rather like Greek thought, Classical Confucian discourse, from its beginnings in the middle of the Chou to its conclusion in the scholasticism of the Han, combined cosmological and ethical reflection in diverse patterns. The germane point here is that the early Confucians, and especially Confucius as he is captured in the *Analects*, were not overly interested in what we would define as cosmology as it came to be understood as reflection on *ch'i*, yin-yang, and the Five Phases. What did concern Confucius were questions of ethical conduct, ritual, good government, education, and self-cultivation. However, as the tradition developed, later Confucians such as Mencius and Hsün Tzu would utilize the work of the early cosmologists in order to defend the Confucian Way against other schools. As the scene shifts from the Chou to the Han, there was a more sympathetic interest in the cosmological speculations of the pre-Han thinkers. The great Tung Chung-shu is credited with finally fusing Chou moral thought with the general background of pan-Chinese cosmological thinking into what has been called Han Confucianism. In many respects this provides all the later schools of Chinese thought with their philosophic vocabulary as well as a pan-Chinese cosmology that is assumed to be the way the world works.

We need to stress that there is nothing contradictory about this fusion of intellectual horizons between the moral and the cosmological. Modern scholarship has shown that there was a generally accepted series of concepts that were the common property of all the Chou schools, so much so that many of the most heated battles were fought over just whose concepts were the best in terms of pristine Confucian origins. For instance, the notion of Tao itself is a perfect example of a word that all the major schools would have used in one way or another. Of course, the specifications of what the Laoist redactors of the *Tao-te-ching* thought the Tao meant[12] and what Mencius taught make the study of the classical Chinese thought of the Chou dynasty the foundation for all later developments of Chinese philosophy.[13] Ideas such as Tao, yin-yang, and *ch'i* appear to have become the common property of all the various philosophic schools at the beginning of the Han dynasty. The genius of Han Confucianism was to explain how the commonplace cosmology of the late classical world related in detail to the axiological speculations of the early Confucian masters. Tung Chung-shu believed that all he was doing was explaining how ideas such as humaneness and ritual were linked to yin-yang and the Five Phases; these cosmological ideas either complemented the Confucian ethical norms or simply served as background to the world in which the specific Confucian values were embodied.

Of course, in the Sung dynasty there was a reflowering of fascination with the cosmological dimensions of the tradition in the work of Shao Yung, Chou Tun-i, and Chang Tsai. These thinkers are remembered for reintroducing the importance of yin and yang, the Five Phases, *ch'i*, and even the equivocal concept of the Supreme Ultimate as the symbol supreme of the cosmological side of their reflections. Even in the more sober times of Ch'ing evidential scholarship, Wang Fu-chih, hardly an enthusiast for the more speculative reaches of Sung cosmology, based his systematic recounting of the original intent of the Confucian Way on a complicated explication of *ch'i* theory. It is also important to remember that Wang argued that he returned to speculation on *ch'i* because it is only out of matter-energy that all object-events emerge, especially those complicated human iconic exchanges known as rituals. Wang went so far as to develop a whole theory of *shen*, or spirit, as that which brings harmony to the constant generative action of yin and yang. Wang believed that if we did not understand the nature of the world, we could not become masters of our fate and competent ritual specialists.

It is also the case that it is probably within the general confines of *ch'i* theory that New Confucians will frame their philosophy of ecology. For instance, the notions of yin and yang have always been

related to *ch'i*, and this is one avenue for arguing about the need
for balance between humanity and nature in terms of large ecological systems. One should also recognize that this whole area will be
one wherein the New Confucians will make use of Taoist as well
as Confucian sources. While the New Confucians are committed to
Confucianism as they interpret it, they tend to be more ecumenically
open to Taoism and Buddhism than were some of their stricter
ancestors. Here, for instance, the typical argument runs that the
Taoists may well have been generally more sensitive to human
relations to nature than most Confucians and therefore that modern
New Confucians need to open themselves to the richness of the
thought, art, and symbolism of Taoism in order to restore an
ecological dimension to the Confucian Way.

The eighth trait is given two names (*summum bonum* as *chih
shan*, or highest good, and *ho*, or harmony) because it adds a final
element to Confucian reflection in line with the kind of work that
Mou Tsung-san was doing at the end of his long and productive
career. His last constructive book, published in 1985, was called
Yüan shan lun, or *Discourse on the Summum Bonum*. Rather like
Whitehead at the end of *Adventures of Ideas*, Mou argued that the
end of life ought to be the ultimate good, or what Whitehead called
peace. In Mou's case he reflected on a comparison of T'ien-t'ai
Buddhist thought and his beloved Kant—both sources caused him
to speculate on what is the highest good for humanity. In terms of
a patron text, the concluding phrase of the first sentence of *Great
Learning* teaches that the final task for becoming human is to learn
how to reside or come to rest in perfect or ultimate goodness, *chih
shan*.[14] Along with perfect goodness it also seems appropriate to
suggest the concept of harmony, or *ho*, as a further specification of
just what is entailed by the trait of perfect goodness, to move from
the generality of perfect goodness to the specifics of a harmonious
life lived with other people. Without a sense of harmony, perfect
goodness would be a hollow bell, an abstract notion. The source
texts for harmony are, of course, the first section of the *Doctrine
of the Mean* and the *Analects*, 13.23.

The first section of the *Doctrine of the Mean* teaches that what
follows from the balanced and measured issuance of the emotions
in the mind-heart is what is called harmony. It is a state that comes
about when the person has achieved not only the inner cultivation

of one's human nature but also an appropriate encounter with what is in the world beyond the human person. Hence, the classic teaches that harmony is the most excellent or perfect functioning of the Way for human flourishing. In the *Analects*, 13.23, one of the characteristics of the *chün-tzu*, or profound person, is that of agreeing with what is good and not merely echoing or accommodating the thoughts of others.[15] Hence, the profound person resides in a state of harmony but not indifferent conformity with the world, *ho erh pu-t'ung*. There are certainly strong grounds to end any list of Confucian traits or core teachings by returning to the *Analects*.

Is this synopsis of core traits or historically enduring motifs an essential reading of the tradition?[16] Of course it is at one level, and Mou Tsung-san knew this as well as anyone else. In fact, Mou argued repeatedly that a more systematic, coherent, and logical presentation of Confucian first principles was one of the crucial things called for because of the encounter of Chinese thought with modern Western thought. Mou believed that Western thought, with its attention to system, logic, and epistemology, demanded from New Confucians a more focused presentation of the Confucian Way in these terms, terms of philosophical discourse that Mou presumed to be part of any respectable modern global philosophy and theology. However, Mou's reading is not a dogmatic or closed interpretation because it is open to addition and subtraction by other Confucians. Mou, as an innovative intellectual historian, knew that some Confucians, like Tung Chung-shu, Shao Yung, Chang Tsai, and Wang Fu-chih, were more interested in cosmology whereas Mencius, Ch'eng Hao, and Wang Yang-ming stressed the more purely human and ethical dimensions of the tradition. Because of Mou's reverence for the specifics of the historical ramification of the Confucian Way over time, he would probably have held that philosophers could enumerate these various traits in remarkably different ways, even as he believed that some of these were more mainline than others. Mou's image of the tradition is that of a great tree with one main trunk but with many other huge branches that spread out over time and space. Mou argued that while there is a "main" trunk to the tree, and that it is this trunk that truly sports the rest of the tree, the more extravagantly spread branches are beautiful in their own divergent ways.

Nonetheless, if one adds the trait of critical reason, hopefully recognizing and including Hsün Tzu as a patron of this style of thought, along with a due recognition that Confucians always want to find concrete ways to embody their ethical and social ideals in a form of social praxis and structure as manifested in the protean and creative matrix of *ch'i*, then we do have one portrait of how the post-Sung moral philosophers went about their business in their relentless search for the highest good.[17] But along with reason as systematic discourse, there is always a concern for history as the arena of action, passion, and thought within the Confucian tradition. History for the Confucians is always material for philosophy in the sense that it is real as contrasted to Taoist and Buddhist doctrines of the void and emptiness. Most Confucians believed that they needed to pay careful attention to the realities of the world in order to encourage human flourishing.

Another way to look at this short lists of traits is to apply the notion of *nei-wai*, or outer and inner, to the categories. If we accept Mou Tsung-san's claim that his vision represents a modern re-interpretation of the Mencian mainline of the Confucian Tao, then we could call this the inner elements of the synopsis. The three additional traits, selected with more of an eye on Hsün Tzu and Chu Hsi, could then represent the outer dimensions of the tradition. And if we accept the non-reductive nature of Chinese dialectical thinking, we need to see the inner and outer dimensions of the synopsis as complementary rather than antagonistic. In fact, proper attention to these inner and outer elements allows for a kind of harmony of the inner and outer elements of human consciousness: it provides a balance between the intuition of the mind-heart and the observation of the external world necessary for broad study and reflection on things at hand. One could further argue that this kind of synthesis is necessary for any realistic tradition that takes the world seriously. To paraphrase a rather enigmatic remark of Confucius: It is better to study than meditate when confronted with a problem that needs solving (*Analects*, 15.31).

Of course, yet another traditional way to analyze the list of eight traits is to break them down into yin-yang polarities. If we accept Mou's first four as crucial to the Mencian mainline, then we can call these four the yang elements of the tradition. The remaining three are then to be viewed as the yin components of the set. There may be some merit in this if we remember that in classical Chinese medical theory, always closely related to the Confucian tradition, yin *ch'i* has the characteristic, according to Manfred Porkert, of structive action. Porkert means by this that matter-energy always provides a structure for reality and that this is seen as a yin function.[18] If principle and form are yang, then those elements that relate more to matter-energy are structive in Porkert's sense of that term in that they provide the living structure for the form or principle. While it is easier to see how this analogy applies to matter-energy and ritual action, it is harder to fit critical reason as reflection and study neatly into the yin-yang categories. However, if we understand the role of *tao wen-hsüeh* as preparing the mind-heart—itself the most refined and cognitive part of the human allotment of *ch'i*—for the recognition and realization of principle, then critical reason is also structive in this yin aspect of its role in the Confucian tradition.

The Ecological Connections

Stimulated by a growing realization that all is not well with the health of the planet, intellectuals committed to the great religious communities of humankind are now engaging in ecological self-criticism. The reasons for this are both practical and religious in nature. First, breathing the air or trying to look at the sky in almost any major urban area is generally enough to convince intellectuals (religious or secular) that it is high time that they begin to think seriously about ecology. Second, because religions all make the claim that they are "ways of life" sufficient unto every need, it is obvious that the religions had also better attend to the question of ecology because there will be no way of life if the habitat for life is destroyed. This has meant a lively theological debate, begun by Lynn White in his classic 1967 article entitled "The Historical Roots of Our Ecologic Crisis," wherein he argued that classical Christian doctrine helped to foster the conditions that led to the modern ecological crisis by promoting a view of the natural world as the realm of the nonsacred or as merely dead matter to be dominated by humankind for the greater glory of God.[19] White's article has spawned a minor cottage industry of scholars seeking either to sustain White's point or to discover that Christian theology is really more nature-friendly than it seems on the surface. Similar attempts are now under way in other traditions. While each tradition finds its own way to answer to charges of ecological insensitivity, none wants to be left in a position of defending the continued degradation of the environment.

The negative and positive charges laid against the axial age religions are generally of two kinds. The first is whether or not the basic assumptions of the tradition make it ecofriendly or not. For instance, it has been alleged that ancient, medieval, and early modern Christianity characteristically held a view of matter and the world that was essentially negative because the world was a source of corruption and would be replaced by some other state at the end of days. An analogous case has been made that Buddhism is unconcerned about the world because the physical world is mere illusion and that liberation from *saṃsāra*, or suffering, ends with *nirvāṇa*, a state beyond any worldly concerns. Second, even if the charge of basic hostility toward nature can be avoided, as it often is by those interested in Taoism for instance, then there is still an urgent need to search for those principles and practices that can be reaffirmed and expanded to deal with the contemporary ecological crisis. The theory here is that modern technology has transformed the whole scale of debate because, for the first time in human history, human beings are capable of literally destroying the environment as a place fit for human habitation.

The conference on Buddhism and Ecology held at the Harvard University Center for the Study of World Religions, 2–5 May 1996, demonstrated a version of the second strategy. It was first argued that Buddhism is essentially a nature-friendly tradition and that some of its fundamental teachings, such as the universality of Buddha-nature, could become the basis for a carefully crafted Buddhist philosophy of nature. Along with the recognition that there is nothing ultimately antinature in the Buddhist tradition, there was the concomitant realization that the modern situation is unique because modern technology is qualitatively different from anything that had been the case in the Buddhist world before and that the modern ecological crisis demanded a fresh review of the tradition in light of contemporary reality. However, some examples were given from the rich history of Japanese Buddhism illustrating that conservationist strains were already part of early modern Japanese Buddhist sensibility.

Following the second strategy of seeking to renew the tradition from within, New Confucians, representing a reformed Sung-Yüan-Ming-Ch'ing systematic philosophy, argue that there is nothing intrinsically antinature to be found within the eight traits of the composite synopsis. The only caveat might come from those both within and without the tradition when it comes to the fact that Confucians fairly persistently focused their philosophical approach on the human realm. However, Confucians can point to figures such as Chou Tun-i, Chang Tsai, Ch'eng Hao, and Wang Fu-chih as examples of Confucians who took nature seriously indeed. And modern New Confucians also do not believe that they need to reject as severely as did their forerunners their Taoist inclinations for a deep reverence and love of nature. Many of the sectarian quarrels of the early modern past, New Confucians argue, need not constrain the present reformation of the tradition, and dealing with the ecological crisis is a perfect test case for the need for a more ecumenical worldview to be articulated and commended as part of the Confucian Tao.

Of course, it should be noted that the first trait, that of *t'ien-ming* as the boundless creativity of the cosmos, is not merely applied to human life but rather encompasses all that has been, presently is, and can be in the future. One of the criticisms of Confucianism as a religion, namely, that it has a weak sense of ultimate transcendence, is now turned into a strength in the sense that Confucians in their more Taoist moments have always had a reverence for the world, or at least a love of its beauty. For instance, in Japan the Confucian tradition, building on Mencius, developed a defense of conservationist theory of nature as an integral aspect of solid Confucian learning and administrative lore as witnessed by the forestry policies of the Tokugawa bakufu.[20] In this cosmological and pragmatic sense, there is no ontological distinction that can be made between humanity and nature.[21] In fact, a case could be made that this foundational account of the cosmos is predicated on a view that makes humanity only one aspect of a much larger reality. The typical Confucian argument would very quickly move to articulate another primordial Confucian claim that Heaven, Earth, and humanity form a unity of lived experience wherein no one element of the triad can be elided in favor of the others. This is really an organic union of Heaven, Earth, and humanity in which each must play a role in the proper constitution of the others. As Cheng Chung-ying has argued at length, this is a dialectic of mutual relations and not the sublation or elimination of one element in favor of some new and grander synthesis.[22]

The perennial Confucian affirmation of the world is yet another reason why modern Western scholars have understood there to be an affinity of Confucian thought with American pragmatic and process philosophies. The Confucians are, for the most part, pluralists and realists who are also committed to a processive and relational view of reality. This means a closure to the world, but only in the sense that the world is the only locus of cosmological interaction between creatures and hence the only place that the creatures can sustain or destroy their own habitat. As the *Chung yung* so long ago argued, and as someone like Wang Fu-chih reaffirmed, it is self-conscious humanity that completes the triad of Heaven and Earth in a harmonious dialectic. From the mainline Confucian point of view there is no appeal for assistance from outside of the triad, though this does not mean that the world is deterministic or without recourse to the comparison of what is with what ought to be. Confucians have made a living on being prophets of the right against wrong; what needs to be added to this persistent Confucian moral vision is an expansion of its range from the typically human to the engaged cosmic.

A quick review of the other eight traits also shows that none of them can be directly construed as antinature, although again only *ch'i* theory deals concretely with human-nature relations. In fact, another case could be made that one of the prime traits of all proper human activity—from embodiment of *t'ien-ming* as humaneness, to the functioning of the active moral mind-heart, to the cultivation and articulation of human nature by means of a broad and comprehensive intellectual quest within a world of civility as expressed in ritual interaction—is an expression of concern-consciousness for every aspect of the world as embodied experience within the matrix of *ch'i*. Although *ch'i* in its ecological role has not been a dominant focus of the tradition, it certainly informs a great deal of nature poetry and painting, landscape gardening, and travel narratives as appreciations of the beauties of the natural world.[23]

A Confucian philosopher must now envision the task of cultivating humanity as part of a larger ecological system wherein human beings must cultivate a sense of reciprocal concern for the whole cosmos as the context for human flourishing itself. The specific task of embodying concern-consciousness as the epitome of human self-cultivation must be expanded to embrace a proper sense of what this concern for humanity must mean in order to create a sustainable and balanced ecosystem. Heaven, Earth, and humanity must truly learn to cooperate in ways not previously contemplated in the tradition.

The Confucian tradition has always been interested in the experience of the person who seeks to embody the Way. The praxis of self-cultivation was always aimed at helping the person become someone of integrity with the ability to face the trials of the world with a measure of equanimity. Wherein would an ecological sensitivity fit in the range of tradition and modern Confucian experience? Here again the cultivation of the aesthetic dimension of *ch'i* is probably the place to begin to look for answers. For instance, Confucians often wrote wonderful travel narratives that focused on the scenic beauty and purity of famous landscapes all over China. What does a modern Confucian make of visits to terribly polluted cities? Like Mencius's point about how the ruler's mind-heart could not remain unmoved to pity when observing the suffering of sacrificial animals, surely such sights ought to cause the same feeling or seed of ecological morality to emerge into consciousness. Therefore, linking reflection on matter-energy and how it interacts with the mind-heart as the seat of human moral sentiment is one promising place to look for the experiential seat for ecological theory and praxis. Mencius's point still holds today, even though it must be expanded to include a scale of the destruction of the environment that would have been beyond even Mencius's fertile imagination—though we need again to remember that it was Mencius who looked at the ruin of Ox Mountain and was moved to comment on this mindless deforestation of North China.

Much more can and should be said about exploring a contemporary elaboration of a Confucian philosophy of nature. Although such a philosophy of nature has never been a major interest of the tradition in the past (and the same could be said for all the Eurasian axial age religions), there is nothing within the tradition that is not conducive to addressing the modern ecological crisis. In fact, if Confucians are truly concerned about human flourishing, then they will have to find a way to contribute to the pan-human and pan-nature conversation that is beginning within and among all the religions and philosophies of the world. New features will be noticed; older points of interest will be modified or even returned to the storehouse of tradition; alliances with other religions and philosophies will be explored; perhaps here will even be a recognition of the worth of all those Taoist ancestors lurking around the beautiful grottoes and waterfalls beyond the typical Confucian purview. Even Confucius once said that he wanted to swim in a stream during the spring with his friends. If the stream is polluted, then this Confucian aspiration will be aborted. As the great Ch'ing critics of Sung-Ming moral philosophy never tired of pointing out, Confucianism should and must be a tradition concerned with the practical nature of human life, and nothing could be more practical these days than our collective responsibility to address the ecological crisis. All our streams need to be cleansed for their own sake and for the sake of humanity.

Appendix

An Alternative Thematic Worldview Outline Based on the Eight
Confucian Core Motifs

1. Root metaphor of concern-consciousness = A fundamental axiology.

2. Form = Relational and dynamic notion of *t'ien-ming* and *jen*; because of the nature of *jen* as relational, this is a correlational model that leads to the third statement concerning the plurality of object-events.

3. Ontological as well as cosmological pluralism of autotelic (self-organizing) object-events.

4. Object-Events are self-creating and sustaining = Autotelic, or self-organizing, worldview; there is only this world and no other.

5. *Ch'i* provides the field of dynamic energy for the autotelic and relational generativity of the object-events to occur. This is where ecological issues find their most persistent place. Object-events, because they are connected by and in *ch'i*, must respect each other if they are not to cause harm one to the other. This concern-consciousness is made aware of the need for ecological balance and responsibility on the part of humanity.

6. Relationships are not static or dialectical qua a higher sublation but rather a dynamic balance of changing balance and imbalance.

7. The final aim of life is harmony as the highest good, both for humanity and the cosmos.

Notes

1. See Wm. Theodore de Bary, *The Trouble with Confucianism* (Cambridge, Mass.: Harvard University Press, 1991). De Bary does a brilliant job of setting the stage for the revival of Confucianism, as well as showing just where the problems in any such attempt will lie.

2. One can make a good case for Eurasia forming one cultural world with varying degrees of intellectual contact over the last four thousand years. There have been periods, such as during the Roman Empire and the Han dynasty, when there was a great deal of trade and even some knowledge of other cultures. The golden age of Buddhism during the middle of the first millennium of the common era is another example of a period when people, products, and ideas moved across the Eurasian landscape. Compared to this kind of constant interchange, the roles of sub-Saharan Africa, the Pacific beyond Japan, and the Americas are not as sustained or as intellectually rich until after the expansion of the European powers in the sixteenth century.

3. See Walter Watson, *The Architectonics of Meaning: Foundations of the New Pluralism* (Chicago: The University of Chicago Press, 1993; with a new preface); and David A Dilworth, *Philosophy in World Perspective: A Comparative Hermeneutic of the Major Theories* (New Haven: Yale University Press, 1989).

4. Included in a special issue of *Philosophy East and West* (48, no. 1 [January 1998]) devoted to the examination of the religious dimension of the Japanese Confucian tradition. Peter Nosco is the guest editor.

5. Sarah Queen has recently argued that it was Tung Chung-shu who first provided the Confucian tradition with a clear and consistent idea of a canon as a way of defining Confucian identity. See Sarah A. Queen, *From Chronicle to Canon: The Hermeneutics of the Spring and Autumn, according to Tung Chung-shu* (Cambridge: Cambridge University Press, 1996).

6. See Chang Hao, "The Intellectual Heritage of the Confucian Ideal of *ching-shih*," in *Confucian Traditions in East Asian Modernity: Moral Education and Economic Culture in Japan and the Four Mini-Dragons*, ed. Tu Wei-ming (Cambridge, Mass.: Harvard University Press, 1996), 73.

7. Ibid.

8. Liu Shu-hsien has also offered another synopsis of Confucian themes in "Confucian Ideals and the Real World: A Critical Review of Contemporary Neo-Confucian Thought," in *Confucian Traditions in East Asian Modernity: Moral Education and Economic Culture in Japan and the Four Mini-Dragons*, ed. Tu Wei-ming (Cambridge, Mass.: Harvard University Press, 1996), 104–5. Liu's list is more extensive in that he deals with a more extended range of issues including government, politics, psychology, education, and economics. Yet Liu has been enough influenced by Mou Tsung-san's reading of the tradition that his longer list supports the basic eight elements given in my synopsis even as it goes into more detail in terms of the specifics of the cumulative tradition.

9. In a lecture on cultural China presented at the Boston Research Center for the 21st Century, Cambridge, Massachusetts, 10 March 1996, Tu Weiming suggested that this characteristic Confucian reading of "reason" can be called "analogical reason." By this I take Tu to mean a kind of reason that is critical in function yet not merely a form of technical rationalism. This is a kind of reason in service to the other key Confucian concerns and virtues.

Yet another way to get at the Confucian use of "reason" is to borrow the term "metic reason" or intelligence from Lisa Raphals's study of Chinese and Greek images of the process of knowing. Raphals writes that ". . .metic intelligence operates with a peculiar twist, the unexpressed premise that both reality and language cannot be understood (or manipulated) in straightforward 'rational' terms but must be approached by subtlety, indirection, and even cunning" (Lisa Raphals, *Knowing Words: Wisdom and Cunning in the Classical Traditions of China and Greece* [Ithaca, N.Y.: Cornell University Press, 1992], 5). What Raphals is trying to tease out here is how Chinese philosophers, and certain classical Greek thinkers, used this kind of cunning thought that is not precisely what Aristotle meant by phronesis but is still close to it. While many have suggested that Chinese thought has affinities with phronesis, Raphals suggests that the situation needs more thought and even a new designation of a special kind of reasoning, namely, what she calls metic intelligence.

10. The *Kuan tzu* has never been part of the Confucian canon, but modern scholars have recognized that its eclectic collection of materials contains elements from all the major intellectual movements after Confucius. For instance, the medical treatises are just as important to the Confucians as they are to the Taoists. It is perhaps within the protomedical texts in the *Kuan tzu* that we see most clearly how *ch'i* becomes the trait of matter-energy that will play such an important role in the later Confucian tradition. See Chang Li-wen et al., *Ch'i* (Beijing: Chung-kuo jen-min ta-hsüeh ch'u-pan she, 1991), 18–43.

It is always important to keep in mind that our labels for Confucianism and Taoism were only invented in the Han by scholars of that period trying to make sense and systematize the wealth of material that they had inherited from the classical age of pre-Han thought. Some texts, such as the *Kuan tzu*, were called eclectic because they did not conform to the way the Han historians believed the various classical schools evolved.

11. For instance, Whitehead once suggested that perhaps the ideas of identity, overlap, contact, and separation are about as general as we are going to get. He confessed that he personally could not imagine any cosmic epoch that would not be governed by these kinds of very abstract considerations.

12. The term Laoist has been suggested by Michael LaFargue, *Tao and Method: A Reasoned Approach to the Tao Te Ching* (Albany: State University of New York Press, 1994), to designate the various editors who helped to assemble the *Tao-te-ching* out of earlier teachings of what we have come to call the school of philosophic Taoism.

13. The major exception to this development of Chinese thought was the introduction of Buddhism in medieval China. The arrival of the West also witnessed a similar addition of novel terms to the Chinese intellectual vocabulary. Over time, Buddhism was itself incorporated, as it in turn enriched the classical Chinese tradition.

14. For a discussion of Chu Hsi's interpretation of this text, see Daniel K. Gardner, *Chu Hsi and the Ta-hsueh: Neo-Confucian Reflection on the Confucian Canon* (Cambridge, Mass.: Harvard University Press, 1986), 88–90.

15. My reading of this short text is guided by both Arthur Waley's and D. C. Lau's translations and interpretations of Confucius.

16. Some scholars have recently been bold enough to argue that an essential reading of a tradition is what we really might need in these days of ecological crisis. For instance, Seyyed Hossein Nasr, the noted Islamic scholar, makes just this point in *Religion and the Order of Nature* (New York and Oxford: Oxford University Press, 1996). Nasr believes that one of the problems with modern Western thought is that it has lost its proper way of dealing with nature because of the rise of a purely mathematical science and acosmic humanism. In passing, Nasr points out that Classical Confucianism and Neo-Confucianism were traditions with essential teachings about the sacred nature of nature and that we in the West had better learn to listen to these kinds of essential teachings if we want to help save ourselves from the worst effects of our modern folly. The footnotes to Nasr's book provide a bibliography for those interested in his reading of the essential features of universal wisdom.

17. The one school that I have avoided in this regard is that of the Ch'ing evidential research school. However, I would argue that in most ways they too could live with this list if we understand critical reason to include the historical sciences as well as the more purely speculative forms of fundamental axiology. It would be hard, for instance, to think of any Ch'ing thinker who would not want to start with humaneness and end with proper ritual.

18. See Manfred Porkert, *The Theoretical Foundations of Chinese Medicine: Systems of Correspondence* (Cambridge, Mass.: MIT Press, 1974), 9–54. Porkert's point is that yin is something that accomplishes something, something that is responsive to other things. Yin is a response to a stimulus. Hence, to say that yin is passive is not completely correct. It is better to say that yin is something sustaining.

19. I have found Roger S. Gottlieb, ed., *This Sacred Earth: Religion, Nature, Environment* (New York: Routledge, 1996) to be an excellent collection of primary statements on the issue. For instance, the anthology reprints the short text of White's 1967 article in full. It was first published in *Science* 155 (March 1967):1203–7.

20. See Conrad Totman, *Early Moden Japan* (Berkeley: University of California Press, 1993), for a discussion of conservation policies.

21. One could argue that this reading of the Confucian tradition links it to what Justus Buchler has called "ontological parity." By this Buchler means that we can no longer privilege any one element of our world over any other. Hence, dreams and ideas must be seen as ontologically "real" as concrete things. This would mean that nature must be seen as real as humanity. See Justus Buchler, *Metaphysics of Natural Complexes*, 2nd, expanded ed., edited by Kathleen Wallace and Armen Marsoobian with Robert S. Corrington (Albany: State University of New York Press, 1990).

22. See Chung-ying Cheng, *New Dimensions of Confucian and Neo-Confucian Philosophy* (Albany: State University of New York Press, 1991), 185–218.

23. For a collection of travel narratives, see Richard E. Strassberg, *Inscribed Landscapes: Travel Writing from Imperial China* (Berkeley: University of California Press, 1994).

Orientation, Self, and Ecological Posture

Robert Cummings Neville

The attempt to broaden the concerns of individuals and communities in order to be able to frame ecological issues fairly is sorely taxed by customary Western and South Asian conceptions of the self. The former are shaped by a strong distinction between self and other, magnified by concerns about internal contradiction and expressed in languages that use reflexive pronouns extensively to talk about the self.[1] The result is that it is barely possible to relate to other selves, except perhaps as mirrors of our own, let alone to natural processes and contexts that have their integrities in irrelevance to human selves.[2] The latter are deeply preoccupied with consciousness and, at least in their popular expressions, have been coupled with belief in reincarnation that has relativized selves to the environment of each life, with the accumulation of lives being more important than any one life. The doctrine of *karma* has mitigated this to some extent, but the result has been an interest in the multilived careers of sentient beings to the depreciation of the environment, especially its nonsentient parts.[3]

I propose a reconstruction of some parts of the East Asian tradition, especially a certain line of Confucian thinking, so as to define the habitual or ritual part of the self in terms of how the self 1) is oriented to various orders of reality and 2) integrates those orientations. In this way of thinking, to be a person is to have, as constituent elements of the self, orientations, well or badly formed, to ecological matters as well as to all the other orders of the "ten thousand things." A self should not be conceived at all except as framed by how it is oriented to the many dimensions or orders of nature.

The collection of orientations and their integration is by no means a full characterization of the self. That one is oriented to a domain of reality is not a sufficient condition for exactly what one does in that respect, although the orientation contextually shapes the possibilities of more specific action and relation. To be oriented so as habitually to recycle food containers does not determine what one does with this bottle now. Nor does a moral orientation determine a specific moral choice where there are alternatives within that orientation. But much of the character of the self is a matter of orientation. The orientations provide the hermeneutical frames within which more specific habits and actions, stimuli and responses, are meaningful.

The first thing to understand about orientation is that there are a great many things and dimensions of existence to which to be oriented, and the orientation to each can have a character of its own different from other orientations. There are the great cosmic processes we see in the stars and grasp theoretically in the language of astrophysics. There are the more earthly processes of the rotation of the seasons that determine the cycles of plant and animal life and the periods of agriculture in the planet's many ecosystems. There are historical forces that are rather like natural ones, such as the migrations of people and transformations of economies because of environmental changes. There are seemingly random phenomena such as famines and typhoons, earthquakes and floods, and the sudden appearances of the barbarians over the hill. Then there are the various dimensions of social life, the history of one's people, economic conditions, the issues in one's community, one's own life cycle in family and work, the dynamics of the family and relations to each of its members, the contingencies of friendships and quarrels, on and on.

The point on which to focus here is that each of these "orders" to which we are willy-nilly oriented in better and worse ways has a kind of career or integrity of its own. It may well be related causally to other orders, but those causal connections might not play out in how we are oriented. Each requires an orientation of its own, sensitive to its own structures and processes.

The result is that a self, and also a community, has many orientations. Hsün Tzu said that we cannot do anything at all with respect to controlling the cosmic rotation of the stars, and so our orientation to that order has to do with aesthetic appreciation and with ritual celebration that calibrates something of our pace and rhythms to the deep peace of those immortal motions.[4] With respect to the rotation of the seasons, however, our orientation takes the form at least of peasant culture, with its seasonal rhythms defining work, leisure, and a variety of things to celebrate (academics have a semester-driven calendar year to which they orient their work). Orientation to seasonal change involves dense and complicated cultural practices, which we pick up less through explicit teachings than by accommodating ourselves to certain rhythms of society. Hsün Tzu pointed out, however, that orientation to unexpected natural disasters and the sudden appearances of barbarians requires high culture, a government capable of thinking ahead, laying plans, and commanding the cooperation of vast numbers of people. Societies without good governments cannot find an adequate orientation to these surprises and are usually overwhelmed by water or warriors.

To define persons and societies primarily in terms of their orientations is to pick up on and reinterpret the observation common to East Asians and Westerners alike that East Asian culture has an extraordinarily aesthetic approach to life. Not that East Asians are more appreciative of art, literature, and music, but that they relate to the aesthetic qualities of nature, society, and persons somewhat before they respond with moral considerations.[5] The East Asian ideals have to do with poise and balance before the shifting processes of nature and society, and of one's own history. Within poise there are specific actions and also efforts at precise rectitude (as in the rectification of names), but only within the balancing act of remaining poised amidst change. Moreover, one needs to be poised in reference to the cosmic processes, poised as well regarding the seasonal shifts, and then poised within the historical, social, and personal currents, each requiring a shaped poise sensitive to its nature, scale, and rhythms. The unity of the self, or the coherence of the society, depends on being poised at large with respect to remaining poised in all those specific ways. Western and South Asian traditions are so concerned with unity that they tend toward monolithic definitions of integrity that suppress or overlook the vagaries required to be poised in orientation to the distant and bizarre elements of the ten thousand things. The East Asian

traditions in various ways urge sensitive orientations to each of the
processes of nature, society, and persons before the orientations are
integrated into the poise of a centered self. Large contradictory
orientations can be harmonized and small ones can be mediated by
irony and humor, all held together in a shifting holistic personal and
social poise.

The question of the "centered self," a Western and South Asian
preoccupation, calls attention to the East Asian variant which is
expressed in the *Doctrine of the Mean* and elsewhere.[6] According
to the *Doctrine of the Mean*, a person is a structured spectrum
between two poles. One pole is the ten thousand things to which
one needs to be oriented with sensitivity to their different natures
and values. The other pole is the pure center or readiness to respond
with aesthetic appreciation and normatively appropriate action; in
Neo-Confucianism, this center (*chung*) was analyzed as principle
(*li*). A person, of course, is not the ten thousand things alone, nor
the center alone (the Confucians criticized the Buddhists for wanting
the center alone, which turned out to be no-self, surprise! surprise!),
but the structured connections between them. The structure consists
of body, mind, emotions, habits, and all the rest, especially the
socially constructed behaviors and symbols, that can be shaped by
orientation. The orientation-theory of the self is East Asian in
inspiration, rather than South Asian or Western, because it locates
the self as the actual and habitual mediation between the ten
thousand things and the pure center, shaped most fundamentally by
orientations.

The discussion so far has combined references to the self and to
society without much discrimination, pointing out that both require
orientation. To sort that out requires that we recognize the importance of semiotic systems, social conventions, and culturally learned
habits in the definition of individuals. All of these are embraced
within East Asian philosophy by the notion of ritual (*li*). Ritual is
as biologically basic as shaping the way we learn to walk and make
eye contact, as socially basic as constituting language and gestures,
as well as the symbolic meaning of dress, feasts, and architecture,
and as religiously basic as court and religious ritual. *Religious* in
this context means the rituals and practices that have to do with
integrating the separate orientations, each poised with regard to its
appropriate order, into a harmonious person and a harmonious

society. Unlike Western and South Asian motifs for the self, which distinguish it sharply from society, the East Asian stress on learned ritual makes the self extraordinarily social.[7] Moreover, human behavior semiotically formed is not just a matter of individuals acting out socially defined roles. It is also a matter of interaction among persons as defined by the roles. To be a person is actively to participate in role-defined interactions with nature, social institutions, and other people.

The contribution to ecology of this conception of the self as an orientation of orientations lies in the focus on rituals.[8] As East Asians have argued, our orientations to nature in its various parts, as well as to the cosmos, society, and items of personal life, are shaped by rituals. We learn the orientations and, in practicing what we learn, also discover better orientations. These can all be conceived as rituals. Therefore, the moral fulcrum in the present situation is to call attention to our rituals and to improve them so as to make them better at poising us in ecological matters.

Particular actions and laws regarding ecological issues are satisfactory if we know what we are doing. But without a prior orientation to nature, without a discriminating set of different orientations to nature, particular actions and laws are likely to be blunt and do more harm than good. To attain proper orientation, it helps only a little to be more aware of nature or to embrace the metaphors of nature romanticism and deep ecology. That little help comes in the feedback they give to the identification of our actual ritual orientations to nature and to the improvement of those rituals.

Sustained attention to the rituals shaping orientations to nature's processes integrates an improved conception of individual selves and their interests, as well as conceptions of social structures as operating within ritually defined orientations. The discipline of improving orientations, and the orientation of orientations, is a contemporary example of the practice of sagehood. Its contributions to grounding morality in realistic sensitivity to the nature of things extend far beyond the domain of ecology, although the novelty of that domain calls attention to what is at stake in poising ourselves for responsibility.[9]

Notes

1. See my essay, "A Confucian Construction of a Self-Deceivable Self," in *Self and Deception: A Cross-Cultural Philosophical Enquiry*, ed. Roger T. Ames and Wimal Dissanayake (Albany: State University of New York Press, 1996), 201–17.

2. For a shrewd, if tortured, expression of skepticism regarding other selves and things, see Stanley Cavell, *The Claim of Reason: Wittgenstein, Skepticism, Morality, and Tragedy* (New York: Oxford University Press, 1979).

3. Ecological issues have caused some Buddhists and Hindus to rethink the exclusiveness of their hereditary stress on sentient beings. See *Buddhism and Ecology: The Interconnection of Dharma and Deeds*, ed. Mary Evelyn Tucker and Duncan Ryūken Williams (Cambridge, Mass.: Harvard University Center for the Study of World Religions, 1997). For a comparative analysis of the practical significance for communities and nature of the reincarnation versus one-lifetime traditions, see my *The Truth of Broken Symbols* (Albany: State University of New York Press, 1996), 247–52.

4. Hsün Tzu's primary discussion is in the essay on heaven or nature, which is chapter 17 in John Knoblock's *Xunzi: A Translation and Study of the Complete Works*, vol. 3 (Stanford: Stanford University Press, 1994), 3–22. See also Edward J. Machle's *Nature and Heaven in the Xunzi: A Study of the* Tian Lun (Albany: State University of New York Press, 1993).

5. One of the earliest expressions was Chang Chung-yuan's *Creativity and Taoism: A Study of Chinese Philosophy, Art, and Poetry* (New York: Julian Press, 1963; Harper, 1970), which uses Alfred North Whitehead's aesthetics to interpret its subject. See also Wu Kuang-ming's "Comparative Philosophy, Historical Thinking, and the Chinese Mind," *National Taiwan University Philosophical Review* 13 (January 1990):255–305; one of the most recent writings in this genre is Tuan Yi-fu's *Passing Strange and Wonderful: Aesthetics, Nature, and Culture* (Washington: Island Press/Shearwater Books, 1993). Among the many Western philosophers who have pressed this point is David L. Hall. See his *The Uncertain Phoenix* (New York: Fordham University Press, 1982) and *Eros and Irony* (Albany: State University of New York Press, 1982); see also his collaborative books with Roger T. Ames, *Thinking through Confucius* (Albany: State University of New York Press, 1987) and *Anticipating China* (Albany: State University of New York Press, 1995). On the problematic balance of aesthetic orientation and moral action, with reference to Confucianism and Western liberalism, see my *The Puritan Smile* (Albany: State University of New York Press, 1987).

6. The texts are quoted and analyzed in my "Confucian Construction of a Self-Deceivable Self," cited above.

7. True, Aristotle and others define the self as social because a person is not human without language; but the stress is not as great as in East Asian philosophy.

8. This theory of ritual is developed at length in my *Normative Cultures* (Albany: State University of New York Press, 1995), chapter 7.

9. There was some gentle teasing at the conference on Confucianism and Ecology about "Boston Confucianism" and its "South of the Charles River School." Bringing the ancient Confucian themes to life in addressing current problems that are no more East Asian than modern Western is the heart of Boston Confucianism. The stress on ritual is a main theme of its South of the Charles River School, though not neglected by the North of the Charles River sages. See Tu Wei-ming's *Humanity and Self-Cultivation: Essays in Confucian Thought* (Berkeley: Asian Humanities Press, 1979), especially chapters 1 and 2.

From Principle to Practice

Confucianism and Garden Design: A Comparison of Koishikawa Kōrakuen and Wörlitzer Park

Seiko Gotō and Julia Ching

Introduction

The ecology movement has made great strides in the West. But arguments for protecting the environment are often derived mainly from utilitarian considerations. There is a need still for comparative studies, for looking at other cultures and their views of nature.

In this study, we wish to call attention to the fact that garden design is considered in today's Japan to be a part of environmental planning, since it contributes to the preservation or enhancement of the natural surroundings. It is our intention here to discuss Confucian influences on two gardens, both in existence today, though designed several hundred years ago and separated by a great distance. These two gardens are Kōrakuen in Tokyo and Wörlitzer Park near Berlin.[1]

We have no record of the exact date Confucianism was introduced to Japan, although it is considered to have been some time during the fifth century C.E. This is an indication of the smooth integration of Confucian thought into Japanese culture, a smoothness facilitated in large part by the Japanese life-style, which was receptive to Confucian influence. The ancient Japanese, under the influence of Shintō, already had strong, though vague, ideas about the relationship between humans and nature, and Confucian thought both reinforced these ideas and systematized them.[2]

From China, Confucianism was introduced into Europe during the Enlightenment. From the sixteenth to the eighteenth century,

European imports from China included not only trade goods but also objets d'art and ideas of philosophy. Far Eastern philosophy was virtually unknown in Europe before the Crusades, but it grew in influence after the discovery of new trade routes during the sixteenth century, finally blossoming during the eighteenth century.[3] Pivotal Enlightenment thinkers, such as Christian Wolff and Immanuel Kant in Germany, Jean-Jacques Rousseau, Voltaire, and François Quesnay in France, and even Isaac Newton in England, were inspired in part by the study of Chinese ideas and images. These included images of a paradise of Taoist immortals, which the Europeans had also encountered. These ideas, both Confucian and Taoist, had a great influence on the aesthetic principles of garden design in both England and on the continent.

The English garden, with its preference for nature as it exists rather than nature formalized, as in French and Italian gardens with their geometrical designs, is an example of how Chinese influence worked. It also incorporated the inspiration of Chinese philosophy, especially of Confucian ideas. Wörlitzer Park, another example of this fusion, with its didactic elements derived from Confucianism married to the picturesque ideas of the emerging tradition of English landscape painting, received its Chinese influence through the intermediary of the English garden.

We shall briefly contrast the design features of traditional gardens in Japan and the West and then demonstrate how Confucian ideas affected the designs of Kōrakuen and Wörlitzer Park, two gardens from these respective traditions.

Notions of Paradise: East and West

In the West gardens are often considered human projections of an earthly paradise. In ancient Japan, the whole of nature was believed to be alive. All the natural forces—water, mountain, or wood—were thought to control human destiny and were worshipped as gods (*kami*). This ancient animistic view, known as Shintō, placed the worlds of human beings, gods, and nature on a continuum. In other words, there was no rigid barrier between human beings and the gods.[4]

In contrast to the Japanese conception of a continuum, the Western Christian worldview presents the exile of humans from

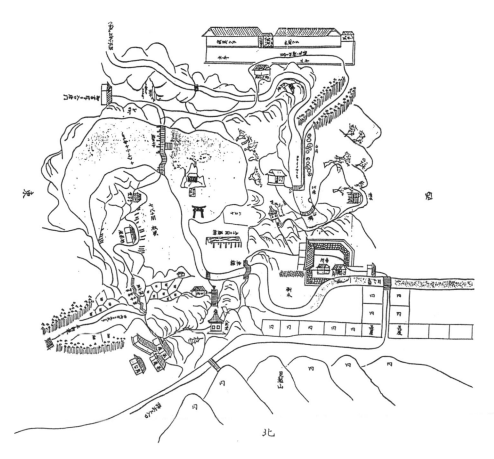

FIGURE 1: PLAN OF KOISHIKAWA KŌRAKUEN
(by permission of Shō-kō-kan, Mitō)

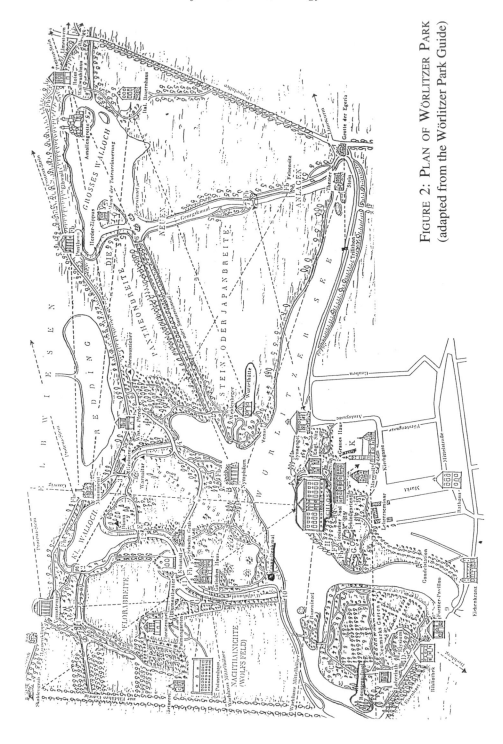

FIGURE 2: PLAN OF WÖRLITZER PARK
(adapted from the Wörlitzer Park Guide)

paradise as a punishment for human sin, with a resulting separation between paradise and the human world. Gardens in the Christian world were thus designed to represent the biblical image of paradise. They were conceived as special, enclosed spaces, which marked the separation between the divine and the human. If we look at the design of the monastic garden, we recognize its characteristic cruciform division into four parts. The perimeter of the garden is enclosed by a covered walk, and fruit trees and herbs are planted around a fountain at the center. The geometric layout of the monastic garden reflects the accepted standard configuration of the Garden of Eden as described in the Old Testament:

> And out of the ground the Lord God made to grow every tree that is pleasant to the sight and good for food, the tree of life also in the midst of the garden, and the tree of the knowledge of good and evil.
>
> A river flowed out of Eden to water the garden, and there it divided and became four rivers.[5]

However, the very continuum between humans and nature that was the result of animistic influence in Japan did not and probably could not dictate any specific form for the garden. In the seventh century the Japanese word for garden, *niwa*, was used to indicate the purified place in which are enshrined the gods of nature. Such identification of the garden with a shrine did not predetermine the physical form of the garden. Shrines were inspired by the surrounding natural features and were built in accordance with this inspiration. Sometimes, places inhabited by the gods were located in areas covered in white pebbles, where a tree might indicate the god's spirit or a large stone his seat. The rocks found in Japanese gardens are representative of such sacred rocks.

With the introduction of Buddhism from China and Korea to Japan in the sixth century, the Japanese began to develop the concept of a paradise separated from the human world. Thus, they began to construct palace and temple gardens in the image of this paradise in which the gods were thought to live. Within the abstract form of the Japanese garden, natural features such as mountains, rivers, or forests were made to represent the world of the gods. In order to represent all of these natural elements within a restricted area, the principles of miniaturization and symbolization were employed.

Nature in miniaturized form was intended to replicate the natural surroundings as they existed on a large scale. The miniaturized features of the Japanese garden were given symbolic meaning through their shapes and names. These techniques stand in contrast to the use in the West of abstractions from nature in order to represent a paradise separated from the human world. Both Kōrakuen and Wörlitzer Park are clearly products of their respective traditions. However, each also demonstrates the direct and indirect influences of Confucian thought on its design.

By Confucian influence, we refer to a love of nature and to a view of the continuum between man and nature, much as we also find in Taoism. These are merged with certain moral teachings, with many references to the Chinese classical past. Without neglecting pleasure, Confucianism places duty before pleasure. Such a spirit is found in the fourth-century B.C.E. Confucian thinker Mencius, who also taught *jen* (humanity) together with *i* (righteousness, or justice). In doing so, he frequently focused on issues of economic and social justice.

In conversations with various rulers of small states, Mencius appears often to put the kings on the defensive regarding their luxurious life-styles. For example, as King Hui of Liang stood over a pond, he asked Mencius: "Are such things enjoyed even by a good and wise man?" The answer was: "Only if a man is good and wise is he able to enjoy them. . . . It was by sharing their enjoyments with the people that men of antiquity were able to enjoy themselves."[6]

In other words, a king might have a beautiful garden with a huge pond. But he is expected to share its enjoyment with his people. Presumably, he is expected to enjoy his garden *after* having performed his duties for the people. The name Kōrakuen reflects this idea. This enjoyment is also to be moderated by a sense of discipline and an understanding of the need to offer a moral example to the people.

Kōrakuen

Kōrakuen today is a national historic garden owned by the Tokyo municipal government. It was first designed and built nearly four hundred years ago. The original idea was conceived by the Daimyo

Tokugawa Yorifusa in conjunction with the Shōgun Tokugawa Iemitsu on a site which was once as large as 290,172 square meters. Today, only 6,050 square meters of the inner garden and a part of the back garden remain. Kōrakuen was designed according to the traditional Japanese philosophy of garden-making, which shows admiration for nature through its depiction's of natural beauty. Famous scenic locations were miniaturized, and small temples were built in the garden, dedicated to the gods of nature. However, the garden differed from other Japanese gardens because it incorporated Confucian elements in its design. This happened with Yorifusa's son and successor, Mitsukuni.

In 1661, thirty-three years after Kōrakuen's construction, Mitsukuni, the third son of Yorifusa, succeeded his father as the second lord of the Mitō clan. He was chosen over Yorishige, his eldest brother, for various political reasons. An active youth, Mitsukuni did not excel in his studies. However, this changed when he was eighteen, after he read the story of the two legendary Chinese hermits Po-yi and Shu-ch'i. Neither Po-yi nor Shu-ch'i succeeded their father to become head of their family. Instead, they yielded their place to their brother. Mitsukuni was very impressed by the relevance of this story to the circumstances surrounding his own succession, and it motivated him to reconsider his attitudes. He subsequently devoted himself to his studies, especially Confucianism.

After his succession, Mitsukuni founded an institution called the "Shō-kō-kan," which he gave the task of editing *The Great History of Japan* (*Dainihonshi*) at his Koishikawa residence. He invited about one hundred and thirty scholars from all over the country to study Confucianism and Japanese history. In July 1665, Mitsukuni invited the Confucian scholar Chu Shun-shui (1600–1682) to his residence. Shun-shui's knowledge ranged from agriculture to Confucian thought, and he placed particular value on the practical application of this knowledge. Shun-shui, who had a tremendous influence on the establishment of the Mitō school, a branch of Japanese Confucianism,[7] remained Mitsukuni's advisor until his death at his residence in Komagome.

Confucian principles permeated Mitsukuni's contributions to policy, education, and culture. Among his greatest accomplishments was the embellishment of the Kōrakuen. Mitsukuni made several significant additions to the garden. He erected statues of his admired sages, Po-yi and Shu-ch'i, in the existing Tokujin Temple, as well as a statue of a scholar given to him by the Shogun Iemitsu when Mitsukuni was eight years old. The latter was placed in the Octagonal Temple. Mitsukuni was also responsible for the naming of a structure in the garden where guests could be served liquor. This he called the "Nine-Eight Shop," which refers to the fact that one should drink only until one is 90 percent satisfied during the day and 80 percent at night. This is an allusion to the Confucian belief that it is best to be satisfied with 80 percent—the complete fulfillment of one's desires leads only to a decline in one's expectations.

In addition to these modifications to the garden, Mitsukuni asked Shun-shui to create miniaturized views recalling scenic locations with important literary significance. Many Japanese sites known for their natural beauty through waka poetry had already been constructed by Yorifusa. To these, Mitsukuni added landscapes recalling renowned Chinese references, such as "West Lake" and "Moon Bridge." Shun-shui also selected the name "Kōrakuen" as a reference to the words of Fan Chung-yen (989–1052), a Neo-Confucian scholar from the Sung dynasty: "A scholar is the first to worry about the world and the last to enjoy its pleasures." The Chinese word for "scholar" (*shih*) is also understood in Japanese as "lord" or "warrior." Mitsukuni presumably understood the phrase as: "The lord worries before the people and enjoys after the people"—that is, while loving nature and enjoying its pleasures, the Confucian remains morally conscious of the need to share this enjoyment with others. This saying of Fan Chung-yen's may at first sight appear joyless.[8] It actually assigns priorities, placing duty before pleasure without denying either.

Mitsukuni frequently held performances and parties in the garden during which he and his retainers composed poetry. The parties were held, not only during the day, but also after dark, lit by moonlight and bonfires. For example, on 24 March 1678, a flower-viewing party was held, during which twelve poems were recorded, including one by Mitsukuni. The following month, on 17 April, a firefly-viewing party took place in the evening, and twenty-two poems were recorded. These writing parties reflected the value placed on talented writers during the Heian period (794–1192), when such writers were considered the most important figures at court. The competitions were organized in order to improve the quality of poetry among the retainers. However, the gatherings in Kōrakuen also had political overtones: they were occasions for the lord to become better acquainted with his retainers. The natural beauty of the garden setting was used for social and diplomatic exchanges. Thus, in Mitsukuni's time, Kōrakuen's design, informed by Confucian ideals, also became a setting for the teaching and practical application of those ideals.

Wörlitzer Park

Prince Franz of Dessau and Wörlitzer Park

Wörlitzer Park is an English-style garden in Germany. The formal layout of the garden reflected the physiocratic beliefs of the Enlightenment, which were derived from the agriculturally based Confucian economic models introduced to Europe from China throughout the eighteenth century. Wörlitzer Park was laid out as an English garden, a style developed during the eighteenth century and characterized by its avoidance of strict geometric forms, embracing instead natural scenery as part of the garden design. This change in style was related to current trends in European landscape painting. Many English-style gardens were direct attempts at three-dimensional replication of landscape paintings, like those of such artists as Claude Lorrain. In addition, many English-style gardens contained Chinese-style buildings, such as pagodas and Chinese towers, reflecting a decorative style fashionable at that time, inspired by the steady influx into Europe of Chinese lacquer ware and porcelain. Wörlitzer Park was the first English-style garden to be built in Germany, an example of the spread of this style to the continent.

Wörlitzer Park was constructed by Prince Leopold Friedrich Franz von Anhalt-Dessau (1740–1817) in 1770, a time when the Enlightenment had a vigorous hold on Western Europe. During his three grand tours, Prince Franz learned about the most recent developments in contemporary European philosophy and their influence on European culture. The inspirational effect that these new and exciting ideas had on him are evident in the design of the garden. Enlightenment notions are woven into the garden, and the influence of chinoiserie and the picturesque are evident.[9]

With the construction of Wörlitzer Park, Prince Franz reproduced a Claudian landscape.[10] The natural scenery of woods and lakes that he devised drew on the designs of such gardens as Stourhead, which he had visited while in England.[11] The rustic was represented by a loggia he had built in the woods, while a Chinese tower, similar to the pagoda at Kew Garden in England, incorporated the exotic into the design. These exotic and picturesque elements were the direct influence of the English architect Sir William Chambers (1723–1796), whom Prince Franz had visited.[12] Chambers, the designer of Kew Garden in London, was influenced by Chinese garden design.

Even more integral to the design of Wörlitzer Park than the picturesque and the exotic was the incorporation of a didactic element. During his second grand tour Prince Franz was influenced by the art and architecture of Italy and met with such influential Enlightenment thinkers as Jean-Jacques Rousseau (1712–1778) and François Quesnay (1694–1774). In addition to serving as the personal physician to the king of France and to the king's mistress, Madame Pompadour, Quesnay was an avid student of economics. The influence of Quesnay's physiocratic ideas on the design philosophy of Wörlitzer Park was especially important.

Quesnay and Physiocracy

François Quesnay's physiocracy is at the core of the Enlightenment influence on the French Revolution and represents a cornerstone of modern economic thought.[13] The French economy was suffering under an enormous debt as a result of the excessive expenditures of Louis XIV. In addition, involvement in the Thirty Years War and other European conflicts during the seventeenth century had devastated the population and, as a result, agricultural production was reduced to one-third of its previous output. Quesnay's philosophy sought to establish economic stability through the reform of agricultural communities.[14]

During this period, Jesuit missions in Asia were also at the height of their influence. There was a continuous flow of correspondence between the missionaries and Rome, and the information contained in this correspondence was published throughout Europe. Through these letters, knowledge about Asia was widely disseminated during the eighteenth century. In particular, scholars looked to Confucianism and other Chinese philosophies as models for social reform.[15] Those missionaries who were in Paris were frequent visitors to Madame Pompadour, and as her physician, Quesnay benefited from his patron's interest in discussions about China. Especially influential was Kō, a Chinese scholar brought to Paris by the missionaries around 1750, from whom Quesnay learned many of the details of Confucian thought. Quesnay was so enthusiastic about Confucian ideas of physiocracy that he was called "the continuator of the work of Confucius" by his students.[16]

Central to Confucian doctrine is the responsibility of the ruler to his country. Quesnay was also impressed by the Chinese agricultural system, which inspired him to write *Tableau Economique*, in which he proposed land as the basis of the economy. Quesnay also stressed the importance of education. Hence, all of the ideas central to physiocracy, a political theory based on agricultural reform, were derived from Chinese Confucianism.[17]

The Design of Wörlitzer Park

In the design of Wörlitzer Park, several islands were set in an artificial lake connected by a series of streams. The island nearest the park entrance was named "Rousseau's Island" and was modeled on the island of Ermenonville in Paris, the location of Rousseau's residence for several months before his death and the site of his tomb. As at Ermenonville, a monument was built with a description of Rousseau.[18]

On other islands, Prince Franz created amphitheaters, labyrinths, and even an artificial volcano. The volcano spouted magma made of red glass, which, lit at night, made the room within the volcano an ideal site for parties. The hilltops of the garden, visually connected with each other across open vistas, were crowned with temples and statues displaying philosophical inscriptions.

The many architectural styles and the variety of sculpture and artwork, as well as of the inscriptions, served to teach the visitor about world culture and philosophy. Open to the public, visitors to Wörlitzer Park were allowed to stay in the guest house. Thus, the park served a didactic purpose as a place from which people could both learn and derive pleasure, according to Confucian teachings. Through its design, the landscape of Wörlitzer Park represented an Enlightenment response to Confucianism.

Wörlitzer Park and Kōrakuen

We now turn to a comparison of the ways in which Confucian ideas are expressed in the designs of both Kōrakuen and Wörlitzer Park. With the Pantheon and the Temple of Venus at Wörlitzer Park and the Temple of Tokujin and the Octagonal Temple at Kōrakuen, both gardens provided locations for inscriptions intended to provoke moral enlightenment. The two gardens also incorporated bridges built using the most advanced technologies of the time. The iron bridge at Wörlitzer Park reproduced in miniaturized form an iron bridge in England that was at the forefront of current bridge-building technology. Similarly, the moon bridge in Kōrakuen was built by Chu Shun-shui using technologies previously unknown in Japan at the time.[19]

Furthermore, the design of Wörlitzer Park included farmland modeled on English agricultural practices in order to demonstrate modern cultivation techniques. Though Prince Franz had never been to Japan, this feature of the garden was called "Japanische Breite" (Japanese Field). It is quite possible that this reference to Japan is purely coincidental, since it is likely that contemporary uses of the word "Japan" were references to a specific geographical region of China rather than to a distinct country.

In contrast to the aesthetic belief of the time, which held the value of beauty to be unique to each individual observer, Prince Franz ascribed to the philosophy that "real beauty is beautiful and useful." This is a reversal of the Kantian belief asserting the "independence of beauty" and represents instead a return to the ideas of Greek thinkers such as Socrates, who asserted that "all beauty is fitted to its use." In accordance with Franz's philosophical views, a haystack became an integral element of the garden, as did oak trees planted to prevent flooding. Architectural features of the garden also reflected this philosophy, built as refuges for visitors to the park. By building Wörlitzer Park to embody his philosophy,

FIGURE 3: RICE PADDIES, KOSHIKAWA KŌRAKUEN (photograph by Seiko Gotō)

FIGURE 4: FARMLAND, WÖRLITZER PARK (photograph by Seiko Gotō)

Prince Franz intended his garden to broaden the knowledge of the people and to bring about social reform by teaching the importance of agriculture, the basis of the economy according to Confucian thought. Thus, the agricultural efficiency and the return to Greek aesthetics represented by Wörlitzer Park exhibited the influence of Confucianism on the garden design.

At Kōrakuen, Mitsukuni laid out rice paddies for similar educational purposes. Since the Heian period, many poems throughout the history of Japanese literature mention rice paddies, but none had been constructed in gardens until the Edo period. Though poetic techniques varied, common to all periods was an appreciation for the green and golden colors of the rice paddy and the way in which rice paddies express the changing seasons. However, Mitsukuni intended the rice paddies not only to be inspirational poetic subjects but also to teach about the hardships endured by farmers. Knowledge about the nature of farmers' work is considered essential for the ideal Confucian ruler, and Mitsukuni demonstrated both farming and weaving techniques to the wife of the third lord. The rice paddies at Kōrakuen, like the farmland of Wörlitzer Park, were important, not merely for their poetic inspiration, but also for didactic purposes. In addition, several features of the garden are compatible with the philosophy of practical beauty valued by Prince Franz. At Kōrakuen, Mitsukuni created a bamboo forest that would provide bamboo for spears and planted a forest of plum trees that could be harvested in time of war.

Conclusion

Both Kōrakuen and Wörlitzer Park stand out from other gardens of their time in their concern for the Confucian ideal of self-cultivation through an integration of history, literature, and art with nature. In the case of Japan, a new relationship between humans and nature was developed, which lent nature a practical and political dimension. In the case of Germany, the correspondence between humans and nature was established. Rather than viewing nature as a force to be fought and brought under the control of human will, nature in the European garden was considered to be in harmony with the economy and with human social systems. Though the gardens differed in many aspects, including size, time period, and country of location, both gardens served a didactic purpose in addition to presenting beautiful scenery. At Kōrakuen, horseback-riding demonstrations exhibited the military arts, temples recalled Confucian stories, and rice paddies showed the work of the farmers. Wörlitzer Park was open to the public, which learned about diverse world cultures, agricultural practices, and technological advancements through the park's design, which incorporated a variety of architectural styles, temple designs, and sculptural and farming techniques.

We can learn from these two examples of the possible didactic roles garden design can play—roles that in turn remind us of the important part nature plays in human existence. Though most of the Confucian allusions found in Kōrakuen are hardly recognized as such by visitors today, the didactic purpose of the garden is still served, as neighborhood elementary school children cultivate the rice paddies. The ascription of a didactic role to nature, as exemplified in Wörlitzer Park, was adopted in the planning of the public spaces of Central Park in New York City, as well as in other urban parks built since the late nineteenth century. It would not be unreasonable to say that the philosophical foundations underlying the design of these gardens have led to a heightened sensibility to the importance of gardens in both countries. These foundations still actively inform contemporary notions about self-cultivation through nature as well as about the role of nature in urban environments in both East Asia and the West.

Notes

1. The garden named Kōrakuen we examine here is in Koishikawa, in central Tokyo. There is another Kōrakuen in Okayama. This study was first presented by Seiko Gotō as a paper at the conference on Confucianism and ecology at Harvard University in the summer of 1996. Shortly before that, Julia Ching had the pleasure of meeting Seiko Gotō and of discussing Confucianism and Kōrakuen, a topic of shared interest. Both authors wish also to thank Graham Mayeda for his kind help.

2. Confucian thought flourished in Japan during the Tokugawa, or Edo, period (1600–1868), an era in which Confucian ideas were promoted in the areas of politics, ethics, and education. Consult *Principle and Practicality: Essays in Neo-Confucianism and Practical Learning*, ed. Wm. Theodore de Bary and Irene Bloom (New York: Columbia University Press, 1979), introduction; Robert Bellah, *Tokugawa Religion: The Cultural Roots of Modern Japan* (New York: Free Press, 1957); and *Tokugawa Japan: The Social and Economic Antecedents of Modern Japan*, ed. Chie Nakane and Shinzaburo Oishi (Tokyo: University of Tokyo Press, 1990), introduction.

3. Consult Julia Ching and Willard G. Oxtoby, *Moral Enlightenment: Leibniz and Wolff on China* (Sankt Augustin: Institut Monumenta Serica; Nettetal: Steyler Verlag, 1992), introduction, 1–36.

4. Consult Jean Herbert, *Shinto: The Fountainhead of Japan* (London: George Allen and Unwin, 1967); William K. Bunce, *Religions in Japan* (Tokyo: Charles E. Tuttle, 1955), chaps. 6–8.

5. Genesis 2:9–10 Revised Standard Version.

6. *Mencius* 1A.2; see D. C. Lau's translation, *Mencius* (Harmondsworth: Penguin, 1970), 50.

7. Consult the *Giko Jitsuroku* (The records of Tokugawa Mitsukuni), kept in the National Diet Library, Tokyo. See also Julia Ching, "The Practical Learning of Chu Shun-shui," in *Principle and Practicality*, 189–229.

8. *Fan Wen-cheng kung wen chi* (Ts'ung shu chi ch'eng edition), 1st series, 3:19.

9. See Gert Gröning, "The Idea of Land Embellishment," *Journal of Garden History* 12 (1992):164–85; Dusan Ogrin, *The World Heritage of Gardens* (New York: Thomas and Hudson, 1993), 291.

10. The reference is to Claude Lorrain, an eighteenth-century French painter to whose influence we owe the "picturesque garden." Consult Monique Mosser and George Teyssot, *The Architecture of Western Gardens: A Design History from the Renaissance to the Present Day* (Cambridge, Mass.: MIT Press, 1991), 302.

11. Stourhead was begun by Henry Hower (1705–1785) in 1735 and completed in 1783. He collected landscape paintings, such as those of Claude Lorrain. The scenery of Stourhead was created to replicate these landscape paintings. The

garden is surrounded by hills and has a lake with an island. There are grottos and temples on the lake's shore that represent Virgil's *Aeneid*. See Ogrin, *World Heritage of Gardens*, 133–34; Christopher Thacker, *The History of Gardens* (Berkeley: University of California Press, 1979), 192–94; Derec Clifford, *A History of Garden Design* (London: Faber and Faber, 1962), 143.

12. Sir William Chambers was a gardener for the Princess of Wales and taught painting to her son, George III. Chambers visited China and wrote *A Dissertation on Oriental Gardening* (London: Griffin, 1772). He designed Kew Garden in 1761. Ogrin, *World Heritage of Gardens*, 131; Thacker, *History of Gardens*, 216; R. C. Bald, "Sir William Chambers and the Chinese Garden," in *Discovering China: European Interpretations in the Enlightenment*, ed. Julia Ching and Willard G. Oxtoby (Rochester, N.Y.: University of Rochester Press, 1992), 142–75.

13. François Quesnay, *Quesnay's Tableau Economique*, trans. Marguerite Kuczynsk and Ronald L. Meek (London: Macmillan; New York: A. M. Kelley for the Royal Economic Society and the American Economic Association, 1972); Henry Higgs, *The Physiocrats: Six Lectures on the French Economists of the Eighteenth Century* (Hamden, Conn.: Archon Books, 1963), 22–48; Ronald L. Meek, *The Economics of Physiocracy: Essays and Translations* (Cambridge, Mass.: Harvard University Press, 1963), 43–56; Elizabeth Fox-Genovese, *The Origins of Physiocracy: Economic Revolution and Social Order in Eighteenth-Century France* (Ithaca, N.Y.: Cornell University Press, 1976); Adolf Reichwein, *China and Europe: Intellectual and Artistic Contacts in the Eighteenth Century* (New York: Kegan Paul, 1925), 99–110.

14. Consult Lewis A. Maverick, *China, A Model for Europe* (San Antonio: Paul Anderson, 1946), translated from François Quesnay, *Le Despotisme de la Chine* (Paris, 1767).

15. Reichwein, *China and Europe*, 15–22, 73–98, 107–8; Donald F. Lach, *Asia in the Making of Europe* (Chicago: University of Chicago Press, 1965).

16. Reichwein, *China and Europe*, 104.

17. Ching and Oxtoby, *Discovering China*, 113.

18. This is a picturesque garden constructed by Marquis Girardin (1735–1803) in 1764 and completed in 1773. Ogrin, *World Heritage of Gardens*, 92; Dora Wiebenson, *The Picturesque Garden in France* (Princeton, N.J.: Princeton University Press, 1978), 81–88.

19. Seiko Gotō, *Koishikawa Kōrakuen no Sakutei ni okeru Tetsugaku* (The philosophy of garden making at Koishikawa Kōrakuen) (Chiba: Chiba University, 1997).

Some Thoughts on Confucianism
and Ecofeminism

Huey-li Li

Introduction: Paradoxes on Treasure Island

Recent discourse on environmental ethics focuses on extending our moral concern for human interests to all other livings beings and to nature as a whole. To many environmentalists, such a nonanthropocentric perspective is the fundamental ethical solution to today's ecological crisis.[1] Although the unity of humans and nature is not a novel idea, its widespread attention in the current environmental movement can be attributed to American historian Lynn White's controversial argument that today's ecological problems are rooted in the Christian doctrine of human dominion over nature. According to White, Judeo-Christianity is the most anthropocentric religion because it "not only established a dualism of man and nature but also insisted that it is God's will that man exploit nature for his proper ends."[2] White further argues that "more science and more technology are not going to get us out of the present ecological crisis until we find a new religion, or rethink our old one."[3] In seeking a new religion, White and others consider many non-Western religious traditions as favorable alternatives to Christianity.[4] These religious traditions share ecologically congenial features, such as a reverence for nature, a nonanthropocentric worldview, and a belief in the organic interconnection among all living beings. At a theoretical level, these religious traditions appear to provide us with a ready-made conceptual foundation for a global environmental ethic.

However, as a baby boomer growing up in Taiwan, I have been amazed at the fact that the Taiwanese people continue to cherish ecologically congenial religious beliefs (such as an organic world-view, a reverence for nature) at the same time that they appear to be indifferent to the far-reaching effects of ecological disasters. In view of such a paradox, I have been skeptical about Lynn White's argument that Christianity is the principal conceptual root of today's ecological crises. Furthermore, I am puzzled that some scholars have represented Asian religious traditions as congenial to the environment, while others have acknowledged Asian religious traditions' contribution to the successful industrialization of East Asia, challenging Max Weber's argument that Asian religious traditions are fundamentally uncongenial to modernization.[5] More specifically, these scholars have identified Confucian values as the "functional analogues" of the Protestant values that facilitated the economic development of East Asian countries.[6] I believe that this apparent contradiction in the function of Confucianism—embracing the unity of humans and nature and yet still supporting industrialization—should alert us to the fact that environmental degradation and industrialization are interrelated.[7] In other words, it is problematic to assume that cultural values that contributed to successful industrialization are irrelevant to today's ecological devastation. Despite this obvious paradox, there has been little investigation into why non-Western religious traditions, such as Confucianism, have been ineffective in inhibiting ecologically destructive human actions.

The relationship between the women's movement and the environmental movement presents a similar conundrum. In response to the global ramifications of today's ecological problems, many feminists have focused on the conceptual connections between the oppression of women and the oppression of nature. In 1974, French feminist Françoise d'Eaubonne, in suggesting that women have the potential for solving today's ecological crises, coined the term "ecofeminism."[8] In the United States, Ynestra King started to use "ecofeminism" in her classroom teaching at the Institute of Social Ecology. Gradually, "ecofeminism" has come to be used to refer to a variety of feminist works regarding ecological issues.[9] Regardless of their different theoretical positions, ecofeminists generally believe that the traditional sex/gender-role system has had a significant impact on today's ecological problems. However, despite their apparent agreement on this point, women have never been a unified group because the contents and functions of sex/gender-role systems vary in different historical, cultural, and material contexts. While many Euro-American ecofeminists have endeavored to deconstruct the age-old perception of an affinity between woman and nature in the West,[10] it is not clear how today's ecological problems are related to the oppression of women in Chinese society, where nature has not been traditionally identified with women.

To address the above concerns, it is essential to expand the explanatory framework concerning the conceptual roots of contemporary ecological problems. In this essay, I first examine the relations between ecological degradation and the Confucian conception of the unity of humans and nature. I argue that a recognition of the interconnections between nature and humans need not support an environmental ethic but rather could sanction large-scale transformation of the natural environment for the pursuit of social perfectibility. Next, I explore some major ecofeminist perspectives and their relevance to an inquiry into the connections between the oppression of women and today's ecological devastation in the Chinese cultural context. Ecofeminists' critiques of male cultural hegemony and sex/gender-role differentiation could make us aware that a fundamental reconstruction of patriarchal culture is essential for solving ecological problems.

Confucianism and Ecological Problems: A Preliminary Exploration

Ecological problems have been present throughout human history. Yi-Fu Tuan noted the discrepancies in pre-industrial societies between ecologically congenial religious traditions and their practitioners' indifference toward ecologically exploitative cultural practices in pre-industrial societies.[11] However, today's ecological problems, such as the greenhouse effect, global warming, and the possibility of nuclear meltdown, are distinctively different from those of pre-industrial societies. Thus, I agree with Lynn White, Jr., that an inquiry into the conceptual roots of today's ecological problems must attend to the development of modern science and technology.

Despite its "occidental" origin, modern science has been diffused into non-Western societies owing to Western imperialism and the ensuing Western cultural hegemony since the seventeenth century. While the internationalization of science, technology, and capitalist economy appears to correlate with global ecological degradation, it is problematic to attribute reductively today's ecological problems to Christianity. More specifically, modernity in both Western and non-Western societies represents a radical break from premodern social structures. J. P. Nettl and Ronald Robertson point out that the process of modernization in non-Western societies was fluid, subjective, and cultural.[12] To a large extent, cultural accoutrements indeed are based on strategical calculation. For instance, the Chinese elite, in facing Western imperialism, proposed the integration of *"t'i yung"* (substance and function). *"T'i"* stood for the essence of the Chinese culture—the highest value—whereas *"yung"* was only the technological product of Western culture. In Japan, there was a similar approach to unite "Japanese spirit" and "Western technology." Clearly, there has been an interaction between native ethos and Western cultural import in order to call for national mobilization in the pursuit of modernization.[13] In other words, since cultural traditions have to render crucial support for the widespread and profound transformative process of modernization, human actions are not simply a mechanical reaction to antecedent events and conditions. Modernization is indeed a reflexive project, and it is important to undertake a further inquiry into some of the particular factors that have contributed to successful industrialization and to the ensuing ecological problems in Chinese cultural contexts.

As mentioned above, many scholars have identified Confucianism as the functional analogue of the Protestant ethic in East Asia. However, Confucianism is by no means a monolithic religious tradition. It is debatable whether there is justification in characterizing contemporary East Asia as "Confucian": while East Asians may attribute their values to Confucian tradition, they may not be truly motivated by Confucian concerns. Although Confucianism may not be the deterministic cultural system, it has at times functioned like an orthodox religious tradition,[14] and its impact on daily Chinese cultural practice certainly cannot be underestimated.

In view of the long, complex, and evolving history of Confucianism, an attempt to inquire into its relationship with contemporary ecological devastation in East Asian countries is a formidable task indeed.[15] Confucius's conception of *t'ien* (Heaven) as recorded in the *Analects* offers an important clue for an under-standing of the unity of humans and nature (*t'ien-jen ho-yi*) that has been widely regarded as the long-lasting foundation of Confucian ethics.[16] Undoubtedly, it can be problematic to draw sociological implications from a textual analysis. However, I believe that a preliminary textual analysis of the conception of Heaven in the *Analects* might be helpful for the sake of prompting further research on the conceptual factors of today's ecological problems within a Chinese context.

The Chinese character "*t'ien*" conveys a wide range of mean-ings—from the sky, the firmament, the heavens to the immanent natural environment.[17] In the *Analects*, Confucius does not define the concept of *t'ien* clearly. Robert Eno notes that only seventeen of the five hundred chapters in the *Analects* have references to Heaven.[18] In fact, Confucius's disciples remark that "one cannot get to hear his views on human nature and the Way of Heaven" (5:13).[19] Correspondingly, Confucius never spoke of "prodigies, force, disorder, and gods" (7:21). A lack of elaboration on the idea of Heaven should not be attributed to the philosophical insignificance of Heaven in Confucian ethics. Rather, we need to be aware of Confucius's disinclination to engage in metaphysical speculation. He exhorts his students to respect gods and spirits but to keep them at a distance (6:22).[20] "You are not able even to serve man. How can you serve the spirits? You do not understand even life. How can you understand death?" (11:12). Consequently, Confucianism is frequently described as a secular humanism rather than as a formal religious organization with priests, scriptures, regular worship, and other ecclesiastical aspects.[21]

In his rare discussion of Heaven, Confucius inherits the tradi-tional immanent and naturalistic characterization of Heaven. In essence, the teaching of Confucius stresses the cultivation of human morality. When his students complain that his unwillingness to talk about Heaven would deprive them of the opportunity to learn about human ethics, he states: "What does Heaven ever say? Yet there are the four seasons going round and there are the hundred things coming into being. What does Heaven ever say?" (17:19). Implicitly, Confucius suggests that regularity and constancy of the immanent natural order corresponds with the ethical norms that human beings ought to observe. Instead of preaching a set of moral codes,

Confucius urges his students to become aware of how human moral behavior reflects the immanent natural order.

Moreover, Confucius considers that an ideal political leadership represents a counterpart to the immanent cosmic order.[22] Specifically, there is no equivalent Christian conception of God as a creator in Confucianism. Instead, Confucius affirms the effort of the paradigmatic "sage-kings," such as Yao, Shun, Wen, Wu, and the Duke Chou, in establishing a civilized social order that reflects the virtue of Heaven. To illustrate this, Confucius acclaims that "Great indeed was Yao as a ruler! How lofty! It is Heaven that is great and it was Yao who modeled himself upon it" (8:19). It is clear that the political leadership is supposed to assume a profound ethico-religious significance within the Confucian tradition.

On the other hand, Confucius seems to suggest that human virtue derives from Heaven and Heaven can safeguard his mission of transmitting an ideal cultural tradition. In confronting the threat from Huan T'ui,[23] he states, "Heaven is author of the virtue that is in me. What can Huan T'ui do to me?" (7:23). When Confucius was under siege in K'uang, he also stated that, "With King Wen dead, is not culture (*wen*) invested here in me? If Heaven intends culture to be destroyed, those who come after me will not be able to have any part of it. If Heaven does not intend this culture to be destroyed, then what can the men of K'uang do to me?" (9:5). Here, Confucius seems to suggest that Heaven has deterministic influence on human actions. He also associates Heaven (*t'ien*) with *ming*, which is commonly rendered "destiny," "fate," "decree," or "mandate." The popular conception of *t'ien-ming* (the Decree, or Mandate, of Heaven) is assumed to determine the legitimacy of the ruler's continuance in office as well as an individual's longevity, social status, and wealth. For instance, Confucius's disciple, Tzu Hsia, said, "Life and death are a matter of *ming*; wealth and honor depend on *t'ien*" (12:5).

The Confucian conception of Heaven seems to be intentionally ambiguous. Heaven refers to both the immanent natural order and a transcendent ethical principle. Such an ambiguous conceptual orientation reflects a holistic metaphysical tradition in China. Chung-ying Cheng notes that Chinese metaphysics cannot be viewed as a pure cosmological inquiry, because it is closely interrelated to individual ontology. He characterizes such an inquiry as both ontocosmological and cosmo-ontological inquiry.[24] In his survey of the pre-Chin philosophical literature, T'ang Chun-i points out that "the term 'ming' represents the interrelationship or mutual relatedness of Heaven and man."[25] In other words, the Decree of Heaven (*t'ien-ming*) does not predetermine the moral and social order. Instead, human beings must perceive themselves as agents in constructing an ideal social order that would reflect the virtue of Heaven. A moral offense against Heaven is a transgression of one's own ethical commitment. Thus, Confucius believes that no attempt should be made to deceive Heaven. He states that "in pretending that I had retainers when I had none, who would we be deceiving? Would we be deceiving Heaven?" (9:11). By inheriting such a metaphysical tradition, Confucius does not consider Heaven to be the ultimate source and standard of meaning and values. More specifically, Confucius argues that moral cultivation is about holding three things in awe: the Decree of Heaven, the great person, and the words of the sage (16:8). Evidently, the moral authority of the Decree of Heaven does not surpass human moral endeavors in the framework of the Confucian ethics. Above all, Heaven does not reveal a specific set of ethical codes, such as the Ten Commandments. Nor can one redeem one's unethical behaviors by worshipping Heaven. For instance, Confucius warns us that "when you have offended against Heaven there is nowhere you can turn to in your prayers" (3:13). From this standpoint, neither Heaven (*t'ien*) nor destiny (*ming*) can be regarded as a supramundane ethical deity or as a causal principle that exists above or outside human beings. Rather, the Confucian concept of Heaven denotes the organismic unity between humanity and nature. Within such a dipolaristic framework, nature is neither a sacred creation of God nor a profane object. Consequently, there is no clear and definite distinction between the transcendent and the immanent. Tu Weiming points out that "the Confucian perception that human beings are earthbound yet strive to transcend themselves to join with Heaven clearly indicates that Confucians see humanity as more than an anthropological concept but as an anthropocosmic idea."[26]

Western scholars often overlook the Confucian effort to integrate the transcendent and the immanent. For instance, G. W. F. Hegel claims that "the heaven (*t'ien*) of the Chinese is not a world that forms an independent realm above the earth. On the contrary, everything is upon earth."[27] F. W. J. Schelling also remarks that Confucianism is "the absolute secularization of the religious principle."[28] Max Weber considers that the "this-worldly" orientation of Confucianism is in opposition to the Protestant commitment to "rational mastery of the world." Following Weber's argument, Talcott Parsons further argues that the "Confucian ethic failed to move the world precisely because its worldliness denied it a place to stand outside the world. The Protestant ethic, on the other hand, had such a place to stand, its transcendental God and its conception of salvation."[29] To Weber and Parsons, the transcendental basis of the Puritan ethic leads to the pursuit of "modernization," whereas the Confucian sanctification of tradition inevitably inhibits industrial and scientific "progress" in China.

As Hegel, Schelling, Weber, and Parsons fail to grasp the non-antithetical relationship between Heaven and humans, they also fail to understand that the core of Confucian ethics lies on a moral effort to transform the world from within. More specifically, there is no definite distinction between the "natural" world and the "social" world in the framework of Confucian ethics. In fact, neither the "natural" world nor the "social" world is viewed as static. Rather, they are in a constant process of transformation. It follows that technology in the pursuit of social perfectibility does not come in conflict with what would be considered "nature" in Confucian society. In fact, Confucians have made a deliberate effort to affirm and emblazon the sage-king Yi's technological achievement in redirecting the rivers that caused floods.

Allan G. Grapard also notes a similar dialectic between nature and culture in Japan. According to Grapard, there is a clear distinction between the realm of nature and the realm of culture in the creation myth found in the *Kojiki* and the *Nihongi*. Nature captures the beauty of the creation of the female divinity; but it is also the realm of change, decay, and putrefaction, which is in opposition to culture, represented by the processes of purification, undertaken by the male divinity. The processes of purification all take place in natural surroundings; religious rituals are performed to make communication with nature possible. The rituals of purification usually involve an attempt to manipulate or influence nature. Moreover, various geographical areas are designated as sacred places that are to be "decoded" in order to reveal their hidden meanings. For instance, Mount Kunisaki is regarded as the "natural form" of the most important scripture of Buddhism, the *Lotus Sūtra*. However, it is not clear whether this *sūtra* is "en-mountained" or the mountain has been "textualized." In view of the dialectic between nature and culture, Grapard concludes that "the Japanese love of nature" actually might be the Japanese love of cultural transformation and the purification of a natural world.[30]

Furthermore, the perfectibility of human nature, as an embodiment of Heaven's virtue, has been central to the Confucian doctrine. Tu Weiming notes that "the Confucians' optimistic attitude is predicated on the ontological assertion that if human nature is conferred by Heaven, the realization of our human nature is tantamount to the fulfillment of a Heavenly-ordained mission."[31] In particular, the realization of human nature must take place in concretely interpersonal and social contexts rather than in a social vacuum. Tu points out that "a defining characteristic of Confucian religiousness is its emphasis on the fiduciary community as an irreducible reality in ultimate self-transformation."[32] In other words, self-transformation is a communal act; and an individual's self-cultivation is to contribute to the establishment of an ideal social order that is by no means predetermined. The fiduciary community must function as a cohesive polity as it strives for societal perfectibility.

Anthony Giddens notes that the emergence of the modern nation-state has been intertwined with capitalism, industrialism, and military power because the modern nation-state plays an important role in regard to the mobilization of social and economic resources.[33] The Confucian ideal of a cohesive polity might have been conducive to the establishment of the modern nation-state in consolidating collective efforts for the pursuit of industrialization in the face of Western imperialism in East Asia. Specifically, political leadership is parallel to the ethical principle of Heaven. To a certain degree, Confucianism renders crucial support for government's leadership in the process of social transformation, such as the project of industrialization.

In short, the Confucian conception of unity between humans and nature actually stresses a dialectic interaction. It does not inhibit human intervention in nature, which after all does not represent a static and immutable order. At the same time, the unity of humans and nature can foster a cohesive support for the process of social transformation leading to industrialization, technological development, and economic growth. Thus, an organic worldview is not necessarily a panacea for resolving environmental problems.

Gender and Ecological Problems[34]

As mentioned before, ecofeminist analyses focus on the conceptual connections between sexual oppression and today's ecological problems. In general, patriarchal cultural values and the association of women with nature[35] appear to be the major issues in ecofeminist discourse. Although Chinese women's lived experiences are different from other women's, it is evident that the sex/gender role system has become entrenched in the construction of major cultural institutions (i.e., Confucianism) and cultural process (i.e., modernization). In order to gain a more comprehensive and inclusive understanding of the conceptual roots of today's ecological problems, it is essential to examine the relevance of ecofeminist perspectives from within a Chinese cultural context.

The affinity of women and nature has played an important but polemic role in the theorizing of ecofeminism. In 1974, Sherry B. Ortner argued that the distinction between female and male is related to the more basic distinction between nature and culture.[36] Ecofeminist Susan Griffin further pointed out that there are perceived similarities between woman and nature—such as passivity and life-giving, nurturing qualities—that make them equally vulnerable to male domination.[37] At the same time, ecofeminists, such as Ynestra King and Ariel K. Salleh, proclaim that women's association with nature might give women a special stake in healing the alienation between humanity and nature and, eventually, in solving some of today's environmental problems.[38]

Beyond the perceived similarities between woman and nature, some ecofeminists offer a further analysis of the development of male gender identity. According to Nancy Chodorow, most human beings experience a sense of oneness with their mother in the state of infantile dependence.[39] Dorothy Dinnerstein argues that the feminization of nature can be traced to the human infant's failure to distinguish clearly between its mother and nature.[40] Drawing from the theories of Chodorow and Dinnerstein, Elizabeth Dodson

Gray further claims that men's need to conquer women and feminized nature is the result of sexual differentiation in gender role development. Specifically, the female infant's sense of oneness with her mother is sustained by modeling her own gender identity after her mother, whereas the male infant's gender development leads to rejection and denial of his dependence on and attachment to her. Gray argues that man's ambivalence toward dependence upon the mother has enormous psychosexual repercussions on his relationship with women and with whatever is perceived as feminine, such as nature. In order to ensure men's continuous independence from the mother and the female in general, it is essential for patriarchal culture to prescribe the wife's role as submissive and inferior. To Gray, the advancement of technology mainly aspires to "transform [men's] psychologically intolerable dependence upon a seemingly powerful and capricious 'Mother Nature' into a soothing and acceptable dependence upon a subordinated and non-threatening 'wife.' "[41]

In *New Woman, New Earth*, Rosemary Ruether argues that both the human destruction of nature and women's oppression are legitimized and perpetuated by a hierarchical social structure that allows one group to dominate another. According to Ruether, this hierarchical social structure is rooted in a dualistic ideology, a "transcendent dualism," that stresses separation, polarization, and detachment between sexes, classes, and human and nonhuman beings. In these binary oppositions, man/upper-class/white/human beings are considered superior to woman/lower-class/people of color/nature.

"Woman as Mother" is a central issue in Ruether's demystification of transcendent dualism. Although she considers the concept of early matriarchal societies lacking in historical evidence, she still presumes that there was a woman-identified culture prior to the present patriarchal one. Ruether implies that in this woman-identified culture, the female capacity for human reproduction led women to an implicit acceptance of and identification with the cyclical ecology of death and rebirth. In contrast, men's inability to bear children induces them to contrive a male deity who creates human beings and transcends finite bodily existence. Rooted in transcendent dualism, patriarchal religion seeks to pursue the infinitude of human existence. Following patriarchal religion, science and technology also seek to "realize infinite demand through infinite material 'progress,' impelling nature forward to infinite expansion of productive power. Infinite demand incarnate in finite nature, in the form of infinite exploitation of the earth's resources for production, results in ecological disaster."[42]

In line with Ruether's perspective, Carolyn Merchant claims that "the ancient identity of nature as a nurturing mother links women's history with the history of the environment and ecological change." According to Merchant, the identification of nature with a nurturing mother prevented human destruction of nature in early history. However, Merchant reminds us that nature can also be identified as a disorderly woman who called forth human control over nature in the scientific revolution. She points out that the early scientists, such as Francis Bacon, utilized the image of the disorderly woman to develop scientific objectives and methods. As a whole, the Baconian doctrine of domination over nature is correlated with the perception of disorder in feminized nature.[43] In brief, Merchant's critique of mechanism complements Ruether's demystification of transcendent dualism. It is dualism that lays the foundation for a mechanistic worldview, and it is mechanism that eventually severs the organic relationship between humans and nature.

The above ecofeminist perspectives focus on biological differences between men and women, but these essentialist perspectives are based on a circular, simplistic, and reductionistic argument.[44] If there were no well-established sex/gender-role system, the development of masculinity would not require a rejection of man's early dependence upon his mother. Although the presence of a woman as the child's primary caretaker reduces the influence of male adults, especially a father, on the development of male infants, "the total and exclusive exposure of mothers to their young children" is a myth rather than reality.[45] In reality, the formation of men's gender identity, like women's, is a continuous process. Men's abrupt rejection of their mothers appears to be misleading and illusory.

Furthermore, Val Plumwood points out that "the reproductively related features of masculinity and femininity. . .were (until recently at least) universal, but the alleged consequent, the transcendent apriority of the rational, is not a universal feature."[46] Also, the feminization of nature and the accompanying devaluation of nature are not cross-culturally the same phenomenon.[47] Specifically, nature as a whole has not been associated with woman in Chinese society. The traditional yin-yang cosmology, while revealing dyadic thinking, does not associate the yin (female) principle with all-encompassing immanent nature. Undoubtedly, the supposedly gender-neutral Confucian conception of *t'ien*, or *ch'ien*, has been gendered. For instance, the Neo-Confucian scholar Chang Tsai stated that "Heaven is my father and Earth is mother, and even such a small creature as I finds an intimate place in their midst."[48] Still, it was clear that neither Heaven as father nor Earth as mother symbolizes nature. Nevertheless, the absence of transcendent dualism does not preclude women's being oppressed. In fact, Chinese misogyny coexisted with an organic worldview. And, as discussed before, an organic worldview could sanction massive transformation of the natural environment. This casts doubt on Ruether's and Merchant's claim that transcendent dualism and a mechanistic worldview are the ultimate causes of various forms of oppression. In short, women's closeness to nature is not biologically determined, and the perception of an affinity between women and nature is not an inherent feature of the human psyche. In other words, the association of woman and nature is more likely a social construction.

On the other hand, Carol Bigwood cautions us not to dismiss "nature as a cultural fiction" and leave "culture as the only determining force in the constitution of our reality and the being of all things."[49] She argues that "in affirming women as women, we must also affirm to some extent a link between the female body and woman's way of being, between the sexual body and gender."[50] To Bigwood, such a link is a focal point for us to inquire into the binary oppositions that "have historically developed between the masculine and the feminine (as nonmasculine) and between other categories such as culture and nature, mind and body, and public and private."[51] The affinity of woman and nature as an imported idea has been accepted and popularized in non-Western society, such as Taiwan. In light of Bigwood's perspective, it is also important to explore the symbolic implications of the feminization of nature further. For instance, it has become common for Chinese people to employ the metaphor of "the rape of Mother Earth" to refer to human exploitation of nature. On the one hand, such a recent feminization of nature reflects Western cultural hegemony. On the other hand, it also reveals certain common perceptions of sex/ gender-role differences across cultural boundaries.

It also is essential to note that the image of woman has been used as an available and powerful metaphor to describe and further prescribe the human perception of nature in male-dominated societies. In the process of metaphorization, the subject who utters the metaphor and the metaphoric vehicle usually represent two distinct groups, such as men and women. Eva Feder Kittay points out that women are persistently used as a metaphor for men's activities and projects, while there are no equivalent metaphors using men as vehicles for women and women's activities.[52] Gerda Lerner further argues that "When humankind made a qualitative leap forward in its ability to conceptualize large symbol systems which explain the world and the universal, women were already so greatly disadvantaged that they were excluded from participation in this important cultural advance."[53]

Men also hold a monopoly on cultural formation in Chinese society. The recent affiliation of woman and nature certainly reflects men's hegemonic status in Chinese society. As discussed before, Confucianism contributed to the establishment of a cohesive polity. The patriarchal family is, to a large extent, the cornerstone of this cohesive polity, and an elaborate sex/gender-role system is indispensable for sustaining such a patriarchal structure. A celebrated statement in the *Book of Rites* clearly indicated Chinese women's subordinate status: "The woman follows and obeys the man: in her youth, she follows her father and elder brother; when married she follows her husband; when her husband is dead, she follows her son." The patrilineal social structure also appears to be closely related to the pursuit of transcendence. In order to gain a better understanding of the relationship between Confucianism and today's ecological problems, it is essential to undertake more contextual analyses of how the exclusion of women's experiences affects the Confucian conception of the correspondence between the cosmic order and social order. Therefore, while the recent feminization of nature may not be the main contributing factor in today's ecological destruction, the deconstruction of traditional sex/gender-role systems certainly can shed light on reorienting ecologically exploitative cultural practices. In other words, our attempt to identify and further demystify the conceptual roots of today's ecological problems cannot overlook the fact that the successful transplantation of gender imagery can be attributed to biological sex differences and male cultural hegemony.

Conclusion

Both religion and metaphysical inquiry have shaped our perception of the relationship between humans and the living environment. My examination of the Confucian conception of the unity of humans and nature suggests that this non-anthropocentric religious tradition still might have sanctioned ecologically destructive actions. While the woman-nature affinity is not a cross-cultural phenomenon, ecofeminists' analysis of the interconnections between various forms of oppression shed light on how gender ideology could influence particular worldviews and the construction of cultural institutions.

Above all, we must be aware that human moral reflexivity is essential to address interrelated environmental issues. Resolving value conflicts cannot be an individual endeavor. Rather, we need to make a collective effort to examine critically the existing social norms and to explore the possibilities of establishing new ethical norms in our moral community.

Notes

1. Holmes Rolston, III, *Environmental Ethics: Duties and Values in the Natural World* (Philadelphia: Temple University Press, 1988); J. Baird Callicott, *In Defense of the Land Ethic* (Albany: State University of New York Press, 1989); Fox Warwick, *Toward a Transpersonal Ecology* (Boston: Shambhala, 1990).

2. Lynn White, Jr., "The Historical Roots of our Ecologic Crisis," in *Western Man and Environmental Ethics*, ed. I. G. Barbour (Reading, Mass.: Addison-Wesley, 1973), 25. This article appeared originally in *Science* 155 (March 1967):1203–7.

3. Ibid., 28.

4. Ibid.; William R. LaFleur, "Saigyō and the Buddhist Value of Nature," pts. 1 and 2, *History of Religions* 13, no. 2 (November 1973):93–127, no. 3 (February 1974):227–47; Eliot Deutsch, "A Metaphysical Grounding for Natural Reverence: East-West," *Environmental Ethics* 8 (1986); Hwa Yol Jung, "The Ecological Crisis: A Philosophic Perspective, East and West," *Bucknell Review* 20 (1972):25–44; Kenneth K. Inada, "Environmental Problematics in the Buddhist Context," *Philosophy East and West* 37, no. 2 (1987):135–49; Russell Goodman, "Taoism and Ecology," *Environmental Ethics* 2 (1980):73–80; Roger T. Ames, "Taoism and the Nature of Nature," *Environmental Ethics* 8 (1986):317–50; Huston Smith, "Tao Now: An Ecological Testament," in *Earth Might Be Fair: Reflections on Ethics, Religion, and Ecology*, ed. I. G. Barbour (Englewood Cliffs, N.J.: Prentice-Hall, 1972), 66–69; Po-Keung Ip, "Taoism and Environmental Ethics," in *Religion and Environmental Crisis*, ed. Eugene C. Hargrove (Athens: University of Georgia Press, 1986); Krishna Chaitanya, "A Profounder Ecology: The Hindu View of Man and Nature," *The Ecologist* 13 (1983):127–35; William LaFleur, "Sattva: Enlightenment for Plants and Trees in Buddhism," *Co-Evolution Quarterly* 19 (1978):47–52; J. Baird Callicott, "Conceptual Resources for Environmental Ethics in Asian Traditions of Thought: A Propaedeutic," *Philosophy East and West* 37, no. 2 (1987):115–30.

5. Max Weber, *The Religion of China*, trans. and ed. by Hans H. Gerth (New York: Free Press, 1951).

6. For instance, Peter Berger claims that "Japan and the newly industrialized countries of East Asia belong to the broad area of influence of Sinitic civilization, and there can be no doubt that Confucianism has been a very powerful force in all of them." The Confucian values refer to a strong achievement-oriented work ethic, a sense of collective solidarity in the family and in artificial groupings beyond the family, the prestige of education, meritocratic norms and institutions, and selecting the elite at an early age. See Peter Berger, "An East Asian Development Model?" in *In Search of an East Asian Development Model*, ed. Peter L. Berger and Hsin-Huang Michael Hsiao (New Brunswick, N.J.: Transaction Books, 1988).

7. David L. Hall and Roger T. Ames, *Thinking through Confucius* (Albany: State University of New York Press, 1987); *Man and Nature: The Chinese Tradition and the Future*, ed. Tang Yi-Jie, Li Zaen, and George F. McLean (Lanham, Md.: University Press of America, 1989); Chung-ying Cheng, *New Dimensions of Confucian and Neo-Confucian Philosophy* (Albany: State University of New York Press, 1991); Giancarlo Finazzo, *The Principle of Tien: Essay on Its Theoretical Relevancy in Early Confucian Philosophy* (Taipei: Mei-Ya Publications, 1967); Robert Eno, *The Confucian Creation of Heaven: Philosophy and the Defense of Ritual Mastery* (Albany: State University of New York Press, 1990); Tu Li, *Chung-hsi Che-Hsueh ssu-hsiang Chung ti T'ien-Tao Shang-Ti* (Taipei: Linking, 1978). Like Confucianism, Buddhism, Taoism, folk Taoism, and Japanese Shintoism all stress the interrelatedness between humans and nature.

8. Mary Daly, *Gyn/Ecology: The Metaethics of Radical Feminism* (Boston: Beacon Press, 1978).

9. Karen J. Warren, "Feminism and Ecology: Making Connections," *Environmental Ethics* 9 (1987):3–20; and "The Power and the Promise of Ecological Feminism," *Environmental Ethics* 12 (1990):125–46; Petra Kelly, "Toward a Green Europe and a Green World," in *Into the Twenty-first Century*, ed. Felix Dodds (London: Green Print, 1984).

10. Sherry Ortner, "Is Female to Male as Nature Is to Culture?" in *Woman, Culture, and Society*, ed. Michelle Rosaldo and Louise Lamphere (Stanford: Stanford University Press, 1974).

11. Yi-Fu Tuan, "Discrepancies between Environmental Attitudes and Behavior: Examples from Europe and China," in *Ecology and Religion in History*, ed. David Spring and Eileen Spring (New York: Harper and Row, 1974).

12. J. P. Nettl and Ronald Robertson, "Industrialization, Development or Modernization," *British Journal of Sociology* 17, no. 3 (1966); Nettl and Robertson, *International Systems and the Modernization of Societies: The Formation of National Goals and Attitudes* (New York: Basic Books, 1968).

13. Lucian W. Pye, "The New Asian Capitalism: A Political Portrait," in *In Search of an East Asian Development Model*, ed. Peter L. Berger and Hsin-Huang Michael Hsiao (New Brunswick, N.J.: Transaction Books, 1988), 81–98.

14. Charlotte Furth, ed., *The Limits of Change: Essays on Conservative Alternatives in Republican China* (Cambridge: Harvard University Press, 1976).

15. For a detailed discussion on this issue, see *The Confucian World Observed: A Contemporary Discussion of Confucian Humanism In East Asia*, ed. Tu Weiming, Milan Hejtmanek, and Alan Wachman (Honolulu: The East-West Center, 1992).

16. Wing-tsit Chan, *Religious Trends in Modern China* (New York: Octagon Books, 1969); Lauren Pfister, "The Different Faces of Contemporary Religious Confucianism: An Account of the Diverse Approaches of Some Major Twentieth Century Chinese Confucian Scholars," *Journal of Chinese Philosophy* 22 (1995):5–80.

17. For a detailed discussion on the ambiguity of *t'ien*, see Pei-Jung Fu, "The Concept of *T'ien* in Classical Confucianism," *Bulletin of the College of Liberal Arts* (National Taiwan University) 33 (1984):5–140; Robert Eno, *The Confucian Creation of Heaven: Philosophy and the Defense of Ritual Mastery* (Albany: State University of New York Press, 1990).

18. Eno, *The Confucian Creation of Heaven*.

19. *The Analects*, trans. D. C. Lau (New York: Penguin Books, 1986). Quotations from the *Analects* are cited by chapter and paragraph according to the traditional text.

20. Ibid.

21. This issue is debated by many scholars. Several, including Tu Weiming, Julia Ching, Wm. Theodore de Bary, John Berthrong, Rodney Taylor, and Mary Evelyn Tucker, have noted ways in which the tradition is profoundly religious. See Rodney L. Taylor, *The Way of Heaven: An Introduction of the Confucian Religious Life* (Leiden: E. J. Brill, 1986); Tu, Hejtmanek, and Wachman, eds., *The Confucian World Observed*.

22. H. G. Creel, *Origins of Statecraft*, vol. 1 (Chicago: University of Chicago Press, 1970).

23. Huan T'ui was the minister of war during the Sung dynasty who once threatened Confucius's life due to his practicing *li* (ritual).

24. Chung-ying Cheng, "Chinese Metaphysics as Non-Metaphysics: Confucian and Taoist Insights into the Nature of Reality," in *Understanding the Chinese Mind*, ed. Robert E. Allinson (Hong Kong: Oxford University Press, 1989), 167–208.

25. Tang Chun-i, "The *T'ien Ming* (Heavenly Ordinance) in Pre-Ch'in China," *Philosophy East and West* 11 (1962):195–218.

26. Tu Wei-ming, *Centrality and Commonality: An Essay on Confucian Religiousness* (Albany: State University of New York Press, 1989), 102.

27. G. W. F. Hegel, *Lectures on the Philosophy of Religion*, vol. 2: *Determinate Religion*, ed. Peter C. Hodgson (Berkeley: University of California Press, 1987).

28. F. W. J. Schelling, *Philosophy der Mythologie*, quoted in Heiner Roetz, *Confucian Ethics of the Axial Age* (Albany: State University of New York, 1993), 19.

29. Talcott Parsons, *The Structure of Social Action: A Study in Social Theory with Special Reference to a Group of Recent European Writers* (New York: Free Press, 1956), 548–49.

30. Allan G. Grapard, "Nature and Culture in Japan," in *Deep Ecology*, ed. Michael Tobias (San Diego, Calif.: Avant Books, 1985).

31. Tu, *Centrality and Commonality*, 99.

32. Ibid., 96–97.

33. Anthony Giddens, *The Consequences of Modernity* (Stanford: Stanford University Press, 1990).

34. Part of this section has been previously published: Huey-li Li, "A Cross-Cultural Critique of Ecofeminism," in *Ecofeminism: Women, Animals, Nature*, ed. Greta Gaard (Philadelphia: Temple University Press, 1993).

35. Ortner, "Is Female to Male as Nature Is to Culture?" and Carol P. MacCormack and Marilyn Strathern, eds., *Nature, Culture, and Gender* (Cambridge: Cambridge University Press, 1980), offer a cross-cultural analysis of woman-nature connections.

36. Ortner, "Is Female to Male as Nature Is to Culture?"

37. Susan Griffin, *Woman and Nature: The Roaring inside Her* (San Francisco: Harper and Row, 1978).

38. Ynestra King, "Toward an Ecological Feminism and a Feminist Ecology," in *Machina Ex Dea: Feminist Perspectives on Technology*, ed. Joan Rothschild (New York: Pergamon Press, 1983).

39. Nancy Chodorow, "Family Structure and Feminine Personality," in *Woman, Culture, and Society*, ed. Michelle Rosaldo and Louise Lamphere (Stanford: Stanford University Press, 1974).

40. Dorothy Dinnerstein, *The Mermaid and the Minotaur: Sexual Arrangements and the Human Malaise* (New York: Harper and Row, 1976).

41. Elizabeth Dodson Gray, *Green Paradise Lost* (Wellesley, Mass.: Roundtable Press, 1981).

42. Rosemary Ruether, *New Woman, New Earth: Sexist Ideologies and Human Liberation* (Boston: Beacon Press, 1995), 194.

43. Carolyn Merchant, *The Death of Nature: Women, Ecology, and the Scientific Revolution* (San Francisco: Harper and Row, 1980).

44. Janet Biehl, *Rethinking Ecofeminist Politics* (Boston: South End Press, 1991).

45. Ann G. Dally, *Inventing Motherhood: The Consequences of an Ideal* (London: Burnett Books, 1982).

46. Val Plumwood, "Ecofeminism: An Overview and Discussion of Positions and Arguments," *Australasian Journal of Philosophy*, supplement, 64 (1986):120–37.

47. Alison H. Black, "Gender and Cosmology in Chinese Correlative Thinking," in *Gender and Religion: On the Complexity of Symbols*, ed. Caroline Walker Bynum, Stevan Harrell, and Paula Richman (Boston: Beacon Press, 1986).

48. Chang Tsai, "Chang-tzu cheng-meng chu," ed. Wang, 9/2a–4b; trans. Wing-tsit Chan, in *A Source Book in Chinese Philosophy* (Princeton: Princeton University Press, 1963), 497. (Quoted in Black, "Gender and Cosmology in Chinese Correlative Thinking.")

49. Carol Bigwood, *Earth Muse: Feminism, Nature, and Art* (Philadelphia: Temple University Press, 1993).

50. Ibid.

51. Ibid.

52. Eva Feder Kittay, "Woman as Metaphor," *Hypatita* 3, no. 2 (1988):63–86.

53. Gerda Lerner, *The Creation of Patriarchy* (New York: Oxford University Press, 1986).

From Heaven-and-Earth to Nature: Chinese Concepts of the Environment and Their Influence on Policy Implementation

Robert P. Weller and Peter K. Bol

This essay provides background for considering how to win support for ecological and environmental policies in China.[1] On the basis of a historical survey, we conclude that China offers both some useful resources for environmental thinking and some difficult obstacles that differ from those that have developed in the West. The idea that political authority has fundamental responsibility for maintaining harmonious relations between society and environment has a long history in China. On the other hand, this view did not result in the conscious establishment of environmentally sound practices, largely because human utility always received first consideration.[2] Efforts to promote and implement effective environmental policies should thus look to emphasize the traditional responsibility of government and people for environmental harmony (perhaps by drawing on traditional knowledge systems for achieving such harmony) and to emphasize the collective, local, and individual human benefits of such policies.

The report that follows introduces the worldviews that have dominated Chinese political culture during three major historical periods. We have given particular attention to "cosmic resonance theory" from the earliest period (the third century B.C.E. through the ninth century C.E.), because a discussion of it allows us to introduce the vocabulary for organismic thinking in a variety of practices still widespread in China today. The Neo-Confucianism of the second period (eleventh–twelfth centuries), which we outline only in brief, did not depart fundamentally from organismic thought. Neo-

Confuciansim remains relevant today due to its revival among some humanistic intellectuals and certain political commentators.[3] Its original natural-philosophical foundation, however, has lost much of its importance. We conclude with the twentieth century, where we turn our attention to the importation from the West of science and ideas about "nature." We take note in particular of the failure of Western science as adopted in China to provide support for environmentalism and end this essay by referring back to the continuing strength of traditional attitudes and practices. The survival and recent resurgence of many of the ideas we are about to discuss give important clues about fruitful directions for policy.

Cosmic Resonance Theory

The concept of *kan-ying* (literally, "stimulus-response," hereafter referred to as "cosmic resonance") is an ancient and unique element of Chinese cosmology and natural philosophy. In its barest essence cosmic resonance is a theory of simultaneous, nonlinear causality. It posits that events taking place at the same time, but separated in space, may exert a subtle effect on one another. For example, a chess game going on in a house and a softball game being played at the same time in the street just outside might be portrayed as influencing one another's outcome, even though none of the respective partici-pants had any knowledge of or contact with one another. It would not matter if we put our chess players in a soundproof, windowless room or removed the baseball game to the next county, state, or continent, since such contingencies have no effect on the operation of cosmic resonance. To a member of the culture, there is nothing mysterious about these effects, although they occur invisibly; cosmic resonance explains them based on a theory of the fundamental workings of the universe.

Basic Cosmic Resonance Theory

A theory of cosmic resonance was first explicitly articulated in a work of Chinese philosophy in the third century B.C.E. The earliest example we have of such a work is the *Lü-shih ch'un-ch'iu*, an encyclopedic text commissioned by the prime minister of the state of Ch'in (the kingdom that would eventually unify China in 221 B.C.E. and found a dynasty of the same name) and published in 240 B.C.E. Following a century after the *Lü-shih ch'un-ch'iu* and closely related to it in content is the *Huai-nan-tzu*, large parts of which have been translated into readily available English monographs. The *Huai-nan-tzu* was another encyclopedic work commissioned by the imperial prince Liu An (179–122 B.C.E.) and presented to the court of the Han emperor Wu Ti (r. 141–87 B.C.E.) in 139 B.C.E. One significant historical development in the time elapsed between the compilation of the two texts is that the concept of cosmic resonance had grown in status from a novel but intriguing idea to become the central and distinctive hallmark of Han dynasty (206 B.C.E.–220 C.E.) thought. By the time of the writing of the *Huai-nan-tzu*, the validity of cosmic resonance theory had been accepted by most major intellectuals of the day and was featured centrally in the works of writers across the philosophical and political spectrum. No challenge to the universal acceptance of cosmic resonance would be registered until the writings of the philosopher Wang Ch'ung (27–97 C.E.), and even his work was not well received until more than a century after his death. We will quote from the *Lü-shih ch'un-ch'iu* and the *Huai-nan-tzu* interchangeably, as both share a single approach to the concept of cosmic resonance and together provide a full picture of the theory as it was first articulated.

A succinct description of the manifestations of cosmic resonance is contained in chapter nine of the *Lü-shih ch'un-ch'iu*:

> When the magnet seeks iron, something pulls it, when trees planted close together [lean] apart, something pushes them. When the sage faces south and stands with a mind bent on loving and benefiting the people, and before his orders have been issued, the [people of the world] all crane their necks and stand on tip-toe; it is because he has communicated with the people via the Vital Essence. If a criminal is about to harm a person, that person will also be this way. If now an attacker sharpens his weapons, wears lewd clothes, and eats fine food, in anticipation of the day [he will attack], those he will attack will feel uneasy. It is not that someone has told them; the "Spirit" has reported to them in advance. If a person is in Ch'in, and someone he loves dies in Ch'i, his feelings will be upset, there has been a coming and going of Vital Essence.[4]

This passage lays out the most basic principles of cosmic resonance. The examples presented are on a par with the hypothetical chess game-baseball game interaction described above. Events and things separated in space, with no observable linear causal connection to one another, are assumed to have an invisible, instantaneous influence on one another. We have since developed scientific explanations for the first two examples (the magnetism of the iron and the tendency of plants to grow towards sunlight) that do not contradict the principle of linear causality. Yet one can appreciate how, in the absence of modern science, these phenomena would be seized upon as examples of cosmic resonance. The fact that both of these processes are readily observable in nature demonstrates an aspect of cosmic resonance theory as it was understood by its advocates: it was not conceived of as a magical or supernatural force but as a mundane aspect of the natural movements of the universe.

The basic mechanics of cosmic resonance are outlined at the conclusion of the passage. Speaking of the examples of what we would call ESP, the author qualifies that "it is not that someone has told them; the 'Spirit' has reported to them in advance," and "there has been a coming and going of Vital Essence." The meaning of these statements is at first glance opaque. What does the author intend by contrasting being "told" by someone with receiving an advance report from "the Spirit?" Though seemingly obscure, these phrases are essential to understanding the mechanism at the heart of cosmic resonance theory.

"Vital Essence," mentioned twice above, is a translation of the Chinese term *ching*. Vital Essence is the most highly refined form of *ch'i*, the primordial substance (literally, "breath" or "air") which constitutes all phenomena in the universe. In various states of coarseness or refinement, *ch'i* composes all objects in the world and fills all the spaces between them. Everything was assumed to be *ch'i* in some form, from eminently tangible objects like rocks and logs to more rarefied phenomena like light and heat. In its coarser forms, *ch'i* coalesces to form our flesh, blood, and bones. As Vital Essence, it is the vitalizing energy that suffuses and animates our bodies (thus separating us from corpses and inanimate objects).[5]

The term "Vital Essence" is intimately related to another term appearing in the above passage. "Spirit" is the English equivalent of *shen*, a Chinese word with a long history and broad range of meaning. In some contexts, Spirit does literally refer to a spirit, god, or ghost. With reference to the individual human mind and physiology, however, Spirit denotes the entity within the body that is responsible for consciousness. According to the understanding of the ancient Chinese, this entity was (like the body that it animated) also made of *ch'i*, yet in its most highly refined form—the Vital Essence. The key to understanding cosmic resonance was its correlation with both Vital Essence and consciousness.

Our thoughts, feelings, and sense perceptions are conceived of as movements of the Vital Essence, which constitutes the Spirit, in response to events we encounter in the world. The infinitely sensitive responsiveness and seemingly instantaneous activation of our thoughts and feelings are attributed to the native properties of the Vital Essence. Cosmic resonance, like consciousness, is an emergent phenomenon resulting from the dynamic properties of *ch'i*.

The resonance which transpires between objects across space is a movement of *ch'i* analogous to that which takes place within our minds: it is "a coming and going of Vital Essence." The *ch'i*, or Vital Essence, which fills all space conducts sympathetic vibrations between objects. The aptness of this image of "sympathetic vibrations" is illustrated by an experimentally verifiable example that cosmic resonance theorists advanced in support of their ideas: "When the lute-tuner strikes the *kung* note [on one instrument], the *kung* note [on the other instrument] responds; when he plucks the *chiao* note [on one instrument], the *chiao* note [on the other instrument] vibrates."[6] Musical resonance of this type was cited time and again as the prototypical example of cosmic resonance, and this image of two lute strings attuned to one another, vibrating in sympathy, is central to all models of cosmic resonance theory. The speed of the interaction between strings (the speed of sound—too fast for the human ear to notice a significant time lapse) confirmed ancient theorists' assumptions about cosmic resonance. Because its medium was the Vital Essence, the same quintessential *ch'i* which constituted our Spirit and thoughts, cosmic resonance was assumed to transpire at the speed of thought (in other words, to require no time whatsoever).

The word "Spirit" (*shen*) was often used adjectivally to describe just this aspect of cosmic resonance: "Spirit-like," it could traverse any expanse of space in the time it took a thought to arise in the mind. This explains the seemingly puzzling contrast noted above, between being "told" by someone and reported to by the Spirit. The author intends us to understand the "report" of the Spirit to be an instance of cosmic resonance. The Spirit, being itself made of quintessential *ch'i*, receives and responds to vibrations arising from other objects or people and carried by the Vital Essence. It is important to note that within this model the human mind (denoted by the Spirit) is not conceived of as transcending the physical world, yet is composed of the same "psycho-physical stuff" (that is, *ch'i*) as the rest of the universe. Human consciousness is thus implicit in and susceptible to the same processes of cosmic resonance that affect trees, iron, magnets, and lute strings. This is exemplified by the wordless communication that passes between a thief and his intended victim and a sage ruler and his grateful subjects.

Yin-yang and Five Phases Cosmology: The Rules of the Dance

We have noted the most essential aspects of cosmic resonance theory as it was articulated by its earliest advocates in the second and third centuries B.C. In order to develop practical applications for the theory, early Chinese philosophers articulated a larger systematic context in which the forces of cosmic resonance operated. The *Huai-nan-tzu* describes the first building block of this larger context:

> The mutual response of things belonging to the same category is darkly mysterious and extremely subtle. Knowledge cannot explain it, nor discussion unravel it. Thus when the eastern wind arises, clear wine overflows. When the silkworm exudes fresh silk, the string of the *shang* note snaps. Something has stirred them. When a drawing [of the moon] is traced in ashes, the moon's halo becomes incomplete [in accordance with the drawing]. When a whale dies, brush-stars (comets) appear. Something has activated them.
>
> Therefore, when the Sage rules, he treasures *Tao* and does not speak; yet his kindness reaches the Ten Thousand People. [But] when ruler and minister distrust each other in their heart, concave and convex halos appear in the sky [on each side of the sun]. These

are indeed evidences of the mutual influence of the marvellous *ch'i* (*shen-ch'i*). Therefore, mountain clouds are [like] prairie grass. River clouds are [like] fish scales. Drought-land clouds are [like] blazing flames. Torrent clouds are [like] billowy waters. Each thing is affected inasmuch as it resembles [partakes of] the shape and category [of other things].[7]

It is difficult to discern whether the ironic tone of this passage is intentional or not. The authors begin by declaring that cosmic resonance is beyond the capacity of either knowledge or language, then proceed to articulate a general principle whereby it can be understood. This principle comes at the end, after the long list of examples: "each thing is affected inasmuch as it resembles (partakes of) the shape and category of other things." The operations of cosmic resonance are not random, they are rule-based. They occur in accord with certain distinctive affinities that exist between objects, and there are criteria ("shapes" and "categories") according to which these affinities can be observed and identified.

We have already seen this principle at work in the most general sense in the examples of cosmic resonance provided in the passages quoted thus far. Human relationships are the most obvious form of affinity between "objects" consistently acknowledged as significant by cosmic resonance theorists. It is for this reason that the death of a loved one far away produces cosmic resonance, as does the concern of a virtuous ruler for his subjects. "Shape" is another type of obvious affinity guiding cosmic resonance, as in the case of the moon traced in ashes and the image of the moon in the sky. The notion of "category," however, suggests a more systematic method of determining sympathetic links between objects that would not be otherwise obvious. The *Lü-shih ch'un-ch'iu* and *Huai-nan-tzu* do, in fact, describe just such a system of categories—those of yin and yang and the Five Phases of *ch'i*.

Yin and yang are two concepts with which English-language readers have become generally familiar. In general, they refer to the two opposed and complementary forces that pervade the cosmos and that give rise to the myriad bipolar oppositions in the world: soft and hard, dark and bright, male and female, and so on. In the technical vocabulary of cosmic resonance theory, yin and yang represent two states, or polarities, of *ch'i*, one passive and yielding, the other active and dynamic. *Ch'i* was conceived of as constantly in dynamic flux between these polar extremes. Any body of *ch'i* normally consisted of some in the yin state and some in the yang state. Ideally, the amounts of *ch'i* in both states should be balanced. Usually one state predominated over the other. Only very rarely and for brief duration would anything consist of either pure yin or pure yang.

Beyond yin and yang, *ch'i* can be classed into five "phases" (*wu-hsing*), or modes, into which it coalesces to form the building blocks of everyday matter. The Five Phases are fire, water, earth, metal, and wood. They were thought to be locked into a dynamic cycle analogous to the fluctuation between the poles of yin and yang. This was called the "succession cycle of the five phases," within which each prevailing phase emerged from the decay and destruction of the phase preceding it. Fire succeeded to wood, earth succeeded to fire, metal succeeded to earth, and water succeeded to metal. These seven—yin, yang, fire, water, earth, metal, and wood—are thus the basic categories into which all the phenomena in the universe may be classified. Two things that share the same category (for example, two items which are composed primarily of metal *ch'i*) are considered to be sympathetically linked within the field of cosmic resonance.

The phenomenon to which these various categories were most often correlated was time. Any block of time could be analyzed into segments corresponding either to yin and yang or the Five Phases of *ch'i*. The easiest illustrative example is the calendar year. With respect to yin and yang, the year is divided into segments marked by the solstices and equinoxes. The winter solstice is the point of fullest yin, when yang has just been reborn in the frozen land. From this point onward, yin begins to decline and yang to increase. At the spring equinox, yin and yang are in perfect balance. The process continues until the summer solstice, when yang is at its highest point and yin at its nadir. Thereafter, yang declines and yin increases, continuing until the winter solstice when the cycle begins again.

The prime category established at the beginning of the passage is the power of wood (the prevailing phase of *ch'i*), from which all of the succeeding categories and rules follow. For example, the anatomy was analyzed into five "orbs," or systems, each one centered on a specific organ that was in turn associated with one of the Five Phases of *ch'i*. The spleen was the focal organ of the orb correlated with wood; thus, in the first month the spleen is the first organ offered from a sacrificial victim. In like fashion, because blue-green is one of the five colors associated with wood, the emperor wears blue-green clothing and uses blue-green equipment.

The justification and operative principle of this entire complex of correlations and categorizations is the theory of cosmic resonance. By following the rules of resonant affinity between objects, the ruler, as pictured in the "Treatise on Seasonal Rules," brings about harmony within his kingdom by sending positive resonant vibrations out into the cosmos. This point is made explicitly within the text of the treatise itself, although it is made in negative, alarmist terms. At the end of the list of rules and regulations for each month, the *Huai-nan-tzu* includes a warning of what will transpire if the rules are broken:

> If in the first month of spring the ordinances of summer were carried out, then there would be unseasonable winds and rain; plants and trees would wither early, and the state would suffer anxiety. If the ordinances of autumn were carried out, the people would suffer epidemics; briars, and overgrowth would spring up together. If the ordinances of winter were carried out, floods would create ruin; there would be rain frost and great hailstones. The first-sown seeds would not sprout.[8]

These negative consequences, like the positive benefits that accrue from following the rules, are the result of cosmic resonance. Within the universe described in these early texts, all things, people, and events are interconnected by a web of resonant affinities. Every action has consequences surpassing its visible, linear effects in the here and now. No one thing may remain isolated; everything constantly exchanges resonant influences with the situation unfolding around it.

Neo-Confucianism

Neo-Confucianism was formulated during the eleventh and twelfth centuries as a kind of ideology of moral rearmament for the Chinese literati as the national elite. It was officially recognized by successive dynasties as the standard of intellectual correctness during the course of the thirteenth and fourteenth centuries, and it remained the principal content of the civil service examination system until the beginning of the twentieth century. Here we briefly introduce the structure of its organismic worldview to establish that Neo-Confucianism continued to base ideas of personal and political morality on an understanding of "Heaven-and-Earth" as an integrated, coherent organism, largely consistent with the lines initially established by cosmic resonance theory. At the same time, we seek to make clear that the natural world is treated in practice as a metaphor for the integration and coherence that humans should try to establish in social life; it generally did not lead scholars to the investigation of the coherence of the natural order or to a biocentric view of the world.

As developed in the teachings and writings of Ch'eng I (1033–1107) and Chu Hsi (1130–1200) and the various works that set out to codify their views, all phenomena consisted of two aspects. The first was the traditional *ch'i*, the matter and energy of which everything is composed, from human emotions and breath to trees and stone. What sets Neo-Confucians apart is their positing of a second aspect, *li*, which they used in turn to explain the basis for and nature of human morality.

Li, translated as "principle" or "pattern," always exists together with *ch'i*, but it can be treated separately for analytic purposes. The *li* of something is that which gives structure to its *ch'i*, directs its evolution over time, and defines its function in context. To illustrate this consider an oak tree. First, it is a whole composed of interconnected parts, a structure that has connections from root to branch. Second, it follows a course of change over time, through both an annual cycle and a life cycle. Third, it has a function according to context: as the source of material suitable for certain uses in a human context or as part of an ecosystem in a natural context, for example. The *li* of an oak tree is why its *ch'i* can, in this instance, take this structure, this cycle of change, and serve these functions. The *li* of the oak tree—and the *li* of the entire cosmic system—is a single coherent *li*, even though one can speak of the *li* particular to every part (to leaves as a category, to each particular leaf, and so on). The acorn is part of the oak, but it contains the *li* of an entire oak within it.

Neo-Confucians were not, it turns out, particularly interested in oak trees. They were concerned with humans as social and political actors and with the reasons why humans failed to realize the organic model of an integrated, dynamic system in social life. The *li* they were interested in were those they presumed to exist in all human beings as the potential guide for action in the present.[9] Thus, Neo-Confucians 1) used the spontaneous, integrated system of the natural world as the foundation for conceiving of a moral world, 2) viewed humanity as inextricably part of that natural world (but the most advanced of the creatures in it), and 3) supposed that individuals were biologically endowed with principles for structuring perception, thought, and action that would, if realized, result in an integrated social world.

Nevertheless, Neo-Confucians were not concerned with the ecological state of the environment. Later Neo-Confucians came to view *li* as "propositional language," a way of expressing ideas about how things ought to be rather than as something inherent in things, but continued to conceive of the constitution of things in terms of *ch'i*. Yet Neo-Confucians to this day have continued to insist that humanity be seen as part of "Heaven-and-Earth" and that, as "co-creators" of the universe, humankind bears the responsibility for acting on a par with Heaven-and-Earth. Contemporary Neo-Confucians, who have a certain following among mainly academic intellectuals in and outside of China, can easily find an ecological tendency in their tradition and they are generally interested in showing that Neo-Confucianism can include environmentalism. This has received a degree of government patronage in the People's Republic, influenced in particular by Singapore's claims for the role of Confucianism in its economic success.

Science and Democracy in the Twentieth Century

The theory of yin-yang and the Five Phases had already begun to decline by the end of the Ming dynasty in the seventeenth century. This stemmed in part from a new historical scholarship that questioned the authenticity of some early texts and in part from the critique of Neo-Confucian orthodoxy by the radical followers of the philosopher Wang Yang-ming (1472–1529). Its most obvious symbol, however, was the success of Jesuit astronomers in revising the calendar and predicting celestial events, leading to their ultimate take-over of the imperial Bureau of Astronomy. Control over the calendar had always been a core symbol of imperial power and authority, and command over its mysteries was a key to the emperor's role in keeping human and natural forces in balance. Indeed, the Chinese word *t'ien* refers both to the abstract forces of Heaven, which were always political in implication, and to actual movements of stars and planets. The Jesuits sought to undercut this mainstay of the organismic understanding of the world by positing an anthropomorphic Creator and by wielding their knowledge of astronomy.[10] Their views clashed with the Chinese understanding of the spontaneous unfolding of the natural world without prior cause.

In spite of this general decline in earlier conceptions of the cosmology, the organismic understanding of the world remained predominant until Western science began to have a powerful influence on Chinese thinkers in the late nineteenth century. Western thought about nature and humanity had taken a very different path from China. For many people in the West, at least since the Enlightenment, nature and culture became dichotomized.[11] Nature by this time had been reduced to an object for (literal and metaphorical) dissection, to be comprehended and ultimately controlled for human progress. Earlier views that had partially resembled Chinese organismic approaches (for instance, the medieval Great Chain of Being, or astrology) were driven out of the ranks of science.

China had ideas partly comparable to nature/culture in the distinction between Heaven (*t'ien*) and humanity (*jen*). Yet these were never a dichotomy in Chinese thought; they were organismically linked to each other, not opposed to each other. *T'ien* itself was a far broader term than nature, including transcendent forces like deities as much as "natural" forces. The concept of humanity was also different from the Western one, as the discussion of cosmic resonance above implied. The fall of the last dynasty in 1911 and the founding of a modernist regime further cut off Heaven/nature from the human world by removing the emperor and his role in maintaining the cosmic balance. The study of Heaven became simply the study of the heavens.

The New Nature

The modern Chinese term for nature is *tzu-jan* (also sometimes *ta tzu-jan* [great nature] or *tzu-jan chieh* [natural world]). This is a term with a long history in Chinese philosophy, but never in the modern sense of the "natural" (as opposed to the "cultural") world. Instead, the term meant both existence and spontaneity—features of how things worked in the organismic realm of Heaven-and-Earth. Taoists in particular were fond of this word, as it expressed the desirability of following the natural flow of *ch'i*, without imposing social structure on it. They sometimes opposed this ideal to Confucian paeans to ritual, propriety, and other more purely social forms of order. The term never referred to nature as the object of human exploitation.

Tzu-jan in the scientific sense, like many Western technical terms, entered China via Japan. Early Japanese philosophical definitions of the new term focused on *tzu-jan* as 1) the opposite of "civilization," "culture," and "skill," and 2) a totality of actual existence, as opposed to "spirit" and "history."[12] These definitions had appeared in a Chinese dictionary of Western philosophy by 1926 and were widely used from then on. This new way of conceptualizing nature came in on the wave of intellectual enthusiasm for Western science and democracy that swept China, especially after the May Fourth Movement of 1919. The new nature, now made concrete and objective, lay open for scientific analysis. While a small minority of intellectuals continued to hold to an older view, the new view in large part colonized Chinese thought on the issue and would not be challenged by either the Nationalist or Communist regimes. The following section borrows material mainly from Taiwan as well as material from the People's Republic. In general, elite attitudes toward science and nature are similarly modernist in both places and the richer data we have from Taiwan enables us to develop these issues in greater depth.

Official Publications

School textbooks provide clear cases of what had become official orthodoxy on nature. First-grade texts in Taiwan,[13] for example, rhetorically ask, "What is the relation between our daily life and local mountains and rivers?" The answers, shown in pictures, are coal mining, fishing, and farming—the view of nature as object for exploitation. Texts for older elementary students emphasize the importance of dam construction for water control and promote other efforts toward, as they put it, "environmental improvement." One includes a section called "Man Must Conquer Heaven," an idea that shows just how drastically Chinese thinking about nature has changed in just under a century. Texts on ethics and morality make no mention of the environment.

More recent official information in Taiwan continues to promote a scientific view of nature over an organismic one. A recent video cartoon, for example, documents the extent of current pollution through some visiting space travelers.[14] In the style of Dickens's *A Christmas Carol*, the aliens take a group of children on a visit to the island's present problems, its idyllic past, and its potentially horrific future. Yet the children also learn the possibility of an alternative future—a technological wonderland of parks built around the waste water from nuclear power plants—if only they stop littering.

Gazetteers, written over the centuries to compile local natural, social, and cultural histories, show a similar evolution. Traditional gazetteers usually began with a section called *chiang-yü* or *feng-yü* (territory). This included subsections called *hsing-yeh* (star-wilderness), which correlated earthly territory and celestial space, and *hsing-shih* (shape and positional potential), which included geographic features, political boundaries, famous scenery and historical sites, and government buildings. As usual in this Heaven-and-Earth view, political and human history intertwined with natural history. Modern gazetteers instead feature a *ti-li* (geography) section, presenting physical and natural information familiar in the West.[15] Political boundaries and historical sites are gone (or at best awkwardly appended in recollection of the older system) from this section on what has by now become "nature" alone.

Contemporary environmental understandings in the West, of course, have also evolved. Within science, the rise of ecology has partially placed nature into a much wider net of interacting forces than the version we have just been discussing. Outside science, organismic understandings of nature (some of them ironically with Chinese roots) continue to be an important undercurrent. These changes themselves have in turn influenced China. Yet the various modernizing regimes in China have nevertheless remained largely wedded to the earlier Western scientific view of nature.

The Environment in Practice

In spite of these dramatic changes in Chinese intellectual thought about nature over the last millennium, popular practice has continued to follow a partially independent course. This had always been true to an extent—one has only to compare Taoist prescriptions about doing nothing against the natural Way with the widespread deforestation and dramatic geographic transformations through terracing and water control that have always accompanied Chinese agriculture. The contrast between popular practice and intellectual prescription, however, has never been stronger than it is today, in spite of almost a century of modernizing states that always discouraged and sometimes completely outlawed most of these practices.

Elites themselves may continue traditional Chinese relations with nature in some aspects of their life, even if they leave Heaven-and-Earth when they think about science. Chinese gardens, for example, continue to thrive, and so does landscape painting in the traditional style that shows the flow of *ch'i* through rows of mountains. Western styles of painting and gardening are also available to people, but only as slightly exotic supplements to the older Chinese conceptions.

Chinese traditional gardens are thought of as human creations on a par with nature, since both human-made and spontaneous landscapes are products of the same creative forces. They do not attempt simply to emulate nature (as in English romantic gardens, or modern back-to-nature ones) or to bend it to human will (as in European formal gardens). Instead, the idea is to capture the subtlety of nature in miniature, to give life to the creative energies that make up the universe, and thereby to reveal the intent (*i*) of the creator. This intent should be visible to people at all times, intertwined with the image of *ch'i* flowing through the landscape. The prominence of oddly shaped, pock-marked stones (*ch'i-shih*) showed the visible power of *ch'i* in sculpting the stone, but also demonstrated the owner's refinement in choosing an appropriate placement and his financial power in finding and importing such a thing.[16] Such gardens continue to be constructed, and the aesthetic has diffused far beyond the elite, as old elite gardens have been opened to the public and as more people can afford luxuries like dramatically shaped stones.

Almanacs

China has had a long tradition of publishing a kind of farmers' almanac. These almanacs included, at a minimum, a lunar calendar with daily information on the crop cycle and lists of activities appropriate or inauspicious for that day, based on the interactions of the Five Phases. More elaborate versions, of which there were many, added detailed information on positions of the heavenly bodies and various systems of fortune-telling and chronomancy. They thus combined technical farming information with daily details about the flow of *ch'i*, which determined good and bad luck for various activities. This was not a combination of practical knowledge and religion; for readers of these texts, it was all practical knowledge.

Governments also published such almanacs. The modernizing regimes, however, quickly minimized what they considered the superstitious aspects, that is, the parts that most closely reflected the old organismic view. A Nationalist almanac of 1939, for example, dropped the section on proper and improper activities for each day and added bits of political information on the constitution.[17] Another Nationalist almanac, this one from after the move to Taiwan, had only a simple calendar and basic astronomical information.[18] Early People's Republic of China almanacs retained a simple section on appropriate activities but added geography, a history of the Communist Party, regulations for punishing counter-revolutionaries, and other information the government considered important. A simple divination system done by tossing coins was replaced by a game where each coin toss led to a political poem instead of a predicted fortune. By the mid-1950s, the cosmic resonance section on appropriate activities was gone. By the time of the Cultural Revolution, sections attacking "superstitions" had been added.

During these same decades, however, privately published almanacs continued to reach enormous populations, and continued to follow the traditional style. Almanacs in Hong Kong and Taiwan, for example, have extremely elaborate sections devoted to appropriate activities for each day, in addition to other kinds of cosmological information and practical information, ranging from magic charms (*hu*) to ward off disease to information on how to play the stock market. The People's Republic banned such publications for a long time, but they are again common. Major events, such as weddings, funerals, or founding a new business, are rarely scheduled without such an almanac first being checked, often with the help of a paid expert in calendrical divination.

Chinese Geomancy

Another widespread and long-enduring cultural practice based upon cosmic resonance theory is the art of *feng shui* (literally, "wind and water"), or Chinese geomancy—the art of aligning houses and graves to harmonize the flow of *ch'i* between humans and environment, thus to reap benefits for the living through the workings of cosmic resonance. The influence of geomancy is seen in the places Chinese people live, in the planning of their graves and cemeteries, and even extends into the realm of the visual arts. A large-scale survey conducted in Taiwan in 1994 shows that about half the population considers geomancy important for health, wealth, and the future success of children. (In addition, about 80 percent indicated they would consult an expert in the calendrical divination mentioned above to choose appropriate times for weddings, opening a business, or moving into a new house.[19]) We have no comparative statistical evidence for the People's Republic, but qualitative evidence indicates a similar resurgence of geomancy, especially in rural areas. People often say that important public or commercial buildings were sited with the help of famous geomancers.[20]

Geomancy seeks to harness the forces of cosmic resonance to plan environments for the benefit of the living and the dead. It begins from the familiar premise that the perpetually active resonant vibrations of *ch'i* flow around and through us along consistent pathways. These pathways have a set spatial pattern, as well as a predictable temporal sequence. The construction of edifices like houses and graves may fit harmoniously into the prevailing patterns of *ch'i* resonances, thus deriving the maximum benefit from vitalizing forces flowing in and through the structure. On the other hand, a structure can block or impede the natural flow of *ch'i* resonances through an area, causing the environment to exert malignant or even deadly influences on those people associated with the structure. The art of geomancy is to insure the former outcome and avoid the latter. A well-planned house or grave can bring health, long life, and prosperity to the family that dwells in or commissions it (beneficent influences are transmitted to the living descendants of the occupant of a well-planned grave, because *ch'i* flows through lineages as it does through the land). A poorly planned structure will produce precisely the opposite result.

Geomancy is as old as the theory of cosmic resonance itself. Its lore includes all of the cosmological systems discussed above, as well as a long list of newer symbols and correlations which have accrued in the course of its two-millennia history. Here, one Western scholar describes the multiple factors contributing to "essential" *feng shui* theory:

> [*Feng shui*] assumes that the universe is in flux, in continuous change, but that there are patterns of change discernible to [its] experts. . . . The forces of two or more of the Five [Phases] may be in a mutually constructive or destructive relationship. The two principle cosmic forces, Yin and Yang, may be out of balance. The life-breath, Ch'i, may be prospering or decaying. By means of his compass and the rings of symbols inscribed on its dial, the geomancer takes a number of bearings on a prospective site to measure the state of the forces in it. But this is only the Compass side of geomancy. A conventional categorisation of landscape features also helps him in his analysis. The salient features of a landscape are those that can be traced as lines—mountain ridges, alluvial formations, all watercourses and thoroughfares—and those which have definite shapes and outlines, such as mountain peaks, boulders, ponds and pools. The lines and shapes may suggest paths of the life-breaths or manifestations of the [Phases of *ch'i*]. They may also suggest something entirely concrete which has immediate significance. A ridge with five undulations may be a scholar's brush-rest and indicate for the owner of the site overlooked by the ridge a scholar's career. . . . [Only] an expert, a geomancer, can by his finer calculations find the right place for a house or grave. . . .[21]

One can see from the multiplicity of factors mentioned here that the art of geomancy eventually evolved into a system even more complicated than the list of ritual prescriptions in the *Huai-nan-tzu*, yet despite its complexity the popularity of geomancy grew consistently throughout Chinese history. Its effects can be seen even now in most Chinese urban centers. Here, the same scholar quoted above describes the geomantic principles exemplified in the layout of the city of Canton:

> To the north there should be a mountainous shield from malicious influences, yet the mountain, as in the case of Canton, in itself harbours good influences and may even be sacred. The dead are buried on a south-facing slope and to the south of them is the town and the living. A south-facing slope receives the summer sun. Thus the inhabitants of Canton are shielded from malicious influences from behind, and down the slope towards them come the good influences from the mountain and the protection of their ancestors in the graves while from the front they receive the fruitful influence of the summer sun.[22]

A stroll through any commercial district of Hong Kong or Taipei will prove to the casual observer that there is no dearth of work for professional diviners, and geomancy is clearly again increasing in the People's Republic as well. Geomancers' compasses and geomancy manuals are widely available in bookstores. Take, as an example of its continued popularity, the comments of this geomancer on the construction of Singapore's mass transit system:

> When the plan to build the MRT [Mass Rapid Transport] was announced in the early 1980's, many geomancers here and overseas came out against the idea. The brief economic downturn during 1985–1986 helped reinforce their arguments. At the time, when I was just a free-lance geomancer, I did not rush to comment, but simply observed Hong Kong's experience with its own mass transit system.
>
> I was surprised to see that during construction of their mass transit systems, Hong Kong and Singapore each underwent a short period of economic trouble. For Hong Kong, the beginning of construction in the early 1970's preceded a stock-market downturn

in 1973 and the oil crisis of the mid-1970's. In turn, just after MRT construction began, Singapore experienced its first negative economic growth since its independence in 1965. Yet by the time the underground systems were ready, the two economies had not only picked up but were enjoying rapid expansion.

With these events in mind, I looked again at the Golden Eagle pattern of Singapore. Suddenly, I saw the explanation. If you superimpose upon the map of Singapore a map of the MRT lines, what do you notice? The MRT lines are exactly like the eagle's blood vessels, carrying a constant supply of blood to every part of the golden eagle's body, which thus gains its vitality from this wonderfully designed transportation network. The MRT is good for *fengshui*.[23]

Geomantic concerns are given serious attention, not only in Singapore but throughout the Pacific Rim. It is not unheard of for riots or protests to break out over a government project that is perceived to pose a threat to the geomantic well-being of a city or community.

One dramatic incident of the impact of traditional beliefs was reported by the *Hong Kong Standard* on 12 April 1986. The *Standard*'s source was a local newspaper that originally carried the report:

> In central Sichuan province, two brothers were arrested for blowing up a bridge near their house after a geomancer advised them the structure was positioned wrong and would prevent them from ever getting rich. "The geomancer said since the traffic and irrigation bridge was pointed at the middle hall of their home, the brothers would not make their fortune," the *Sichuan Daily News* reported.

This is a rather extreme example, but the number of articles in internal state and party journals in the last decade devoted to the "problem" of "superstitious practices" among the people and even among Communist party members leaves little room for doubt that traditional ideas are alive and well and perhaps enjoying a resurgence of popularity in the People's Republic.

Examples of the survival, and even the resurgence, of cosmic resonance understandings of the world could easily be multiplied. Chinese medicine, after all, is also an application of cosmic resonance theory, which seeks to manipulate the flow of *ch'i* in the body through acupuncture and to balance it with external *ch'i* through diet. *Ch'i-kung*, the wildly popular exercise regimen that has swept Taiwan and the People's Republic in recent years, also strives to balance and shape the flow of *ch'i* between body and environment. The health effects of food also offer an ongoing theme where people manipulate the flow of *ch'i* in their bodies through diet. Indeed, one can hardly sit down at a Chinese feast without being told of the health effects of the various dishes. The publishing industry in the People's Republic has fed these interests.[24]

Implications for Behavior

A brief look at how these understandings of humans-in-nature influence the implementation of environmental policy underscores their continuing importance. Most of the evidence we will draw on comes from Taiwan, whose longer experience with environmental policy, an environmental movement, and national parks provides us with clearer data. The differences between Taiwan and the People's Republic of China, of course, are numerous and deep. Yet there is little reason to expect these broad cultural patterns to vary. Indeed, their survival in Taiwan, in spite of powerful and direct Western influences on environmental policy, suggests a cultural tenacity that will also affect the People's Republic.

Environmental Movements and Nature Tourism

Taiwan's environmental movement has been very active for well over a decade. Taiwan newspapers reported 278 cases of environmental demonstrations in 1991 alone, and the three years between 1988–1990 saw over NT$ 12 billion (about US$ .5 billion) paid to settle environmental suits.[25] The members of the national leadership of this movement sound exactly like Western environmentalist leaders, calling for preservation over development, for valuing nature for its own sake. In some cases, they have organized branches of world-wide environmental organizations, like Greenpeace and Earth First. They are often natural or social scientists, and many earned their higher degrees in the United States.

At the grass roots, however, environmental movements take on a very different character, often organizing through local political factions, community temples, and kinship networks. In several cases, for example, local temples have contributed large sums of money to environmental movements trying to prevent construction of a factory or to discipline a polluting industry. More strikingly, gods sometimes possess spirit mediums who denounce the offending factories as threats to the long-term welfare of the local areas the gods control. In one case, a temple's traditional martial arts performing group, swords and spears in hand, managed to intimidate police into allowing the blockade of a factory gate.[26] National environmentalist elites have never encouraged this use of religion. Typical of modernizing elites anywhere, they generally feel a great distance from tradition-bound local religious practice, especially in the forms most effective in actual movements—possessed mediums, flaming incense pots, powerful divinations. Just as importantly, they reject the localism inherent in the use of religion. The gods of local temples protect their human communities above all and worry about the environment only when it threatens their people. Taiwanese religion structurally and culturally offers little encouragement for a global or even an island-wide view of ecology. It centers instead on the welfare of its people (not so much opposed to nature as living with it), in its specific locality. "Heaven-and-Earth," in this case, encourages local profit to the detriment of national policy. Religion thus supports a general not-in-my-backyard tendency, where people broadly support nuclear power or heavy industry, as long as it is built somewhere else.

Local protests also often borrow the language of kinship. In part, this takes the form of appeals to the welfare of descendants, again emphasizing local and familial concerns with the continuity of the patriline. In part, the use of kinship also appears in funeral symbolism, which is widely borrowed in these movements. Demands to save resources for descendants resonate deeply with the Chinese ideals of filial piety and mesh with economic behavior that attempts to maximize an estate to be handed down. The funeral symbolism furthers the image of filial piety, rebutting state or corporate worries about economic growth with classic Confucian values. Some funerals mourn the slain local land or water as if it were a dead parent and thus imply an accusation that the state or corporation has murdered the environment. At the same time, these "mourners" claim an expanded filial piety in response to the usual accusations that protesters are just out for financial compensation.

Such use of kinship metaphors is again almost entirely absent among the national environmental leadership. The localist and particularist features of kinship make it less appealing to these leaders than to local activists. In addition, the kinship/religious approach brings with it important differences as to how the environment itself should be considered. The metaphors of kinship have no place in the universalist principles of green leaders.[27] Rather than being an inherent good threatened by humanity, as many national environmental leaders see nature, nature in the language of kinship is either part of a local inheritance for the good of the patriline, or a sad invalid requiring human care. Geomancy itself makes this difference of attitude clear—it does not attempt to adjust people to nature, but rather to focus the forces that energize both nature and humanity for the good of certain groups of people. It denies the dichotomy between nature and culture, while putting human benefit at the forefront. Significantly, it can also emphasize very long-term planning. Filial piety, after all, implies a concern for guaranteeing the prosperity of an infinite line of descendants, as well as recognizing a line of ancestors. These local features of Taiwanese environmentalism thus fit with the anthropocentric character of cosmic resonance in practice in China, although it views benefits more from a strictly local level than did the national Confucian elites who expounded on the philosophies we discussed above.

A quick look at nature tourism in Taiwan, which has also boomed in the last ten or fifteen years, shows a very similar pattern. Taiwan's national park system is only about a decade old and has taken the American wilderness park (like Yellowstone) as its model. This model grows out of the Western separation of nature and culture; it valorizes a nature apparently freed of cultural forms. In addition to its five national parks (and several provincial parks, run instead on Japanese models), Taiwan also has several hundred private nature tourism sites. While national parks respond directly to policy decisions, private nature tourism must respond instead to the market. The private sites rarely emphasize unsullied nature, but instead seek to combine scenery (waterfalls are especially popular) with human activities. Chinese or Western gardens are popular, but so are temples, carnival rides for children, and tables for playing mah-jongg. There is little demand for pure nature. Just as traditional landscape painting in China (but not the West) often included people, nature is not separated from humanity but, rather, is shaped for human benefit.

Finally, it is also worth recalling problems with endangered species protection in all Chinese societies. One important implication of cosmic resonance is that all foods contain properties that affect our bodies. Exotic animals, unfortunately, tend to be associated with exotic and desirable medical properties. The market for tiger penis, rhinoceros horn, snake gall, or pangolin scales relates directly to the medical properties traditionally ascribed to them, and demand is intensified by the increasing wealth of these societies. Cosmic resonance is no guarantee of environmental protection, because it serves human ends above all.

Conclusions

The preceding material suggests four tentative conclusions, as well as a direction for further inquiry and policy promotion. Our first conclusion is the most promising. In each of the dominant world-views of the three epochs discussed here—the cosmic resonance theory of the early Chinese empires, the Neo-Confucianism of the later imperial period, and the democratic/scientific model of the twentieth century—the fate of political authority and the well-being of human society are integrally linked to a conception of the larger environment.

Our second conclusion is on the face of it less hopeful. As far as we can tell, these same worldviews, which explicitly recognized the interdependency of the human social/political order and the natural world, did not result in the conscious establishment of ecologically sound environmental attitudes, policies, or practices. We believe this happened for at least two reasons. First, the organismic worldviews we have discussed were developed to address the dominant concerns of political culture—how to maintain political unity and social harmony—and did not concern themselves with the well-being of nature as such. If anything, they assumed that nature was inherently capable of recovering from human action.

Second, the popular practices that emerged from these worldviews were also put in service of human utility, and not infrequently reduced to means for individual and local self-aggrandizement and factional political advantage. From a pragmatic point of view, this consistent utilitarian tendency offers certain possibilities in support of environmental prudence, although it is typically treated in China as evidence for the breakdown of moral commitment.

Our third conclusion, drawn from the preceding, is that in China, too, efforts to establish environmental policies will only work if they appeal to the profit and welfare of those charged with effecting them—from officials to factory managers to farmers. Abstract appeals to the well-being of "nature" are not likely to work. Successful appeals are likely to speak most to local or individual benefit. This problem is especially difficult for those environmental issues—like greenhouse gas emissions—where the global effects are clear but the local area feels little direct detriment. On the other hand, it also suggests that appropriate pricing mechanisms and other techniques for changing the calculation of local profit may be effective. In addition, appeals to very long-term benefits, which are often necessary in environmental planning, may work better in China than they do in the West, because they mesh easily with the need to plan for future generations of the patriline. The clear public health effects of pollution define the venue in which such appeals would be effective.

Our fourth conclusion also relates to the problems of giving effect to environmental policy: we hold that the conceptual resources exist in Chinese political culture and popular practice for promoting two attitudes that seem essential for establishing public support for environmental policies: first, that human beings, and government in particular, are considered directly responsible for the state of the environment; and second, that both individual well-being and communal human welfare are seen as integrally related to the state of the environment. In this regard we suggest that environmental understanding may be usefully linked to practices such as Chinese medicine, geomancy, and *ch'i-kung*, which are based on traditional organismic worldviews. Dismissed as backward and superstitious by urban intellectual elites trained in the modern sciences, these practices in fact remain extremely widespread. They have sophisticated written traditions and the infrastructure for the dissemination of knowledge and techniques. Finally, cosmic resonance offers a view of human life that fits well with contemporary environmental science and forms part of the tradition of Chinese traditional medicine that is already well established.[28]

Notes

1. We are especially grateful to Andrew Meyer and Ping-tzu Chu, who put great effort into the research behind this paper. We are also grateful for the support of the Harvard University Committee on the Environment and for funding from the Kann Rasmussen Foundation. This article is also appearing in Michael McElroy, ed., *Energizing China: Reconciling Environmental Protection and Economic Growth* (Cambridge, Mass.: Harvard University Committee on the Environment, 1998).

2. China is not the only place where a unitary view of nature and society nevertheless supports anthropocentric activity. Seeing humanity and nature as part of a single system can easily support the human right to alter that system. See, for example, J. Kathirithamby-Wells, "Socio-political Structures and the Southeast Asian Ecosystem: An Historical Perspective up to the Mid-Nineteenth Century," in *Asian Perceptions of Nature*, ed. Ole Bruun and Arne Kalland (Copenhagen: Nordic Institute of Asian Studies, 1992), 18–38; and Arne Kalland, "Culture in Japanese Nature," in ibid., 218–33.

3. See, for example, Tu Wei-Ming, "The Continuity of Being: Chinese Visions of Nature," in *On Nature*, ed. Leroy S. Rouner (Notre Dame, Ind.: University of Notre Dame Press, 1984), 113–29, reprinted in this volume; and Huang Chün-chieh and Wu Kuang-ming, "Taiwan and the Confucian Aspiration: Toward the Twenty-First Century," in *Cultural Change in Postwar Taiwan*, ed. Stevan Harrell and Huang Chün-chieh (Boulder: Westview, 1994), 69–87.

4. *Lü-shih ch'un-ch'iu* 9/9a. All citations of the *Lü-shih ch'un-ch'iu* are to the *Ssu-pu ts'ung-k'an* edition.

5. Vital Essence is not limited to humanity. Human vitality and consciousness are merely two of the more important consequences of its activities. Vital Essence, the most rarefied and quintessential form of *ch'i*, was thought to pervade the universe, occasionally coalescing within objects and giving rise to marvelous properties. The vitality of animals was also attributed to Vital Essence, as was the growth of plants and trees and the luster of jade. See *Lü-shih ch'un-ch'iu* 3/4a.

6. Charles Le Blanc, *Huai-nan Tzu: Philosophical Synthesis in Early Han Thought* (Hong Kong: Hong Kong University Press, 1985), 138.

7. Ibid., 116–19. This emphasis on finding keys within cosmic resonance that will help a ruler succeed is typical of the *Huai-nan-tzu.* Other cosmic resonance theorists of the time (like Tung Chung-shu, ca. 179–104 B.C.E.) saw a more complex and multiple causality.

8. John Major, *Heaven and Earth in Early Han Thought: Chapters Three, Four, and Five of the* Huainanzi (Albany: State University of New York Press, 1993), 225.

9. They thus defined "human nature" as the endowment of *li* shared by all humans.

10. *T'ien* is also one of the plausible translations of the Western idea of nature into classical Chinese. Chinese at the time pointed out the apparent contradiction between the Jesuits' rationalist understanding of astronomy and their insistence on an anthropomorphic God.

11. Maurice Bloch and Jean H. Bloch, "Women and the Dialectics of Nature in Eighteenth-Century French Thought," in *Nature, Culture, and Gender*, ed. Carol P. MacCormack and Marilyn Strathern (Cambridge: Cambridge University Press, 1980), 25–41; Carolyn Merchant, *The Death of Nature: Women, Ecology, and the Scientific Revolution* (San Francisco: Harper and Row, 1980).

12. *Tetsugaku Daijisho* (Dictionary of philosophy), ed. Dai Nihon Hyakka Jisho Benshōshu, 5th ed. (Tokyo: Dobunkan, 1924).

13. Kuo-li Pien-i-kuan, ed., *Kuo-min hsiao-hsüeh ch'ang-shih k'o-pen* (Textbook of common knowledge for elementary schools) (Taipei: Kuo-li Pien-i-kuan, 1974). We have not had access to a run of texts from the People's Republic, but there is no reason to expect major differences on this particular issue.

14. *Huan-pao hsiao ying-hsiung* (Little heroes of environmental protection), prod. Hsing-cheng Yüan Huan-ching Pao-hu Chü, Taipei, Taiwan, 1991, videocassette.

15. *Ti-li* is also an early term for geomancy and still carries that meaning in some dialects (like southern Min).

16. Joanna F. Handlin Smith, "Gardens in Ch'i Piao-chia's Social World: Wealth and Values in Late-Ming Kiangnan," *Journal of Asian Studies* 51, no. 1 (1992):55–81; John Hay, *Kernels of Energy, Bones of Earth: The Rock in Chinese Art* (New York: China Institute in America, 1985).

17. Kuo-li Chung-yang Yen-chiu-yuan T'ien-wen Yen-chiu-so, ed., *Erh-shih-pa nien kuo-min li* (Citizen's calendar for 1939) (Nan-ching: Nei-cheng pu, Chiao-yü pu, 1939).

18. Kuo-li Chung-yang Yen-chiu-yuan, ed., *Ssu-shih-i nien kuo-min li* (Citizen's calendar for 1952) (Taipei: Nei-cheng pu, Chiao-yü pu, 1952).

19. Ch'ü Hai-yüan, *Taiwan ti-ch'ü she-hui pien-ch'ien chi-pen tiao-ch'a chi-hua, ti erh ch'i wu tz'u tiao-ch'a chih-hsing pao-kao* (Report on the fifth implementation of the second section of the plan for a basic survey on social change in Taiwan) (Taipei: Chung-yang yen-chiu-yuan min-tsu-hsüeh yen-chiu-so, 1994), 165–66.

20. Such stories may not always be true, of course, but their constant telling as truth shows the importance of the theme.

21. Stephan Feuchtwang, *An Anthropological Analysis of Chinese Geomancy* (Taipei: Southern Materials Center, 1982), 3.

22. Ibid., 2.

23. Peter Gwee Kim Woon, *Fengshui: The Geomancy and Economy of Singapore* (Singapore: Shing Lee Publishers, 1991), 45–47.

24. This is evident in the monthly list of popular books offered by the Joint Publishing Company (the major international distributor of books published in the People's Republic). The monthly list contains between two and three hundred titles on all categories (philosophy, literature, technology, medicine and health, etc.) and an equal number on a monthly "special theme." The October 1995 circular offered two hundred titles on the special theme of "health, physical cultivation, and athletics," covering such topics as *ch'i-kung*, divination, popular remedies, Chinese medicine, techniques for prolonging life, and swimming. In November, when the special theme was culture, the section on medicine and health offered over twenty books on Chinese medicine and about ten on Western medicine. The special theme in both December and January was medicine; in each case about three-quarters of the more than two hundred titles were devoted to Chinese medicine. The January circular also announced the republication of some ten rare books on geomancy and divination, a modern illustrated version of a traditional Chinese herbal, and announced thirty titles in a new series devoted to divination.

25. Data on this comes from joint research conducted by Robert Weller and Hsin-Huang Michael Hsiao. See Robert P. Weller and Hsin-Huang Michael Hsiao, "Culture, Gender and Community in Taiwan's Environmental Movement," paper presented at the Workshop on Environmental Movements in Asia, International Institute for Asian Studies and Nordic Institute of Asian Studies, Leiden, 1994.

26. This is based on interviews with organizers of the protest conducted in 1992. See also ibid.

27. Some local Western environmentalists also talk about preserving resources for future generations. Yet their consideration lacks the Chinese specificity for either the patriline itself or the immediate family. It is a universalist claim, unlike the particularism of the Chinese kinship metaphor.

28. Although modernizing elites are unlikely to embrace such a suggestion, the People's Republic has in fact done something similar with the revival and reorganization of traditional Chinese medicine.

Notes on Contributors

Joseph A. Adler is an associate professor of religion at Kenyon College. He received his Ph.D. in religious studies from the University of California, Santa Barbara. He is the author, with Peter K. Bol, Kidder Smith, Jr., and Don J. Wyatt, of *Sung Dynasty Uses of the I Ching* (Princeton University Press, 1990), and co-chair of the Confucian Traditions Group of the American Academy of Religion.

John Berthrong, educated in sinology at the University of Chicago, is the associate dean for academic and administrative affairs and director of the Institute for Dialogue among Religious Traditions, Boston University School of Theology. Active in interfaith dialogue programs, his teaching and research interests include interreligious dialogue, Chinese religions, Neo-Confucianism and New Confucianism, and comparative theology and philosophy. His most recent book is *Transformations of the Confucian Way*, a history of Confucian thought in Asia.

Peter K. Bol is a professor of Chinese history at Harvard University and chair of the Department of East Asian Languages and Civilizations. He is the author of *"This Culture of Ours": Intellectual Transitions in T'ang and Sung China* (Stanford University Press, 1992) and, with Kidder Smith, Jr., Joseph A. Adler, and Don J. Wyatt, of *Sung Dynasty Uses of the I Ching* (Princeton University Press, 1990).

Chung-ying Cheng is a professor of philosophy at the University of Hawaii, Manoa. He is the editor of the *Journal of Chinese Philosophy* and the author of *Peirce's and Lewis' Theories of Induction* (Martinus Nijhoff, 1969), *Tai Chen's Inquiry into Goodness* (The East-West Center Press, 1971), *Philosophical Aspects of the Mind-Body Problem* (University Press of Hawaii, 1975), *New Dimensions of Confucian and Neo-Confucian Philosophy* (State University of New York Press, 1991), and, in Chinese, *C Theory: Philosophy of Management in the I Ching* (Sanmin, 1995) and *On Spirits of Chinese and Western Philosophies* (Dongfang, 1997).

Julia Ching is University Professor at the University of Toronto and a Fellow of the Royal Society of Canada. She teaches East Asian philosophy and religion and is the author of numerous books, including, most recently, *Mysticism and Kingship in China* (Cambridge University Press, 1997).

Wm. Theodore de Bary is John Mitchell Mason Professor Emeritus and Provost Emeritus at Columbia University, as well as director of Heyman Center for the Humanities. He is the author or editor of more than two dozen works on Asian civilizations, including *Waiting for the Dawn* (Columbia University Press, 1993), *The Trouble with Confucianism* (Harvard University Press, 1991), *Confucianism and Human Rights* (Columbia University Press, 1998), and *Asian Values and Human Rights* (Harvard University Press, 1998).

Seiko Gotō received her Ph.D. in Japanese garden history from Chiba University in 1997, after earning a master's degree from the Graduate School of Design, Harvard University. She is a landscape architect and teaches at the Kasei Gakuin University, Tokyo. She is currently visiting at the School of Architecture and Landscape Architecture at the University of Toronto.

Philip J. Ivanhoe has published work on topics in religious studies, philosophy, and Asian studies. He is the author of *Ethics in the Confucian Tradition: The Thought of Mencius and Wang Yang-ming* (Scholar's Press, 1990) and *Confucian Moral Self-Cultivation* (P. Lang, 1993), editor of *Chinese Language, Thought, and Culture* (Open Court, 1996), and coeditor (with Paul Kjellberg) of *Essays on Skepticism, Relativism, and Ethics in the Zhuangzi* (State University of New York Press, 1996). He is currently an associate professor in the Departments of Asian Languages and Cultures and Philosophy at the University of Michigan, Ann Arbor.

Michael C. Kalton received his Ph.D. from Harvard University in the joint fields of comparative religion and East Asian languages and civilizations. He is professor and director of the Program of Liberal Studies at the University of Washington, Tacoma. He is the author and translator of books and articles dealing with Korean Neo-Confucianism, including *To Become a Sage: The Ten Diagrams on Sage Learning by Yi T'oegye* (Columbia University Press, 1988) and *The Four-Seven Debate: An Annotated Translation of the Most Famous Controversy in Korean Neo-Confucian Thought* (State University of New York Press, 1994).

Toshio Kuwako is a professor of value structure in the Department of Value and Decision Science, Graduate School of Decision Science and Technology, Tokyo Institute of Technology. He is the author of *Energeia: The Creation of Aristotle's Philosophy* (University of Tokyo Press, 1993), *The Philosophy of Ch'i Phase* (Shinyosha, 1996), and *Space and Body: A New Perspective on Philosophical Investigation* (Toshindo, 1998).

Huey-li Li has lived most of her life in Taiwan. She received her Ph.D. from the University of Illinois, Urbana-Champaign, in the philosophy of education. She is currently an assistant professor of educational philosophy at the University of Akron. She has published articles on ecofeminism, ethical foundations of environmental education, and teacher education.

Robert Cummings Neville is professor of philosophy, religion, and theology and dean of the School of Theology at Boston University and has been president of the American Academy of Religion and the International Society for Chinese Philosophy. His works treating Confucianism and/or ecology include *Reconstruction of Thinking* (1981), *The Tao and the Daimon* (1982), *The Puritan Smile* (1987), *Recovery of the Measure* (1989), *Behind the Masks of God* (1991), *Normative Cultures* (1995), and *The Truth of Broken Symbols* (1996), all from the State University of New York Press.

Young-chan Ro is an associate professor of religious studies in the Department of Philosophy and Religious Studies, George Mason University. He is the author of *The Korean Neo-Confucianism of Yi Yulgok* (State University of New York Press, 1989) and coauthor of *The Four-Seven Debate: An Annotated Translation of the Most Famous Controversy in Korean Neo-Confucianism* (State University of New York Press, 1994).

Rodney L. Taylor is a professor of religious studies and associate dean of the Graduate School at the University of Colorado, Boulder. His books include: *The Cultivation of Sagehood as a Religious Goal in Neo-Confucianism: A Study of Selected Writings of Kao P'an-lung, 1562–1626* (Scholars Press, 1978), (with F. M. Denny) *The Holy Book in Comparative Perspective* (University of South Carolina Press, 1985), *The Way of Heaven: An Introduction to the Confucian Religious Life* (Brill, 1986), *The Confucian Way of Contemplation: Okada Takehiko and the Tradition of Quiet-Sitting* (University of South Carolina Press, 1988), (with J. Watson)

They Shall Not Hurt: Human Suffering and Human Caring (Colorado Associated University Press, 1989), *The Religious Dimensions of Confucianism* (State University of New York Press, 1990), and *The Illustrated Encyclopedia of Chinese Confucianism* (forthcoming).

Mary Evelyn Tucker is an associate professor of religion at Bucknell University in Lewisburg, Pennsylvania. She received her Ph.D. from Columbia University in the history of religions, specializing in Confucianism in Japan. She has published *Moral and Spiritual Cultivation in Japanese Neo-Confucianism* (State University of New York Press, 1989) and is coeditor, with John Grim, of *Worldviews and Ecology* (Bucknell University Press, 1993/Orbis Books, 1994) and, with Duncan Williams, of *Buddhism and Ecology* (Harvard University Center for the Study of World Religions, 1997). She and John Grim are currently directing a series of ten conferences on religions of the world and ecology at the Harvard University Center for the Study of World Religions. They are also editors for a series on ecology and justice from Orbis Books.

Tu Weiming is professor of Chinese history and philosophy at Harvard and the director of the Harvard-Yenching Institute. He is the author of *Neo-Confucian Thought in Action: Wang Yang-ming's Youth* (University of California Press, 1976), *Centrality and Commonality: An Essay on Confucian Religiousness* (State University of New York Press, 1989), *Confucian Thought: Selfhood as Creative Transformation* (State University of New York Press, 1985), and *Way, Learning, and Politics: Essays on the Confucian Intellectual* (State University of New York Press, 1993) and the editor of *The Living Tree: The Changing Meaning of Being Chinese Today* (Stanford University Press, 1994), *China in Transformation* (Harvard University Press, 1994), and *Confucian Traditions in East Asian Modernity* (Harvard University Press, 1996).

Robert P. Weller is an associate professor of anthropology and a research associate at the Institute for the Study of Economic Culture at Boston University. His work centers on the relationships between culture and economic change in China and Taiwan, especially in religion, environmental consciousness, and civil organizations. He is the author of *Unities and Diversities in Chinese Religion* (Macmillan, 1987) and *Resistance, Chaos, and Control in China* (University of Washington Press, 1994).

Index

Asia. *See* East Asia
Asian religious traditions,
    environment and, 40–43
Astronomical predictions, of Jesuits,
    324
Astronomy, in gazetteers, 326
Astrophysics, 266
Authenticity, 124
    concept of, 127, 131
    defined, 135
    foundation of, 132–133
    of human beings, 142
    human mind and, 137
    human nature and, 131–136
    responsiveness as, 140–142
    of sages, 125, 130–131, 133–135
Autotelic object-events, 259
Axiology, 67
    "concern-consciousness"
    metaphor as, 243

Bacon, Francis, 304
Balance principle, 61–62, 93, 267
    life systems and, 162–163
Beauty, 227
    of nature, 286–289
    in worldviews, 76*n*
Being, 234*n*
    chain of, 108
    continuity of, 105–118
    inclusive humanism and, 217
    realization of full, 196–197
    state of, 177
    t'ai-chi as first cause of, 179–180
    unity of nonbeing and, 193
Benevolence, 167*n*
    ethics of, 217
    government of, 223–224
    jen as, 154–155
Berger, Peter, 238, 308*n*
Berry, Thomas, 187, 205*n*
Berry, Wendell, 29–33
Big Bang theory, 106
Bigwood, Carol, on nature and
    culture, 305–306

Biocentric thinking, 62
Biological rhythms, 95
Biota, self-regulation of, 60–61
Bipolar complementarity, 51
Bonding, ritual of, 8
Book of Changes. See I ching
Book of Rites, 306
Buchler, Justus, 263*n*
Buddha-nature, 64–65
Buddhism, 262*n*, 270*n*, 301
    environmental issues and, 42–43
    Japanese garden design and, 279–
    280
    of New Confucians, 250
    "oneness" concept in, 74–75*n*
    worldly unconcern of, 254
Buddhism and Ecology conference,
    254
Buddhist idealism, 26

Calendar, control of Chinese, 324
Callicott, J. Baird, 41
Canonical texts, of Confucianism,
    246–247
Capitalism, property in, 62
Caretakers, human beings as, 61–62
"Categorical imperative," 211
Category, concept of, 318–319
Causality, in "cosmic resonance
    theory," 314, 315–316
Celestial movements, 160–161. *See
    also* Astronomy
    supreme good in, 164
"Centered self," in Asian cultures,
    268
Chain of being, 108
    spirituality of, 114
Chambers, Sir William, 284, 292*n*
Chan, Wing-tsit, 107
    on *ch'i*, 190
    on realizing full being, 196–197
Change. *See also* Cyclic change; *I
    ching*; Transformation
    creative, 215–216
    li and, 192

interpretation of *T'ai-chi t'u shuo*
by, 155–157
on *jen*, 165
on *li* and *ch'i*, 188–189
on moral responsiveness, 138–
139, 141
Neo-Confucianism of, 322
on order, 156
on sages, 223
system for accessing ultimate
reality by, 137–138
on time and Five Agents, 162
Ch'un-ch'iu fan-lu (Tung Chung-
shu), 128
Chung, concept of, 268
Chung yung, 18–19, 28–29, 31, 125,
127, 140, 218, 256. *See also*
Doctrine of the Mean
authenticity concept in, 131–132
Mandate of Heaven in, 245
on sincerity, 224
Chün-tzu, concept of, 251
Chu Shun-shui, 286
in Japan, 281
Kōrakuen garden designed by,
282
Chu Tzu yü-lei, 159
Circulation, life systems and, 162–
163
Civility, 244, 246
Civilization
conflicts within, 16
five cultural values of, 227
origin of, 68–69
polarization of, 11–12
Classical Confucian tradition, 43–
45, 218. *See also* Early
Confucianism
ch'i in, 188
human nature in, 198–199
moral responsibility in, 124–125
New Confucianism and, 237–239
patterns of discourse in, 248
Cold War, 20*n*

Commentary on the Decision, 158
Communal feelings, depth of, 12
"Communicative rationality," 6
Communism
early appeal of, 25
fraternity and, 25–26
Communitarian activity, 25
Communitarian ethic, emergence of, 6
Communities, orientations of, 266–
267
Community idea, 5
Community infrastructures, 27
Community schools, 27
Communization, 12
"Companionship with all things," 53
Compass, for geomancy, 330–331
Compassionate mind, 199
Complexity, 82, 83
li as, 89
Comprehension, in relationship of
humans to nature, 224–225
"Concern-consciousness" metaphor,
243, 244, 257, 259
Conduct, *li* as a guide to, 87
Conflict, modernization and, 12
Conformity, of the profound person,
251
Confucian Asia, Westernization of, 7
Confucian culture, 32
creation myths in, 105–106
orientation of self in, 267–268
Confucian discourse, revitalization
of, 16
Confucian ecology, 37–56, 183–184
agenda for, 55–56
"continuity of being" and, 43–44
environmental notion and, 53–56
methodological inquiry into, 49–52
Okada Takehiko and, 45–48
Confucian ethics, 7, 85, 86–87
in Chang Tsai's synthesis, 194–197
toward environment, 183
in human nature, 198–199, 202–
203